THE RECORD OF A

FALLEN VAMPIRE

chubby

I like cats. I prefer plump ones over the slim, cool type, Japanese ones over foreign cats and mixed breeds over purebreds. Yes, I'm the kind of foolish pet owner that thinks her own critters are the best in the world.

–Yuri Kimura

Artist Yuri Kimura debuted two short stories in Japan's *Gangan Powered* after winning the Enix Manga Award. Shortly thereafter, she began *The Record of a Fallen Vampire*, which was serialized in Japan's *Monthly Shonen Gangan* through March 2007.

Author Kyo Shirodaira is from Nara prefecture. In addition to *The Record of a Fallen Vampire*, Shirodaira has scripted the manga *Spiral: The Bonds of Reasoning*. Shirodaira's novel *Meitantei ni Hana wo* was nominated for the 8th Annual Ayukawa Tetsuya Award in 1997.

THE RECORD OF A

FALLEN VAMPIRE

STORY BY: KYO SHIRODAIRA ART BY: YURI KIMURA

7

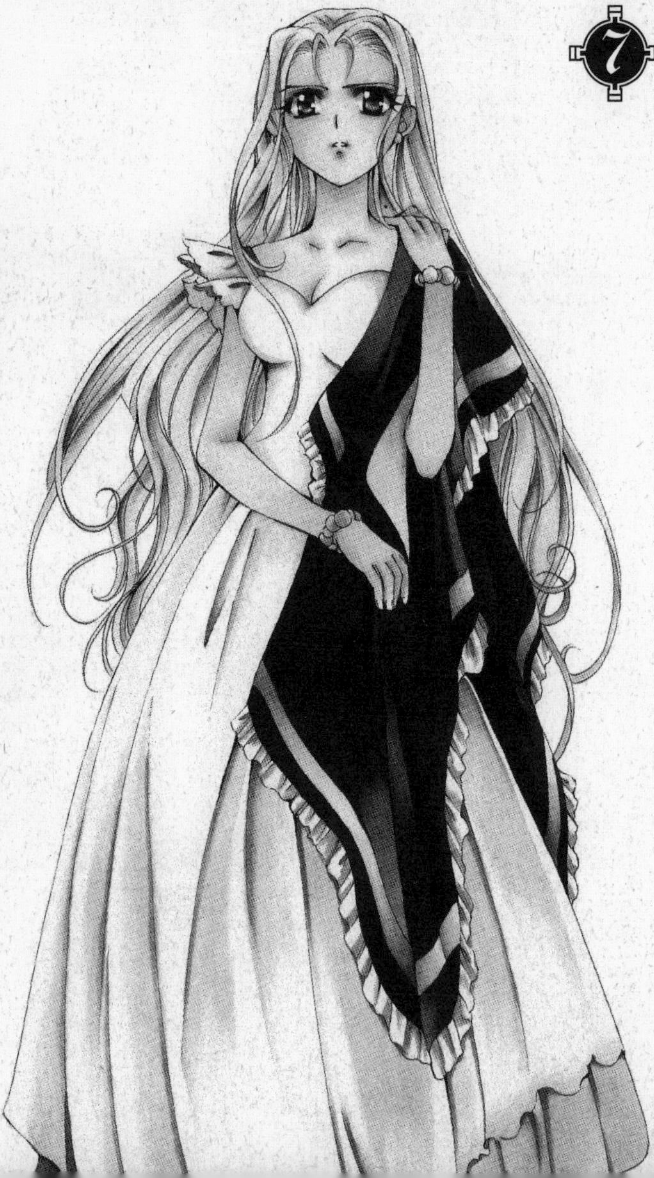

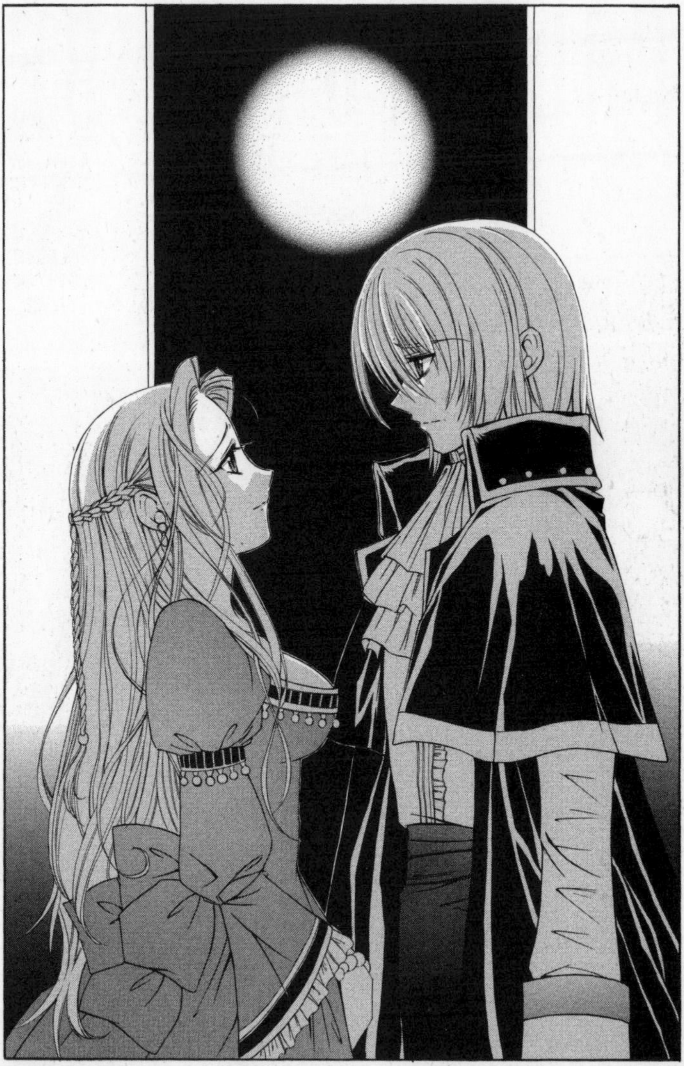

CONTENTS

Chapter 29: Advent

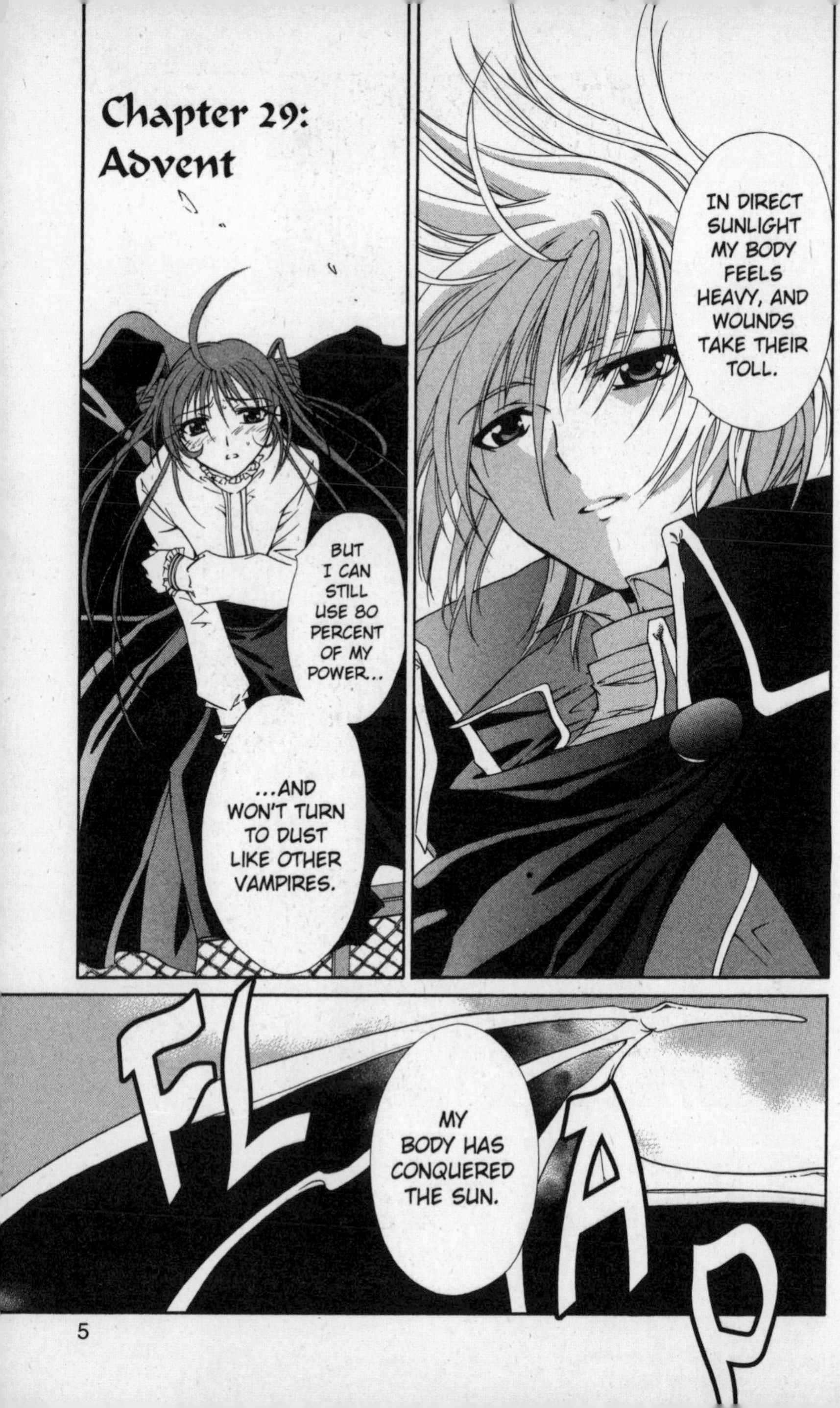
IN DIRECT SUNLIGHT MY BODY FEELS HEAVY, AND WOUNDS TAKE THEIR TOLL.
BUT I CAN STILL USE 80 PERCENT OF MY POWER...
...AND WON'T TURN TO DUST LIKE OTHER VAMPIRES.
FLAP
MY BODY HAS CONQUERED THE SUN.

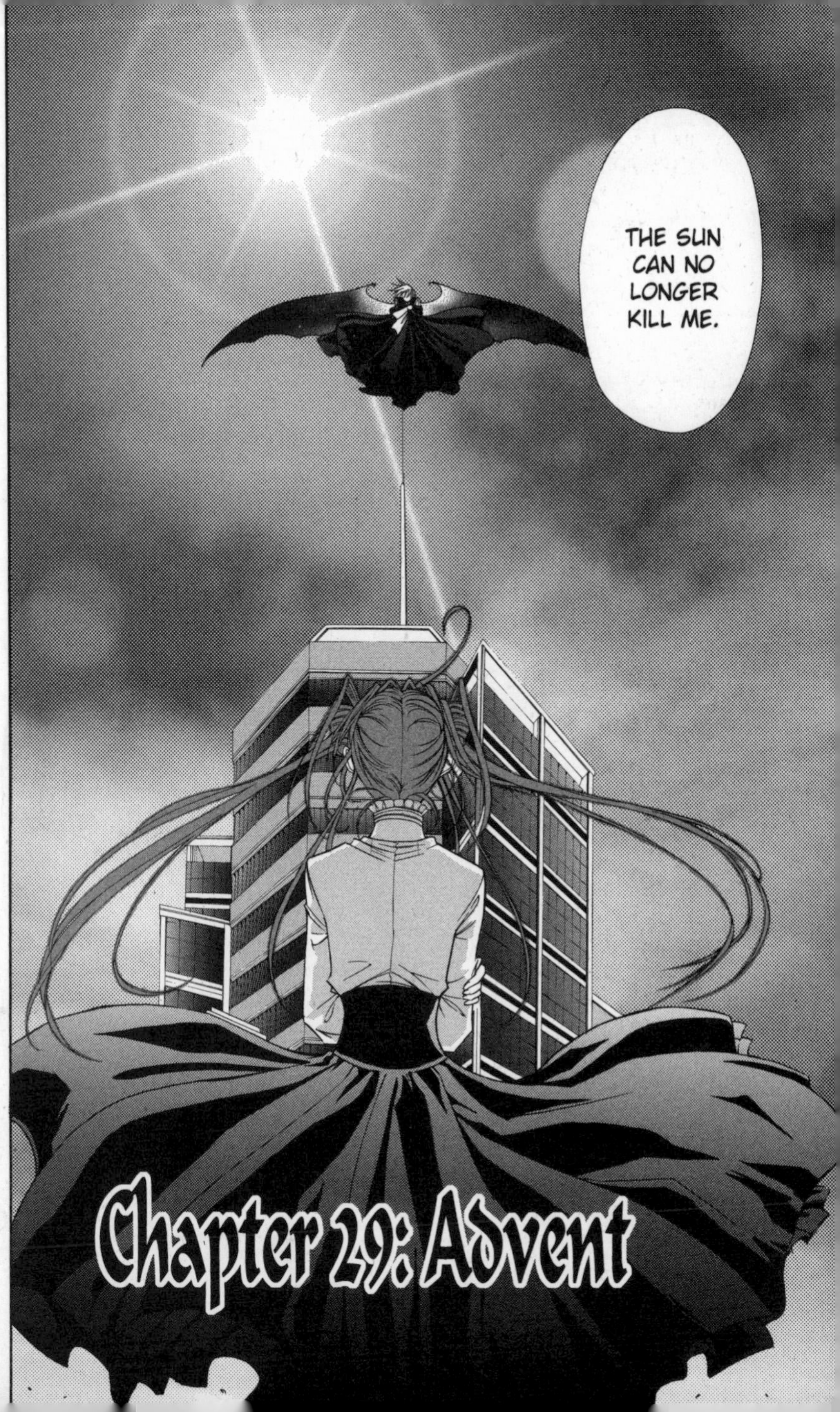
THE SUN CAN NO LONGER KILL ME.
Chapter 29: Advent

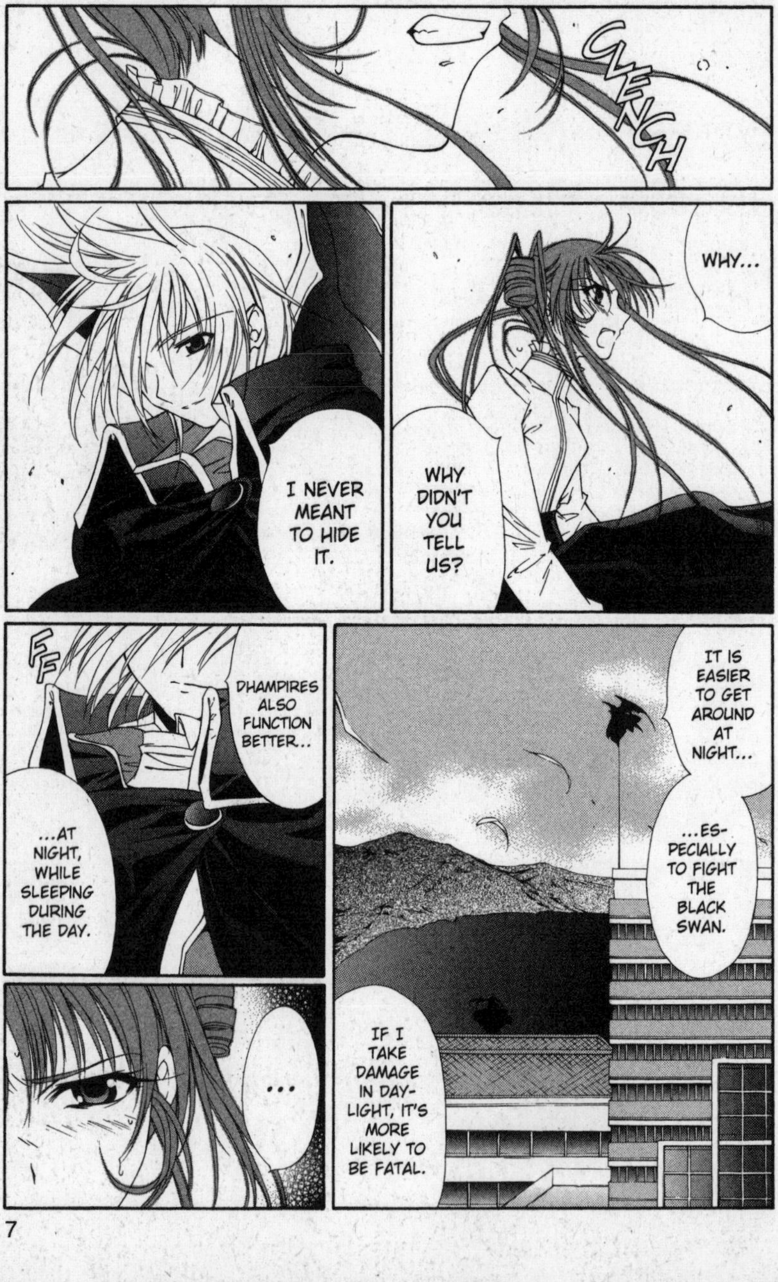
GWENCH
WHY...
WHY DIDN'T YOU TELL US?
I NEVER MEANT TO HIDE IT.
IT IS EASIER TO GET AROUND AT NIGHT...
...ES-PECIALLY TO FIGHT THE BLACK SWAN.
IF I TAKE DAMAGE IN DAY-LIGHT, IT'S MORE LIKELY TO BE FATAL.
DHAMPIRES ALSO FUNCTION BETTER...
FF
...AT NIGHT, WHILE SLEEPING DURING THE DAY.
...

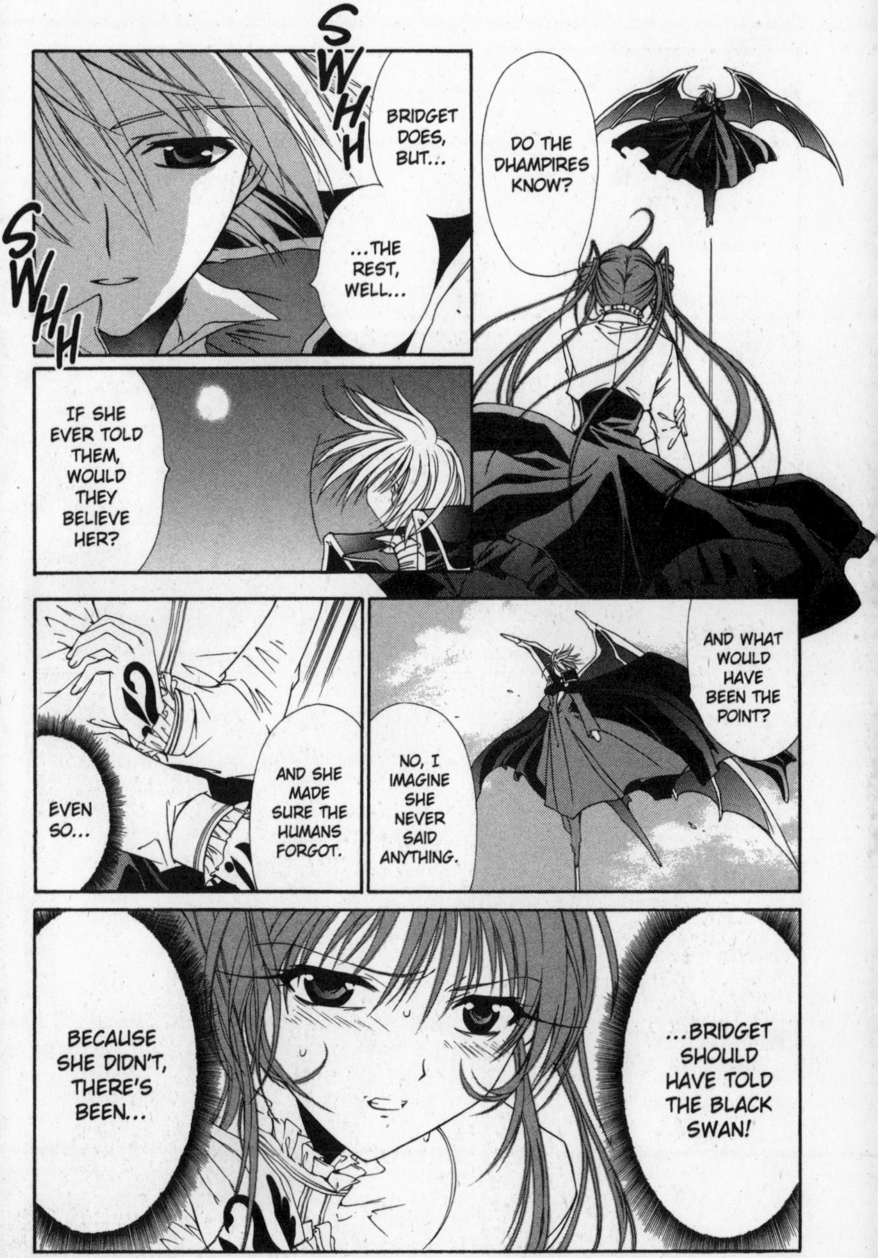
DO THE DHAMPIRES KNOW?
SWHH
BRIDGET DOES, BUT...
...THE REST, WELL...
SWHH
IF SHE EVER TOLD THEM, WOULD THEY BELIEVE HER?
AND WHAT WOULD HAVE BEEN THE POINT?
NO, I IMAGINE SHE NEVER SAID ANYTHING.
AND SHE MADE SURE THE HUMANS FORGOT.
EVEN SO...
...BRIDGET SHOULD HAVE TOLD THE BLACK SWAN!
BECAUSE SHE DIDN'T, THERE'S BEEN...

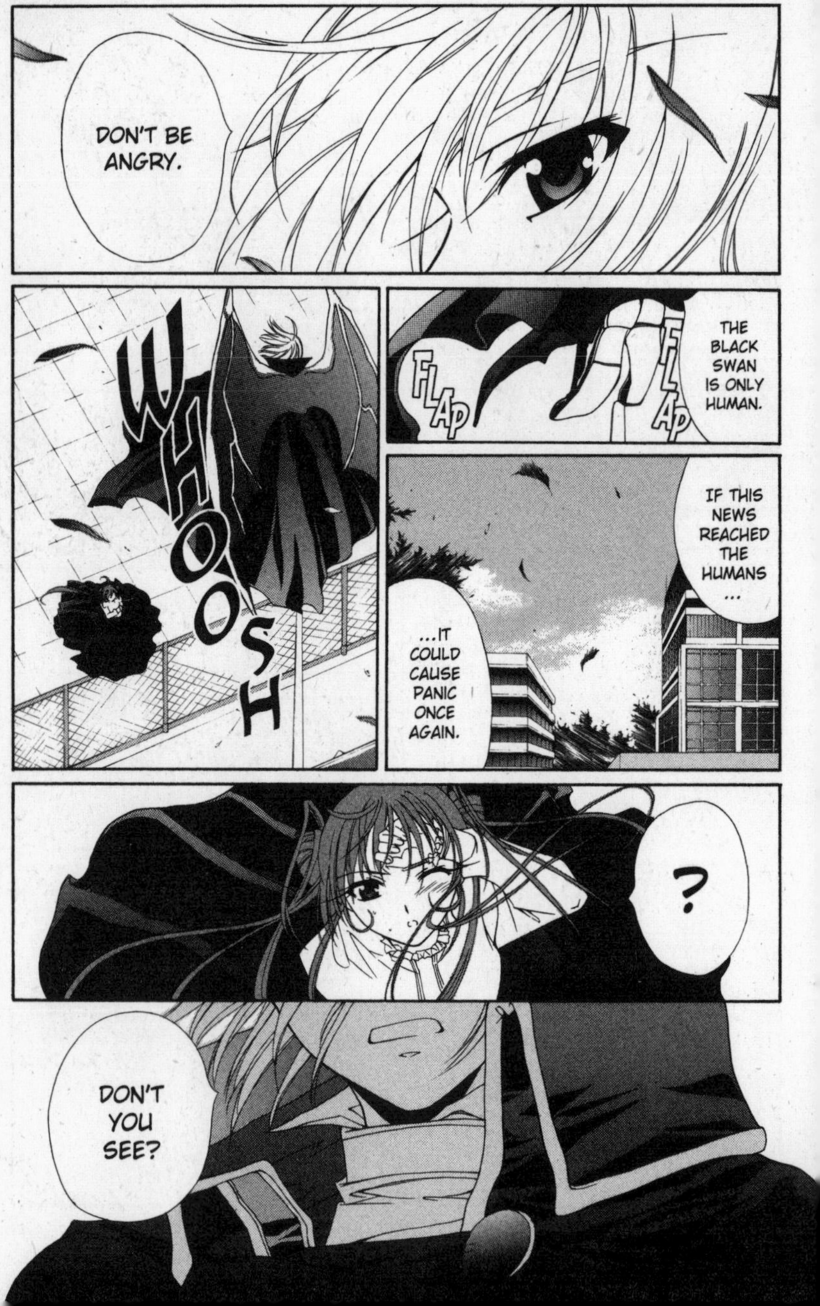
DON'T BE ANGRY.
THE BLACK SWAN IS ONLY HUMAN.
FLAP
FLAP
IF THIS NEWS REACHED THE HUMANS ...
...IT COULD CAUSE PANIC ONCE AGAIN.
WHOOSH
?
DON'T YOU SEE?

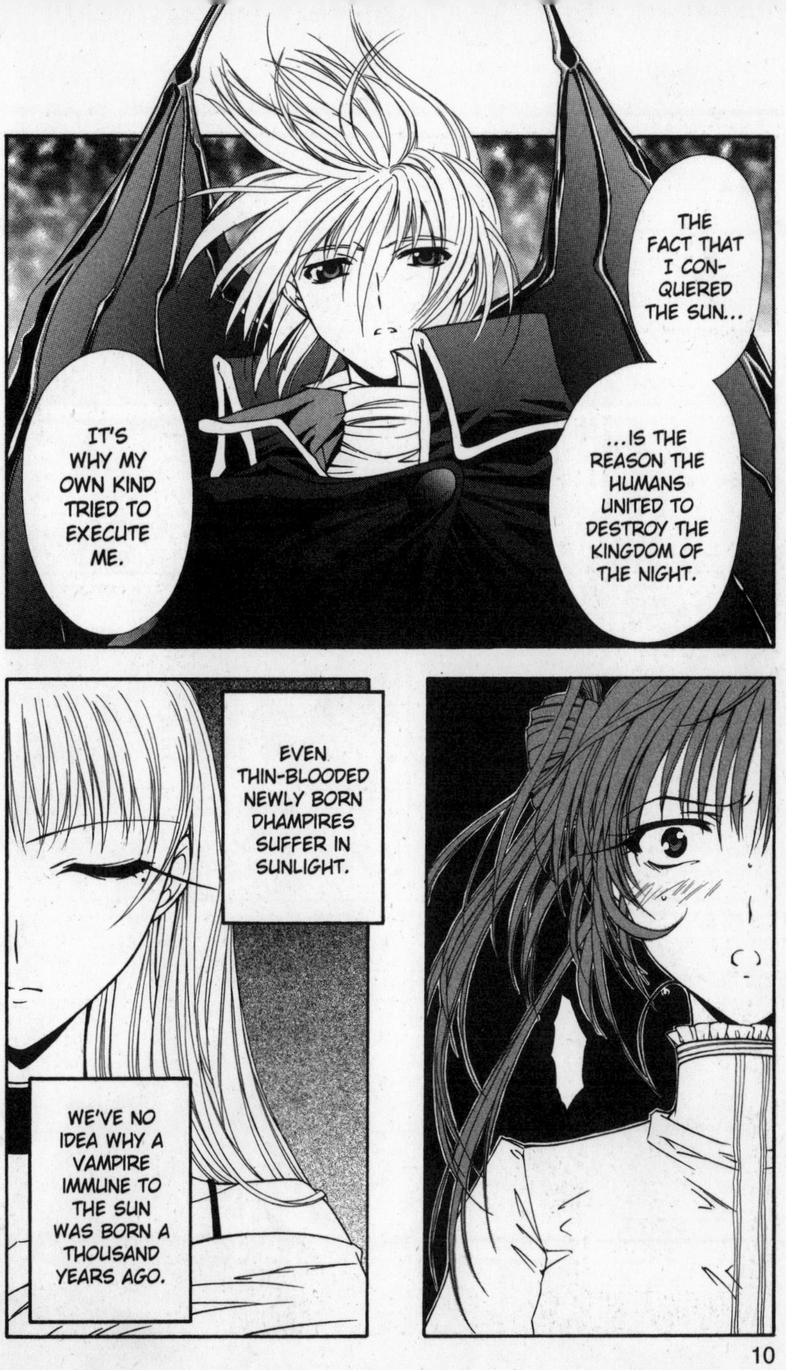
THE FACT THAT I CON-QUERED THE SUN...
...IS THE REASON THE HUMANS UNITED TO DESTROY THE KINGDOM OF THE NIGHT.
IT'S WHY MY OWN KIND TRIED TO EXECUTE ME.
EVEN THIN-BLOODED NEWLY BORN DHAMPIRES SUFFER IN SUNLIGHT.
WE'VE NO IDEA WHY A VAMPIRE IMMUNE TO THE SUN WAS BORN A THOUSAND YEARS AGO.

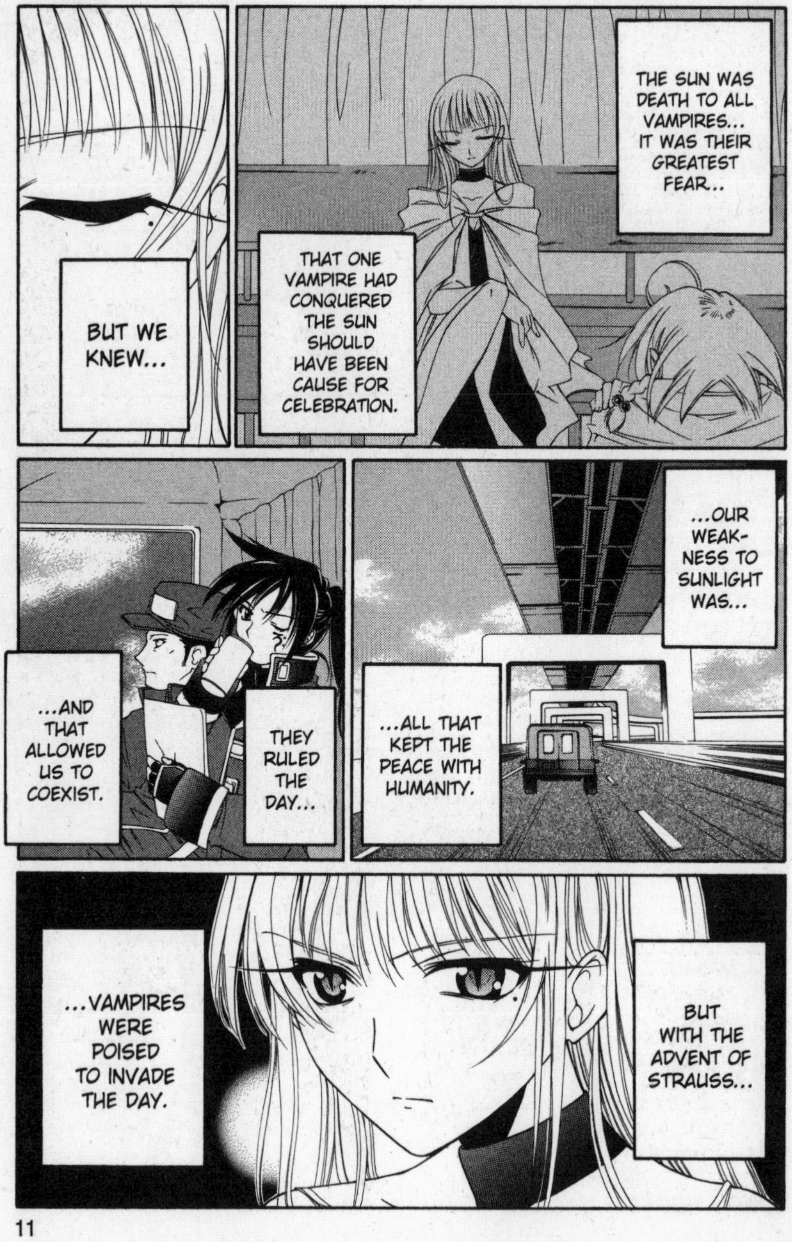
THE SUN WAS DEATH TO ALL VAMPIRES... IT WAS THEIR GREATEST FEAR...
THAT ONE VAMPIRE HAD CONQUERED THE SUN SHOULD HAVE BEEN CAUSE FOR CELEBRATION.
BUT WE KNEW...
...OUR WEAK-NESS TO SUNLIGHT WAS...
...ALL THAT KEPT THE PEACE WITH HUMANITY.
THEY RULED THE DAY...
...AND THAT ALLOWED US TO COEXIST.
BUT WITH THE ADVENT OF STRAUSS...
...VAMPIRES WERE POISED TO INVADE THE DAY.

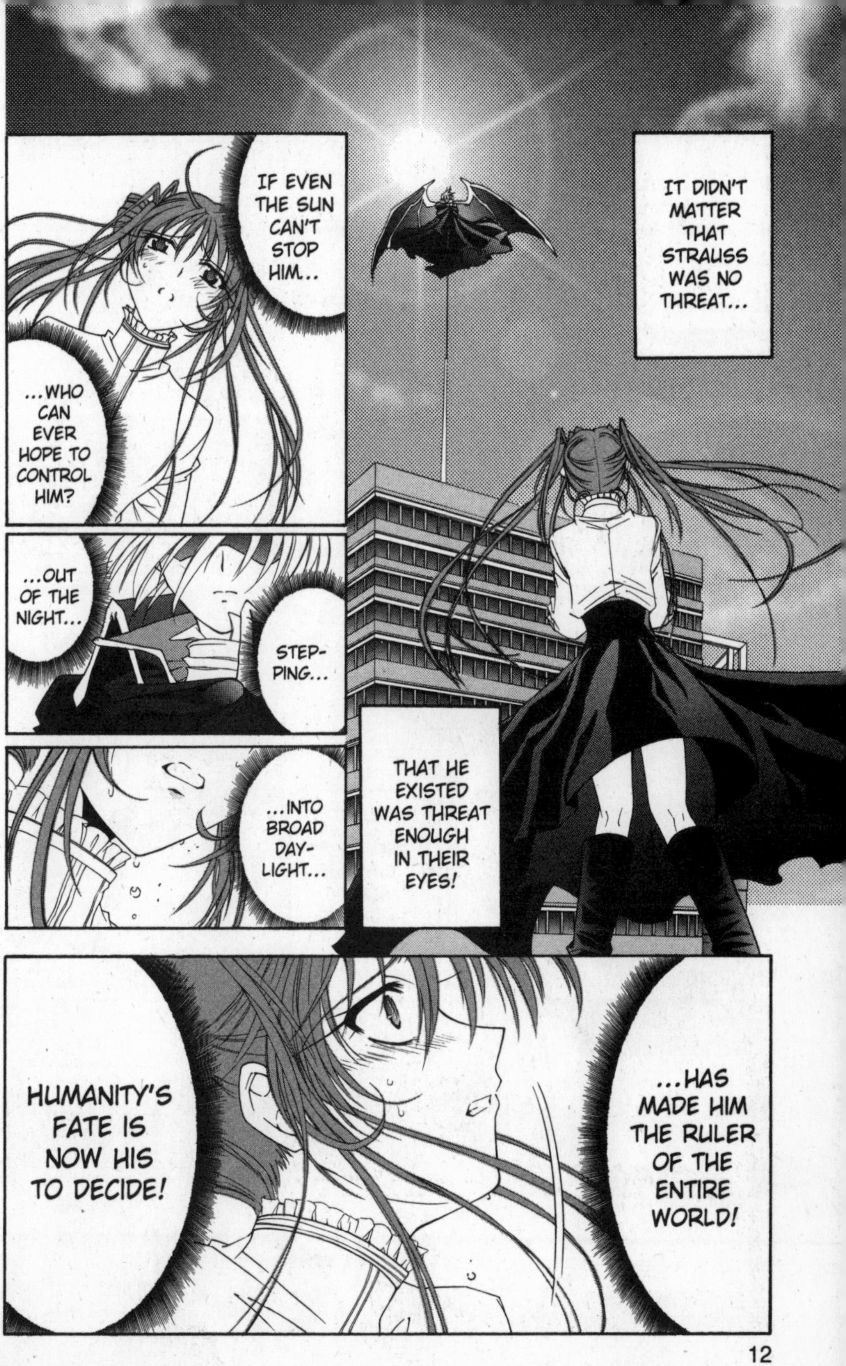
IT DIDN'T MATTER THAT STRAUSS WAS NO THREAT...
THAT HE EXISTED WAS THREAT ENOUGH IN THEIR EYES!
IF EVEN THE SUN CAN'T STOP HIM...
...WHO CAN EVER HOPE TO CONTROL HIM?
STEP-PING...
...OUT OF THE NIGHT...
...INTO BROAD DAY-LIGHT...
...HAS MADE HIM THE RULER OF THE ENTIRE WORLD!
HUMANITY'S FATE IS NOW HIS TO DECIDE!

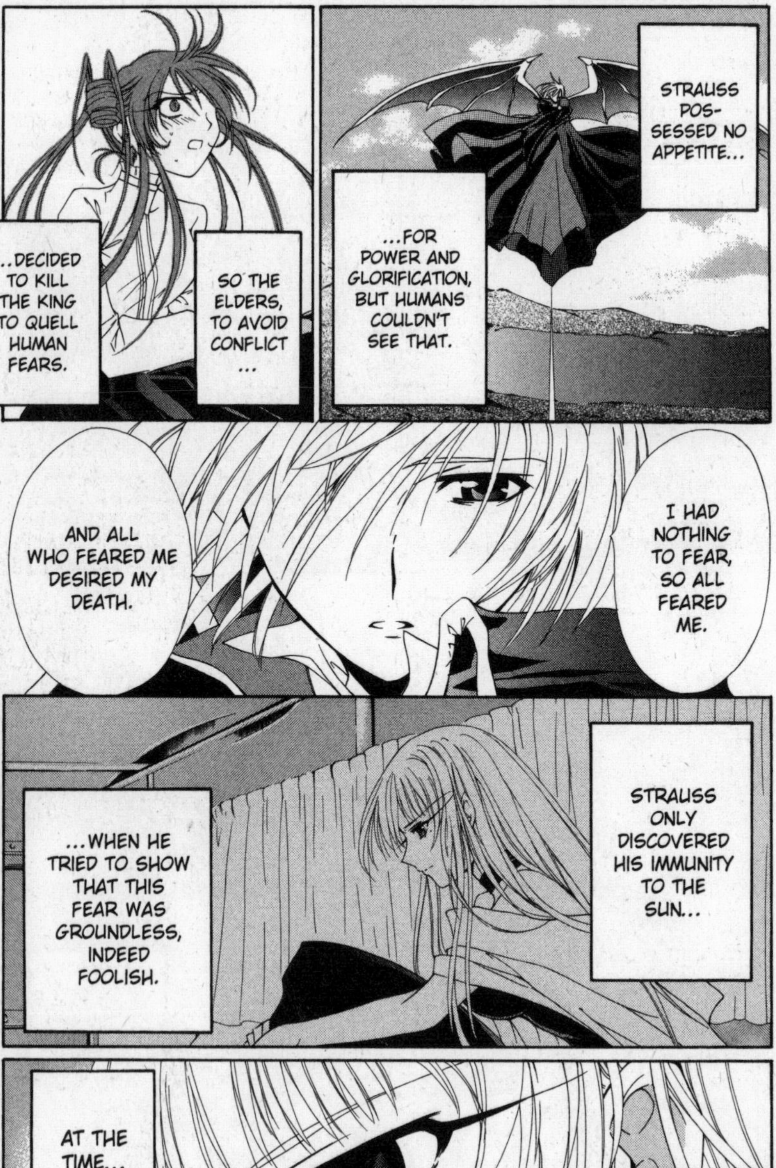
STRAUSS POS-SESSED NO APPETITE...
...FOR POWER AND GLORIFICATION, BUT HUMANS COULDN'T SEE THAT.
SO THE ELDERS, TO AVOID CONFLICT ...
...DECIDED TO KILL THE KING TO QUELL HUMAN FEARS.
I HAD NOTHING TO FEAR, SO ALL FEARED ME.
AND ALL WHO FEARED ME DESIRED MY DEATH.
STRAUSS ONLY DISCOVERED HIS IMMUNITY TO THE SUN...
...WHEN HE TRIED TO SHOW THAT THIS FEAR WAS GROUNDLESS, INDEED FOOLISH.
AT THE TIME...

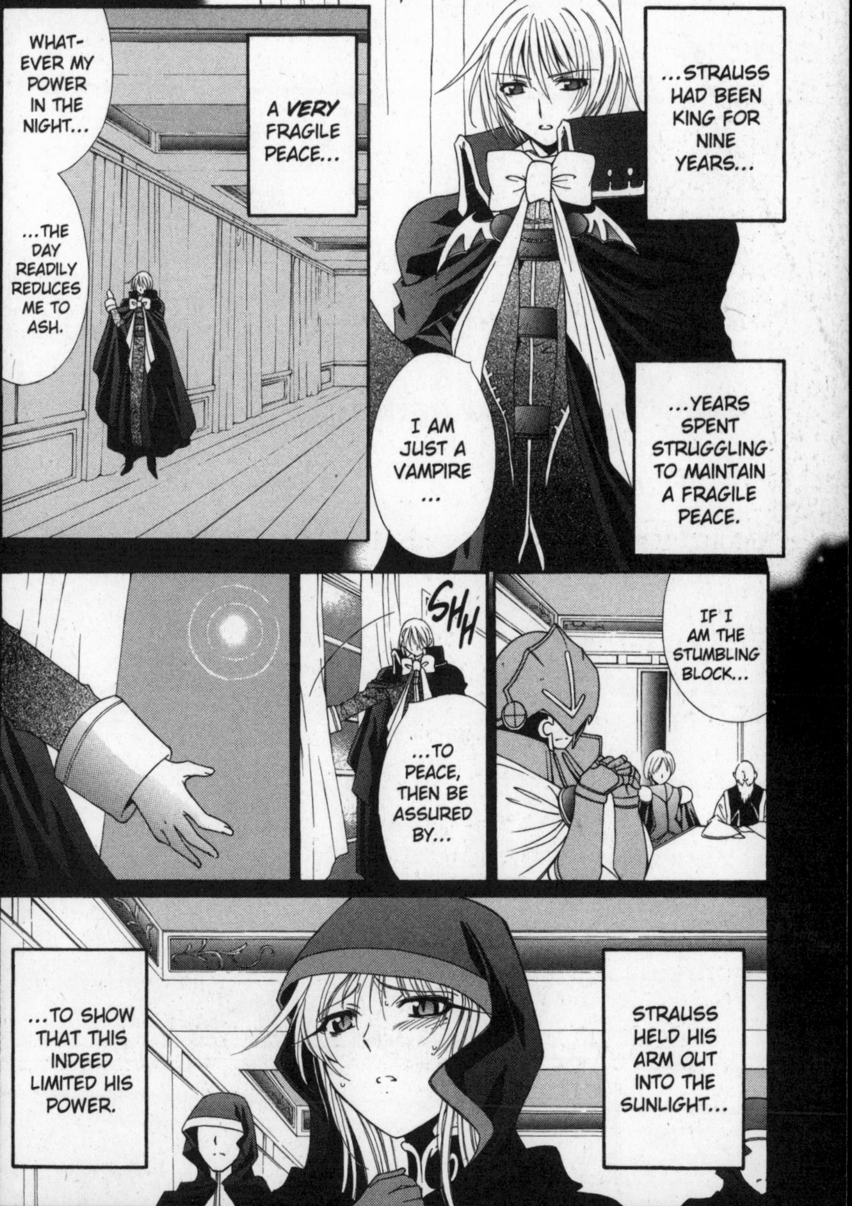
...STRAUSS HAD BEEN KING FOR NINE YEARS...
...YEARS SPENT STRUGGLING TO MAINTAIN A FRAGILE PEACE.
I AM JUST A VAMPIRE ...
A *VERY* FRAGILE PEACE...
WHAT-EVER MY POWER IN THE NIGHT...
...THE DAY READILY REDUCES ME TO ASH.
IF I AM THE STUMBLING BLOCK...
SHH
...TO PEACE, THEN BE ASSURED BY...
STRAUSS HELD HIS ARM OUT INTO THE SUNLIGHT...
...TO SHOW THAT THIS INDEED LIMITED HIS POWER.

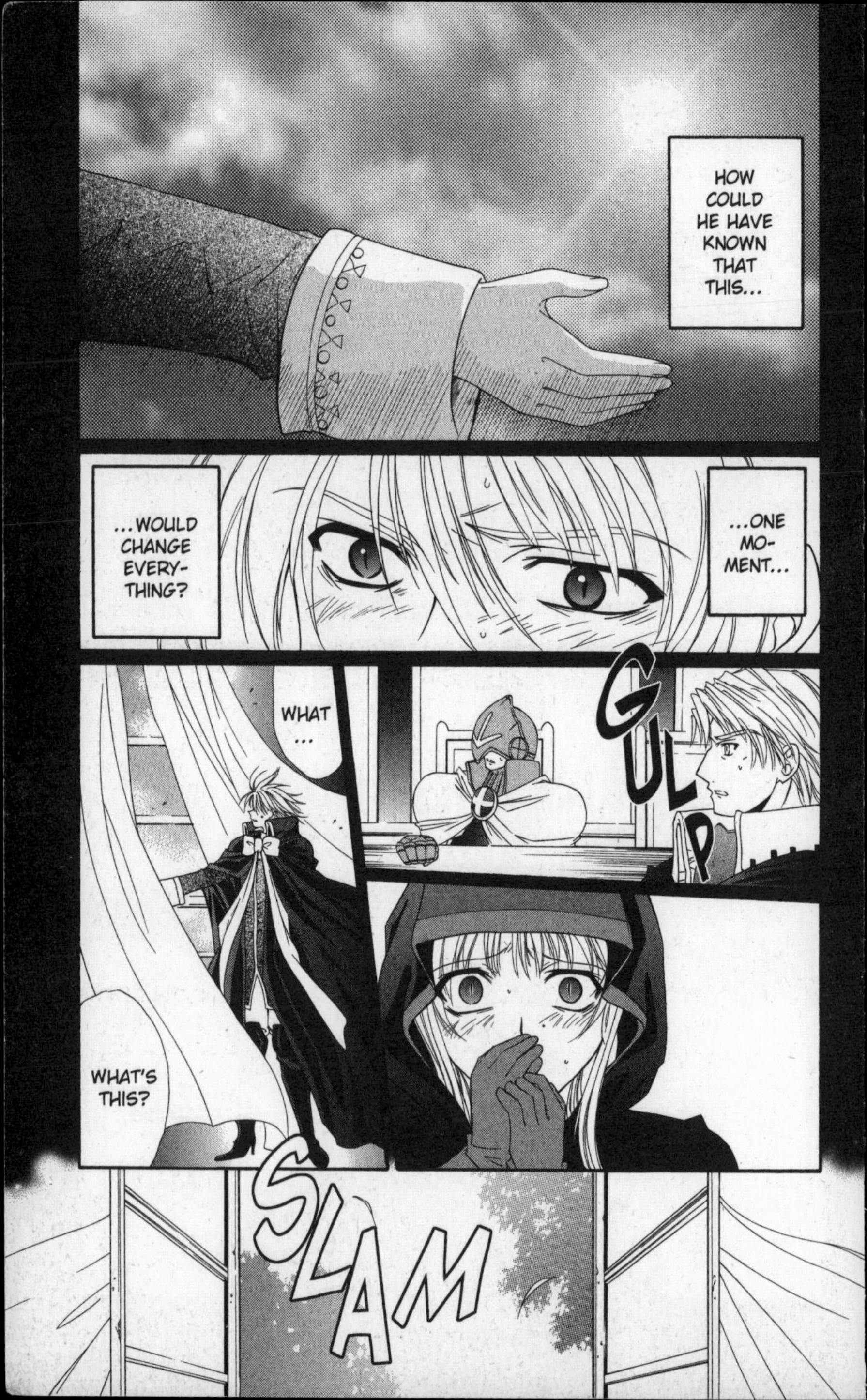
HOW COULD HE HAVE KNOWN THAT THIS...
...ONE MO-MENT...
...WOULD CHANGE EVERY-THING?
GULP
WHAT ...
WHAT'S THIS?
SLAM

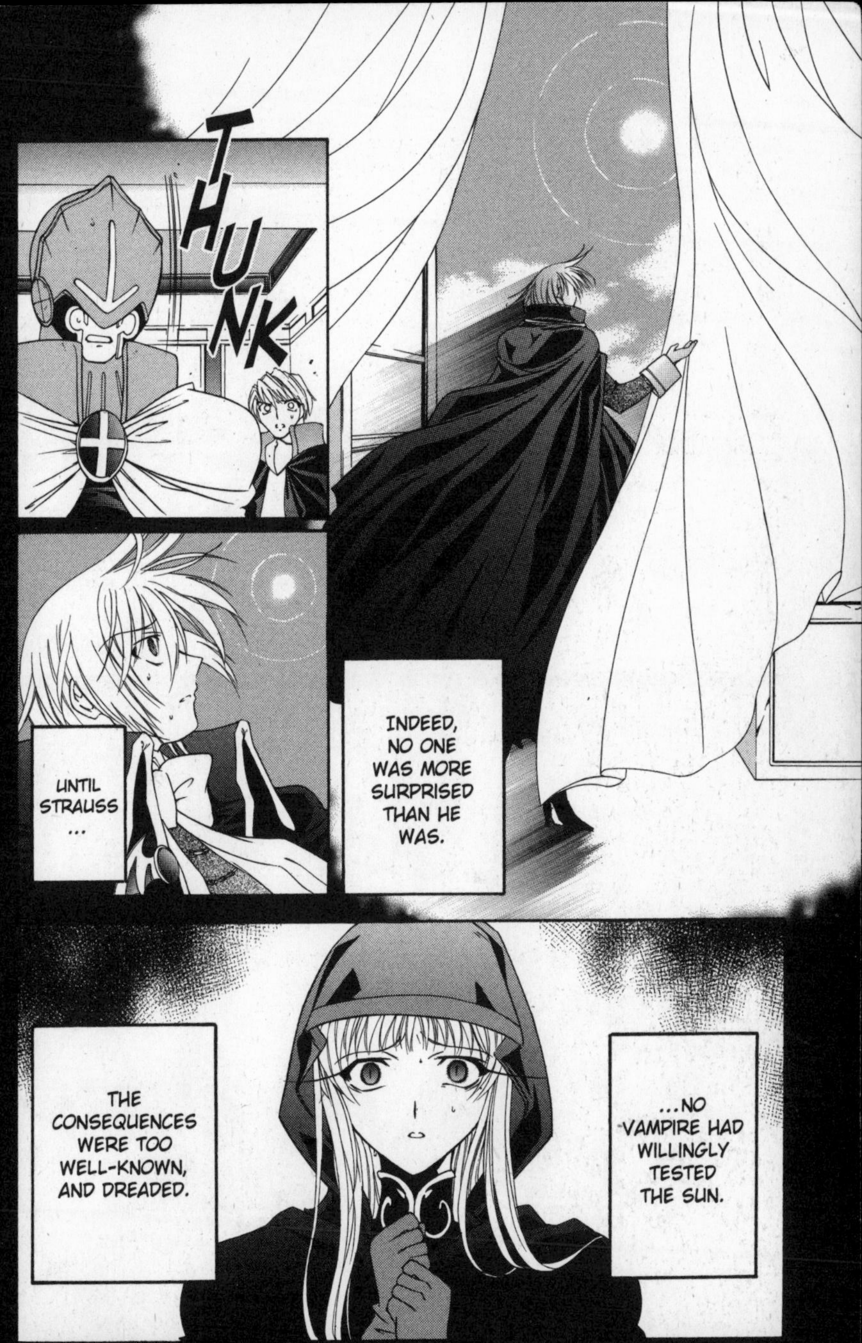
INDEED, NO ONE WAS MORE SURPRISED THAN HE WAS.
THUNK
UNTIL STRAUSS ...
...NO VAMPIRE HAD WILLINGLY TESTED THE SUN.
THE CONSEQUENCES WERE TOO WELL-KNOWN, AND DREADED.

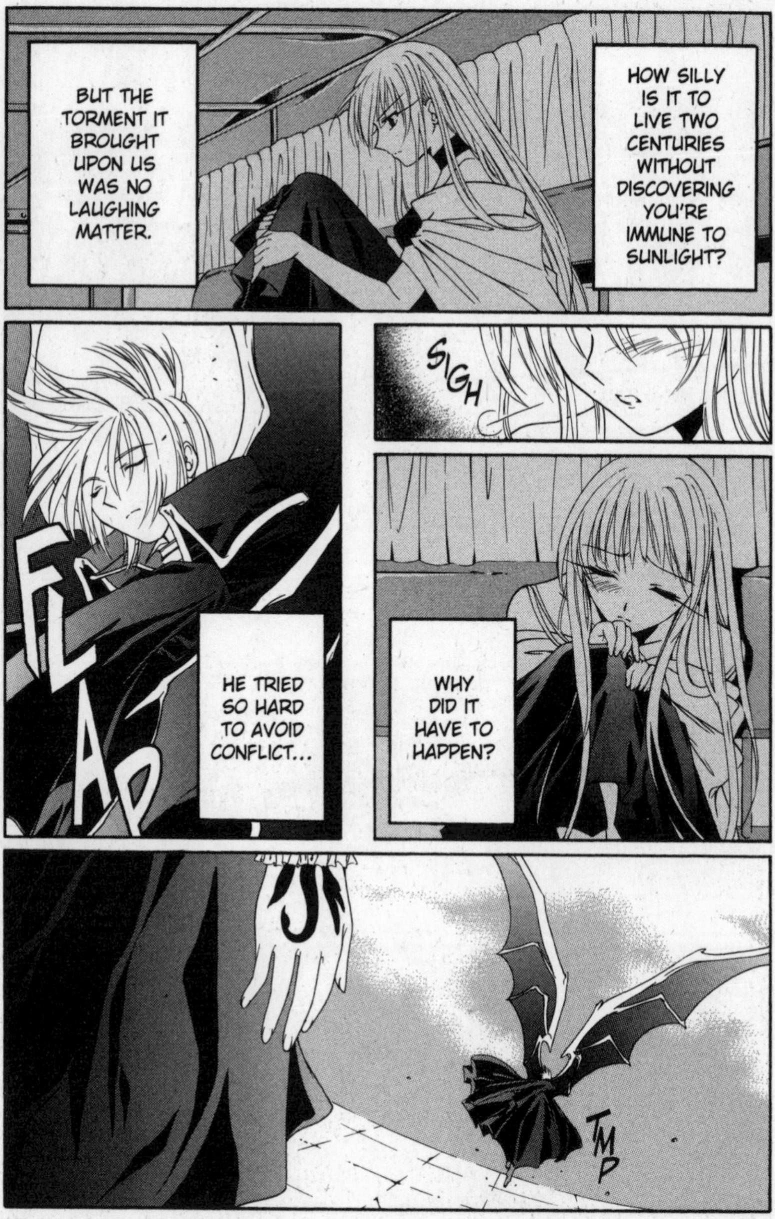
HOW SILLY IS IT TO LIVE TWO CENTURIES WITHOUT DISCOVERING YOU'RE IMMUNE TO SUNLIGHT?
BUT THE TORMENT IT BROUGHT UPON US WAS NO LAUGHING MATTER.
SIGH
WHY DID IT HAVE TO HAPPEN?
HE TRIED SO HARD TO AVOID CONFLICT...
FLAP
TMP

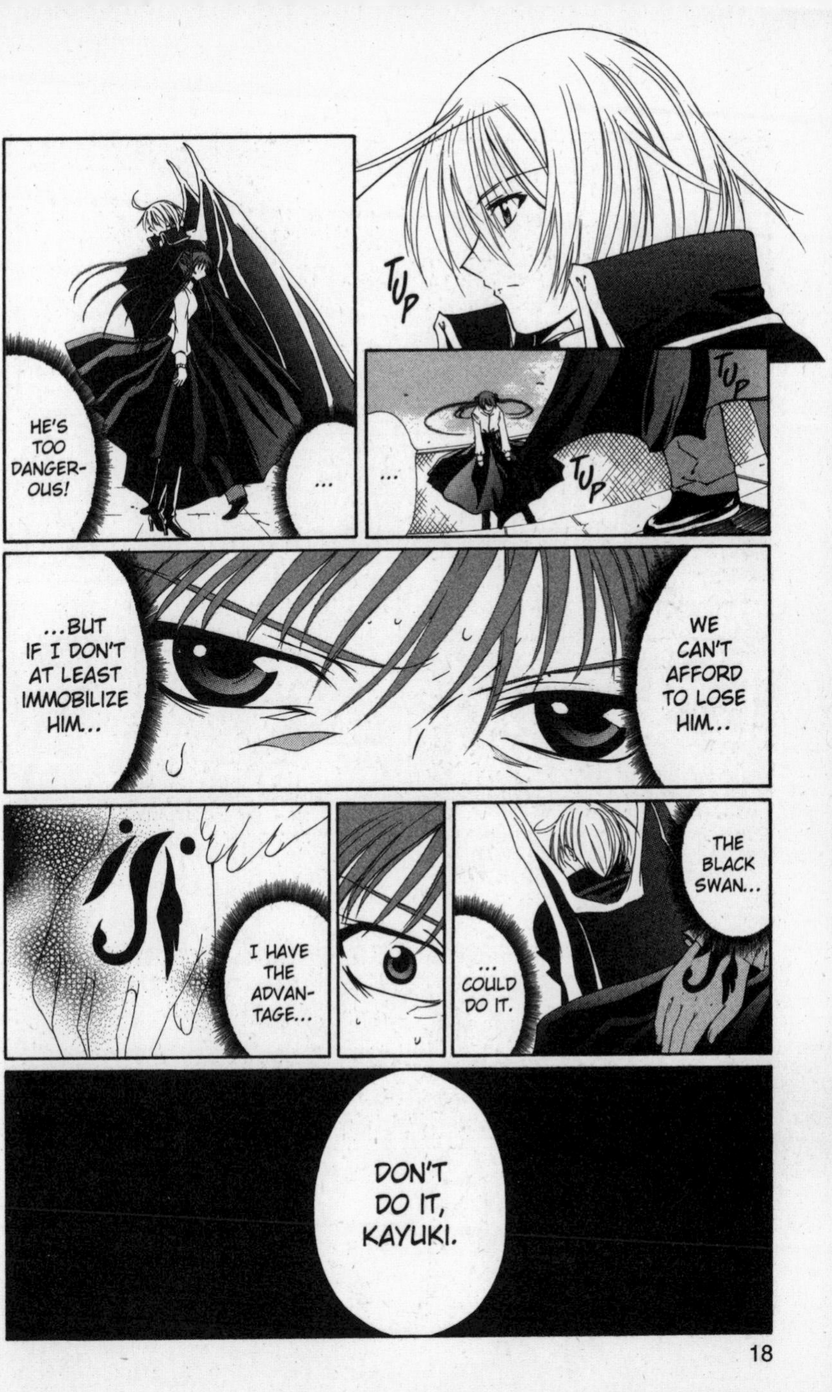
TUP
TUP
TUP
...
...
HE'S TOO DANGER-OUS!
WE CAN'T AFFORD TO LOSE HIM...
...BUT IF I DON'T AT LEAST IMMOBILIZE HIM...
THE BLACK SWAN...
...COULD DO IT.
I HAVE THE ADVAN-TAGE...
DON'T DO IT, KAYUKI.

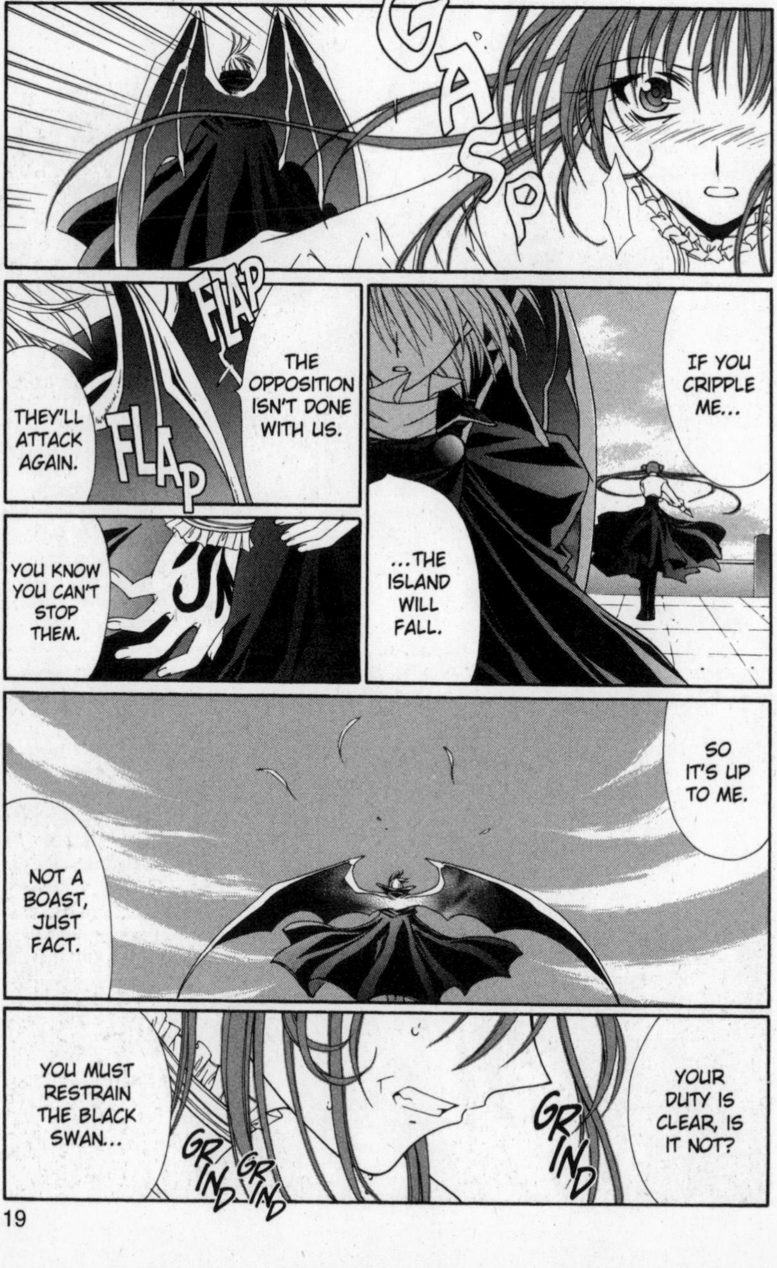
GASP
IF YOU CRIPPLE ME...
...THE ISLAND WILL FALL.
FLAP
THE OPPOSITION ISN'T DONE WITH US.
THEY'LL ATTACK AGAIN.
FLAP
YOU KNOW YOU CAN'T STOP THEM.
SO IT'S UP TO ME.
NOT A BOAST, JUST FACT.
YOUR DUTY IS CLEAR, IS IT NOT?
GRIND
YOU MUST RESTRAIN THE BLACK SWAN...
GRIND
GRIND

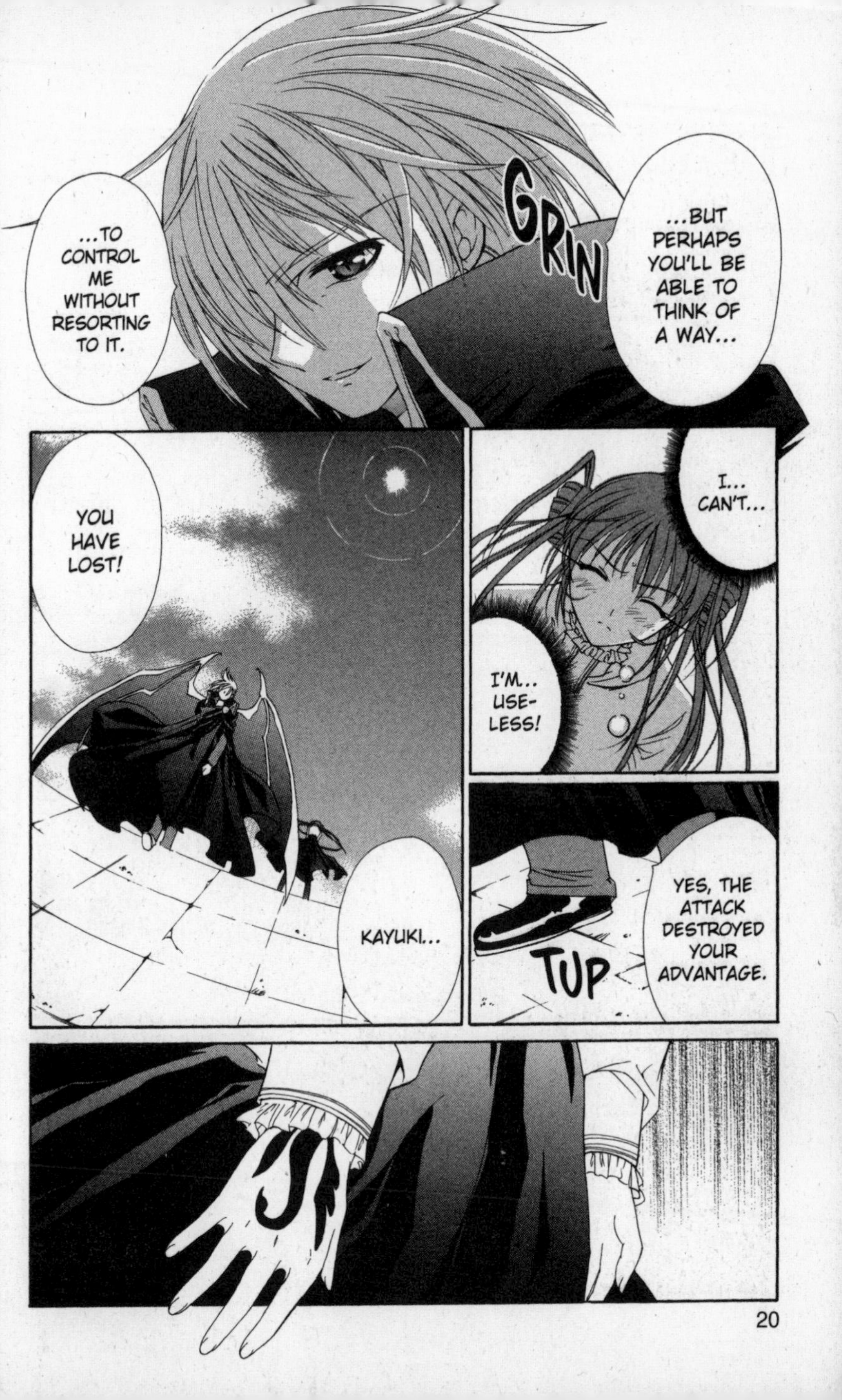
...BUT PERHAPS YOU'LL BE ABLE TO THINK OF A WAY...
GRIN
...TO CONTROL ME WITHOUT RESORTING TO IT.
I... CAN'T...
I'M... USE-LESS!
TUP
YES, THE ATTACK DESTROYED YOUR ADVANTAGE.
YOU HAVE LOST!
KAYUKI...

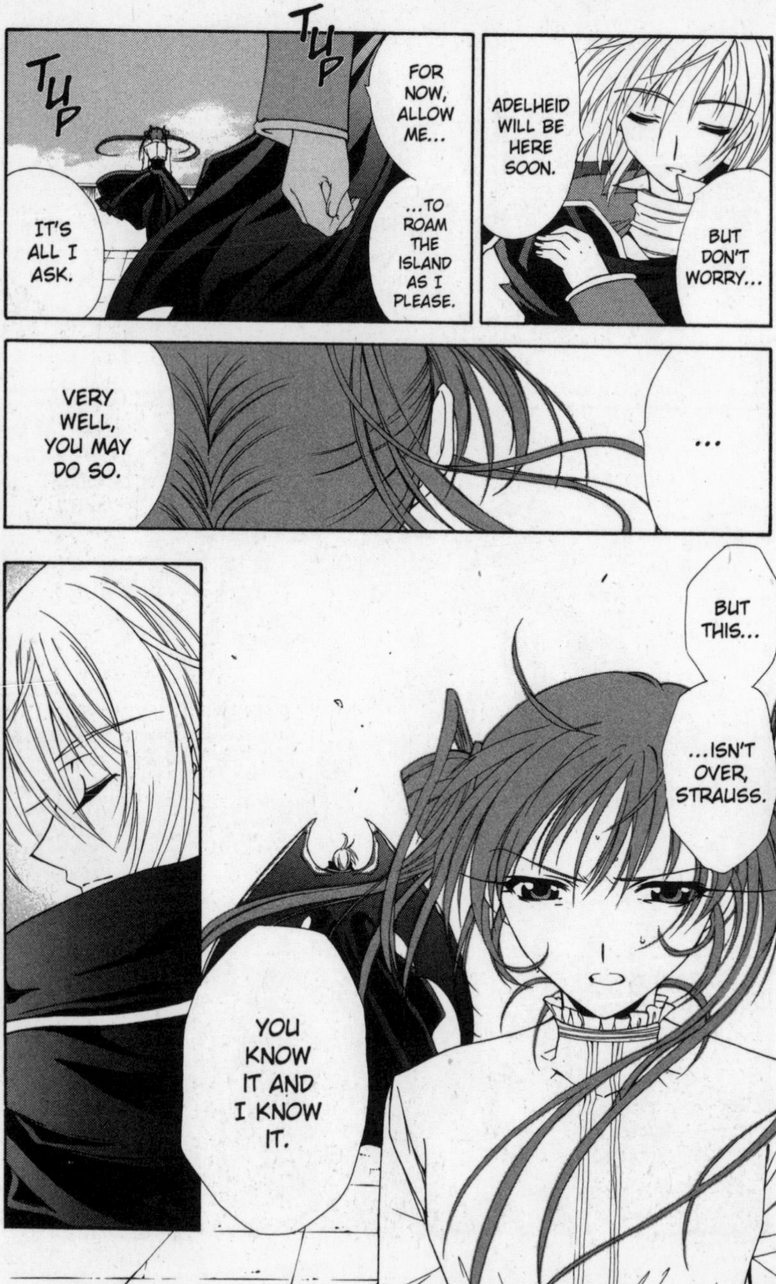
ADELHEID WILL BE HERE SOON.
BUT DON'T WORRY...
TUP
FOR NOW, ALLOW ME...
...TO ROAM THE ISLAND AS I PLEASE.
TUP
IT'S ALL I ASK.
...
VERY WELL, YOU MAY DO SO.
BUT THIS...
...ISN'T OVER, STRAUSS.
YOU KNOW IT AND I KNOW IT.

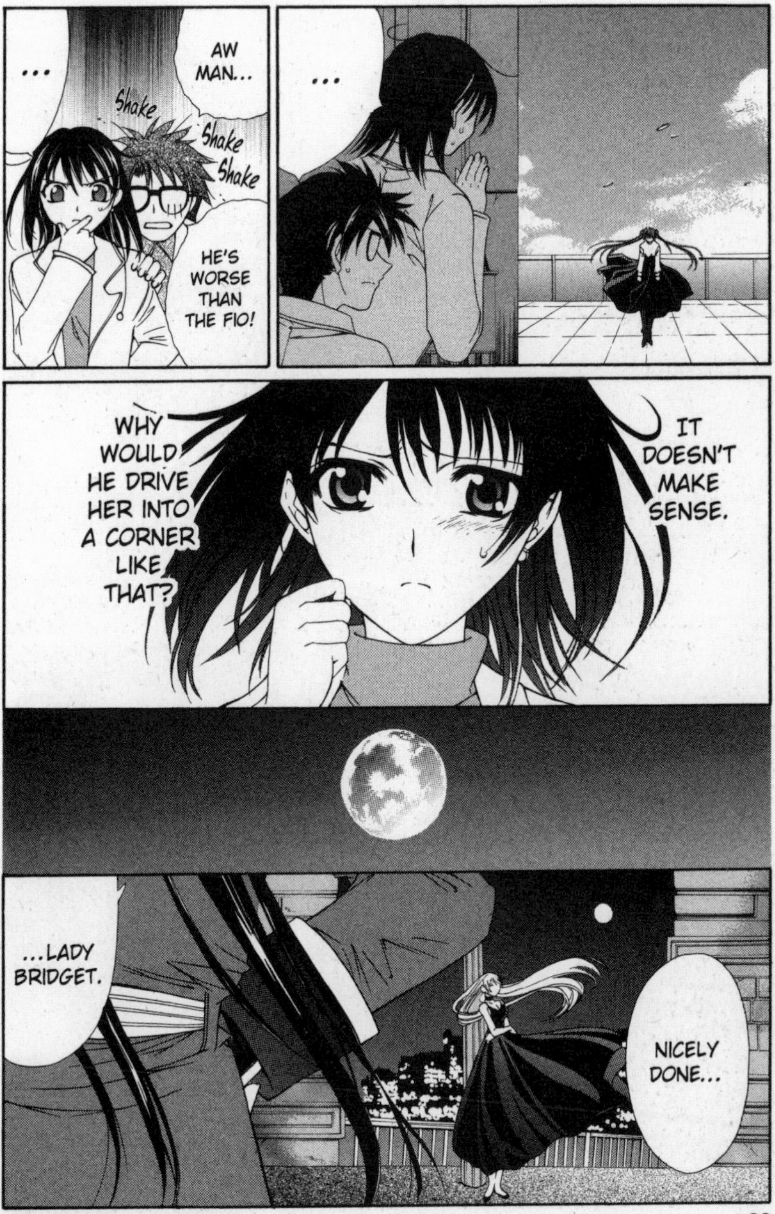
...
AW MAN...
...
Shake
Shake
Shake
HE'S WORSE THAN THE FIO!
IT DOESN'T MAKE SENSE.
WHY WOULD HE DRIVE HER INTO A CORNER LIKE THAT?
NICELY DONE...
...LADY BRIDGET.

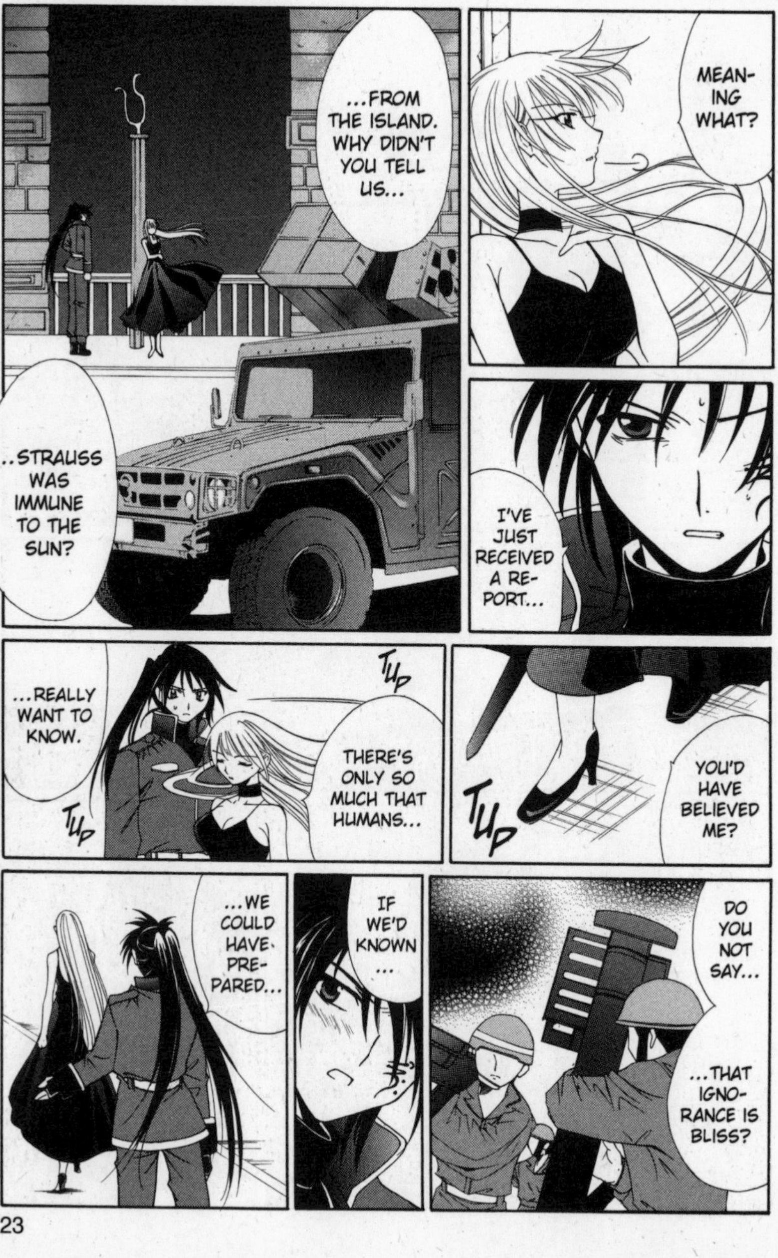
MEANING WHAT?
I'VE JUST RECEIVED A REPORT...
...FROM THE ISLAND. WHY DIDN'T YOU TELL US...
...STRAUSS WAS IMMUNE TO THE SUN?
YOU'D HAVE BELIEVED ME?
TUP
TUP
THERE'S ONLY SO MUCH THAT HUMANS...
...REALLY WANT TO KNOW.
TUP
DO YOU NOT SAY...
...THAT IGNORANCE IS BLISS?
IF WE'D KNOWN...
...WE COULD HAVE PREPARED...

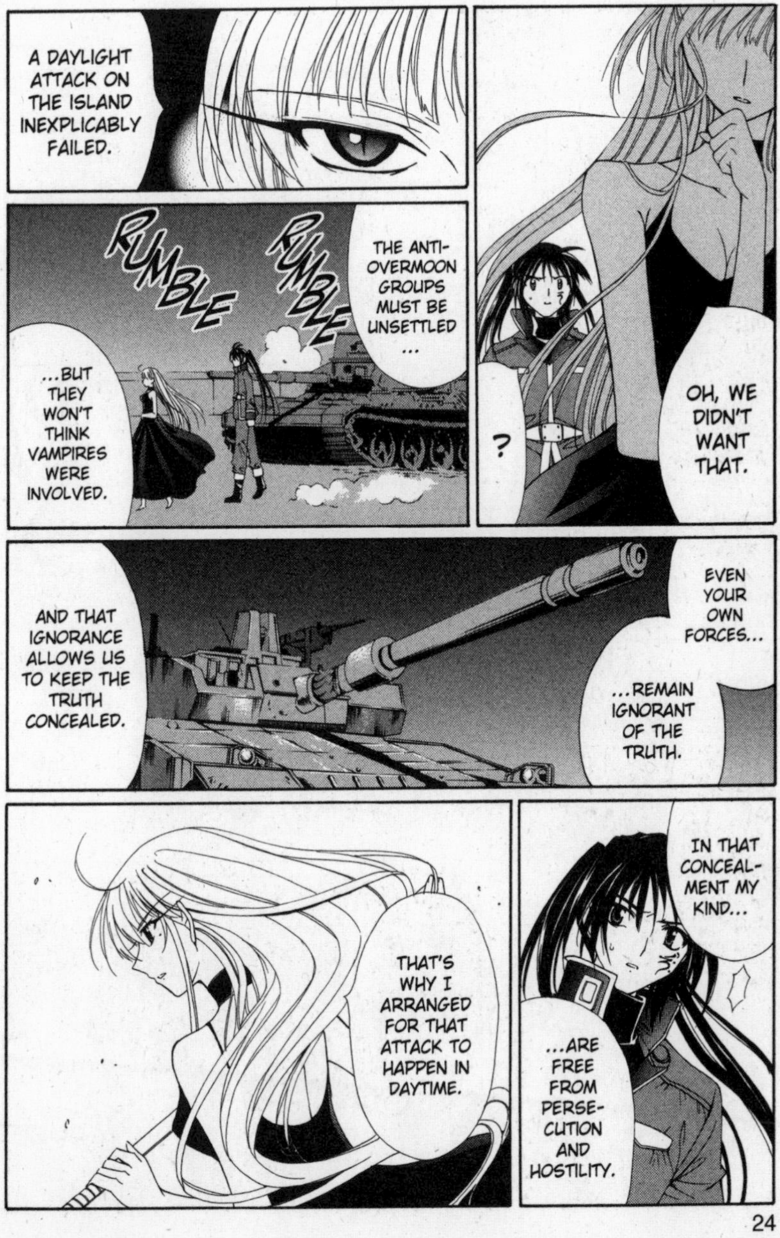
OH, WE DIDN'T WANT THAT.
?
A DAYLIGHT ATTACK ON THE ISLAND INEXPLICABLY FAILED.
RUMBLE RUMBLE
THE ANTI-OVERMOON GROUPS MUST BE UNSETTLED...
...BUT THEY WON'T THINK VAMPIRES WERE INVOLVED.
EVEN YOUR OWN FORCES...
...REMAIN IGNORANT OF THE TRUTH.
AND THAT IGNORANCE ALLOWS US TO KEEP THE TRUTH CONCEALED.
IN THAT CONCEAL-MENT MY KIND...
...ARE FREE FROM PERSE-CUTION AND HOSTILITY.
THAT'S WHY I ARRANGED FOR THAT ATTACK TO HAPPEN IN DAYTIME.

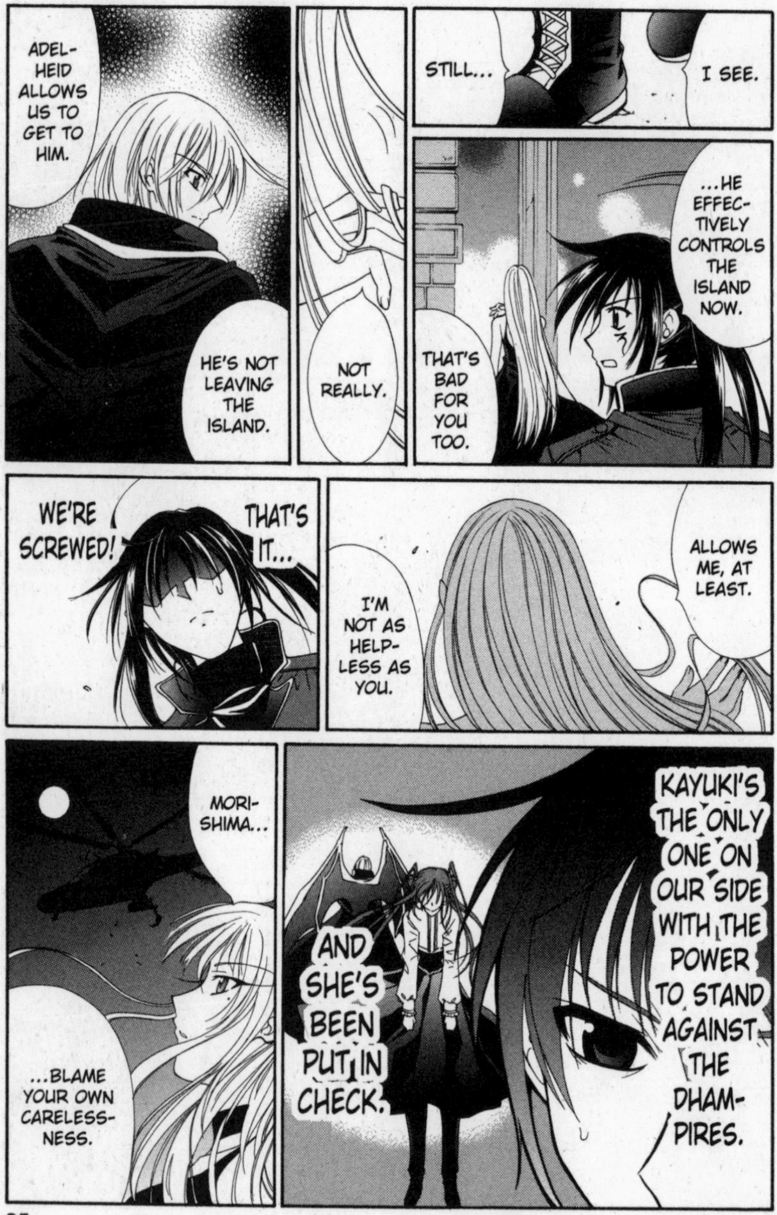
I SEE.
STILL...
...HE EFFECTIVELY CONTROLS THE ISLAND NOW.
THAT'S BAD FOR YOU TOO.
NOT REALLY.
ADELHEID ALLOWS US TO GET TO HIM.
HE'S NOT LEAVING THE ISLAND.
ALLOWS ME, AT LEAST.
I'M NOT AS HELPLESS AS YOU.
THAT'S IT...
WE'RE SCREWED!
KAYUKI'S THE ONLY ONE ON OUR SIDE WITH THE POWER TO STAND AGAINST THE DHAMPIRES.
AND SHE'S BEEN PUT IN CHECK.
MORISHIMA...
...BLAME YOUR OWN CARELESSNESS.

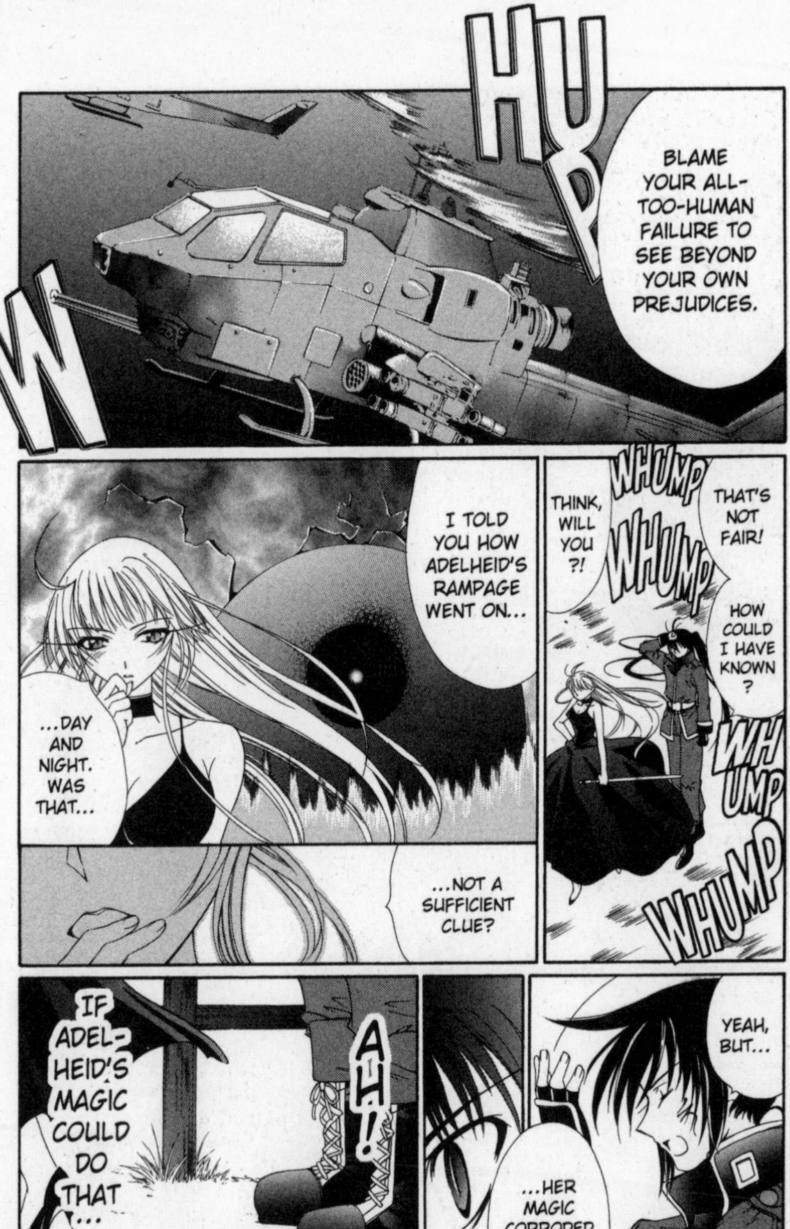
WHUP
BLAME YOUR ALL-TOO-HUMAN FAILURE TO SEE BEYOND YOUR OWN PREJUDICES.
THAT'S NOT FAIR!
WHUMP
THINK, WILL YOU?!
WHUMP
HOW COULD I HAVE KNOWN?
WHUMP
WHUMP
I TOLD YOU HOW ADELHEID'S RAMPAGE WENT ON...
...DAY AND NIGHT. WAS THAT...
...NOT A SUFFICIENT CLUE?
YEAH, BUT...
...HER MAGIC CORRODED SUNLIGHT...
AH!
IF ADELHEID'S MAGIC COULD DO THAT...

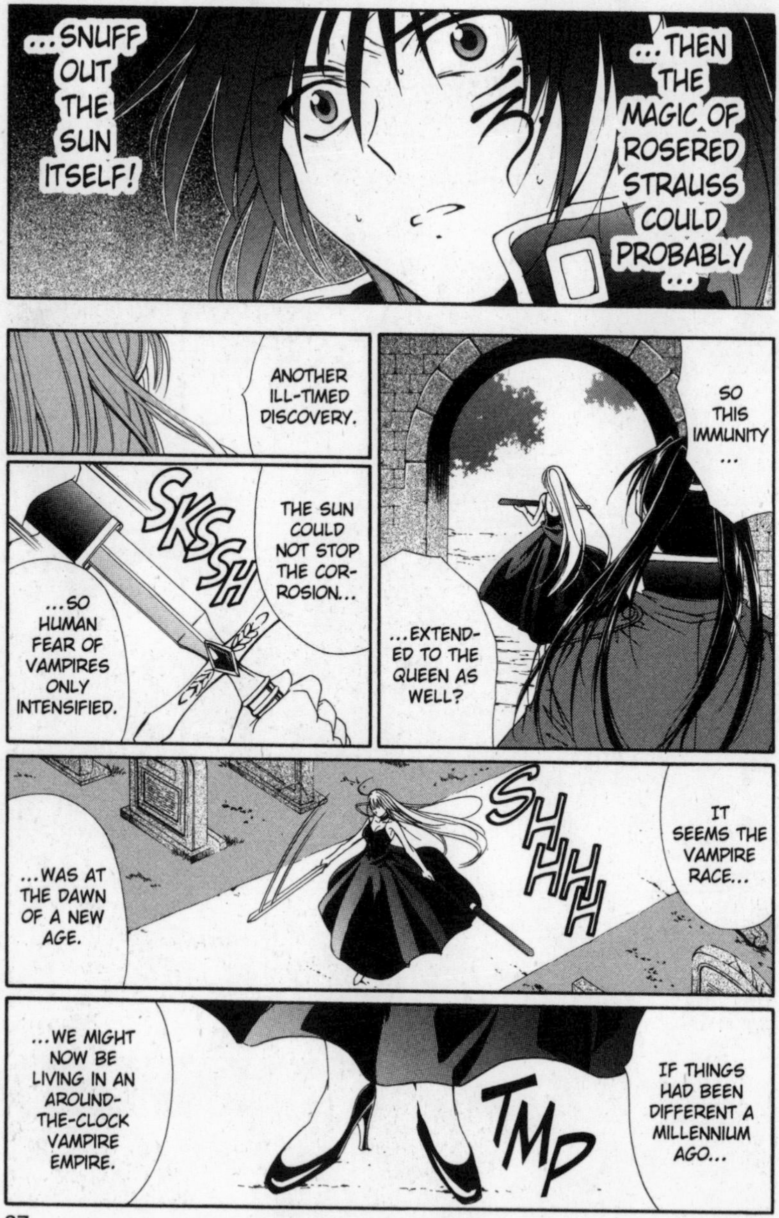
...THEN THE MAGIC OF ROSERED STRAUSS COULD PROBABLY...
...SNUFF OUT THE SUN ITSELF!
SO THIS IMMUNITY...
...EXTENDED TO THE QUEEN AS WELL?
ANOTHER ILL-TIMED DISCOVERY.
SKSSH
THE SUN COULD NOT STOP THE CORROSION...
...SO HUMAN FEAR OF VAMPIRES ONLY INTENSIFIED.
IT SEEMS THE VAMPIRE RACE...
SHHHH
...WAS AT THE DAWN OF A NEW AGE.
IF THINGS HAD BEEN DIFFERENT A MILLENNIUM AGO...
TMP
...WE MIGHT NOW BE LIVING IN AN AROUND-THE-CLOCK VAMPIRE EMPIRE.

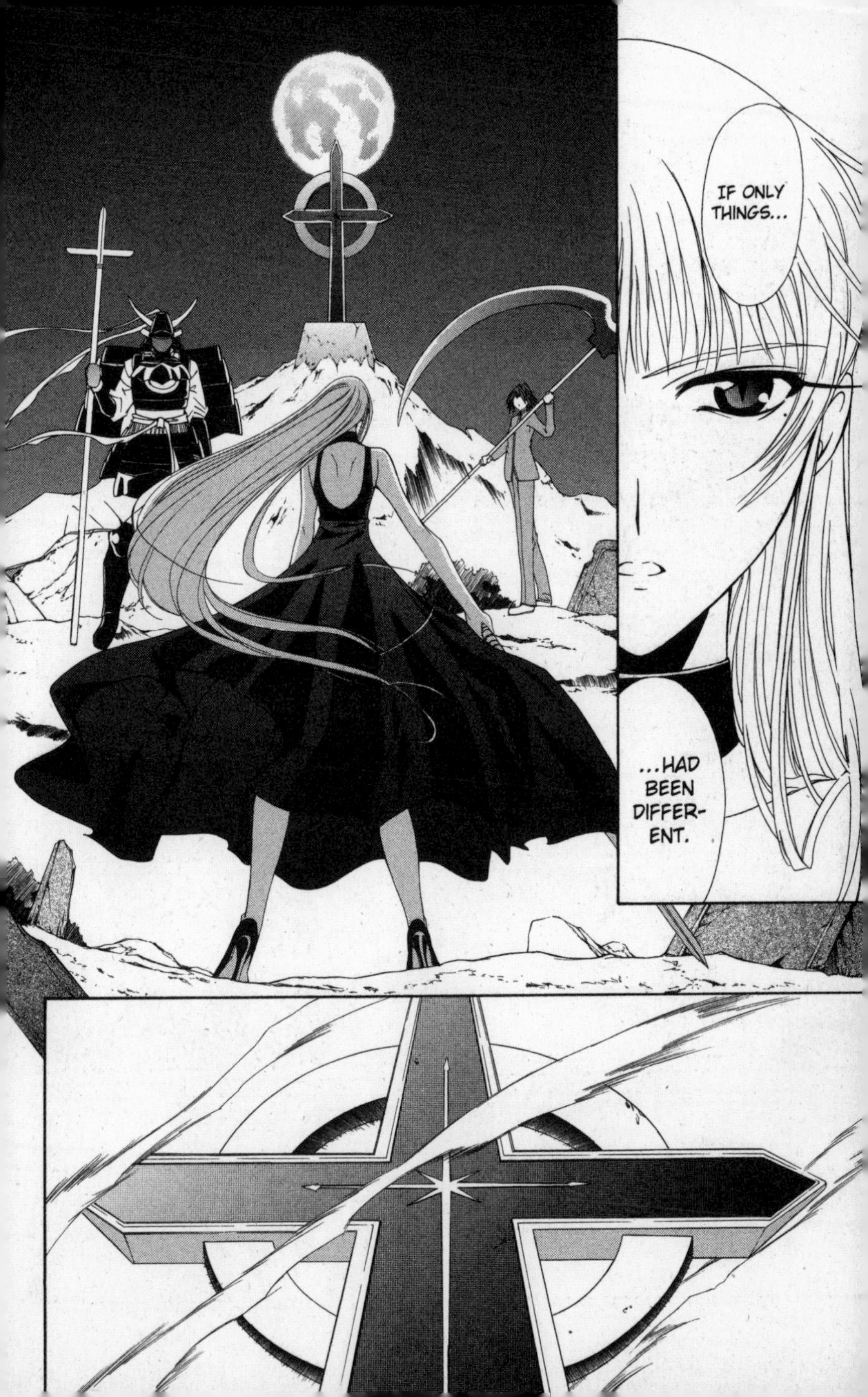
IF ONLY THINGS...
...HAD BEEN DIFFER-ENT.

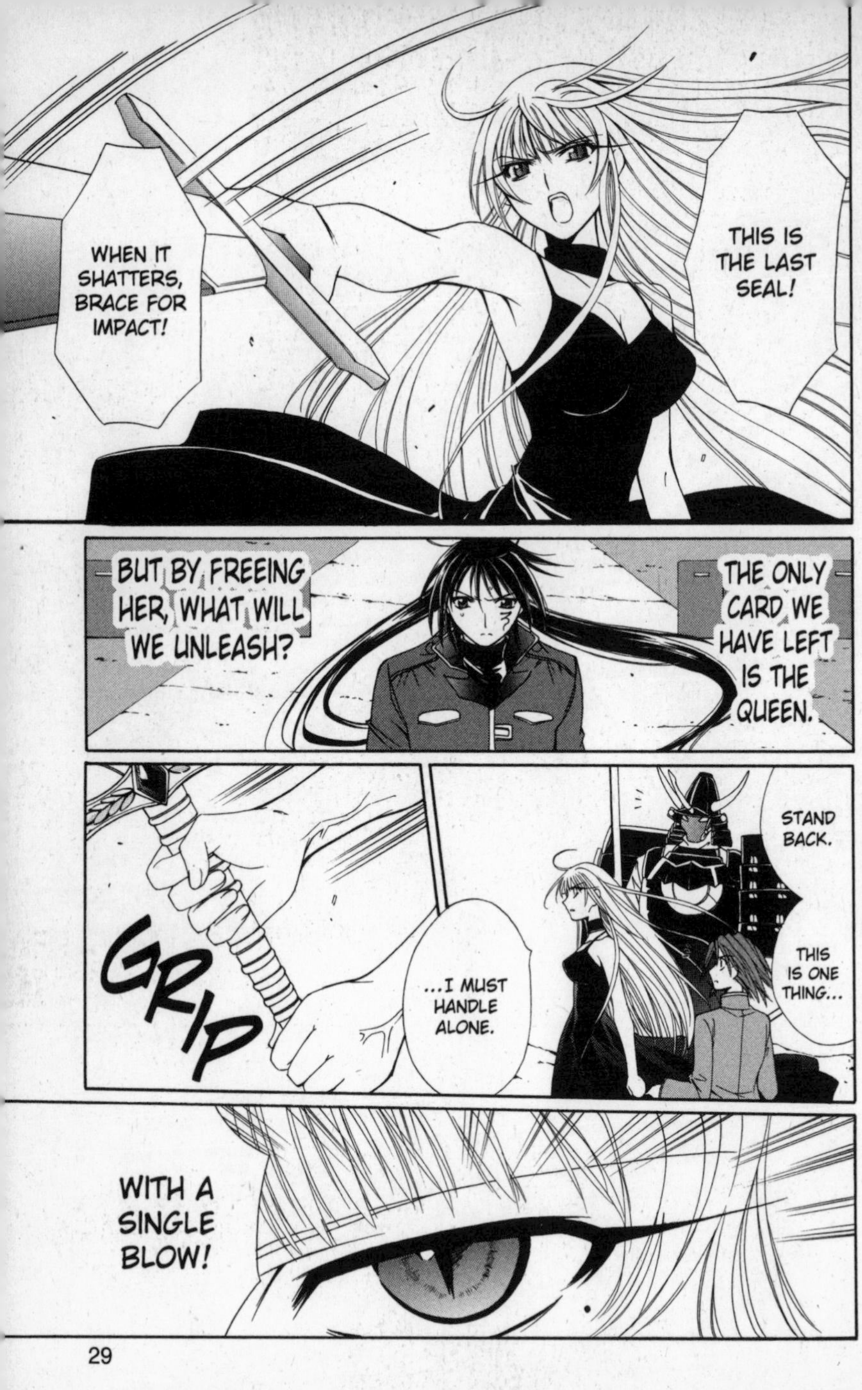
THIS IS THE LAST SEAL!
WHEN IT SHATTERS, BRACE FOR IMPACT!
THE ONLY CARD WE HAVE LEFT IS THE QUEEN.
BUT BY FREEING HER, WHAT WILL WE UNLEASH?
STAND BACK.
THIS IS ONE THING...
...I MUST HANDLE ALONE.
GRIP
WITH A SINGLE BLOW!

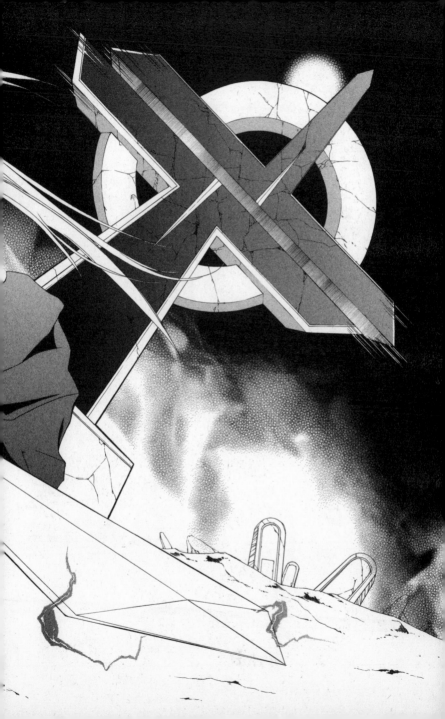

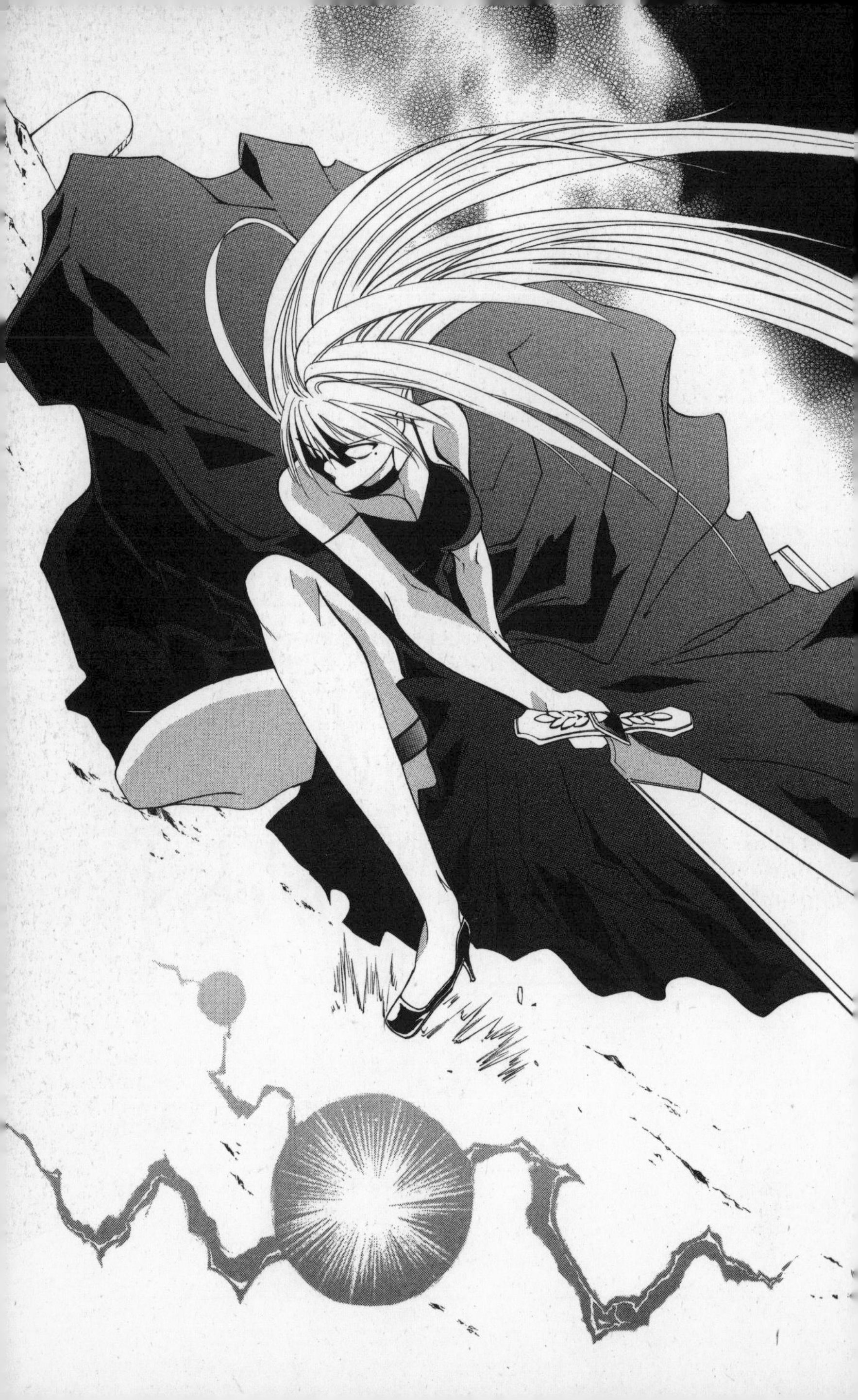

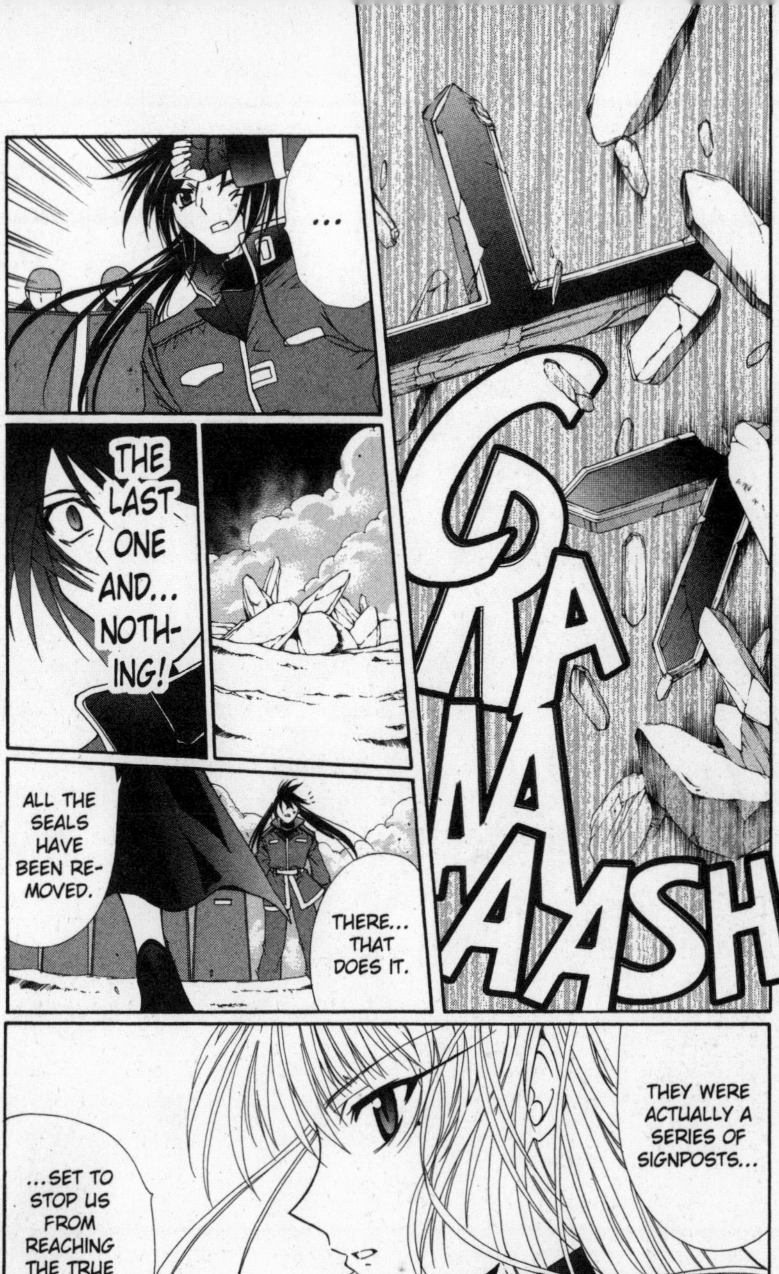
CRAAASH
...
THE LAST ONE AND... NOTHING!
THERE... THAT DOES IT.
ALL THE SEALS HAVE BEEN REMOVED.
THEY WERE ACTUALLY A SERIES OF SIGNPOSTS...
...SET TO STOP US FROM REACHING THE TRUE SEAL.

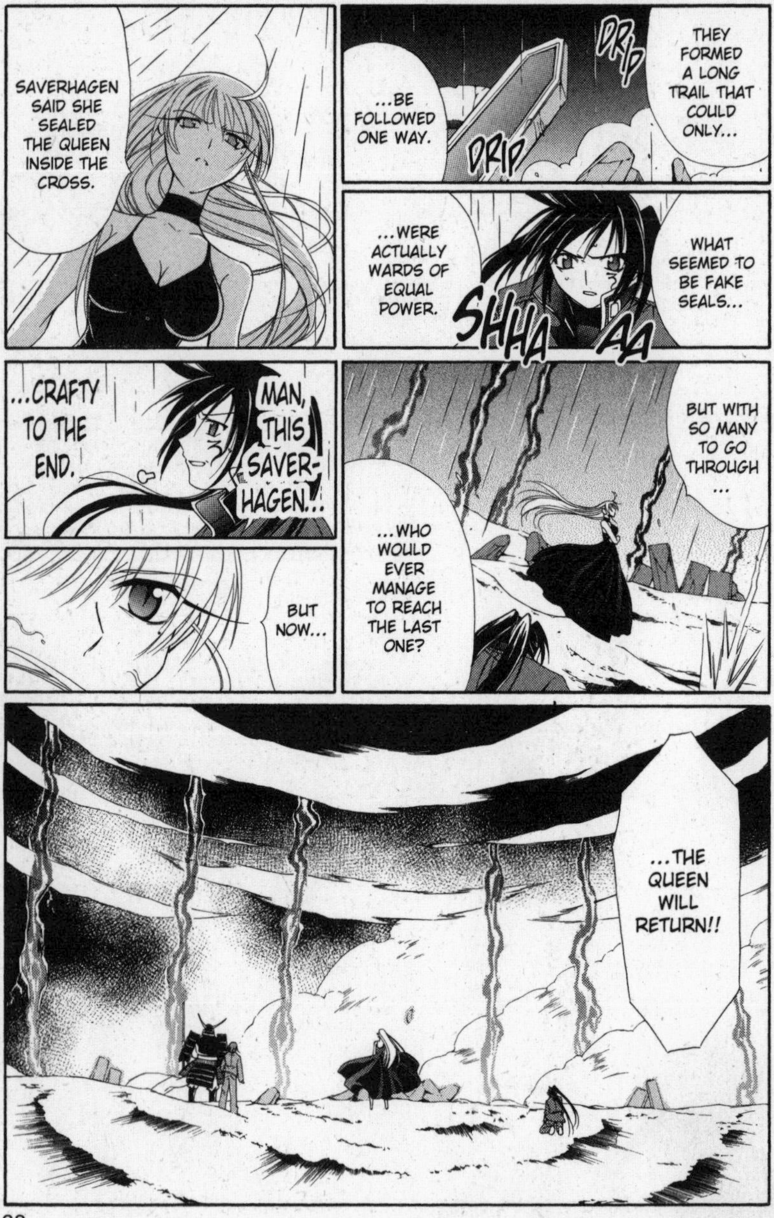
THEY FORMED A LONG TRAIL THAT COULD ONLY...
DRIP
...BE FOLLOWED ONE WAY.
DRIP
WHAT SEEMED TO BE FAKE SEALS...
...WERE ACTUALLY WARDS OF EQUAL POWER.
SHHAAA
SAVERHAGEN SAID SHE SEALED THE QUEEN INSIDE THE CROSS.
BUT WITH SO MANY TO GO THROUGH...
...WHO WOULD EVER MANAGE TO REACH THE LAST ONE?
MAN, THIS SAVERHAGEN...
...CRAFTY TO THE END.
BUT NOW...
...THE QUEEN WILL RETURN!!

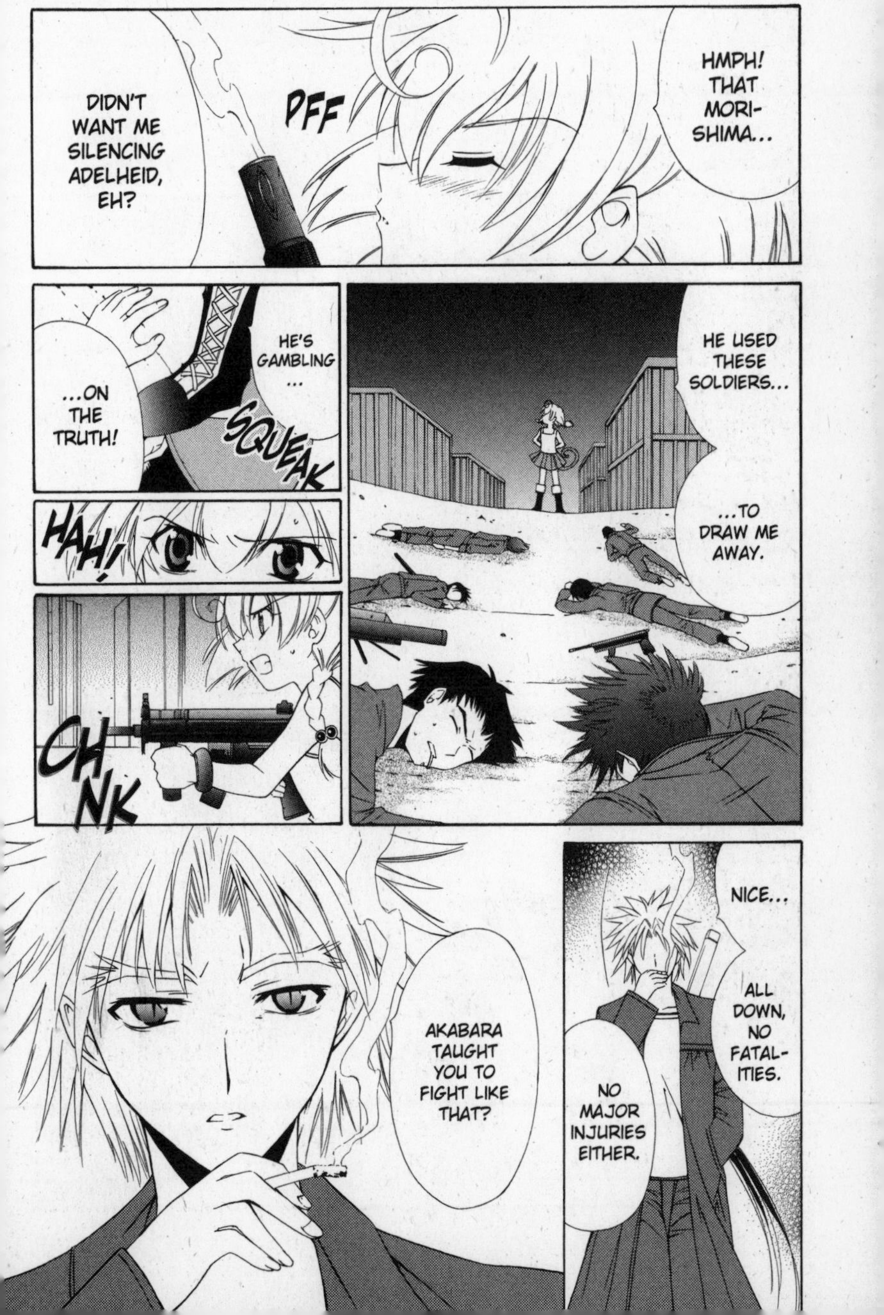
HMPH! THAT MORI-SHIMA...
PFF
DIDN'T WANT ME SILENCING ADELHEID, EH?
HE USED THESE SOLDIERS...
...TO DRAW ME AWAY.
HE'S GAMBLING ...
SQUEAK
...ON THE TRUTH!
HAH!
CHNK
NICE...
ALL DOWN, NO FATAL-ITIES.
NO MAJOR INJURIES EITHER.
AKABARA TAUGHT YOU TO FIGHT LIKE THAT?

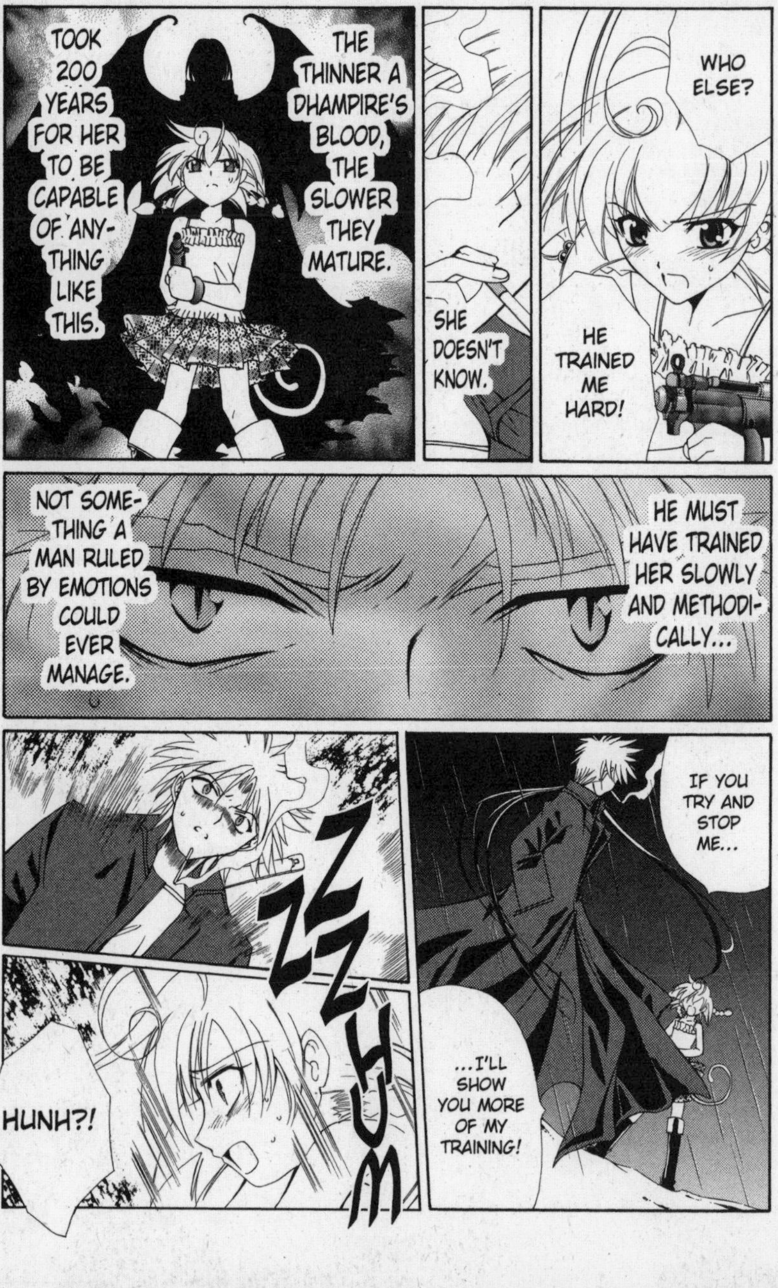
WHO ELSE?
HE TRAINED ME HARD!
SHE DOESN'T KNOW.
THE THINNER A DHAMPIRE'S BLOOD, THE SLOWER THEY MATURE.
TOOK 200 YEARS FOR HER TO BE CAPABLE OF ANYTHING LIKE THIS.
HE MUST HAVE TRAINED HER SLOWLY AND METHODICALLY...
NOT SOMETHING A MAN RULED BY EMOTIONS COULD EVER MANAGE.
IF YOU TRY AND STOP ME...
...I'LL SHOW YOU MORE OF MY TRAINING!
ZZZHUM
HUNH?!

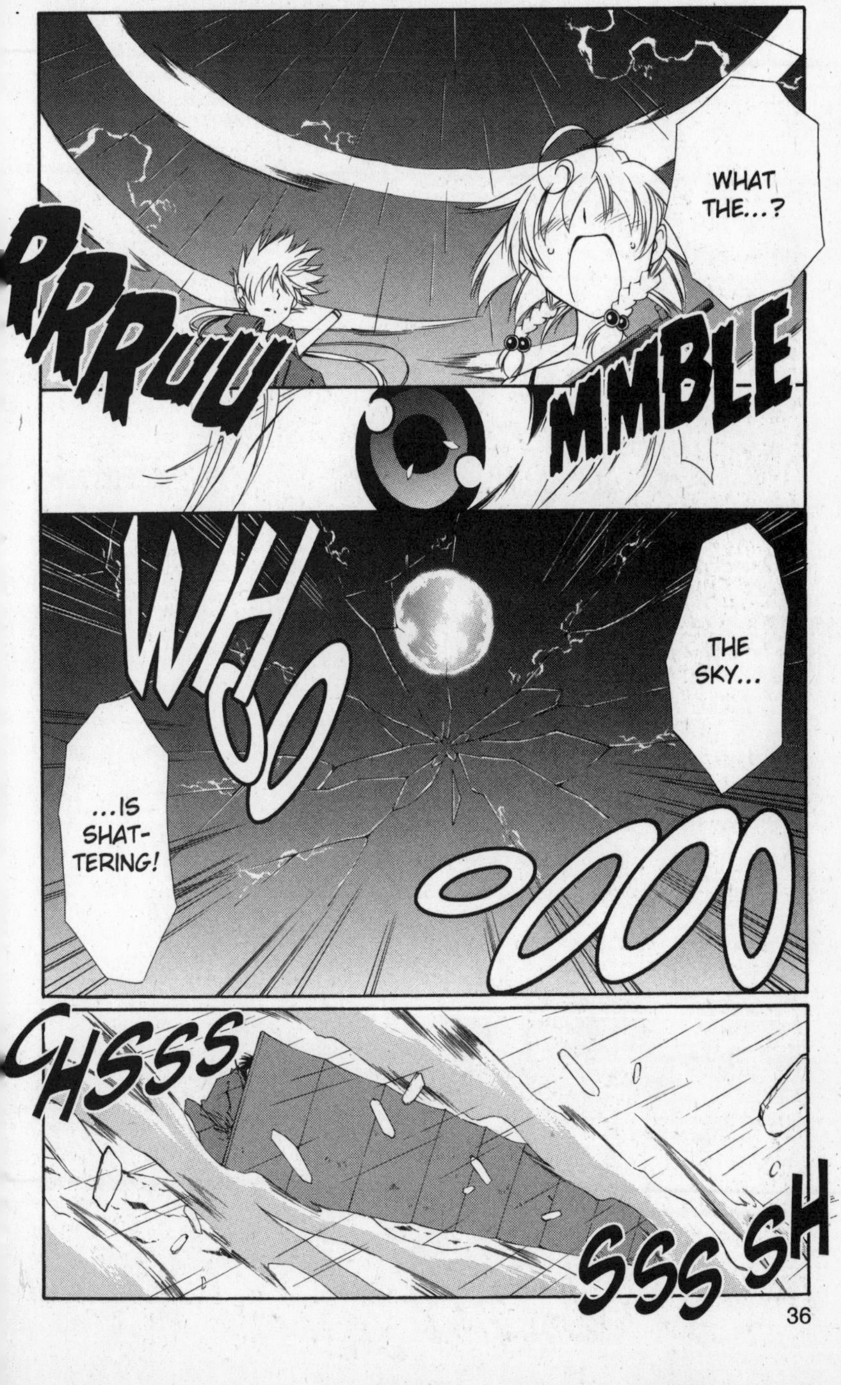
WHAT THE...?
PRRUU
MMBLE
THE SKY...
...IS SHAT-TERING!
WHOO
OOOO
CHSSS
SSSSH

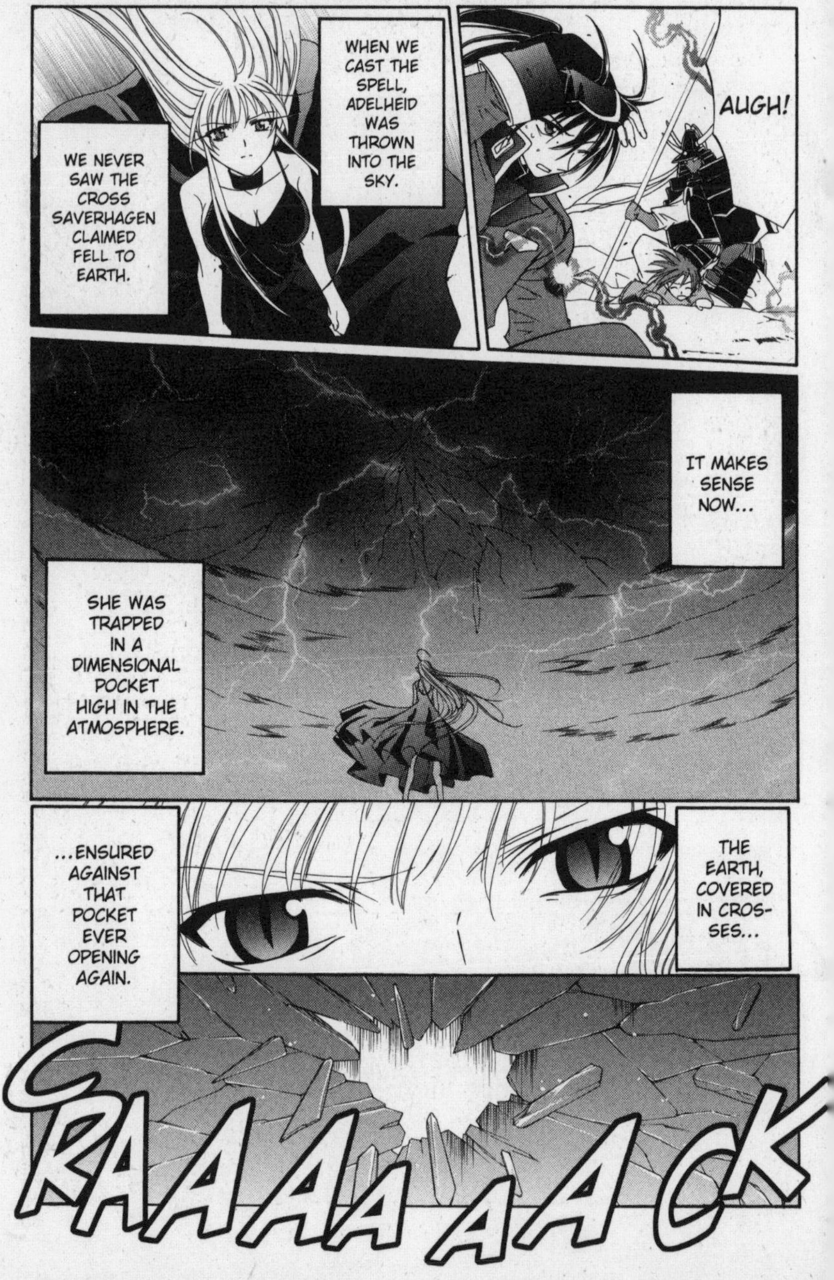
AUGH!
WHEN WE CAST THE SPELL, ADELHEID WAS THROWN INTO THE SKY.
WE NEVER SAW THE CROSS SAVERHAGEN CLAIMED FELL TO EARTH.
IT MAKES SENSE NOW...
SHE WAS TRAPPED IN A DIMENSIONAL POCKET HIGH IN THE ATMOSPHERE.
THE EARTH, COVERED IN CROS-SES...
...ENSURED AGAINST THAT POCKET EVER OPENING AGAIN.
CRAAAAAAACK

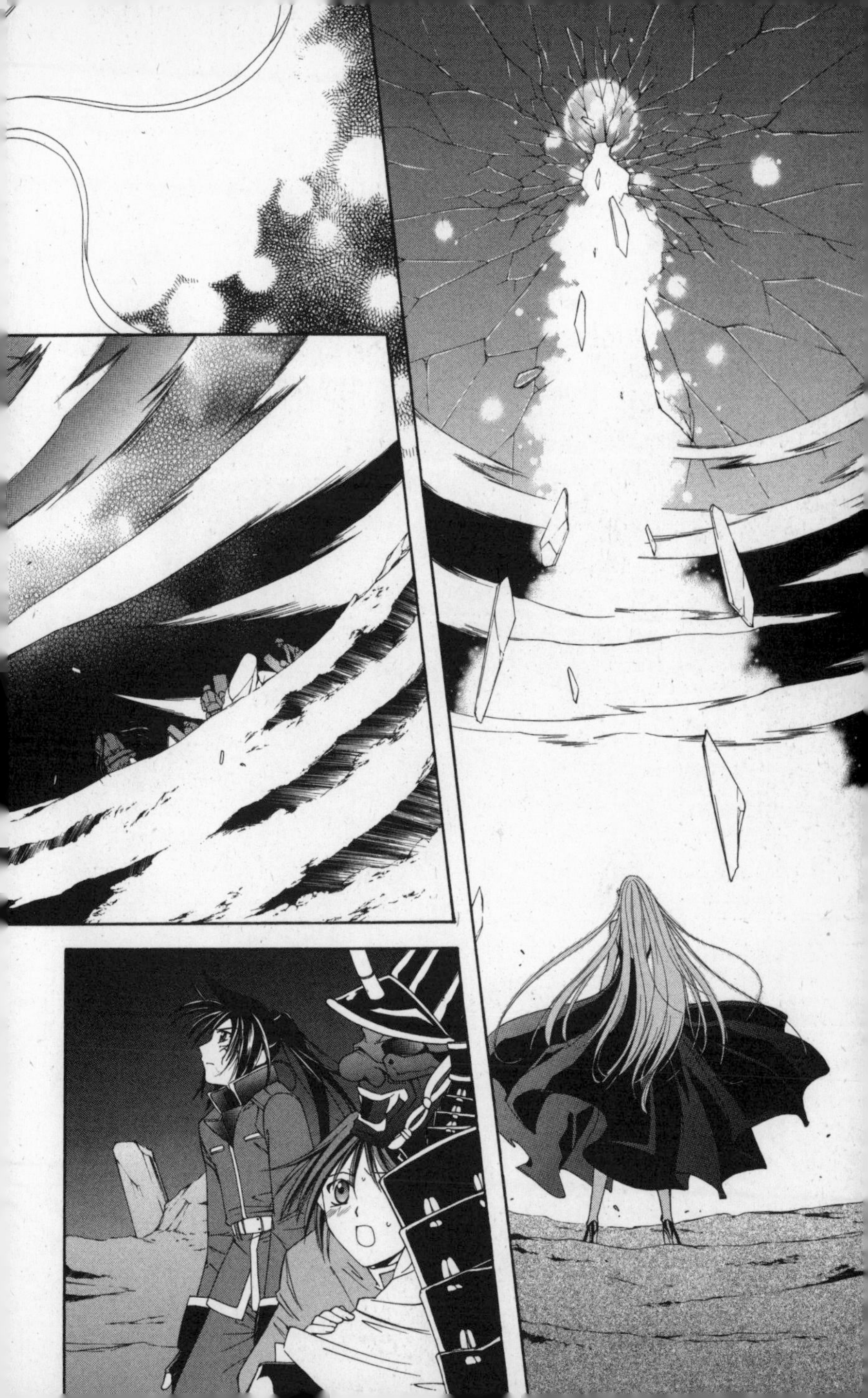

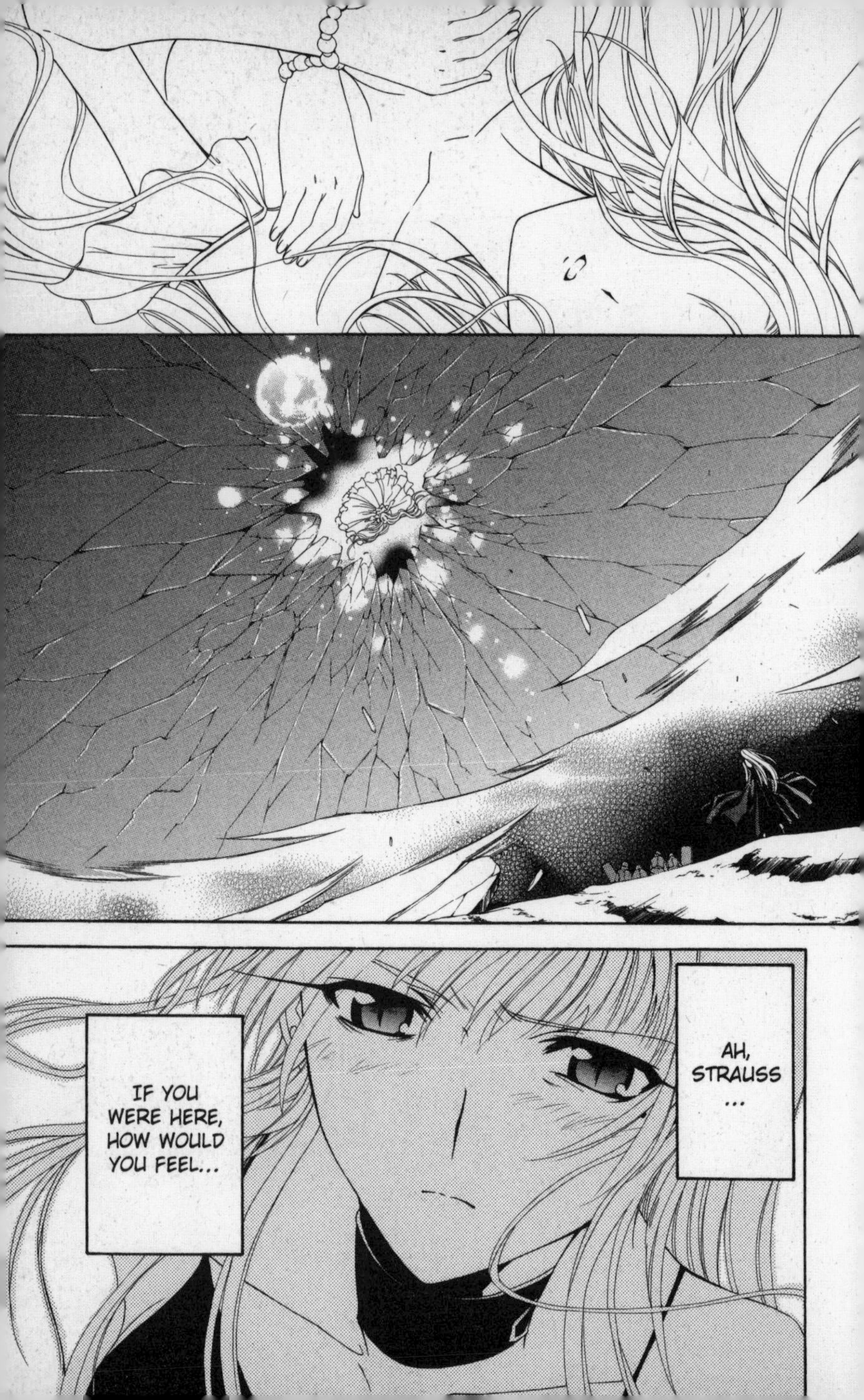
AH, STRAUSS...
IF YOU WERE HERE, HOW WOULD YOU FEEL...

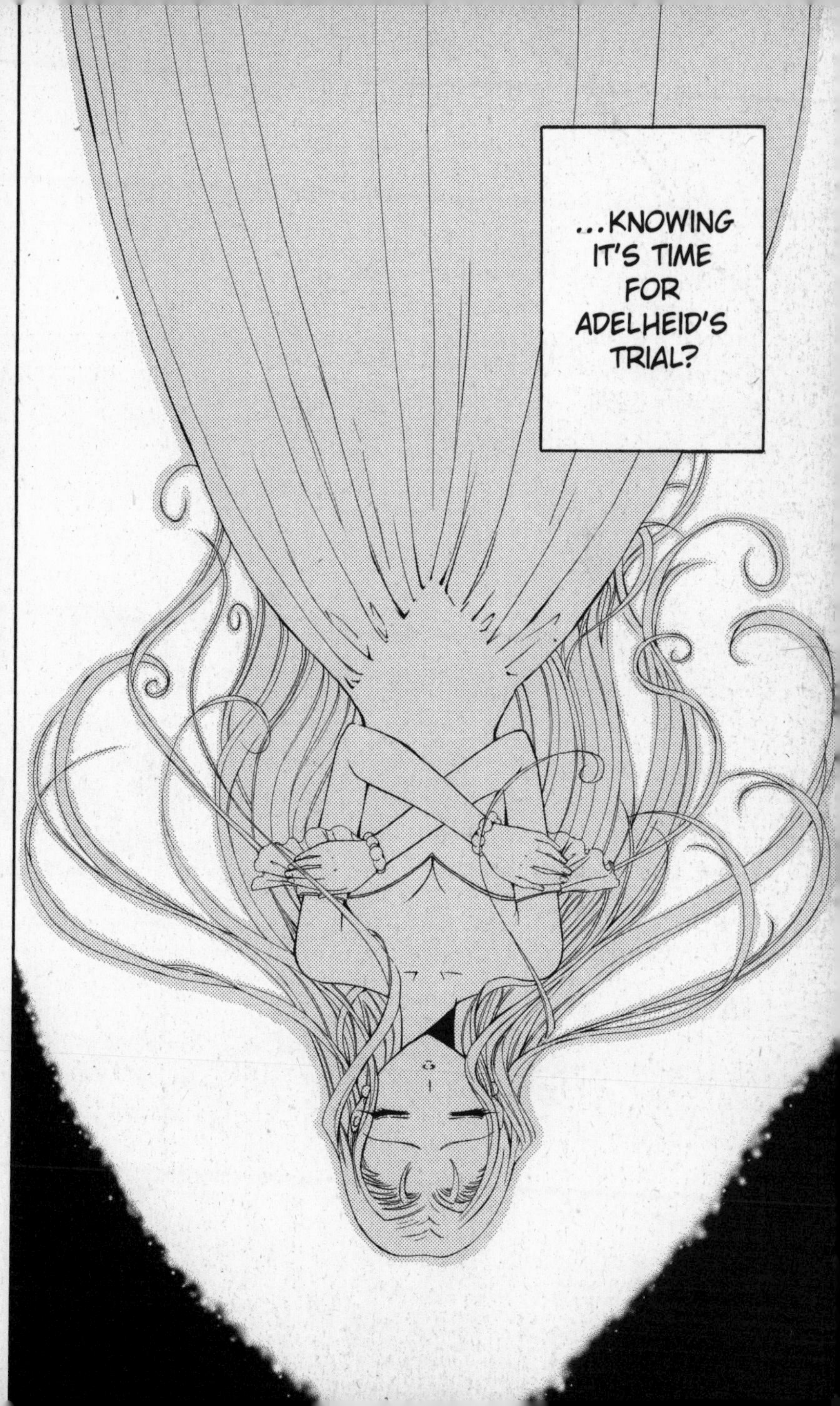
...KNOWING IT'S TIME FOR ADELHEID'S TRIAL?

THE RECORD OF A

FALLEN VAMPIRE

THE RECORD OF A

FALLEN VAMPIRE

Chapter 30: The Queen's Portrait

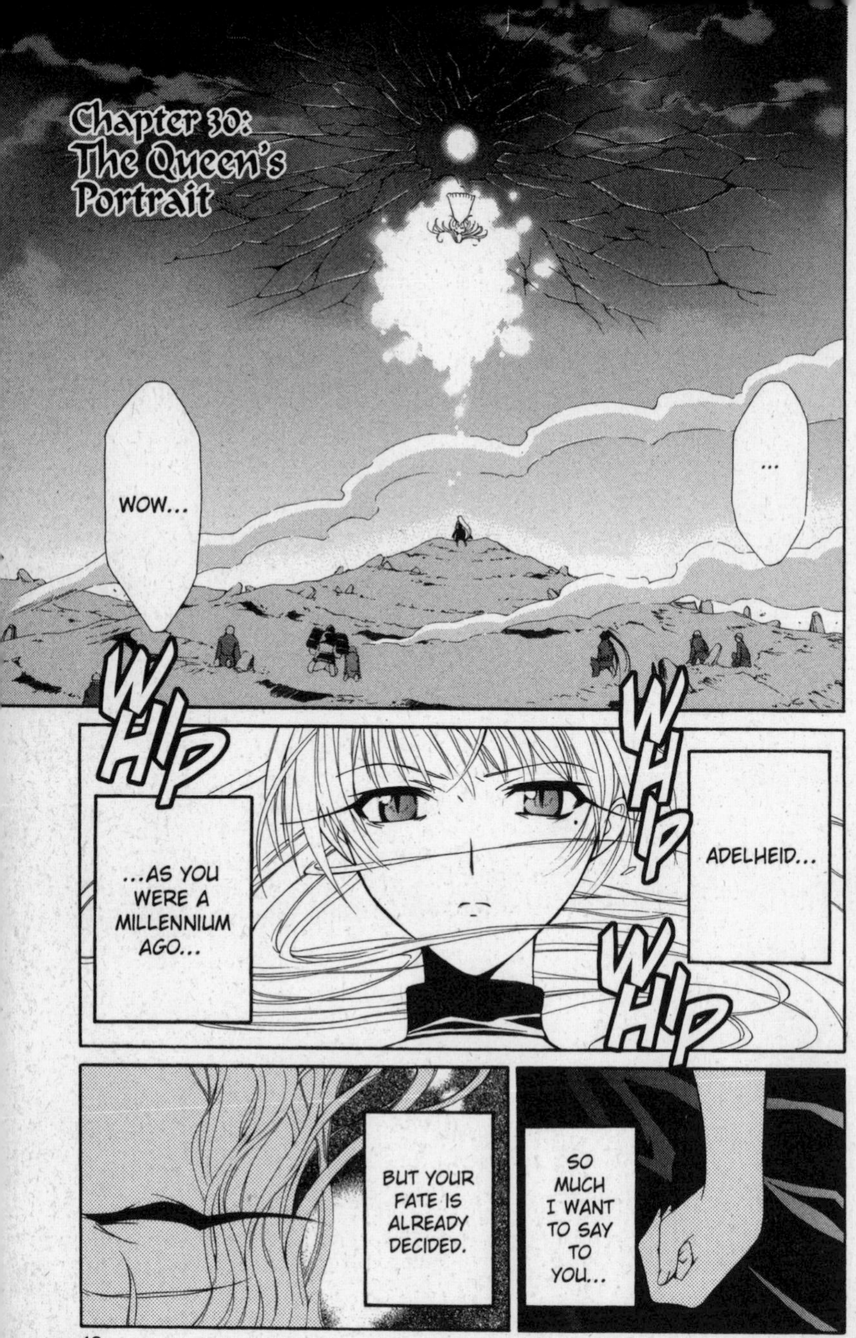
...
WOW...
WHIP
ADELHEID...
WHIP
WHIP
...AS YOU WERE A MILLENNIUM AGO...
SO MUCH I WANT TO SAY TO YOU...
BUT YOUR FATE IS ALREADY DECIDED.

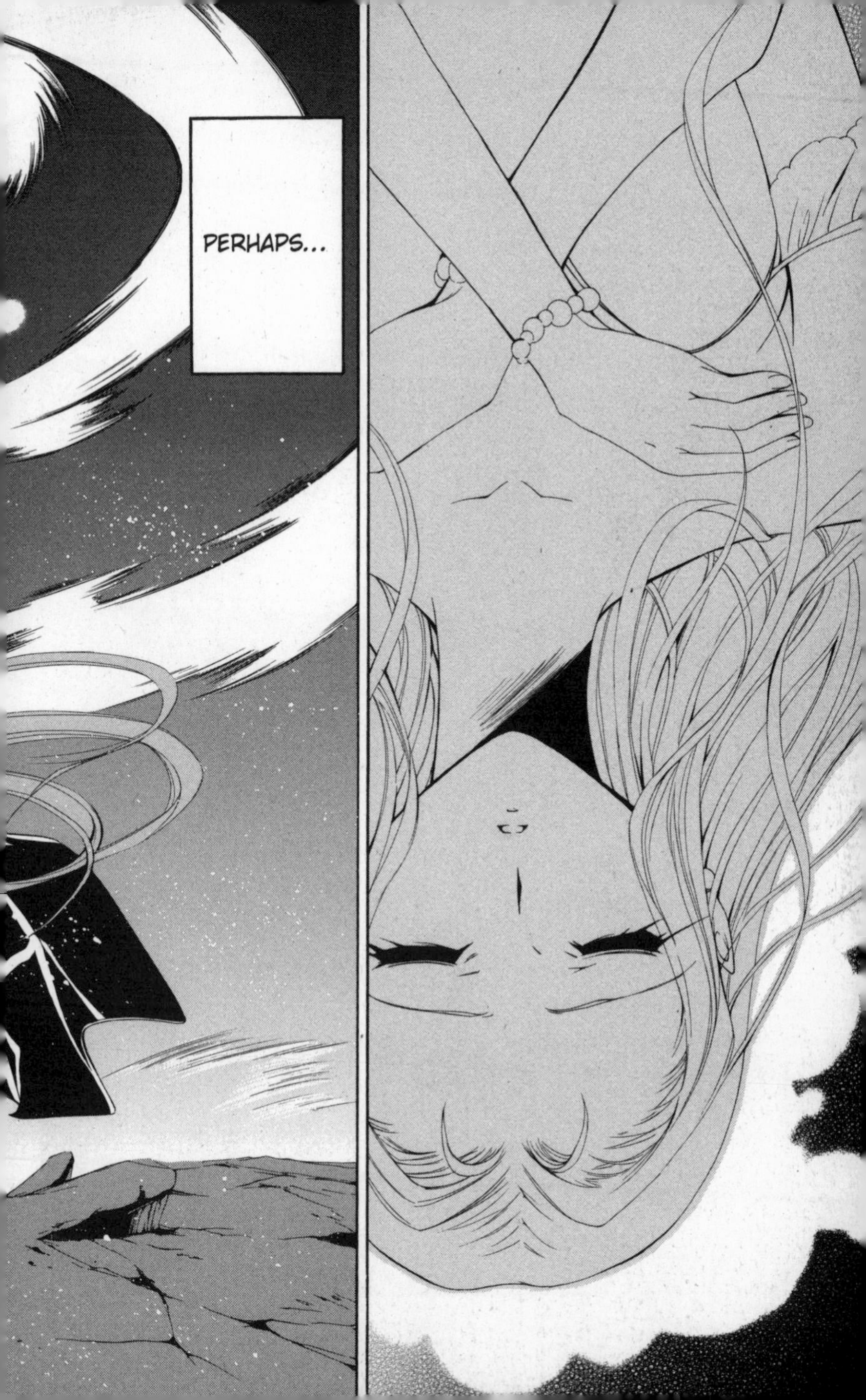
PERHAPS...

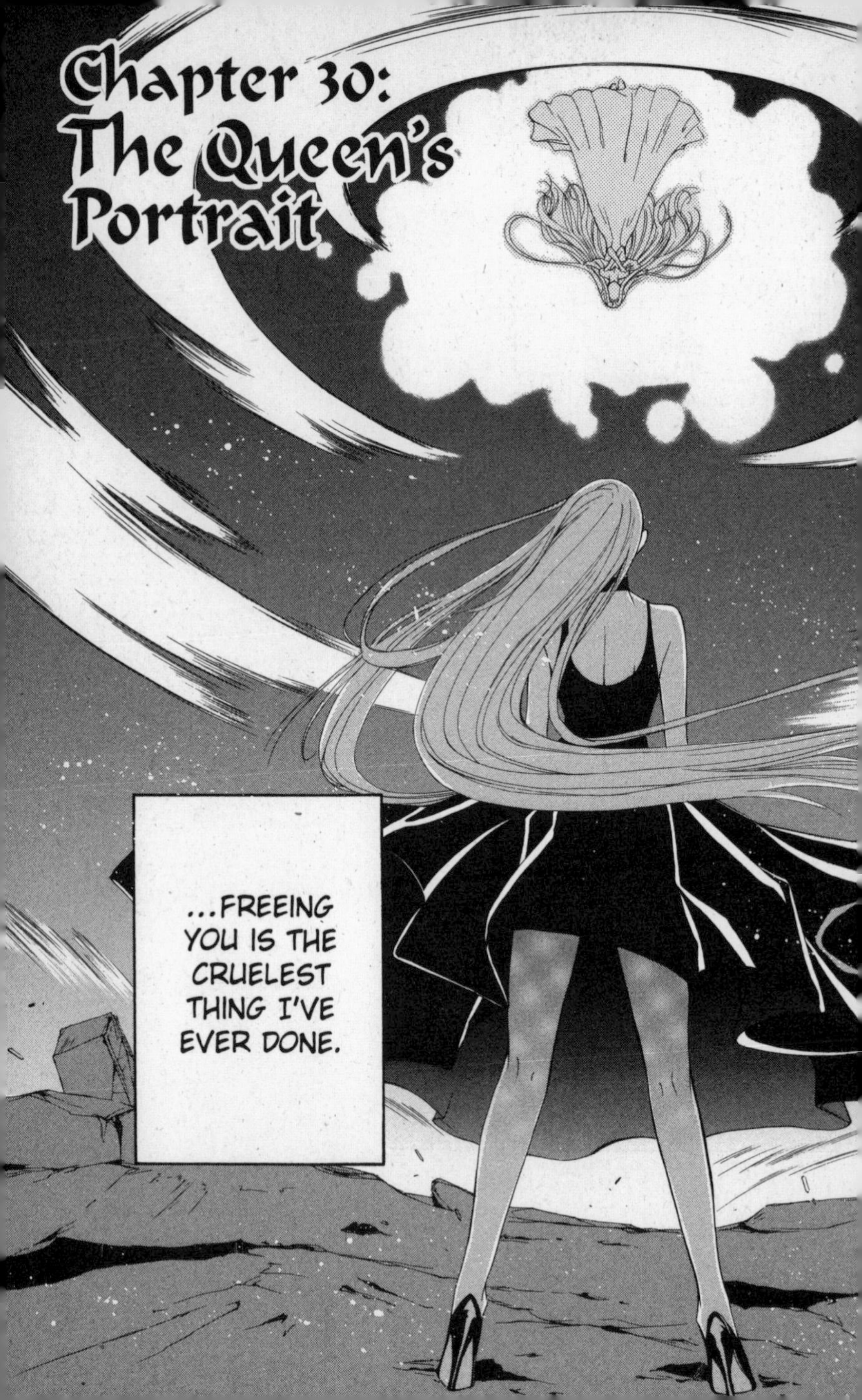
Chapter 30: The Queen's Portrait
...FREEING YOU IS THE CRUELEST THING I'VE EVER DONE.

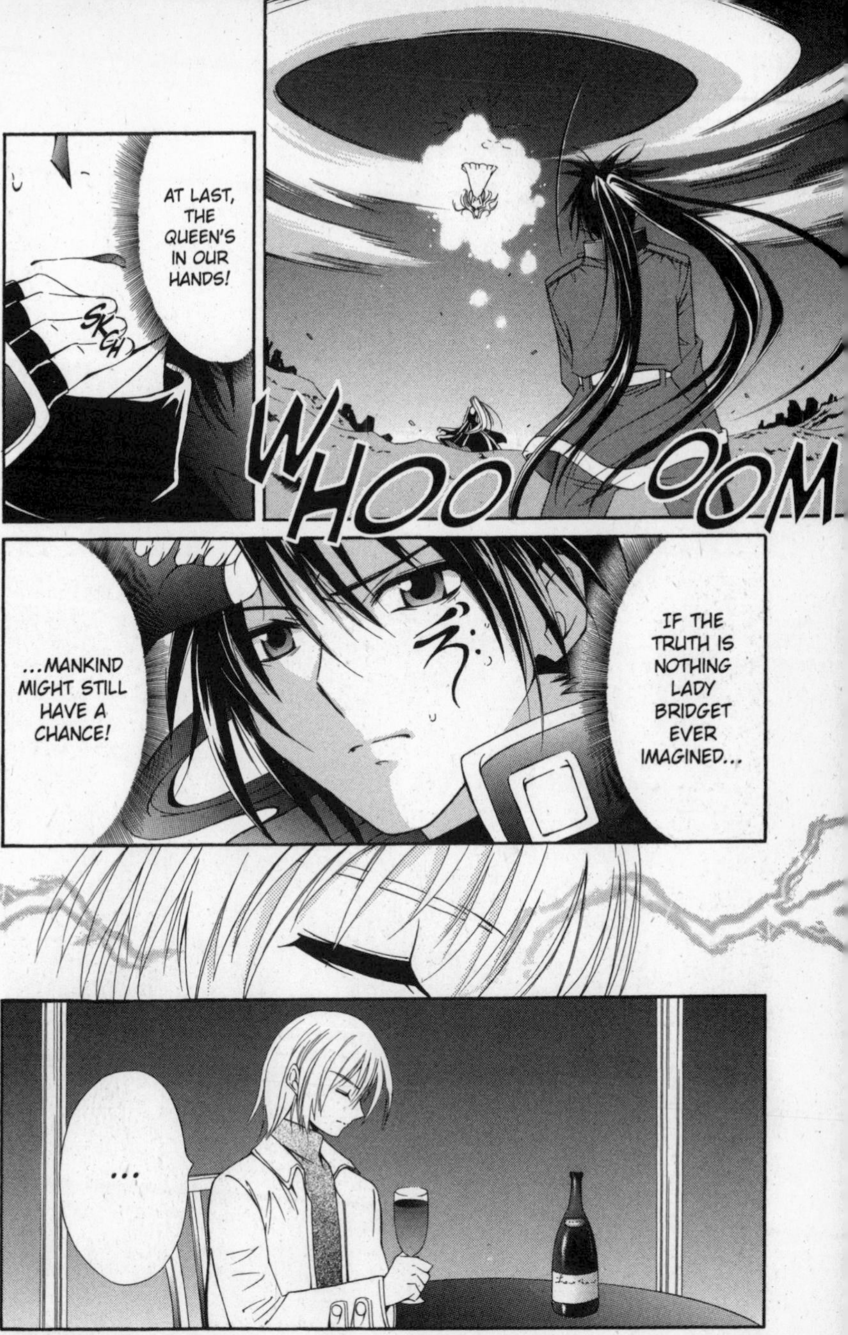
WHOOOOOM
AT LAST, THE QUEEN'S IN OUR HANDS!
SKCH
IF THE TRUTH IS NOTHING LADY BRIDGET EVER IMAGINED...
...MANKIND MIGHT STILL HAVE A CHANCE!
...

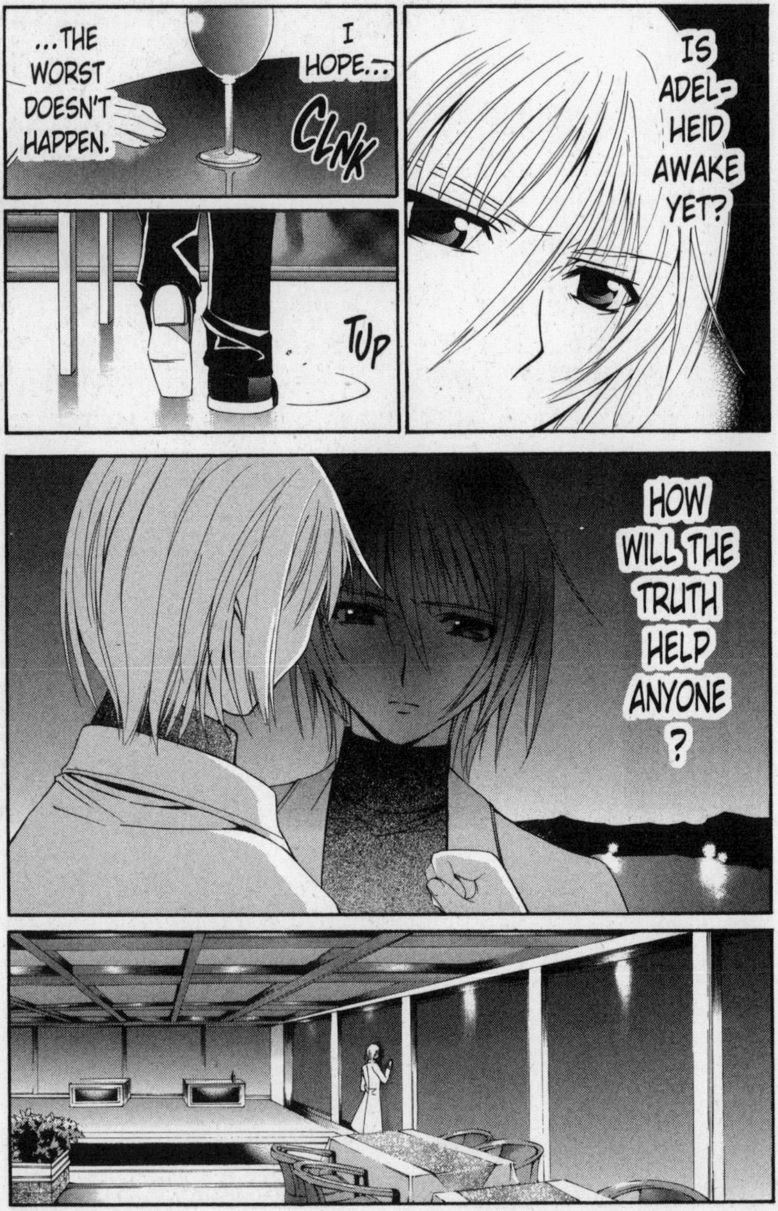
IS ADEL-HEID AWAKE YET?
I HOPE...
...THE WORST DOESN'T HAPPEN.
CLNK
TUP
HOW WILL THE TRUTH HELP ANYONE?

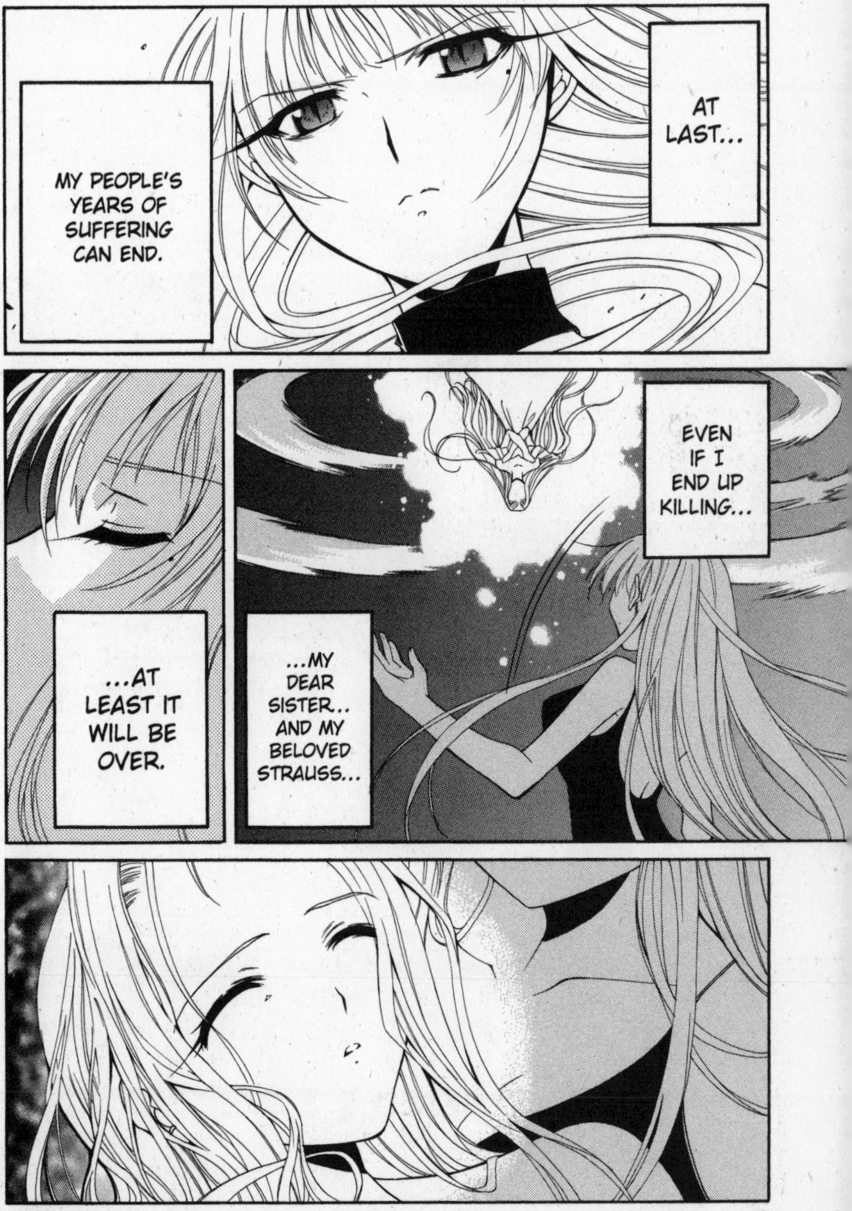
AT LAST...
MY PEOPLE'S YEARS OF SUFFERING CAN END.
EVEN IF I END UP KILLING...
...MY DEAR SISTER... AND MY BELOVED STRAUSS...
...AT LEAST IT WILL BE OVER.

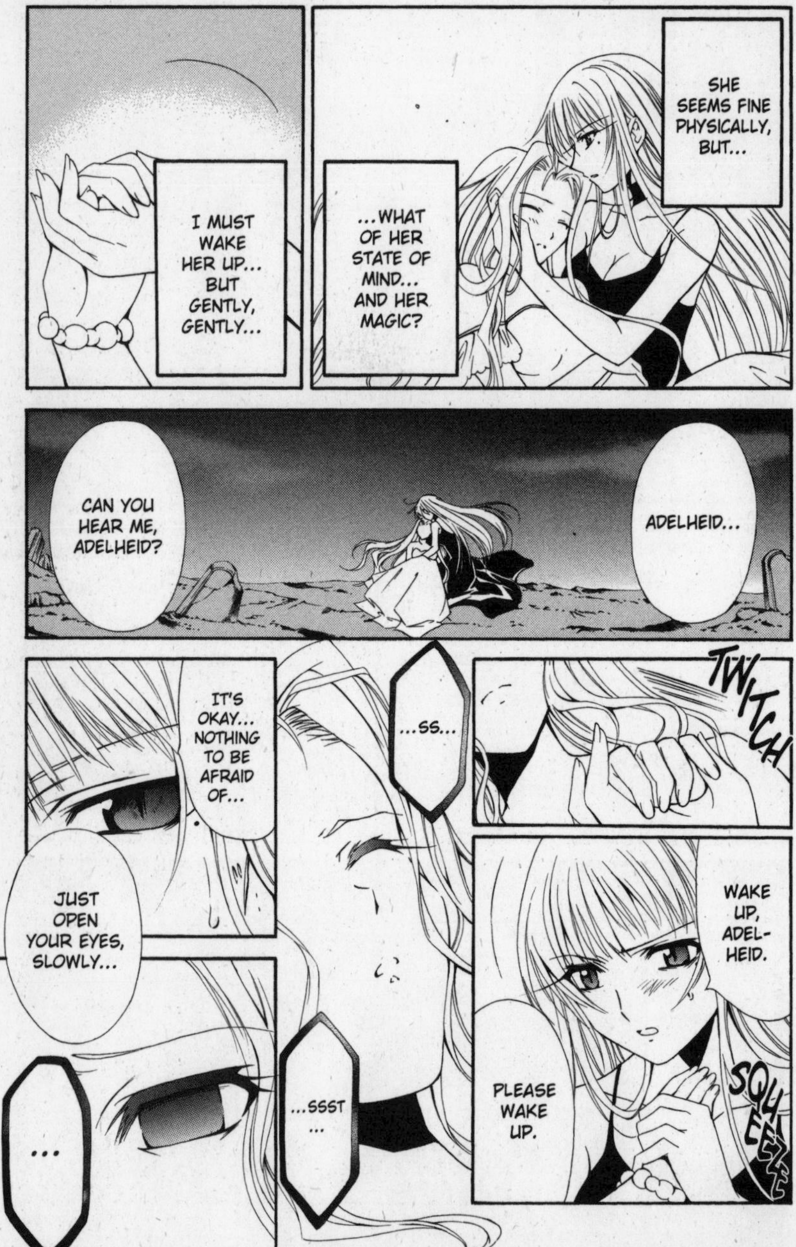
SHE SEEMS FINE PHYSICALLY, BUT...
...WHAT OF HER STATE OF MIND... AND HER MAGIC?
I MUST WAKE HER UP... BUT GENTLY, GENTLY...
ADELHEID...
CAN YOU HEAR ME, ADELHEID?
TWITCH
WAKE UP, ADEL-HEID.
SQUEEZE
PLEASE WAKE UP.
...SS...
...SSST ...
IT'S OKAY... NOTHING TO BE AFRAID OF...
JUST OPEN YOUR EYES, SLOWLY...
...

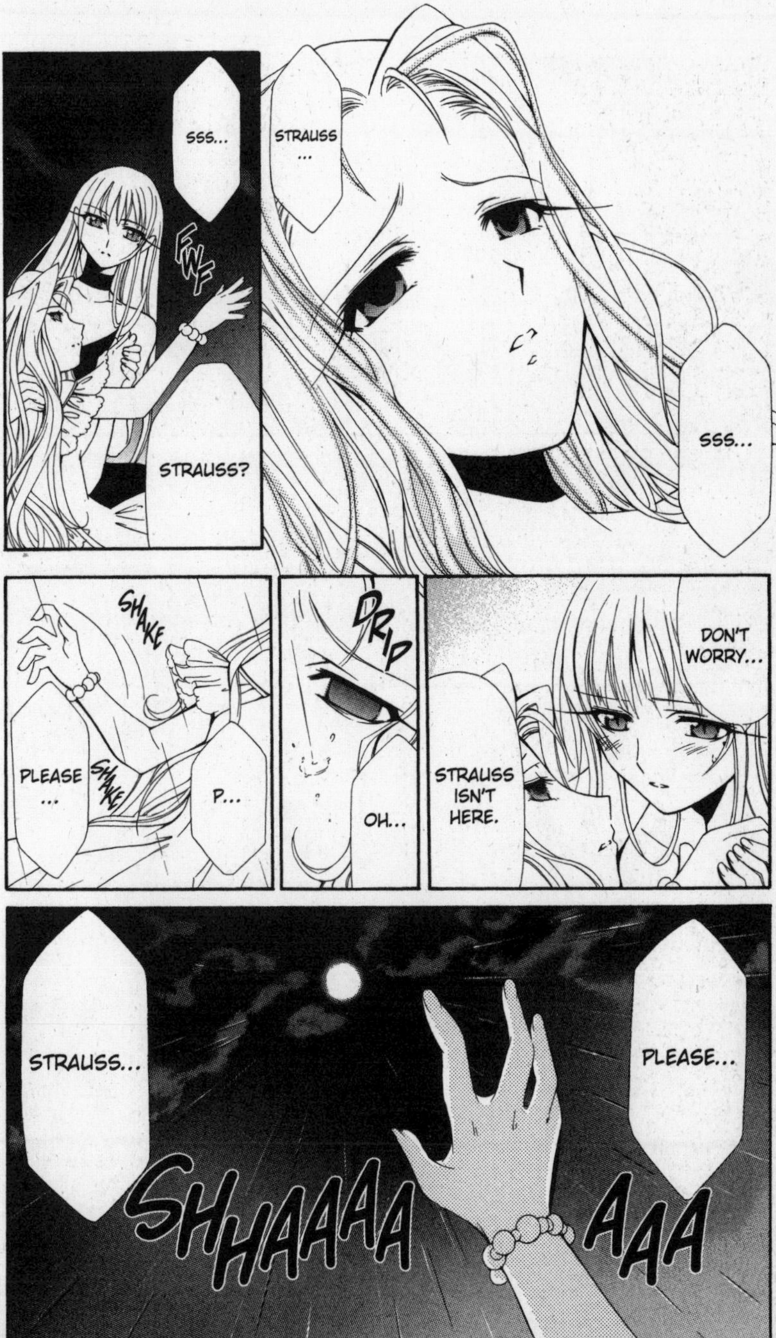
STRAUSS ...
SSS...
SSS...
FWF
STRAUSS?
DON'T WORRY...
STRAUSS ISN'T HERE.
DRIP
OH...
SHAKE
P...
SHAKE
PLEASE ...
PLEASE...
STRAUSS...
SHHAAAAAAAA

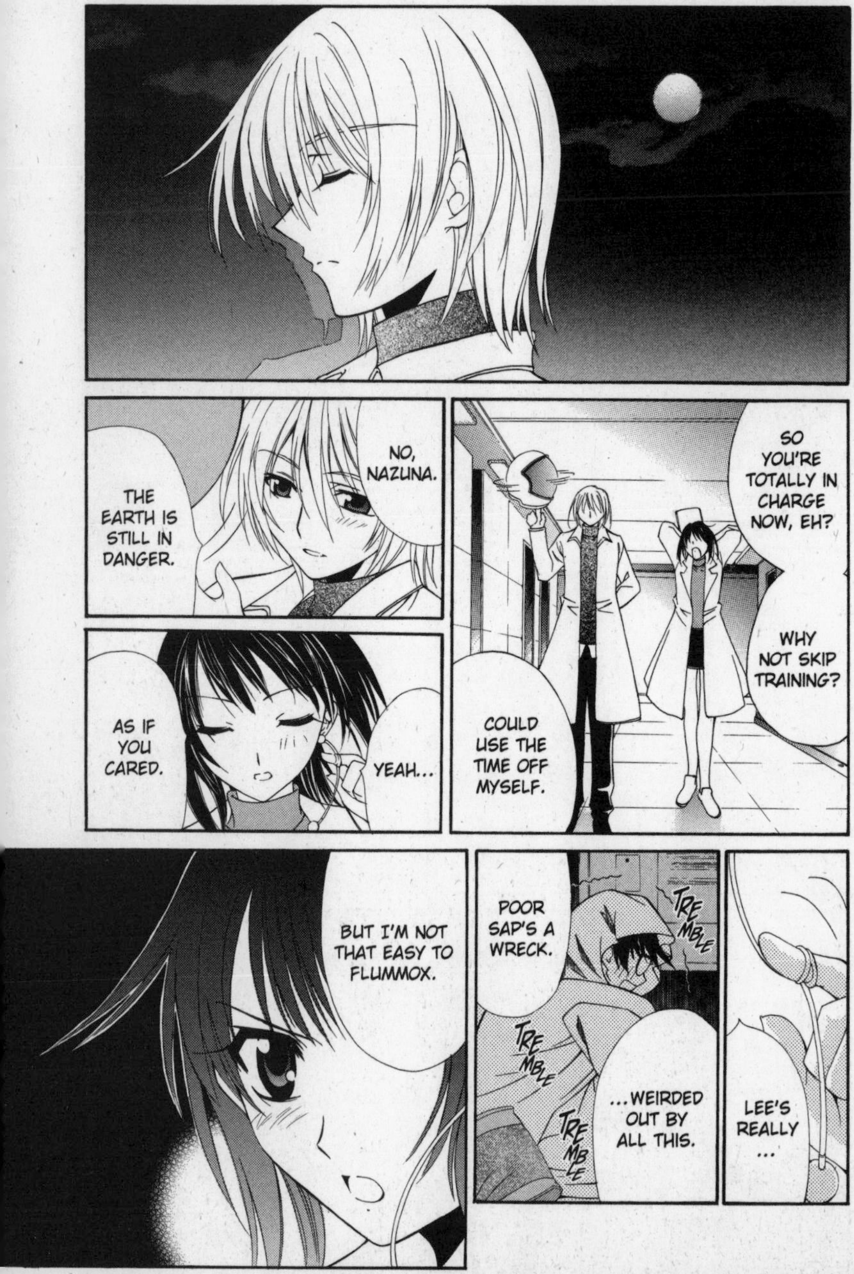
SO YOU'RE TOTALLY IN CHARGE NOW, EH?
WHY NOT SKIP TRAINING?
COULD USE THE TIME OFF MYSELF.
NO, NAZUNA.
THE EARTH IS STILL IN DANGER.
YEAH...
AS IF YOU CARED.
LEE'S REALLY ...
TREMBLE
POOR SAP'S A WRECK.
TREMBLE
TREMBLE
...WEIRDED OUT BY ALL THIS.
BUT I'M NOT THAT EASY TO FLUMMOX.

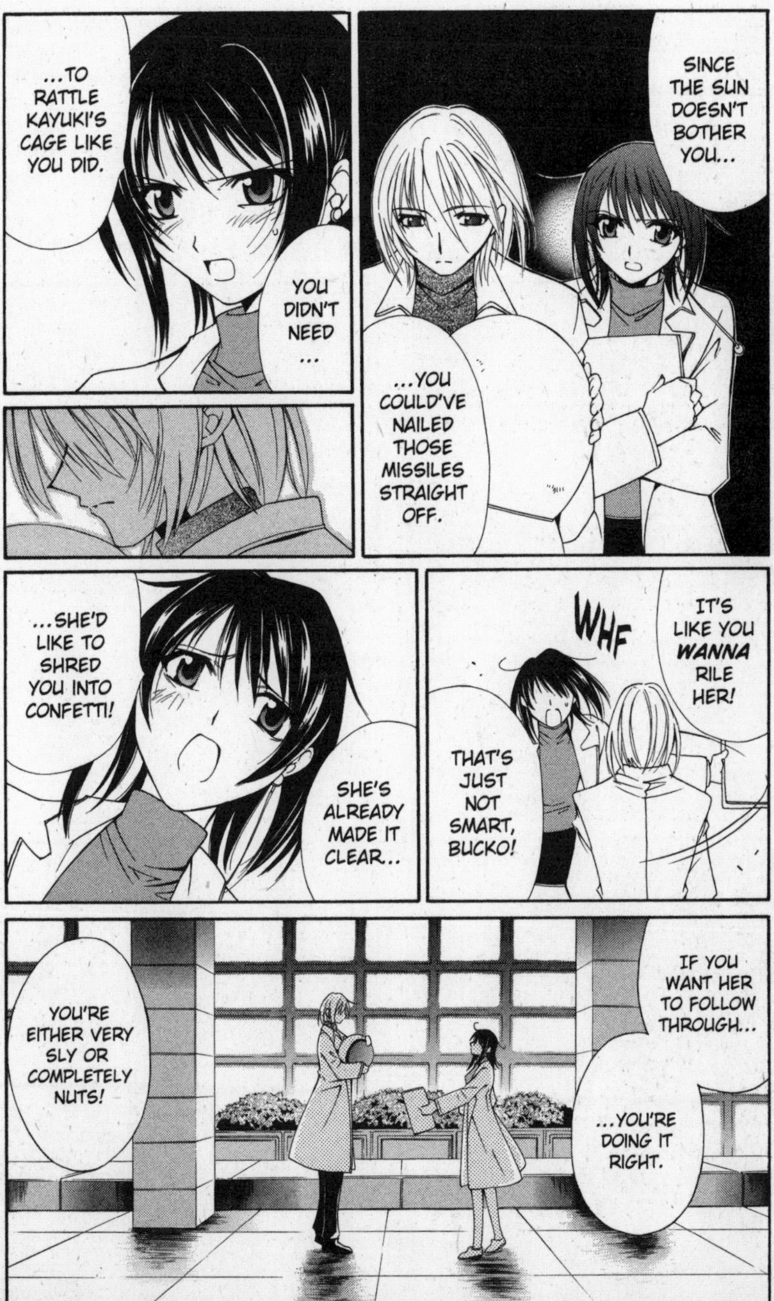
SINCE THE SUN DOESN'T BOTHER YOU...
...YOU COULD'VE NAILED THOSE MISSILES STRAIGHT OFF.
YOU DIDN'T NEED ...
...TO RATTLE KAYUKI'S CAGE LIKE YOU DID.
IT'S LIKE YOU *WANNA* RILE HER!
WHF
THAT'S JUST NOT SMART, BUCKO!
SHE'S ALREADY MADE IT CLEAR...
...SHE'D LIKE TO SHRED YOU INTO CONFETTI!
IF YOU WANT HER TO FOLLOW THROUGH...
...YOU'RE DOING IT RIGHT.
YOU'RE EITHER VERY SLY OR COMPLETELY NUTS!

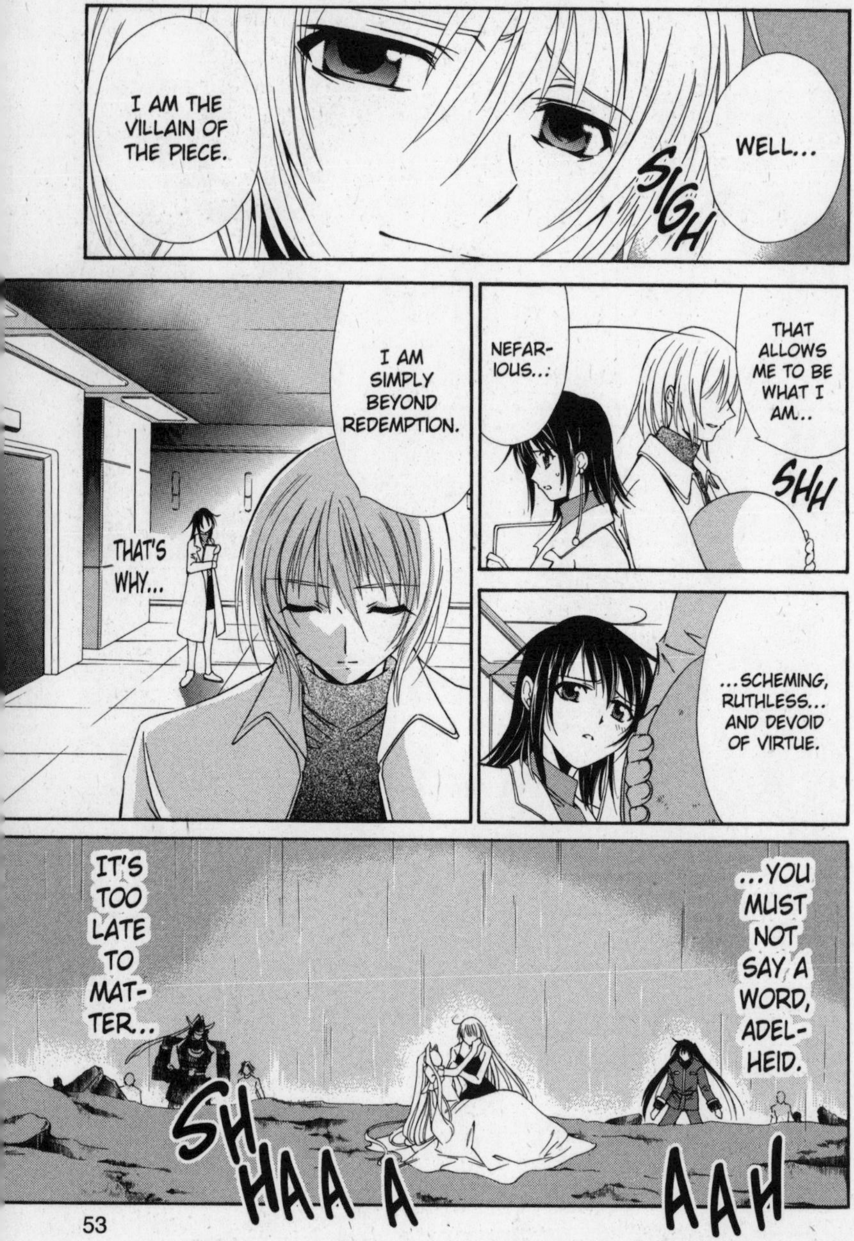
WELL...
SIGH
I AM THE VILLAIN OF THE PIECE.
THAT ALLOWS ME TO BE WHAT I AM...
SHH
NEFARIOUS...:
...SCHEMING, RUTHLESS... AND DEVOID OF VIRTUE.
I AM SIMPLY BEYOND REDEMPTION.
THAT'S WHY...
...YOU MUST NOT SAY A WORD, ADELHEID.
IT'S TOO LATE TO MATTER...
SHHAAAAAH

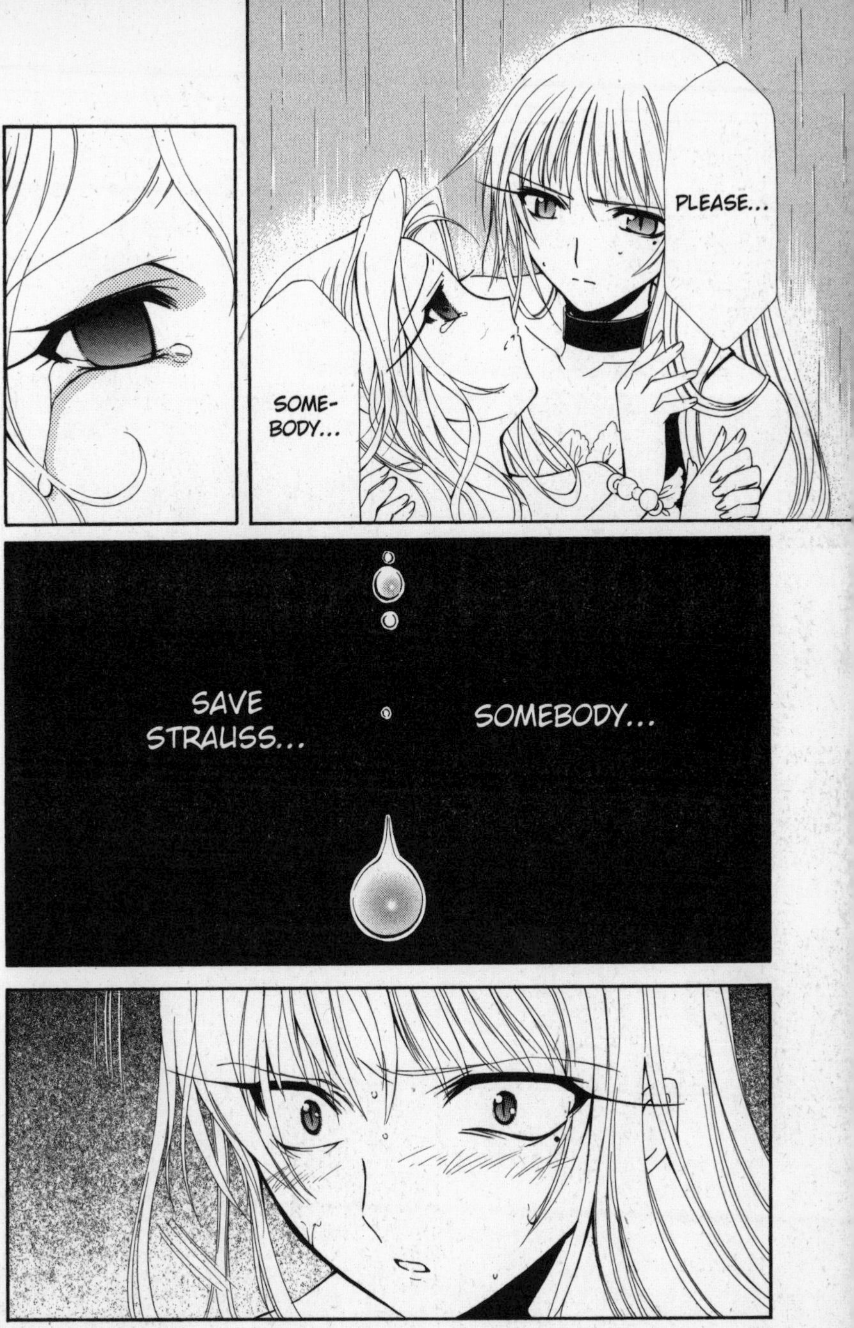
PLEASE...
SOME-BODY...
SOMEBODY...
SAVE STRAUSS...

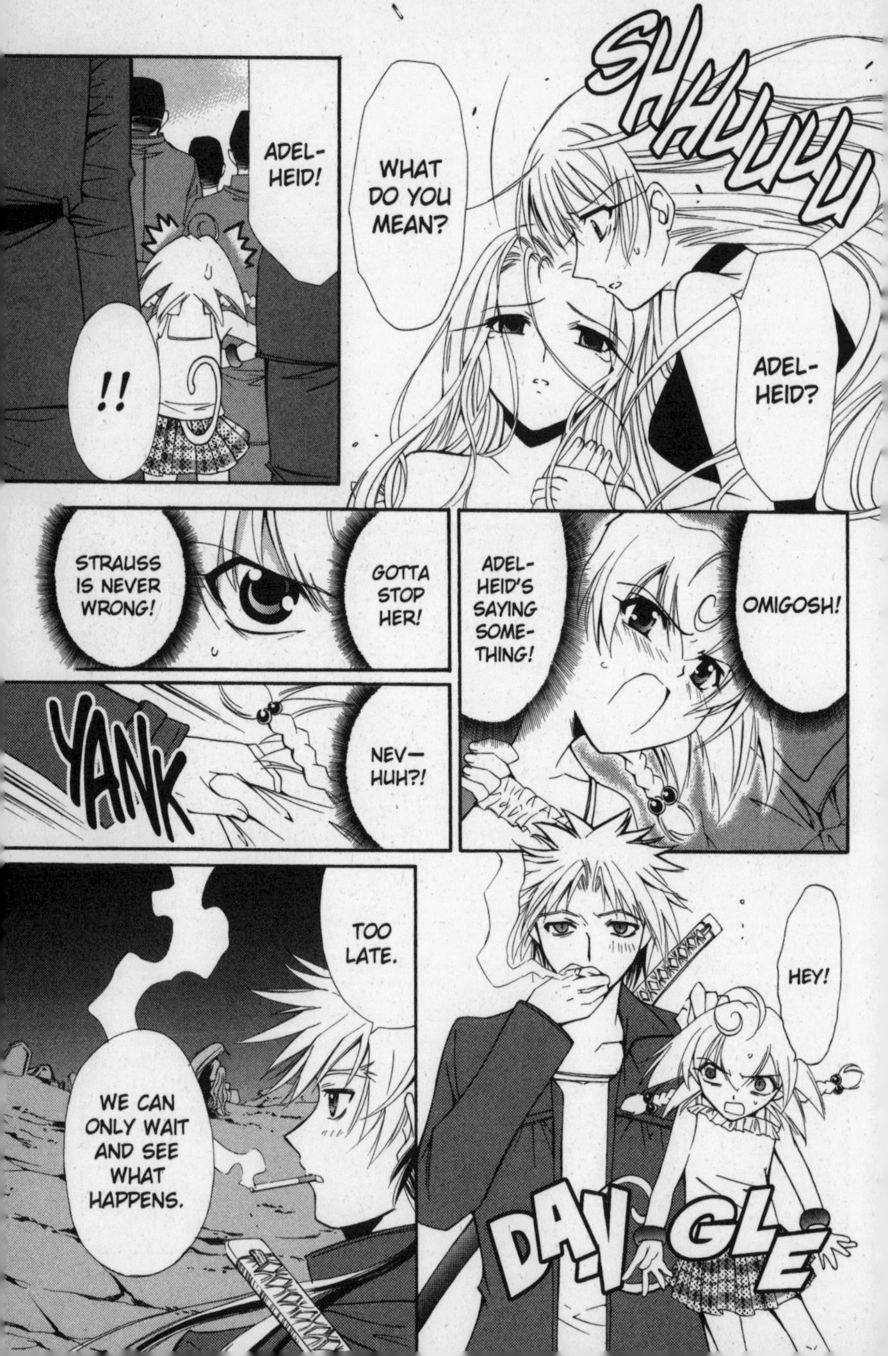
SHULULU
ADEL-HEID?
WHAT DO YOU MEAN?
ADEL-HEID!
!!
OMIGOSH!
ADEL-HEID'S SAYING SOME-THING!
GOTTA STOP HER!
STRAUSS IS NEVER WRONG!
NEV— HUH?!
YANK
HEY!
DANGLE
TOO LATE.
WE CAN ONLY WAIT AND SEE WHAT HAPPENS.

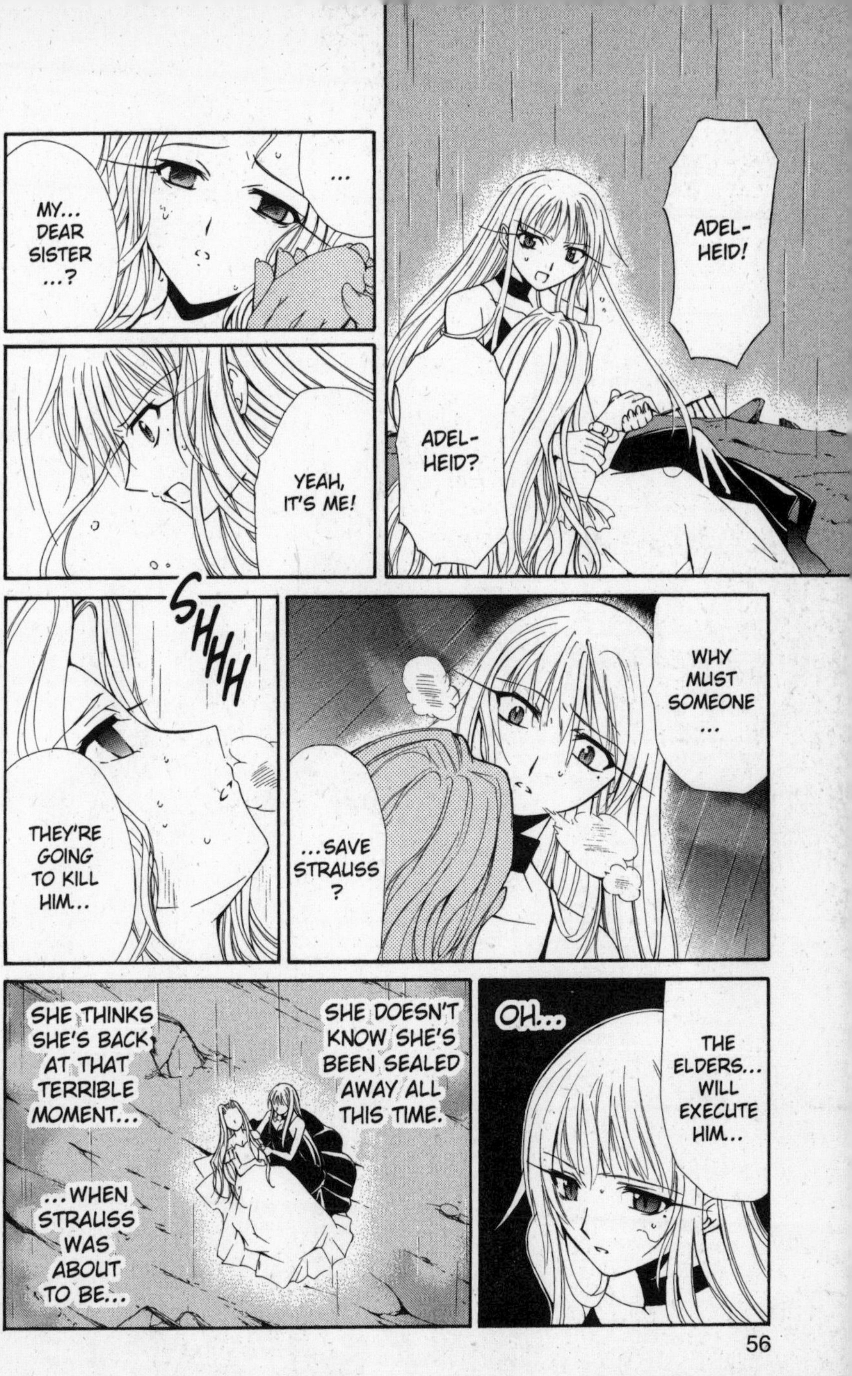
ADEL-HEID!
ADEL-HEID?
...
MY... DEAR SISTER ...?
YEAH, IT'S ME!
WHY MUST SOMEONE ...
...SAVE STRAUSS ?
SHHHH
THEY'RE GOING TO KILL HIM...
OH...
THE ELDERS... WILL EXECUTE HIM...
SHE DOESN'T KNOW SHE'S BEEN SEALED AWAY ALL THIS TIME.
SHE THINKS SHE'S BACK AT THAT TERRIBLE MOMENT...
...WHEN STRAUSS WAS ABOUT TO BE...

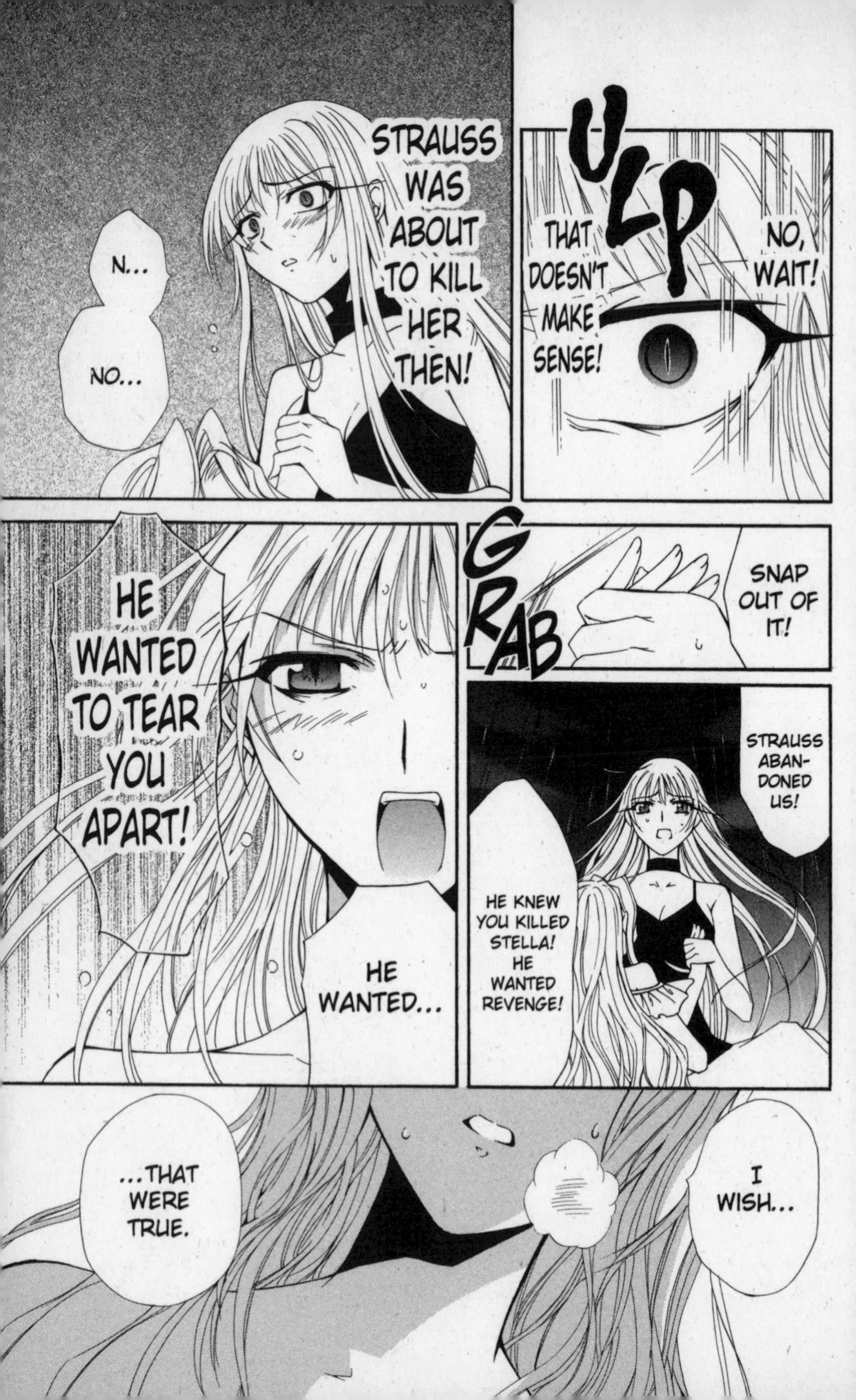
ULP
NO, WAIT!
THAT DOESN'T MAKE SENSE!
STRAUSS WAS ABOUT TO KILL HER THEN!
N...
NO...
GRAB
SNAP OUT OF IT!
STRAUSS ABAN-DONED US!
HE KNEW YOU KILLED STELLA! HE WANTED REVENGE!
HE WANTED...
HE WANTED TO TEAR YOU APART!
I WISH...
...THAT WERE TRUE.

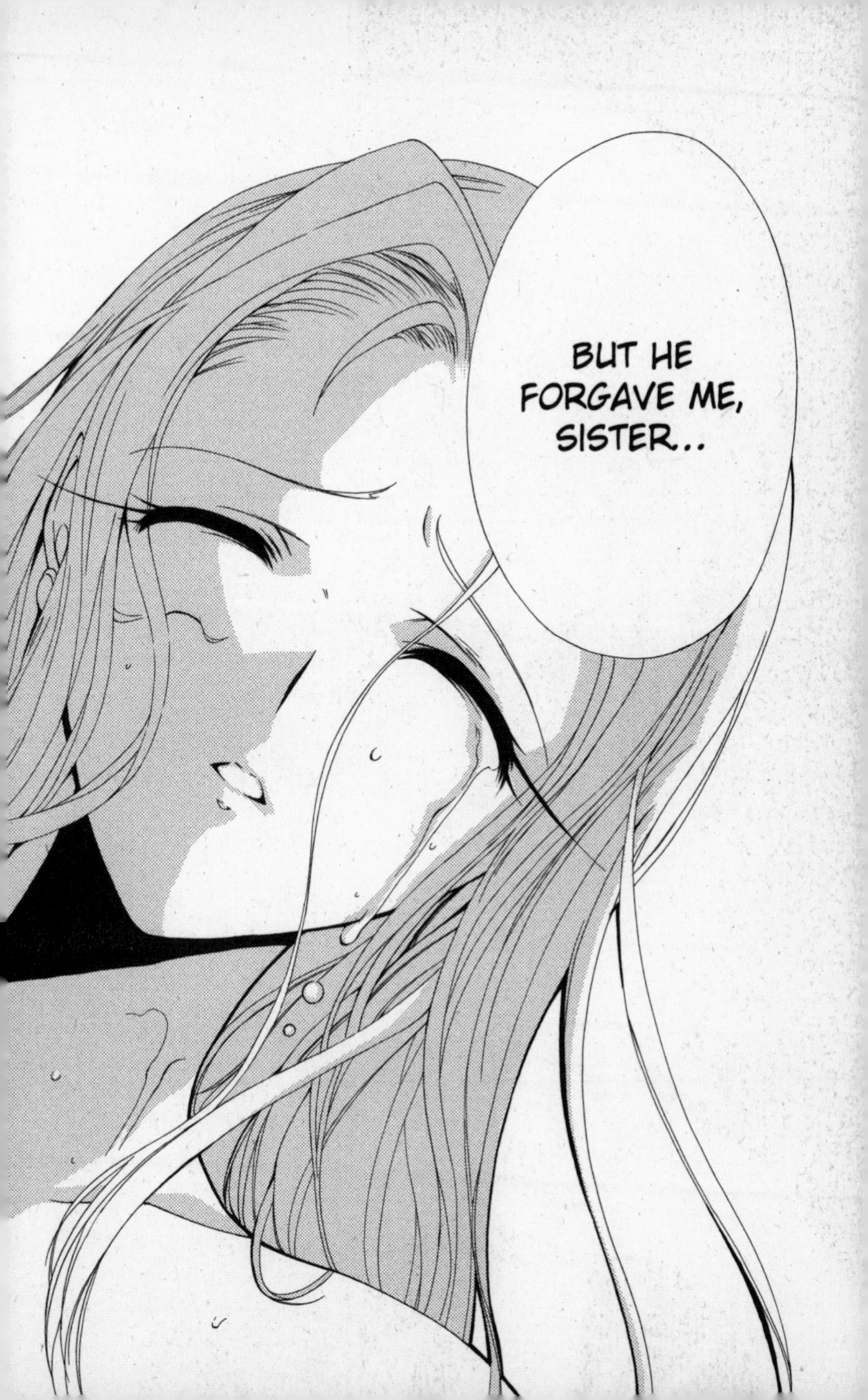
BUT HE FORGAVE ME, SISTER..

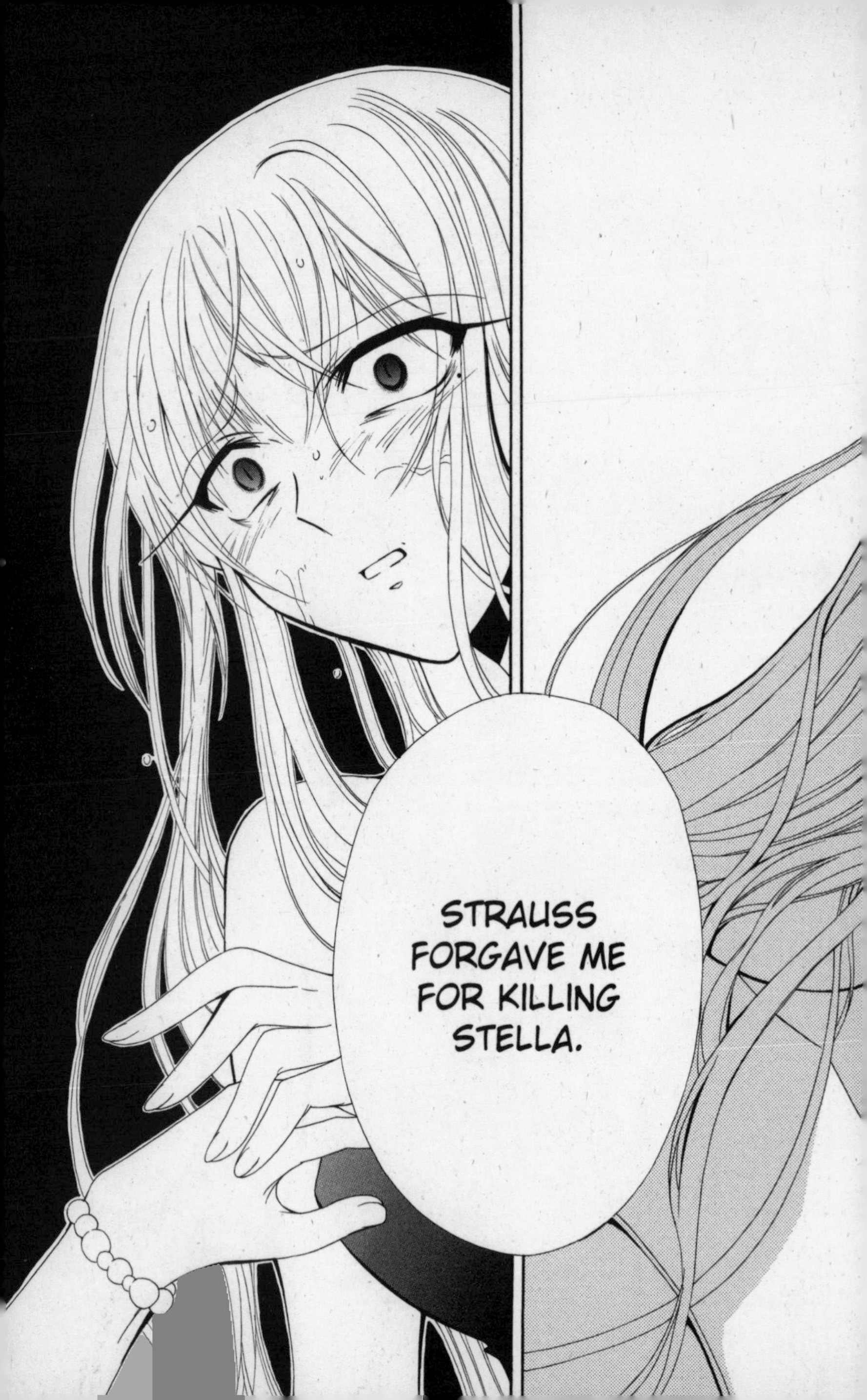
STRAUSS FORGAVE ME FOR KILLING STELLA.

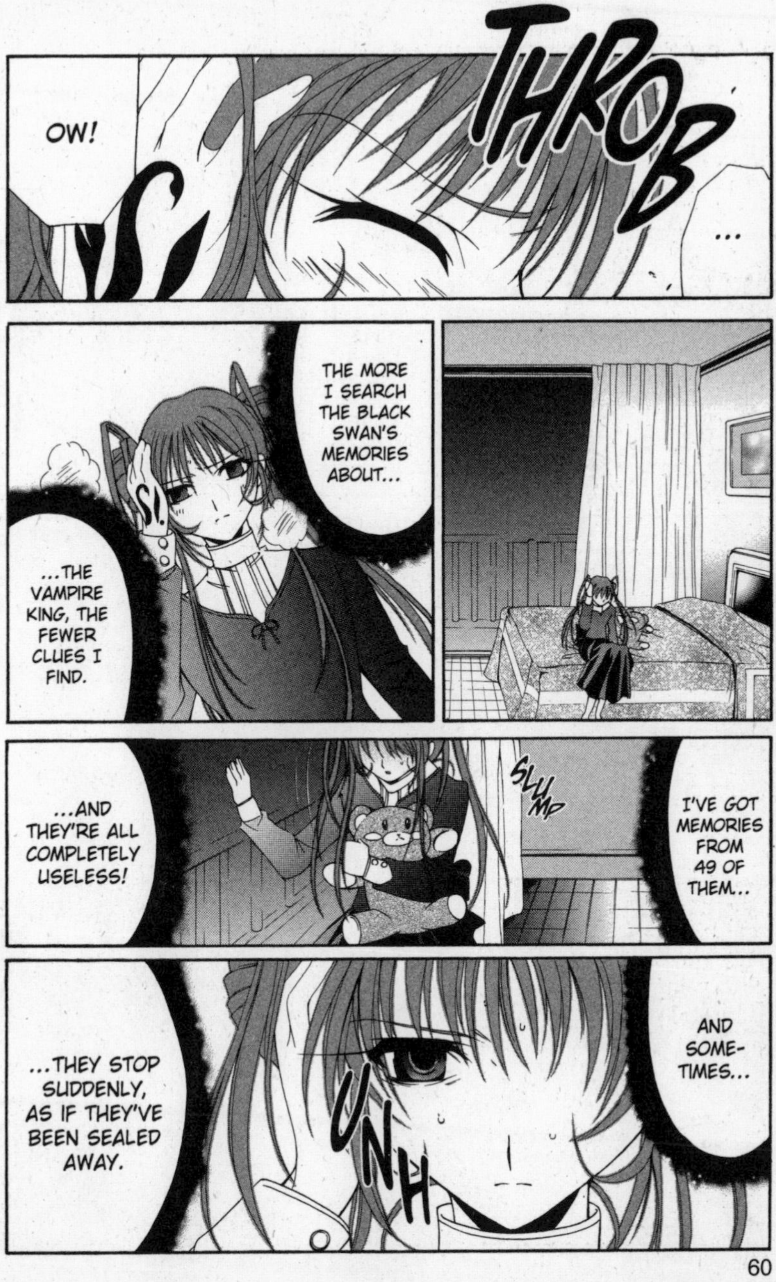
THROB
...
OW!
THE MORE I SEARCH THE BLACK SWAN'S MEMORIES ABOUT...
...THE VAMPIRE KING, THE FEWER CLUES I FIND.
I'VE GOT MEMORIES FROM 49 OF THEM...
SLUMP
...AND THEY'RE ALL COMPLETELY USELESS!
AND SOME-TIMES...
UNH
...THEY STOP SUDDENLY, AS IF THEY'VE BEEN SEALED AWAY.

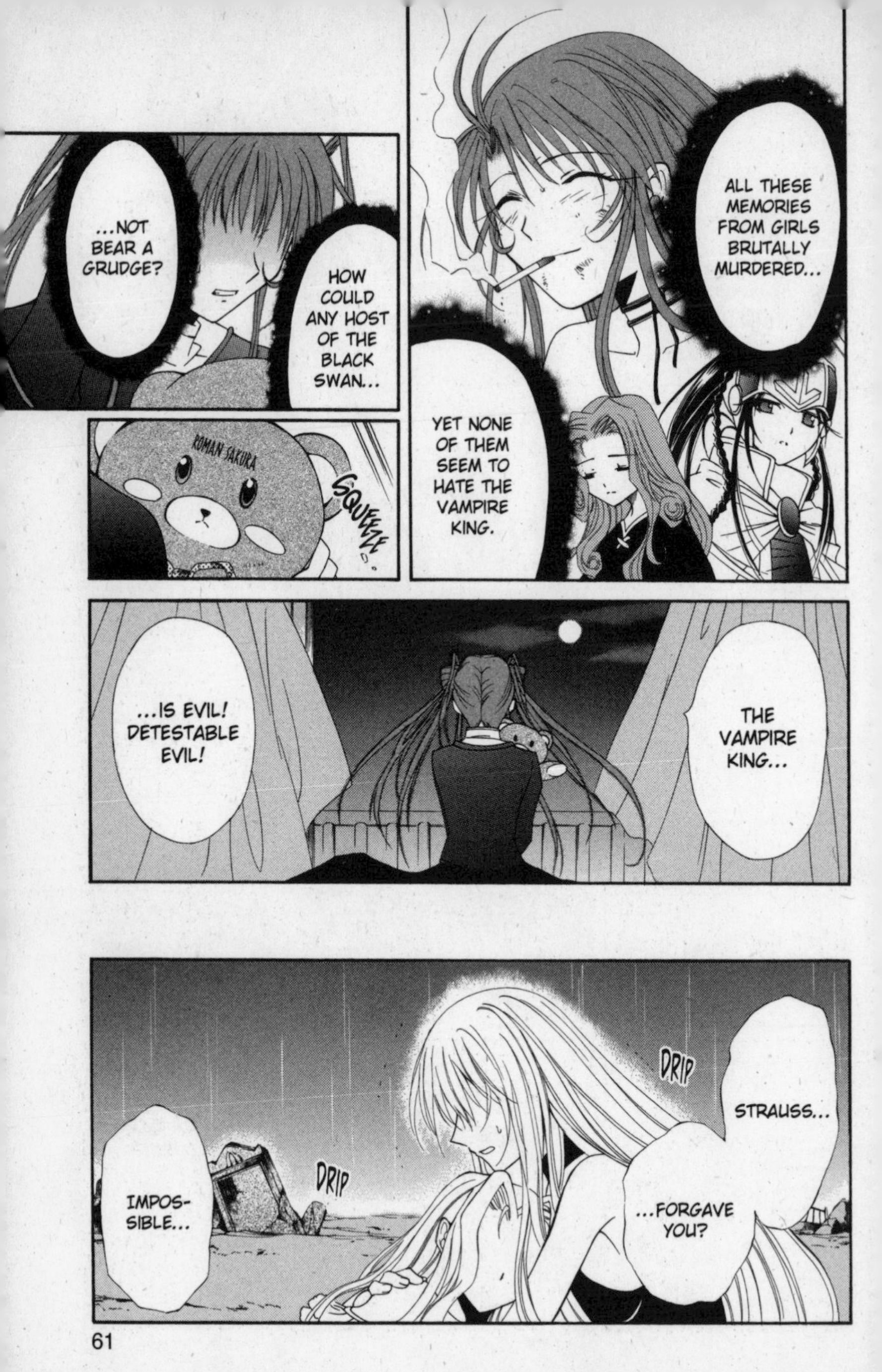
ALL THESE MEMORIES FROM GIRLS BRUTALLY MURDERED...
YET NONE OF THEM SEEM TO HATE THE VAMPIRE KING.
HOW COULD ANY HOST OF THE BLACK SWAN...
...NOT BEAR A GRUDGE?
ROMAN SAKURA
SQUEEZE
THE VAMPIRE KING...
...IS EVIL! DETESTABLE EVIL!
STRAUSS...
...FORGAVE YOU?
DRIP
DRIP
IMPOS-SIBLE...

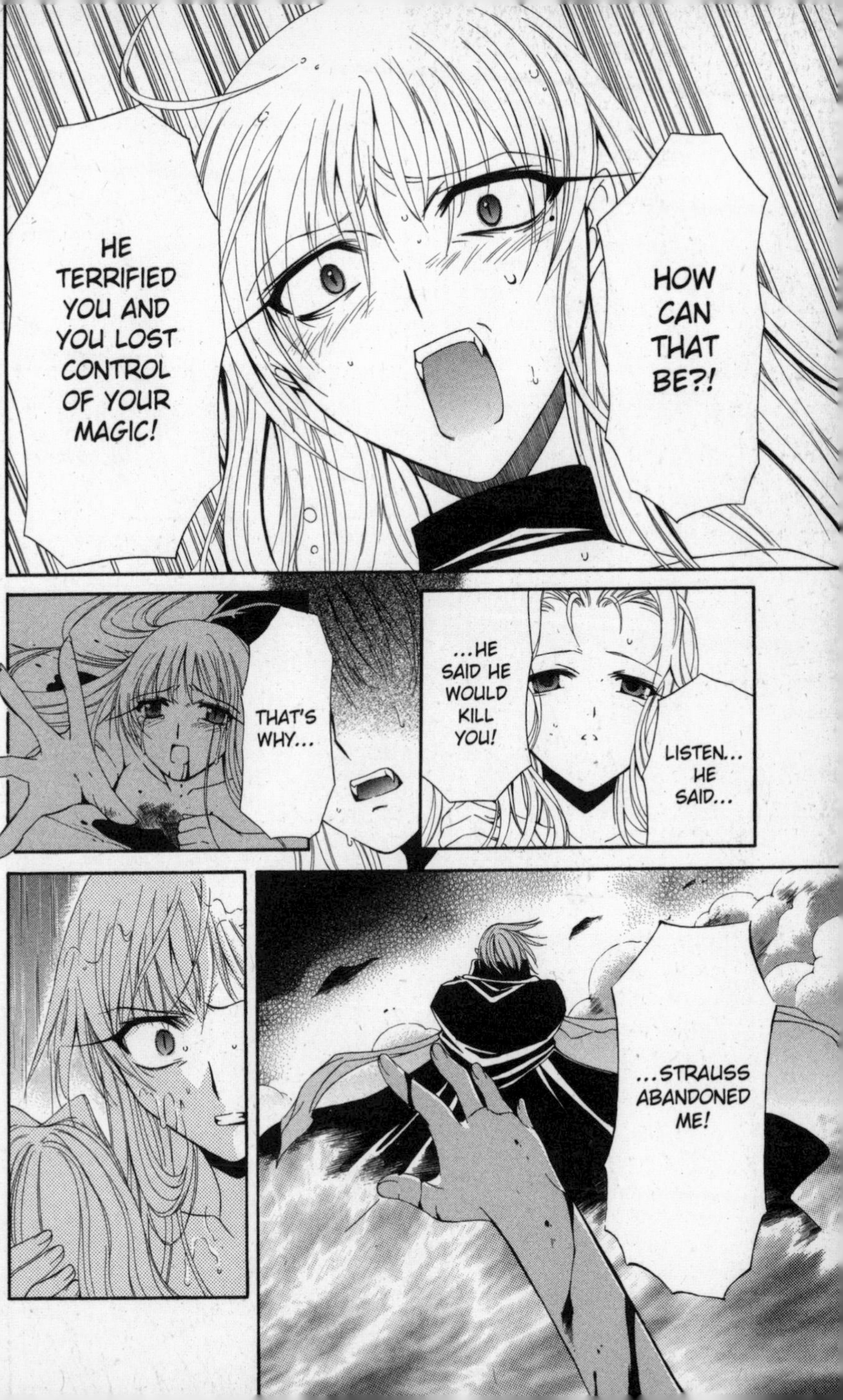
HOW CAN THAT BE?!
HE TERRIFIED YOU AND YOU LOST CONTROL OF YOUR MAGIC!
LISTEN... HE SAID...
...HE SAID HE WOULD KILL YOU!
THAT'S WHY...
...STRAUSS ABANDONED ME!

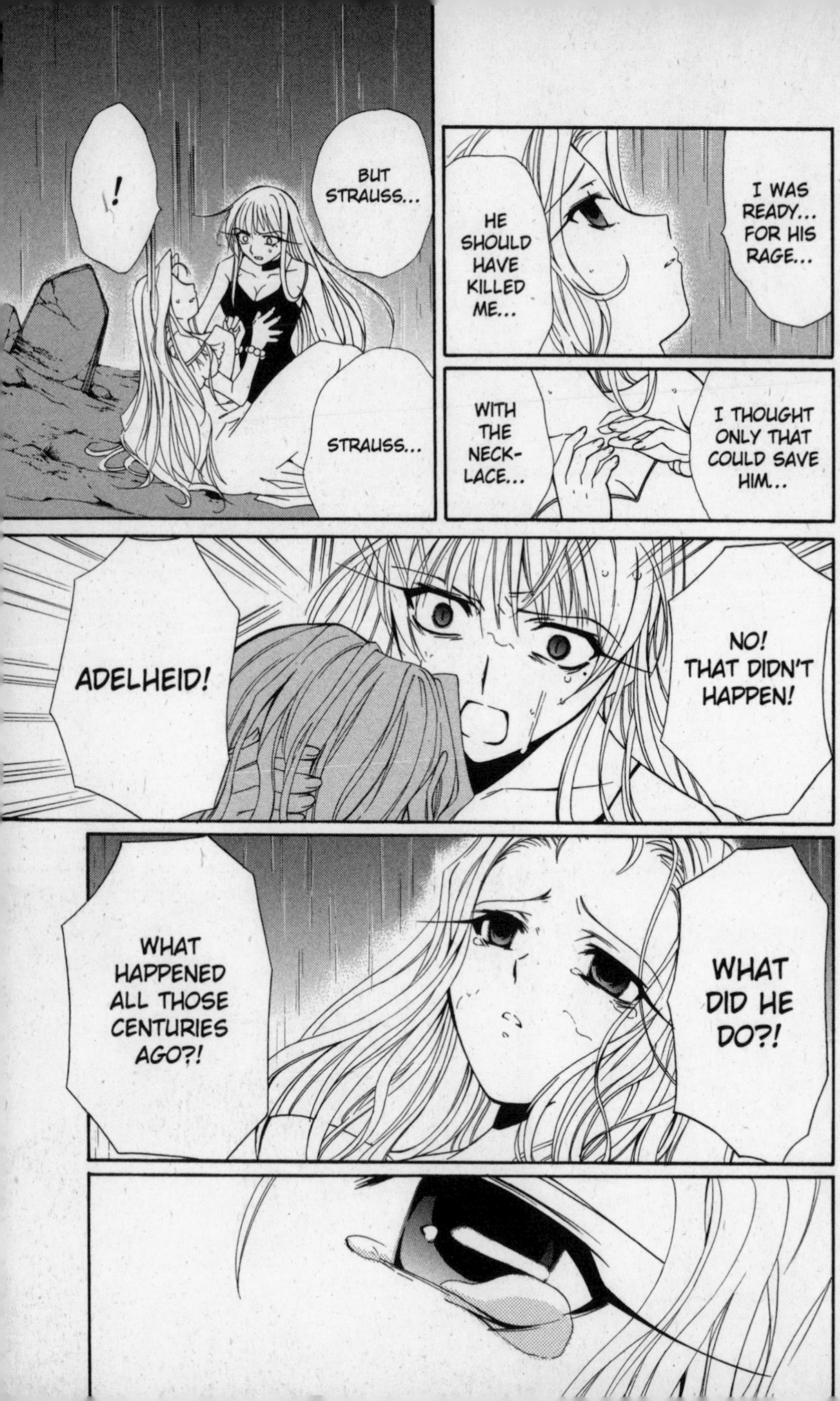
I WAS READY... FOR HIS RAGE...
HE SHOULD HAVE KILLED ME...
I THOUGHT ONLY THAT COULD SAVE HIM...
WITH THE NECK-LACE...
BUT STRAUSS...
!
STRAUSS...
NO! THAT DIDN'T HAPPEN!
ADELHEID!
WHAT DID HE DO?!
WHAT HAPPENED ALL THOSE CENTURIES AGO?!

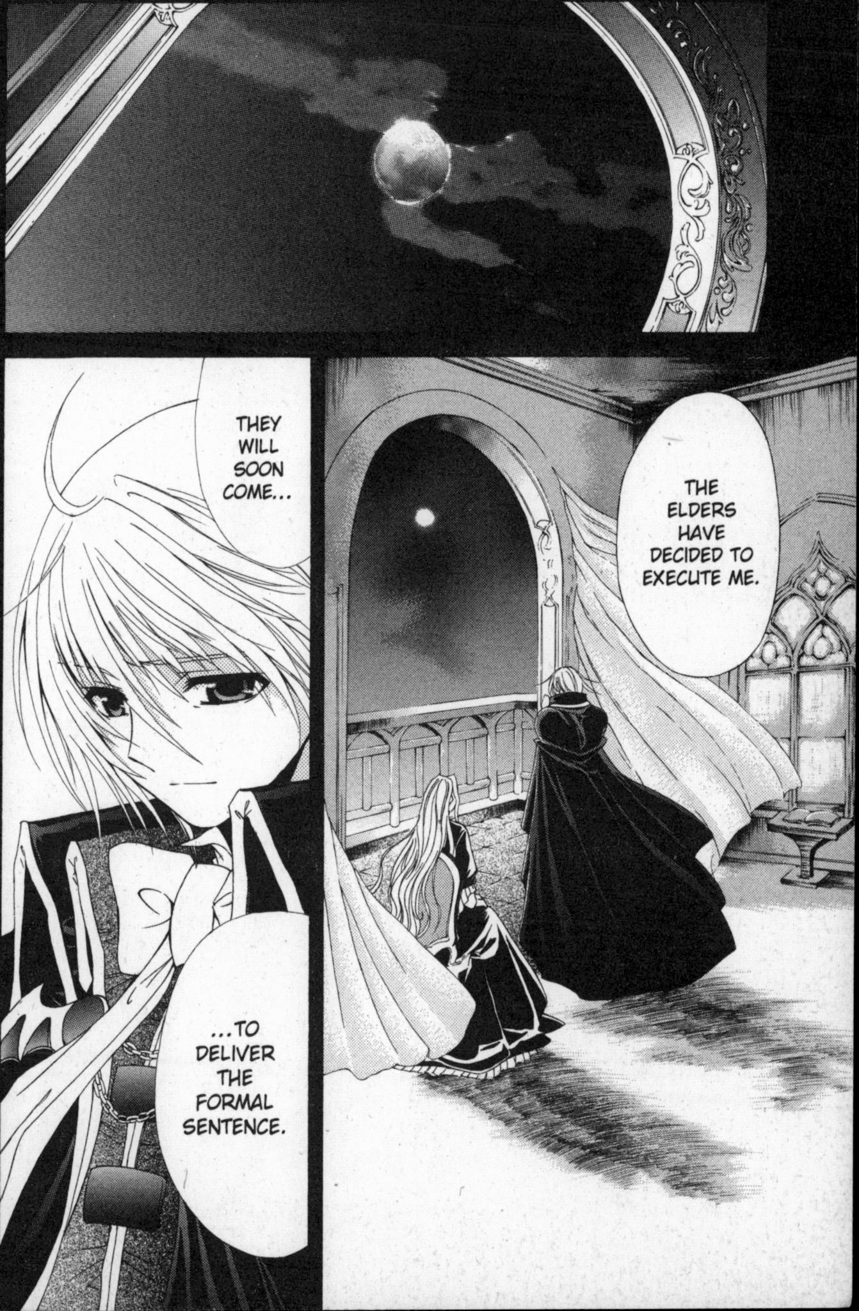
THE ELDERS HAVE DECIDED TO EXECUTE ME.
THEY WILL SOON COME...
...TO DELIVER THE FORMAL SENTENCE.

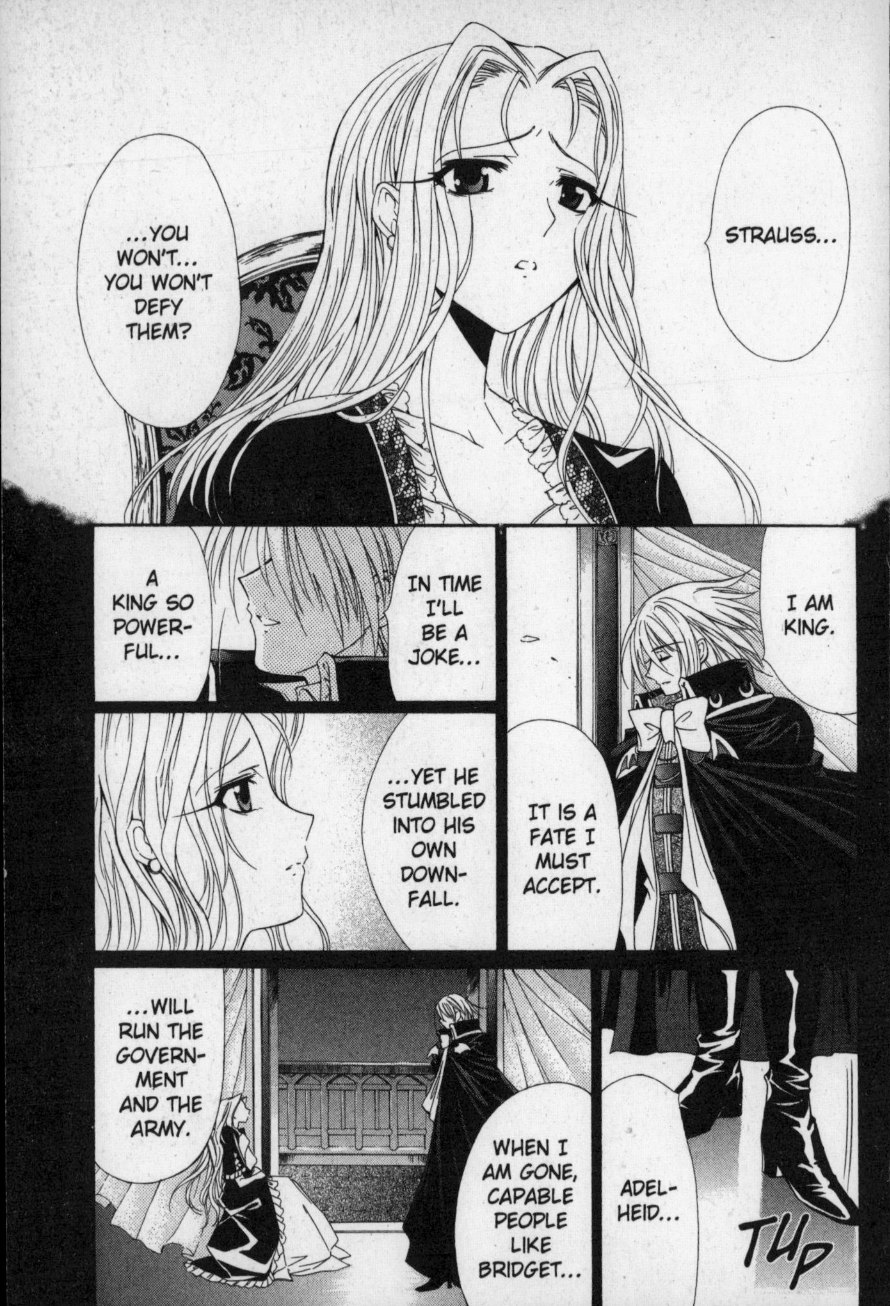
STRAUSS...
...YOU WON'T... YOU WON'T DEFY THEM?
I AM KING.
IT IS A FATE I MUST ACCEPT.
IN TIME I'LL BE A JOKE...
A KING SO POWER-FUL...
...YET HE STUMBLED INTO HIS OWN DOWN-FALL.
ADEL-HEID...
TUP
WHEN I AM GONE, CAPABLE PEOPLE LIKE BRIDGET...
...WILL RUN THE GOVERN-MENT AND THE ARMY.

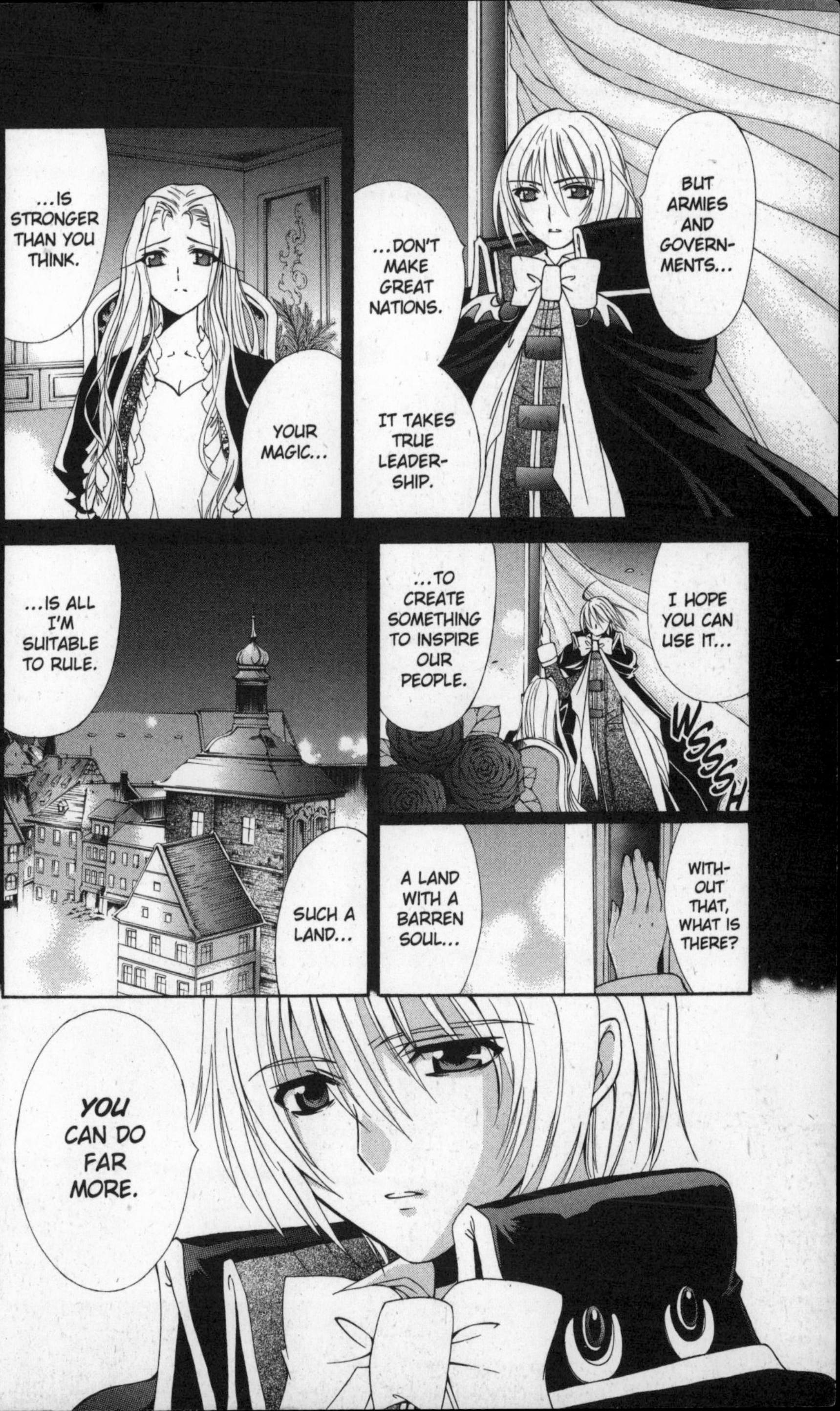
BUT ARMIES AND GOVERN-MENTS...
...DON'T MAKE GREAT NATIONS.
IT TAKES TRUE LEADER-SHIP.
YOUR MAGIC...
...IS STRONGER THAN YOU THINK.
I HOPE YOU CAN USE IT...
...TO CREATE SOMETHING TO INSPIRE OUR PEOPLE.
WSSSH
WITH-OUT THAT, WHAT IS THERE?
A LAND WITH A BARREN SOUL...
SUCH A LAND...
...IS ALL I'M SUITABLE TO RULE.
YOU CAN DO FAR MORE.

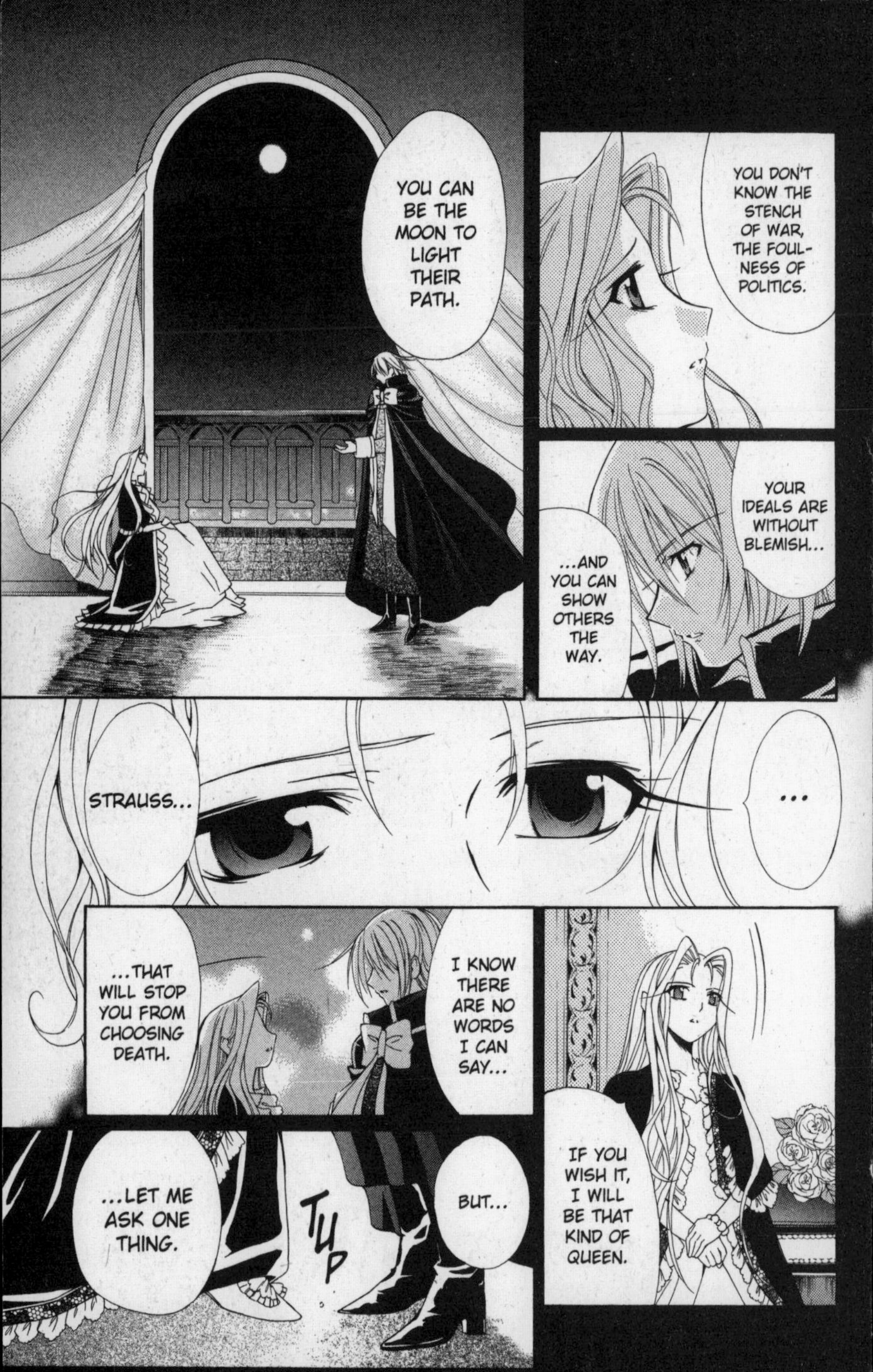
YOU DON'T KNOW THE STENCH OF WAR, THE FOUL-NESS OF POLITICS.
YOUR IDEALS ARE WITHOUT BLEMISH...
...AND YOU CAN SHOW OTHERS THE WAY.
YOU CAN BE THE MOON TO LIGHT THEIR PATH.
...
STRAUSS...
IF YOU WISH IT, I WILL BE THAT KIND OF QUEEN.
I KNOW THERE ARE NO WORDS I CAN SAY...
...THAT WILL STOP YOU FROM CHOOSING DEATH.
BUT...
TUP
...LET ME ASK ONE THING.

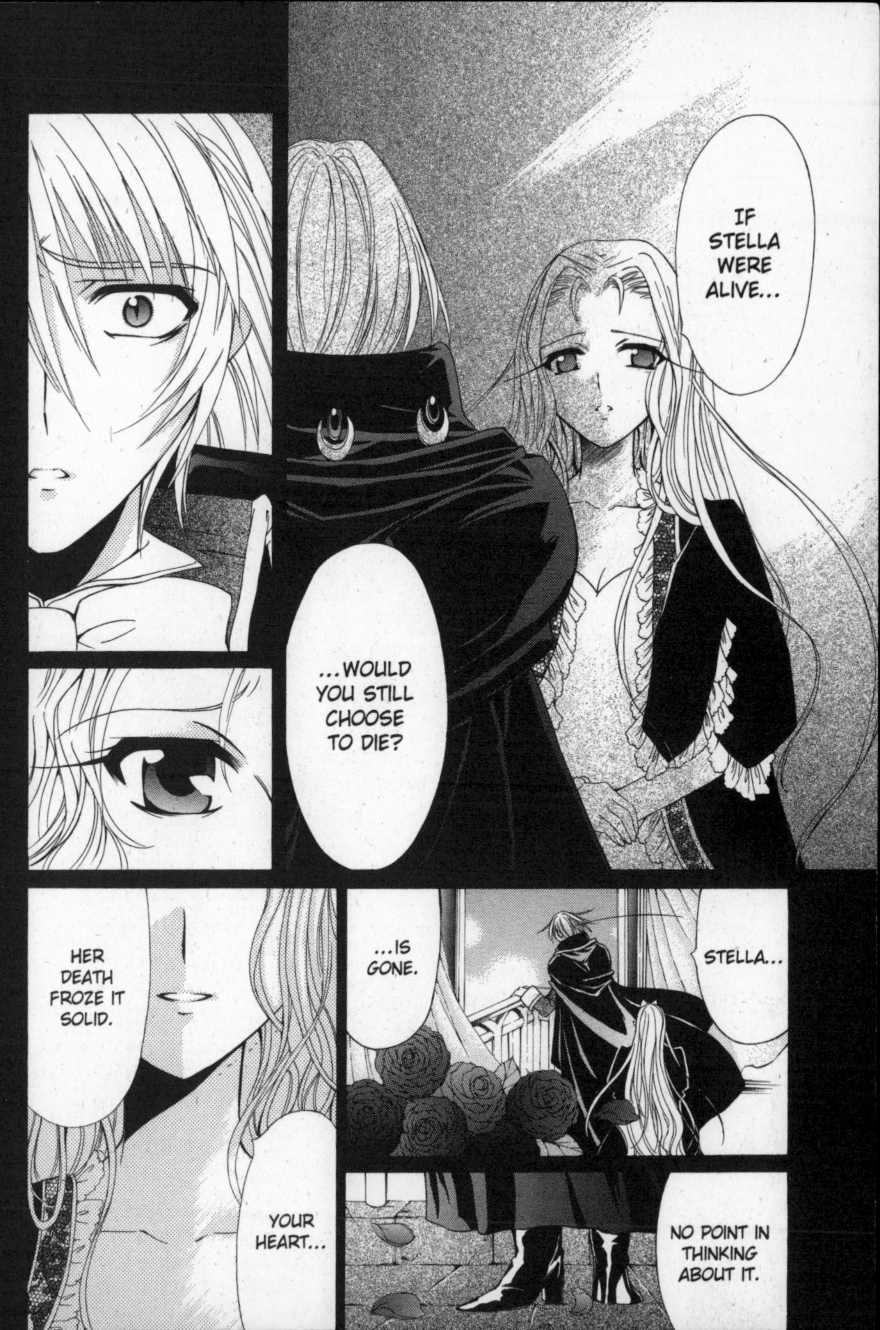

IF STELLA WERE ALIVE...
...WOULD YOU STILL CHOOSE TO DIE?
STELLA...
...IS GONE.
NO POINT IN THINKING ABOUT IT.
YOUR HEART...
HER DEATH FROZE IT SOLID.

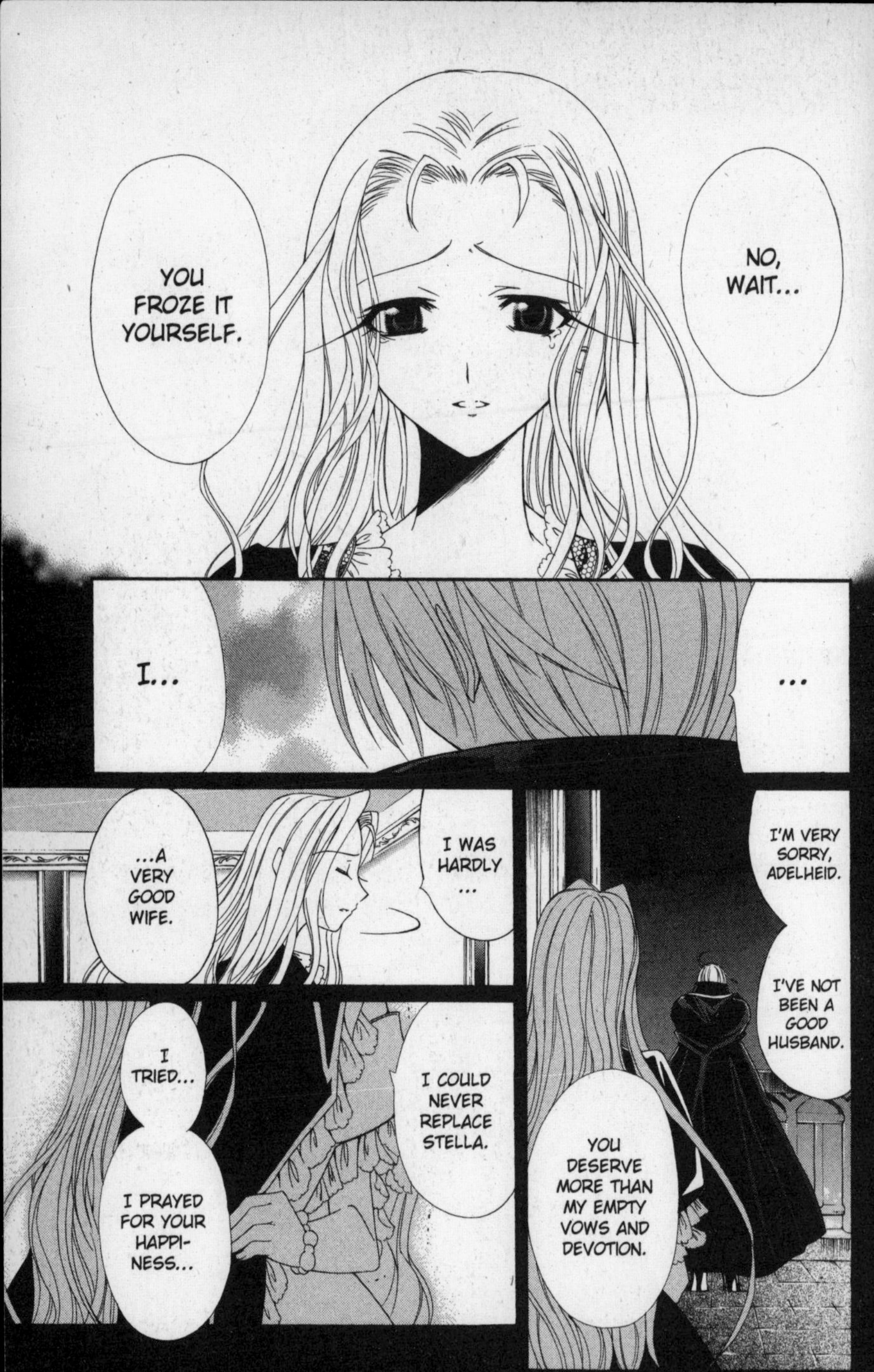
NO, WAIT...
YOU FROZE IT YOURSELF.
...
I...
I'M VERY SORRY, ADELHEID.
I'VE NOT BEEN A GOOD HUSBAND.
YOU DESERVE MORE THAN MY EMPTY VOWS AND DEVOTION.
I WAS HARDLY...
...A VERY GOOD WIFE.
I COULD NEVER REPLACE STELLA.
I TRIED...
I PRAYED FOR YOUR HAPPINESS...

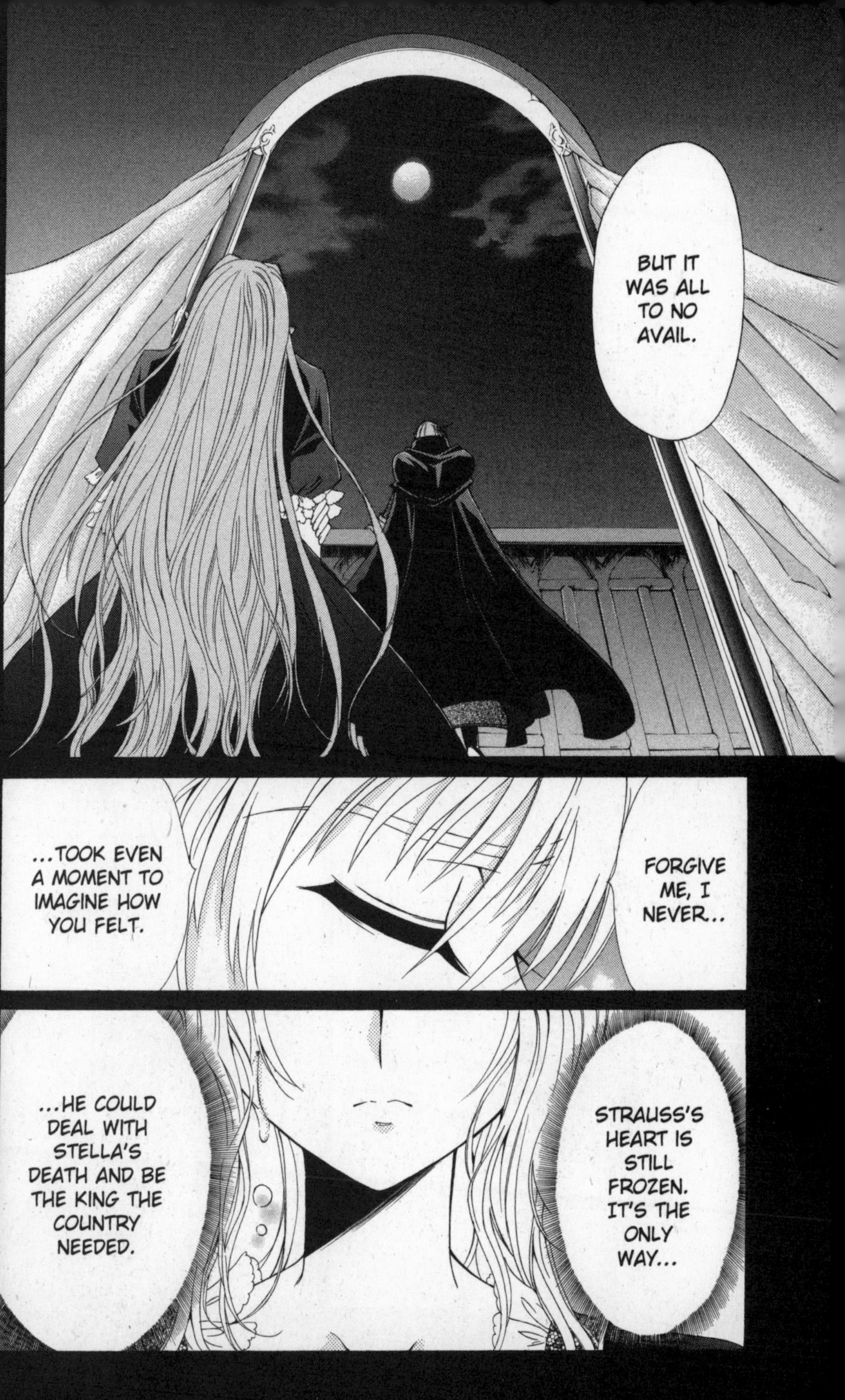
BUT IT WAS ALL TO NO AVAIL.
FORGIVE ME, I NEVER...
...TOOK EVEN A MOMENT TO IMAGINE HOW YOU FELT.
STRAUSS'S HEART IS STILL FROZEN. IT'S THE ONLY WAY...
...HE COULD DEAL WITH STELLA'S DEATH AND BE THE KING THE COUNTRY NEEDED.

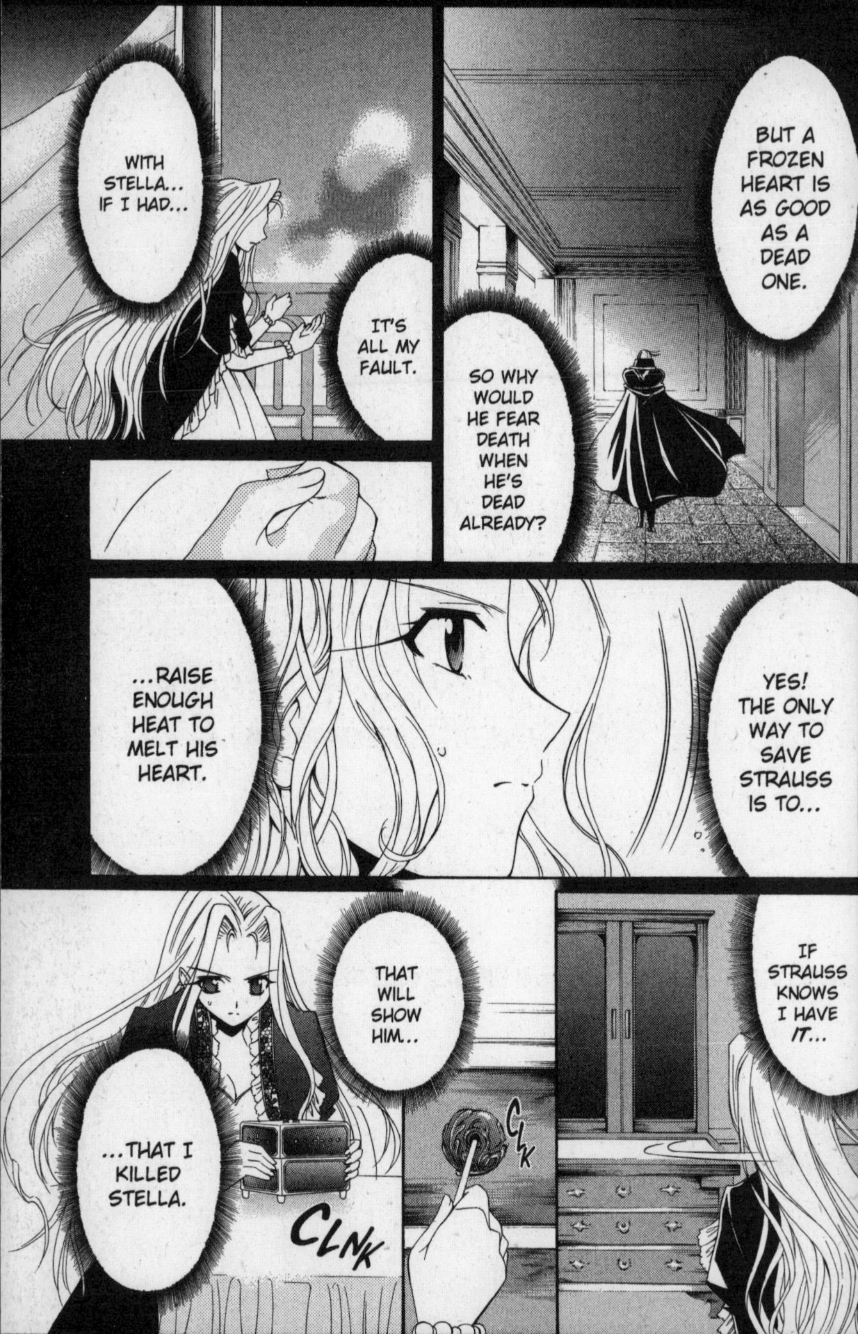
BUT A FROZEN HEART IS AS GOOD AS A DEAD ONE.
SO WHY WOULD HE FEAR DEATH WHEN HE'S DEAD ALREADY?
WITH STELLA... IF I HAD...
IT'S ALL MY FAULT.
YES! THE ONLY WAY TO SAVE STRAUSS IS TO...
...RAISE ENOUGH HEAT TO MELT HIS HEART.
IF STRAUSS KNOWS I HAVE *IT*...
CLK
THAT WILL SHOW HIM...
...THAT I KILLED STELLA.
CLNK

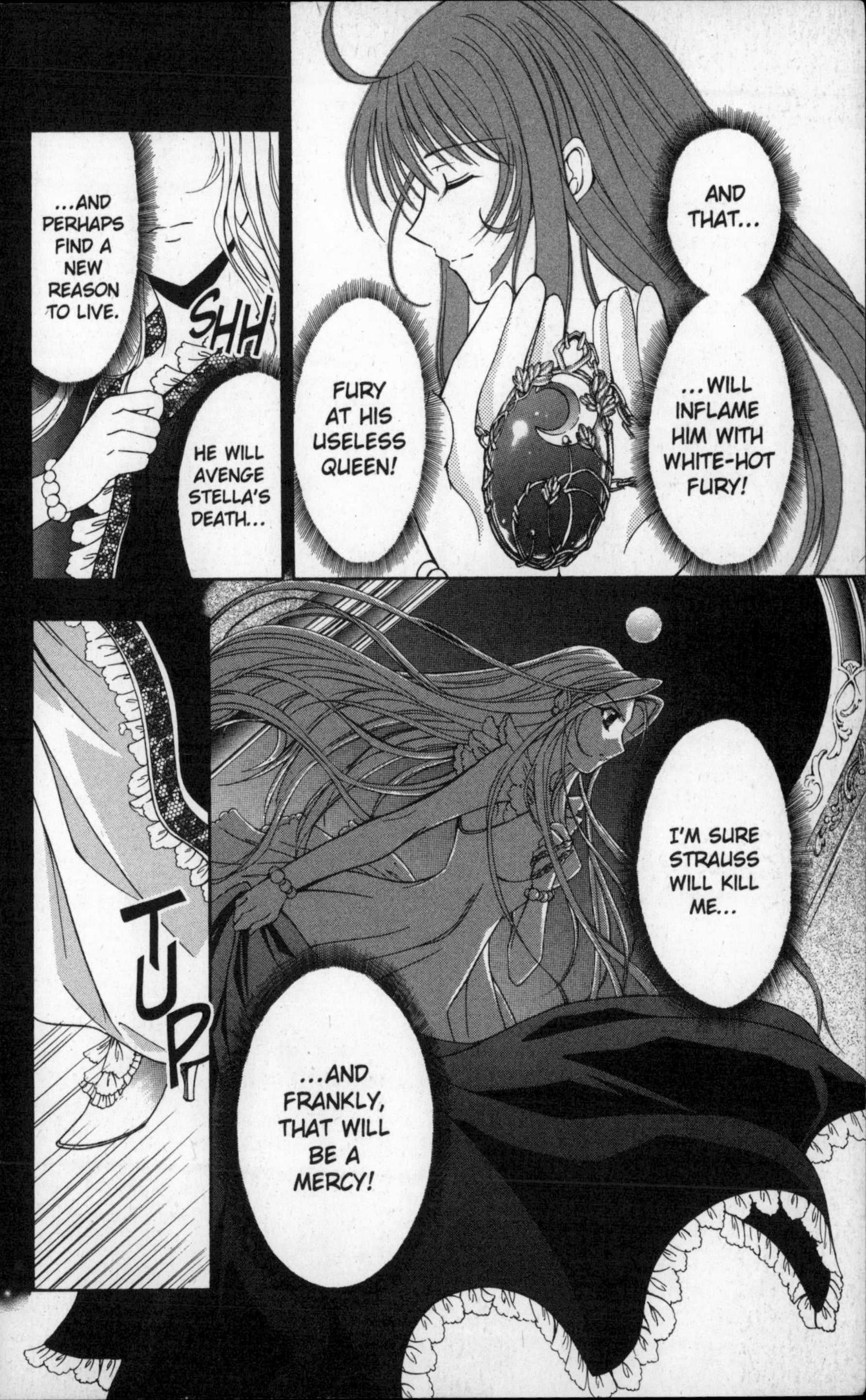
AND THAT...
...WILL INFLAME HIM WITH WHITE-HOT FURY!
FURY AT HIS USELESS QUEEN!
HE WILL AVENGE STELLA'S DEATH...
SHH
...AND PERHAPS FIND A NEW REASON TO LIVE.
I'M SURE STRAUSS WILL KILL ME...
...AND FRANKLY, THAT WILL BE A MERCY!
TUP

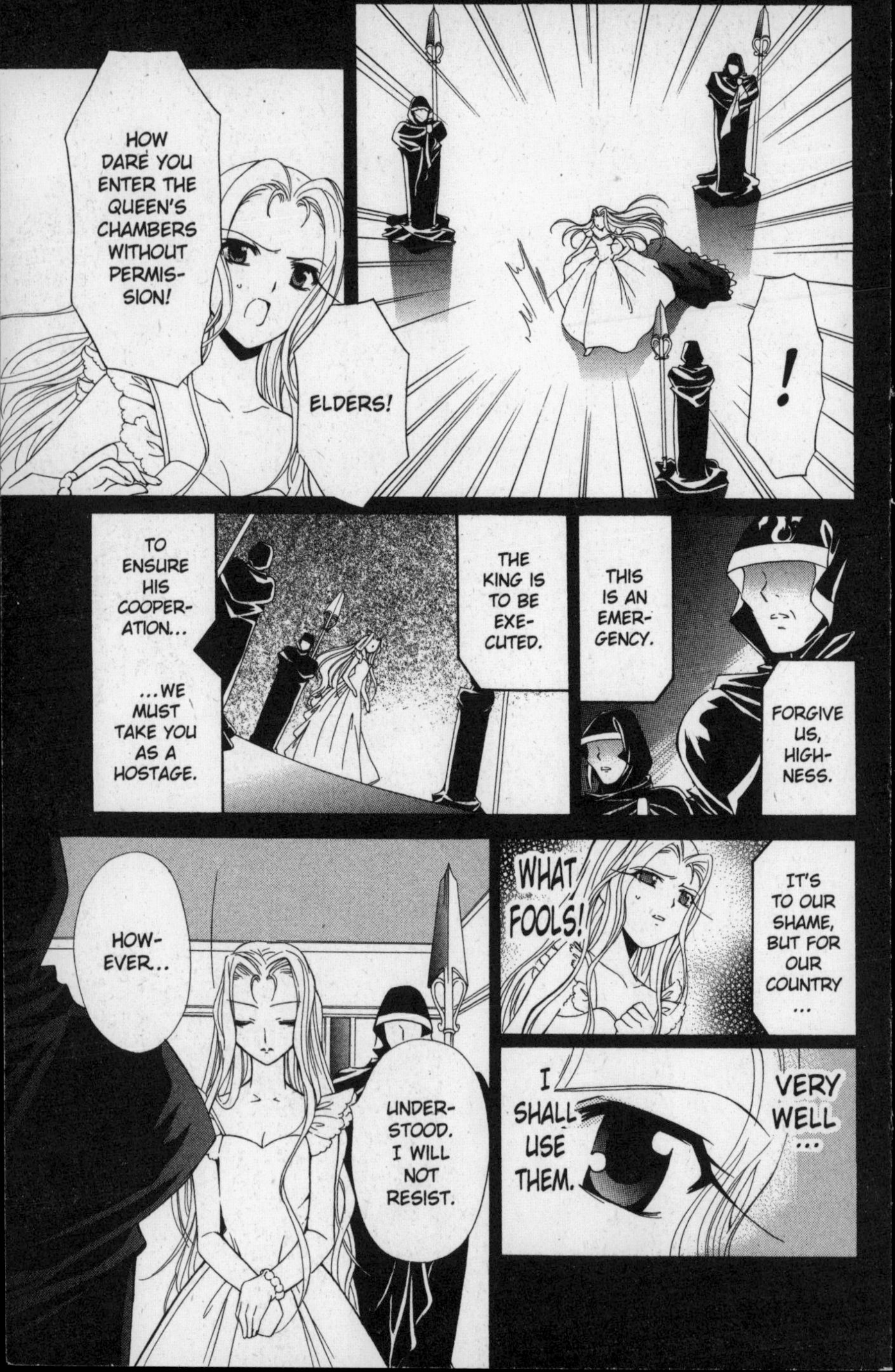
!
HOW DARE YOU ENTER THE QUEEN'S CHAMBERS WITHOUT PERMIS-SION!
ELDERS!
THIS IS AN EMER-GENCY.
FORGIVE US, HIGH-NESS.
THE KING IS TO BE EXE-CUTED.
TO ENSURE HIS COOPER-ATION...
...WE MUST TAKE YOU AS A HOSTAGE.
IT'S TO OUR SHAME, BUT FOR OUR COUNTRY ...
WHAT FOOLS!
VERY WELL ...
I SHALL USE THEM.
HOW-EVER...
UNDER-STOOD. I WILL NOT RESIST.

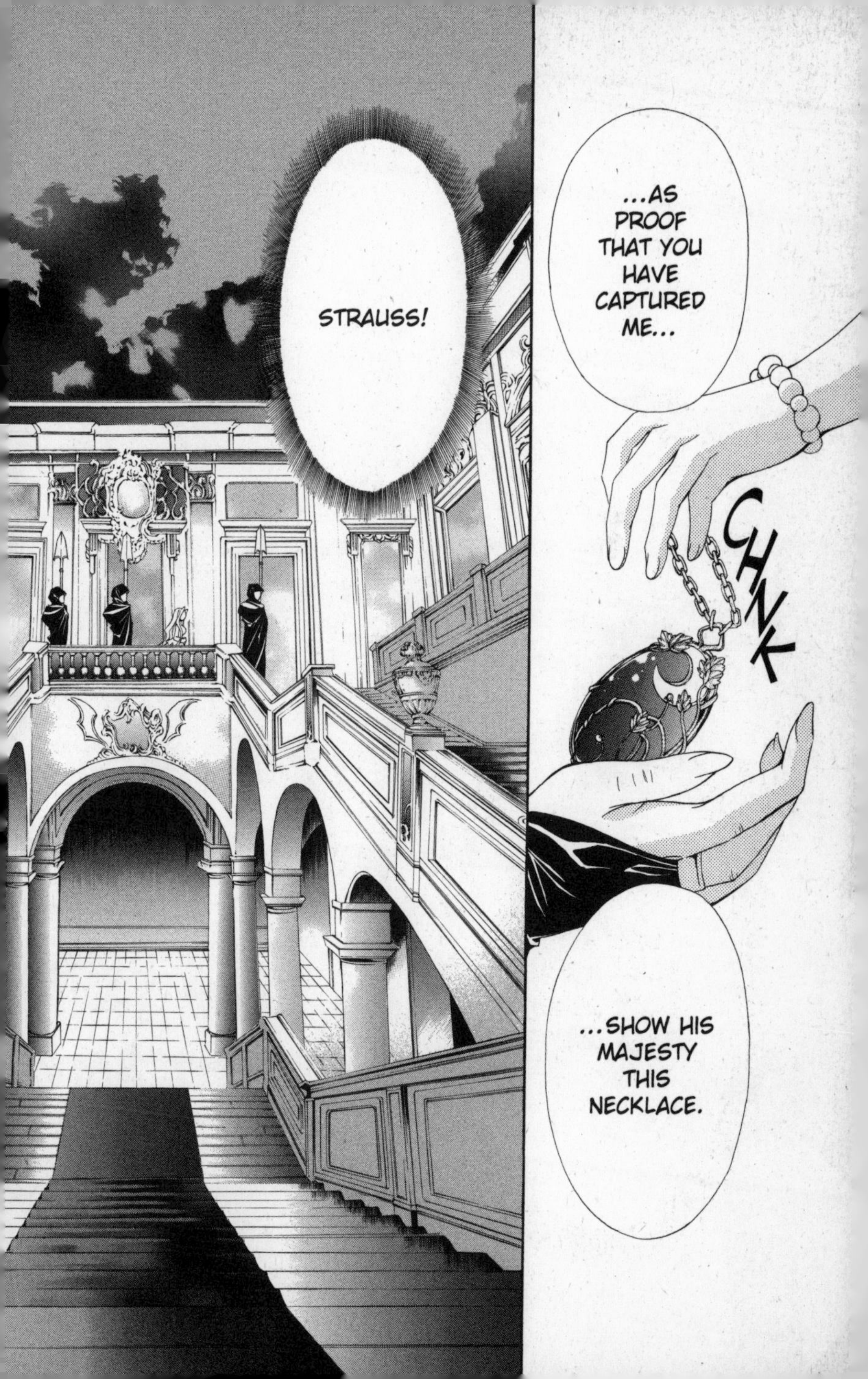
...AS PROOF THAT YOU HAVE CAPTURED ME...
CHNK
...SHOW HIS MAJESTY THIS NECKLACE.
STRAUSS!

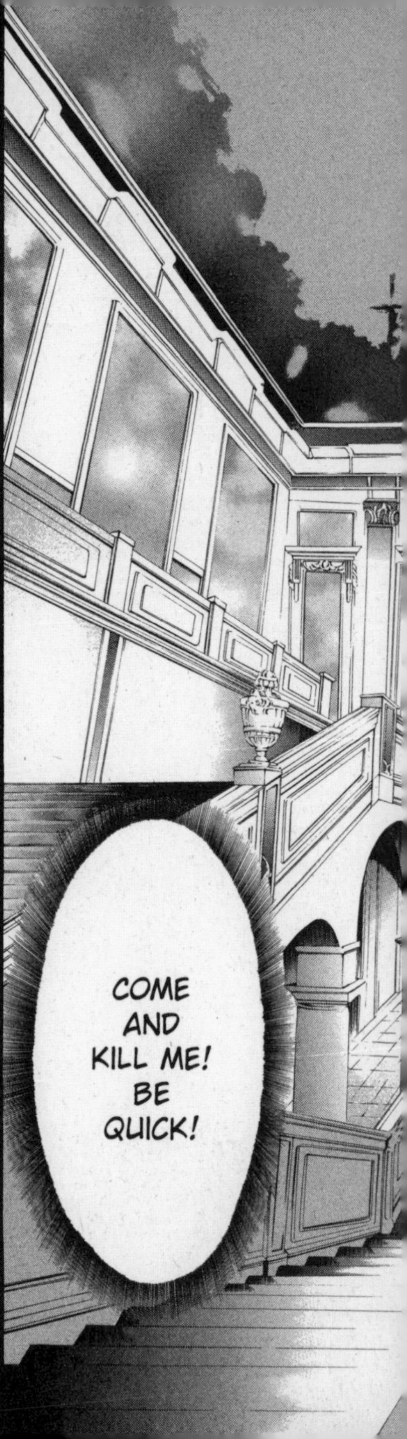
COME AND KILL ME! BE QUICK!
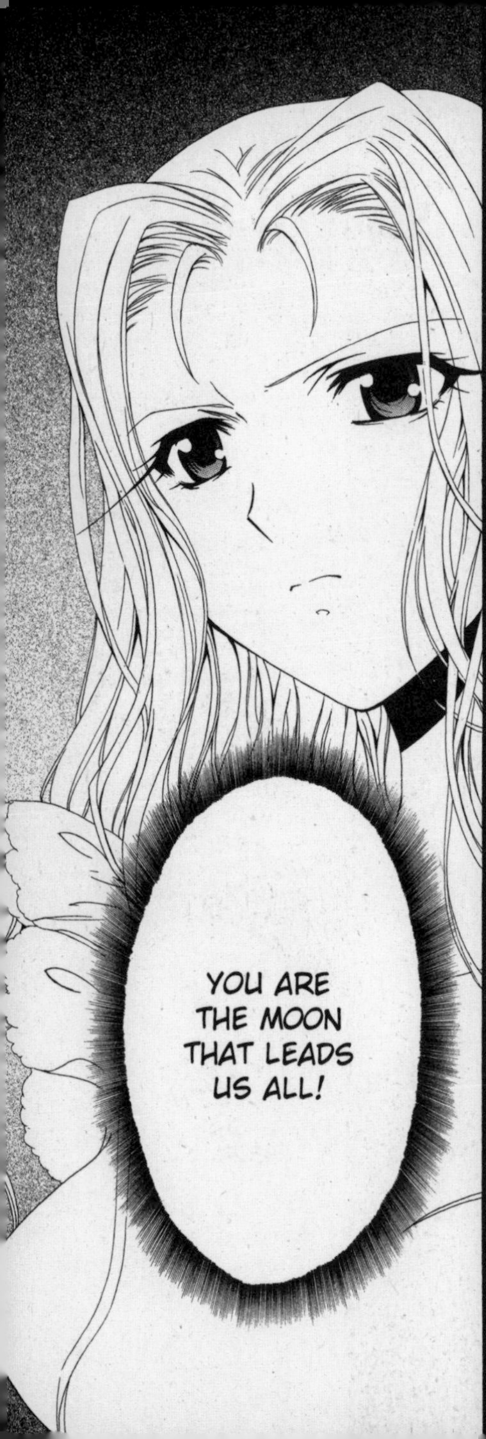
YOU ARE THE MOON THAT LEADS US ALL!

THE RECORD OF A

FALLEN VAMPIRE

Chapter 31: The King's High Moon

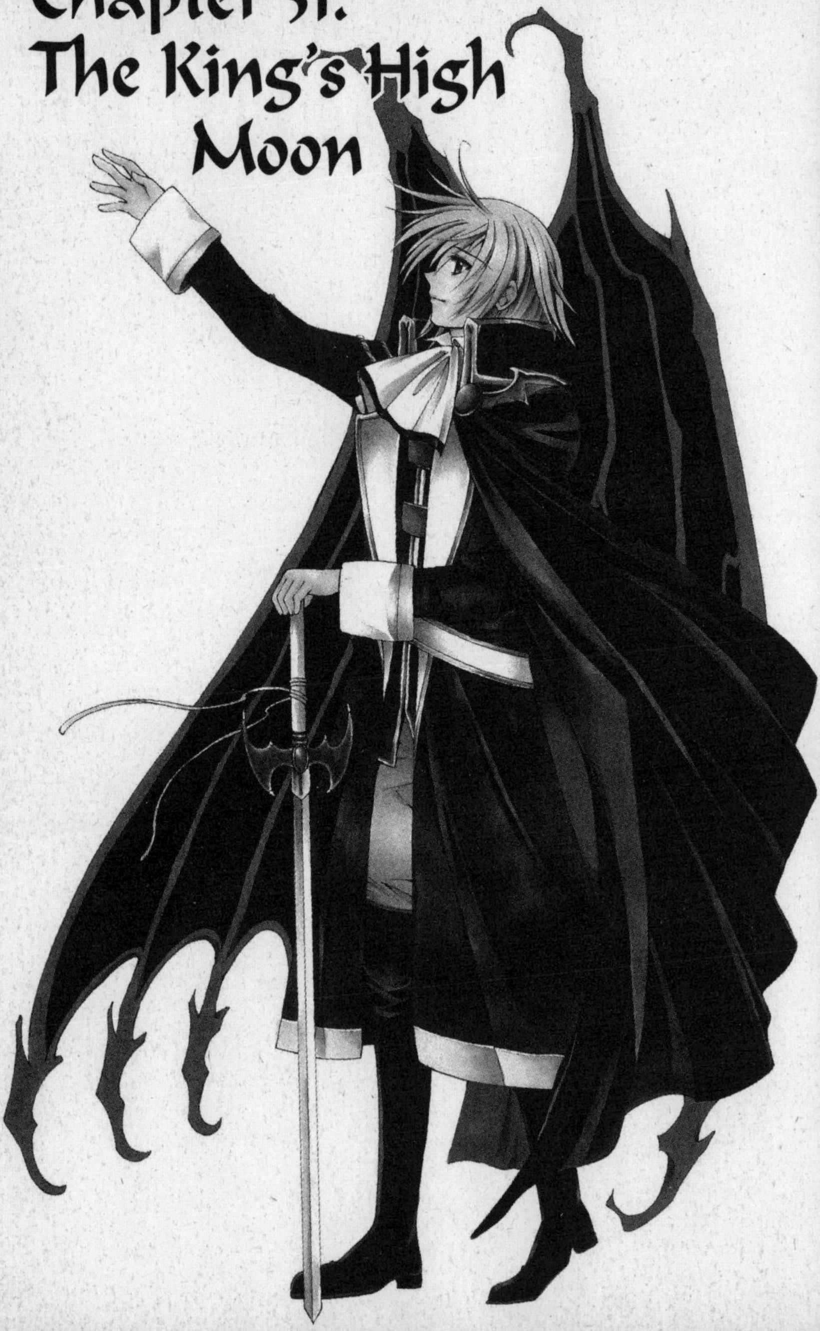

THE RECORD OF A

FALLEN VAMPIRE

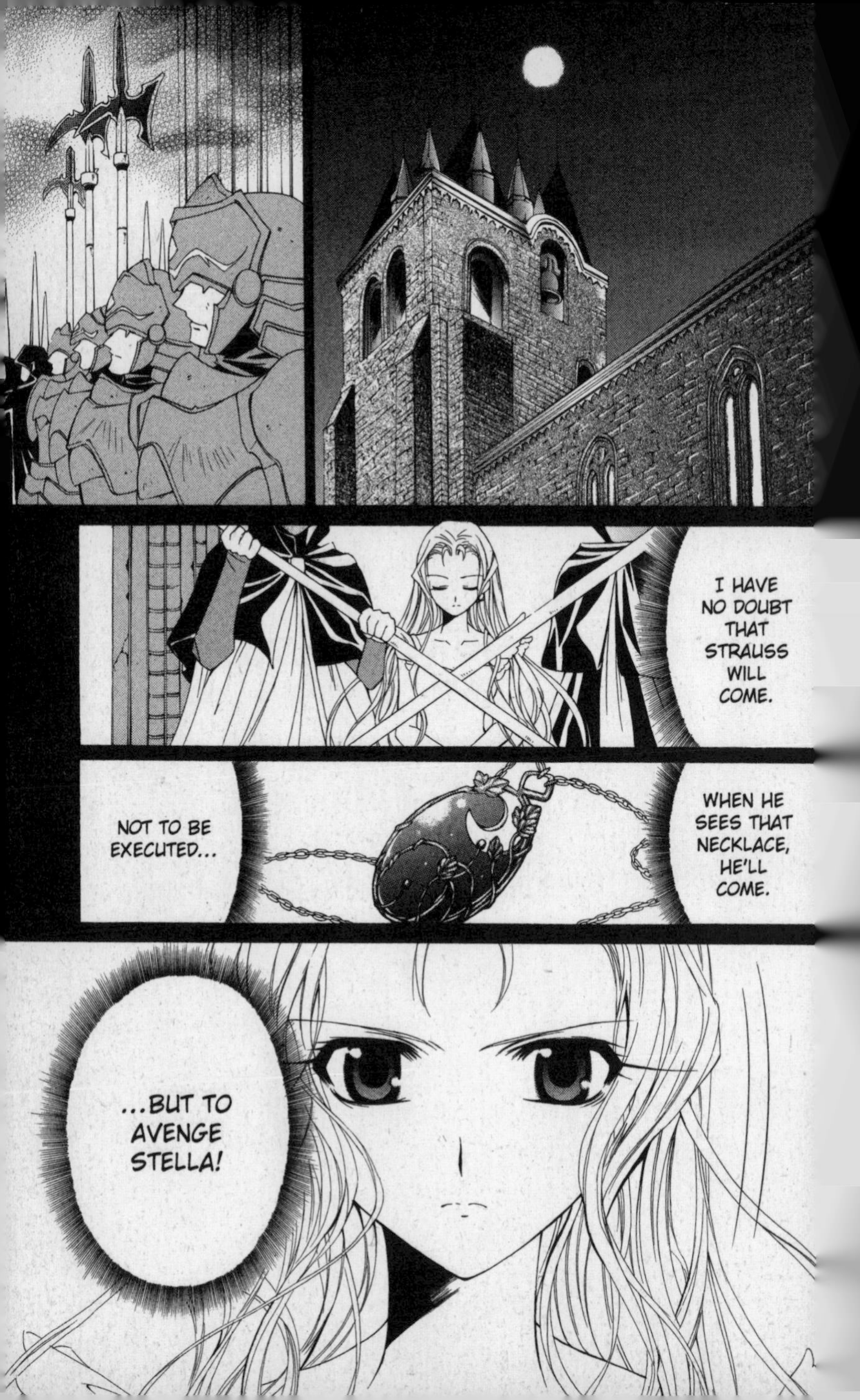
I HAVE NO DOUBT THAT STRAUSS WILL COME.
WHEN HE SEES THAT NECKLACE, HE'LL COME.
NOT TO BE EXECUTED...
...BUT TO AVENGE STELLA!

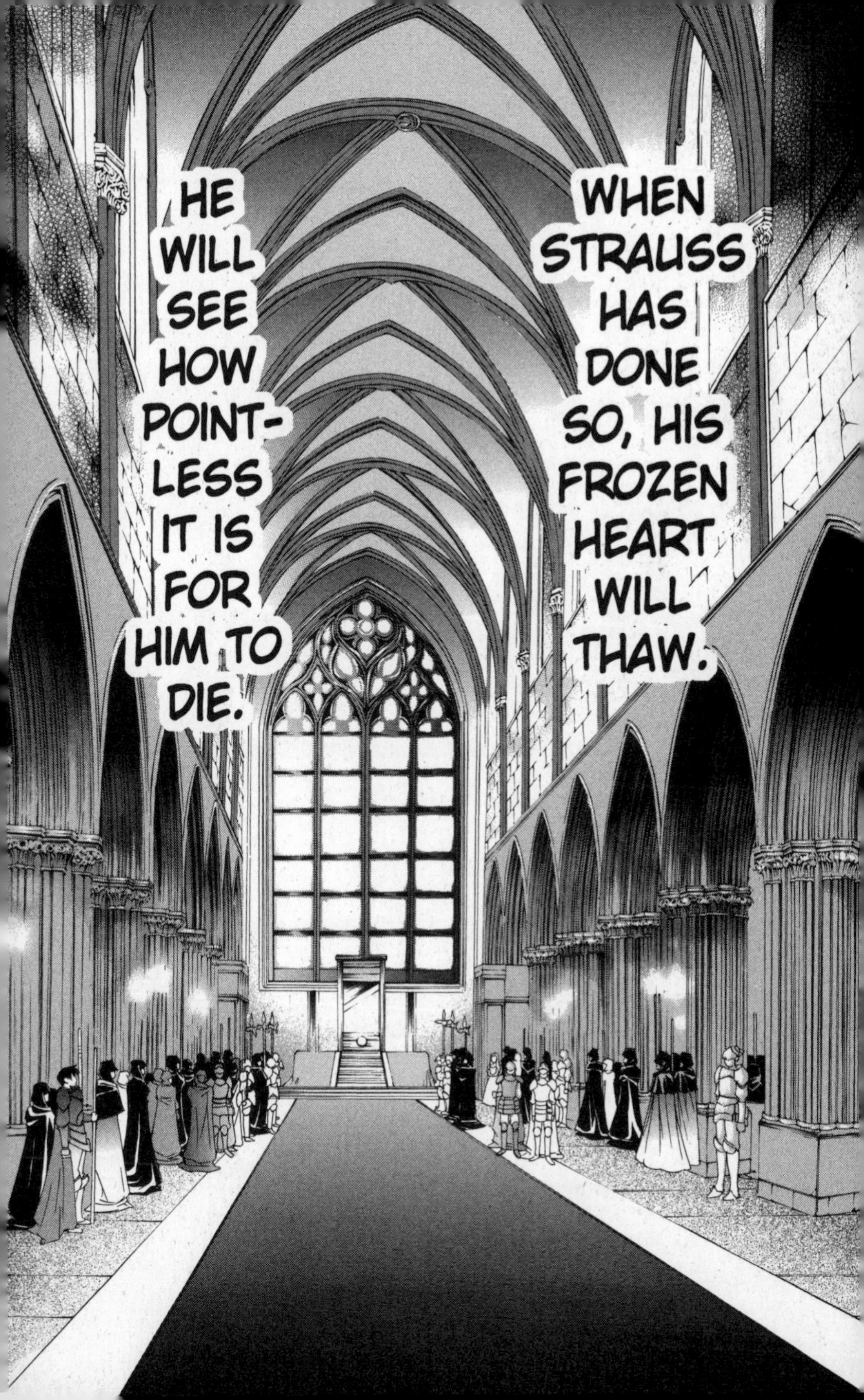
WHEN STRAUSS HAS DONE SO, HIS FROZEN HEART WILL THAW.
HE WILL SEE HOW POINT-LESS IT IS FOR HIM TO DIE.

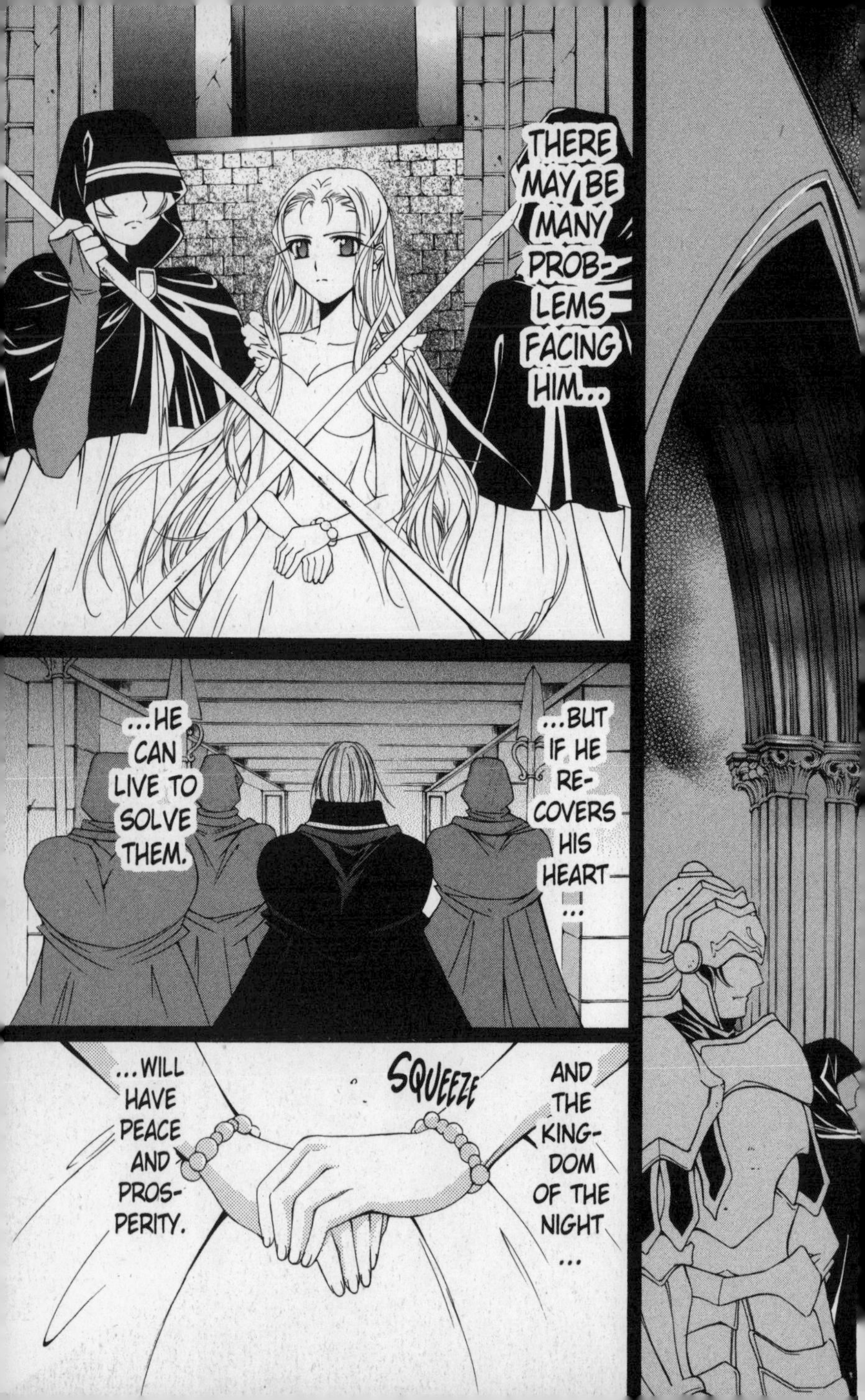
THERE MAY BE MANY PROBLEMS FACING HIM...
...BUT IF HE RECOVERS HIS HEART...
...HE CAN LIVE TO SOLVE THEM.
AND THE KINGDOM OF THE NIGHT...
SQUEEZE
...WILL HAVE PEACE AND PROSPERITY.

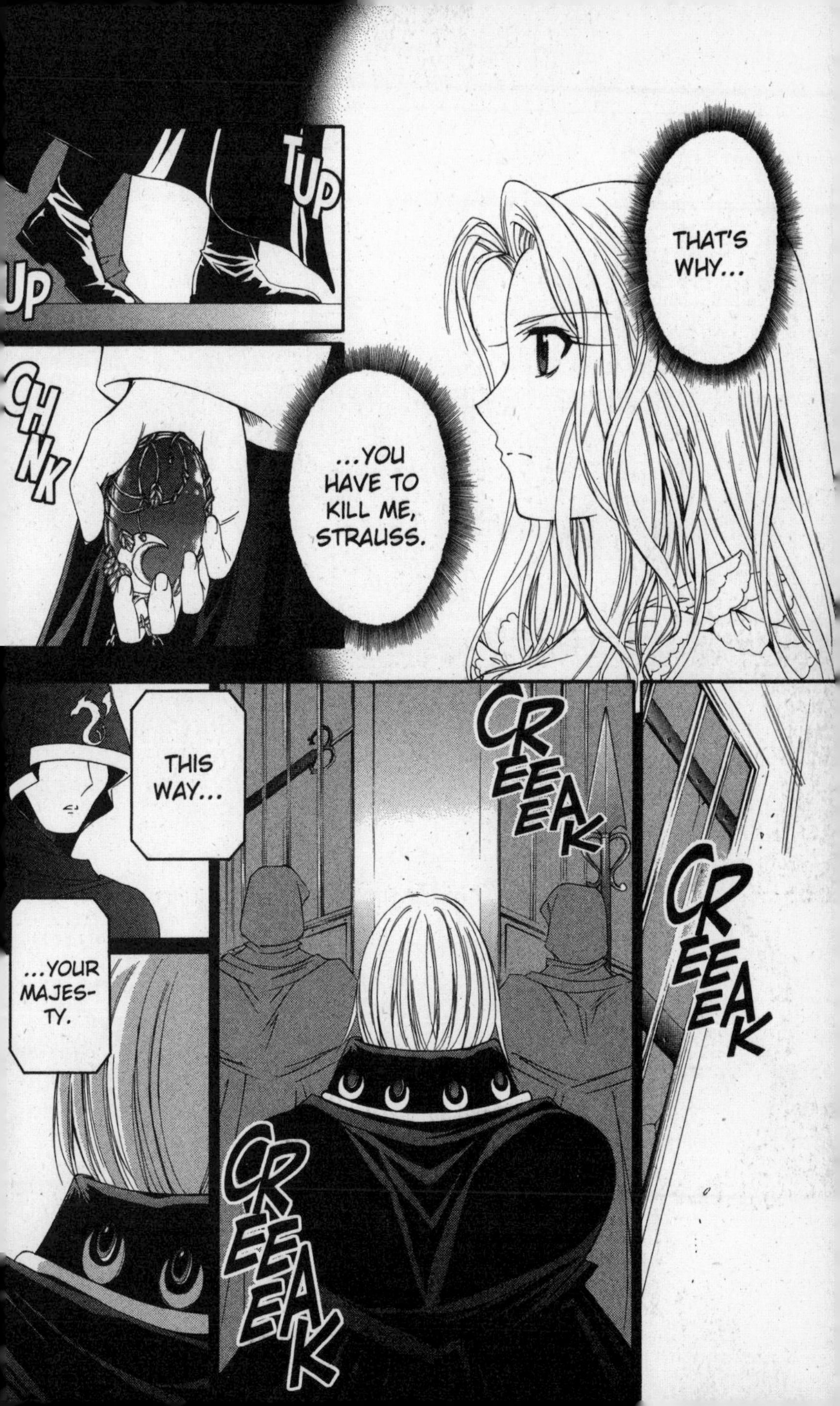
THAT'S WHY...
...YOU HAVE TO KILL ME, STRAUSS.
TUP
UP
CHINK
CREEEAK
CREEEAK
CREEEEAK
THIS WAY...
...YOUR MAJES-TY.

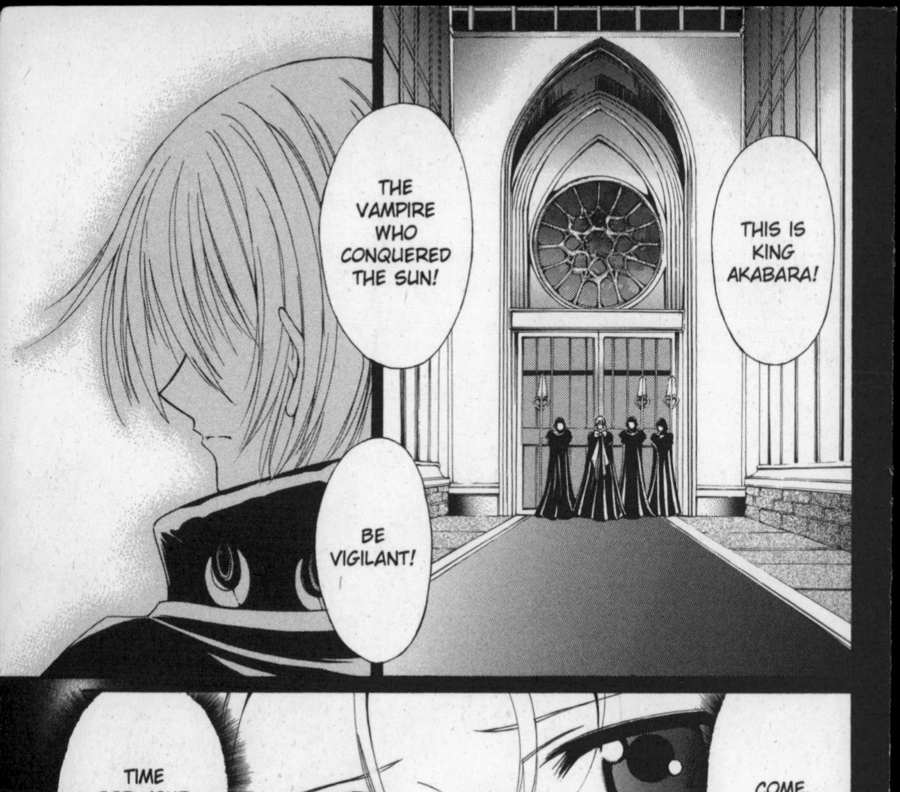
THIS IS KING AKABARA!
THE VAMPIRE WHO CONQUERED THE SUN!
BE VIGILANT!
COME, STRAUSS.
TIME FOR YOUR REVENGE.
DEATH TO STELLA'S KILLER!
LET LOOSE YOUR ANGER AND HATRED...
TUP

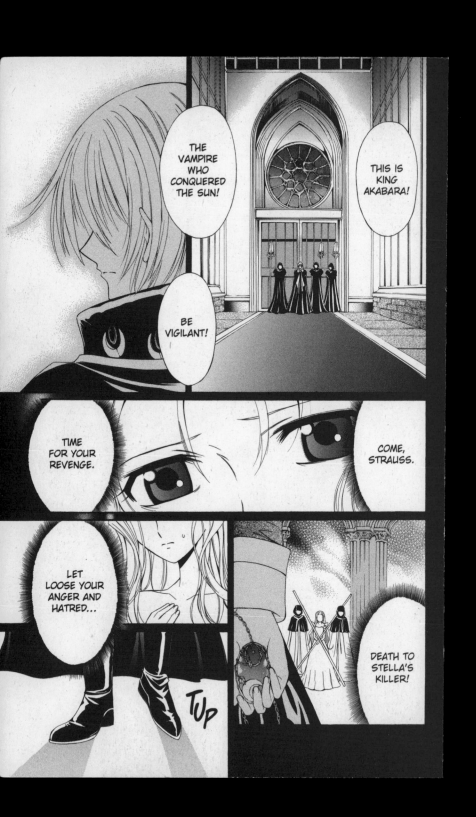

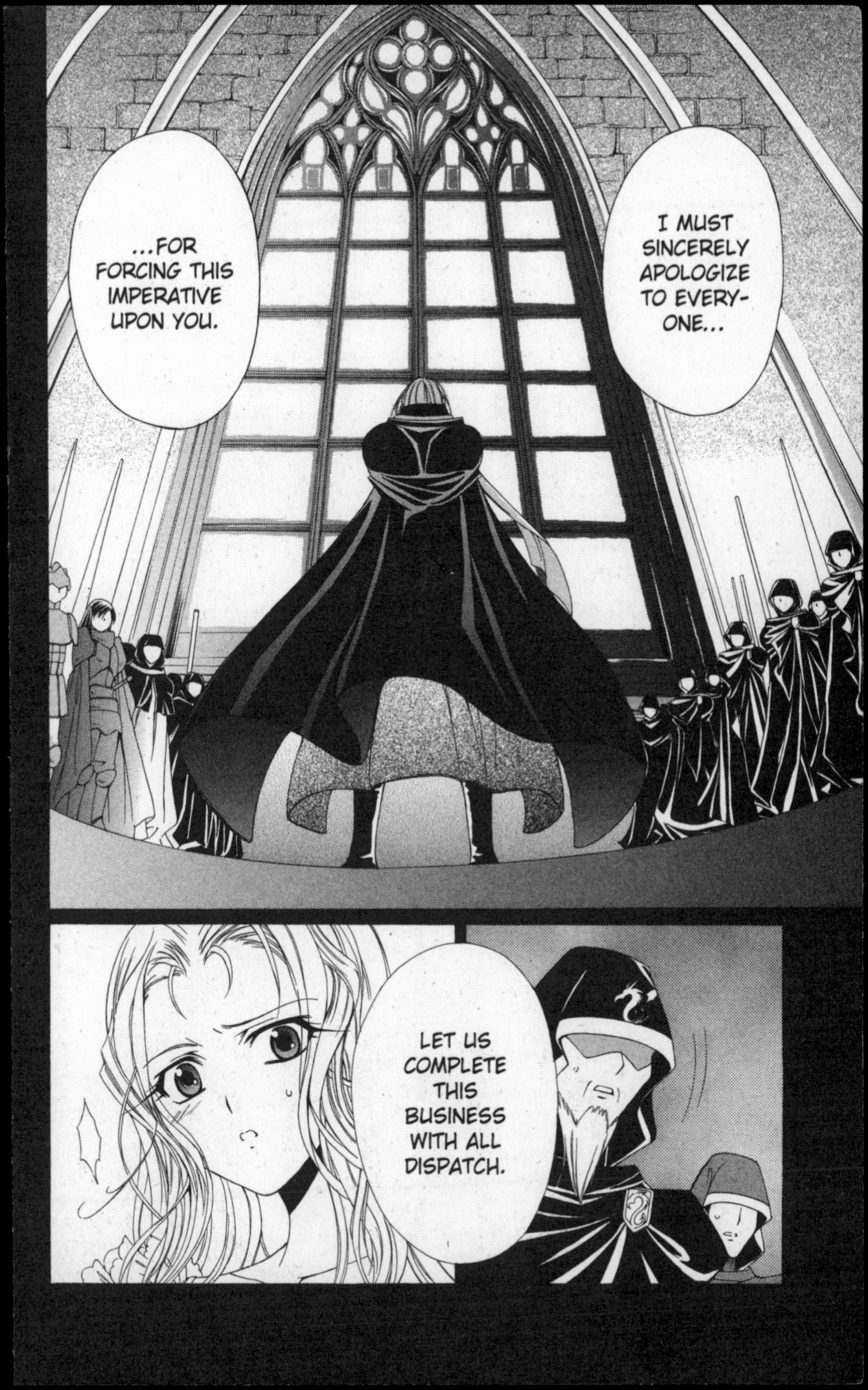
I MUST SINCERELY APOLOGIZE TO EVERY-ONE...
...FOR FORCING THIS IMPERATIVE UPON YOU.
LET US COMPLETE THIS BUSINESS WITH ALL DISPATCH.

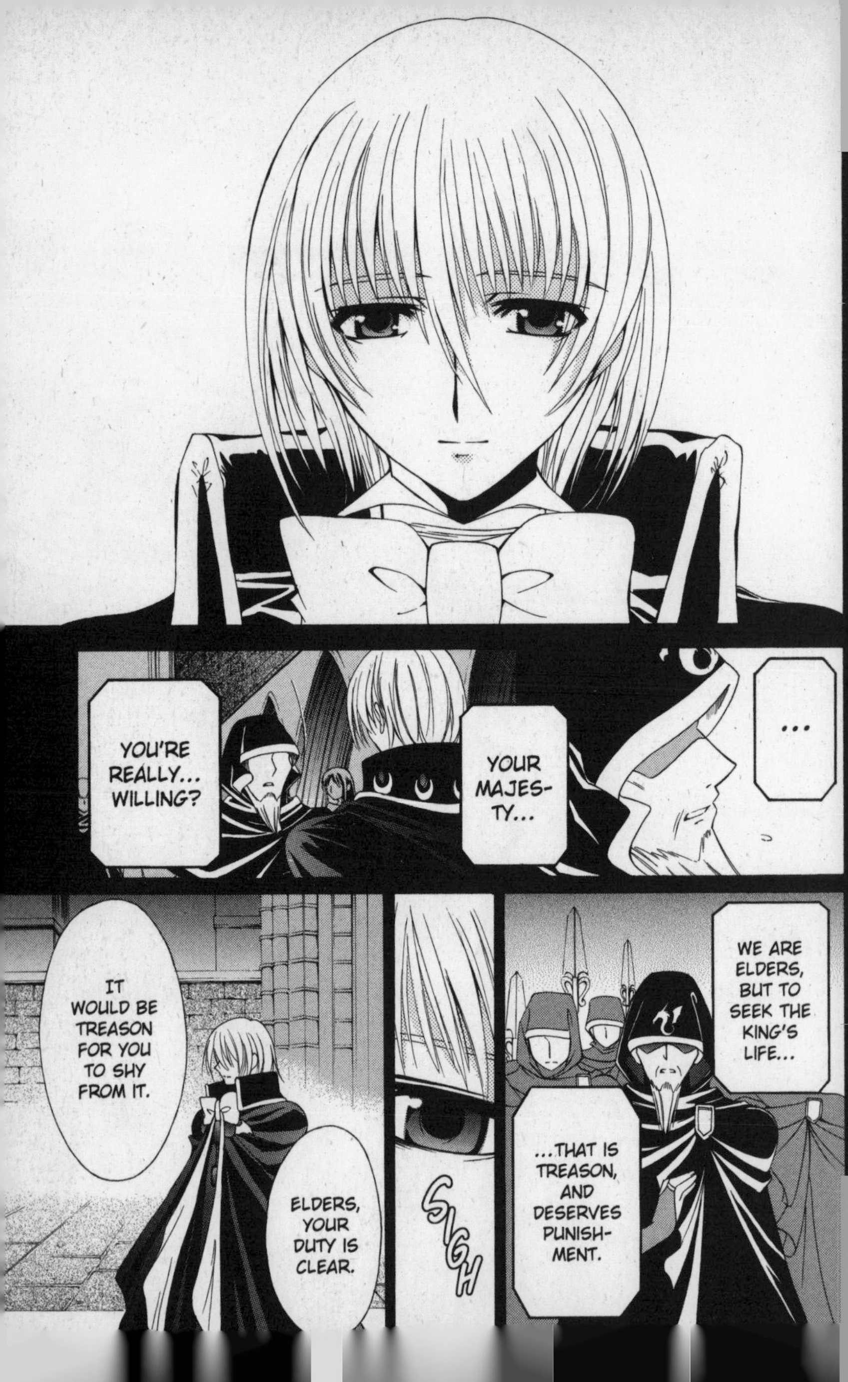
...
YOUR MAJESTY...
YOU'RE REALLY... WILLING?
WE ARE ELDERS, BUT TO SEEK THE KING'S LIFE...
...THAT IS TREASON, AND DESERVES PUNISHMENT.
SIGH
ELDERS, YOUR DUTY IS CLEAR.
IT WOULD BE TREASON FOR YOU TO SHY FROM IT.

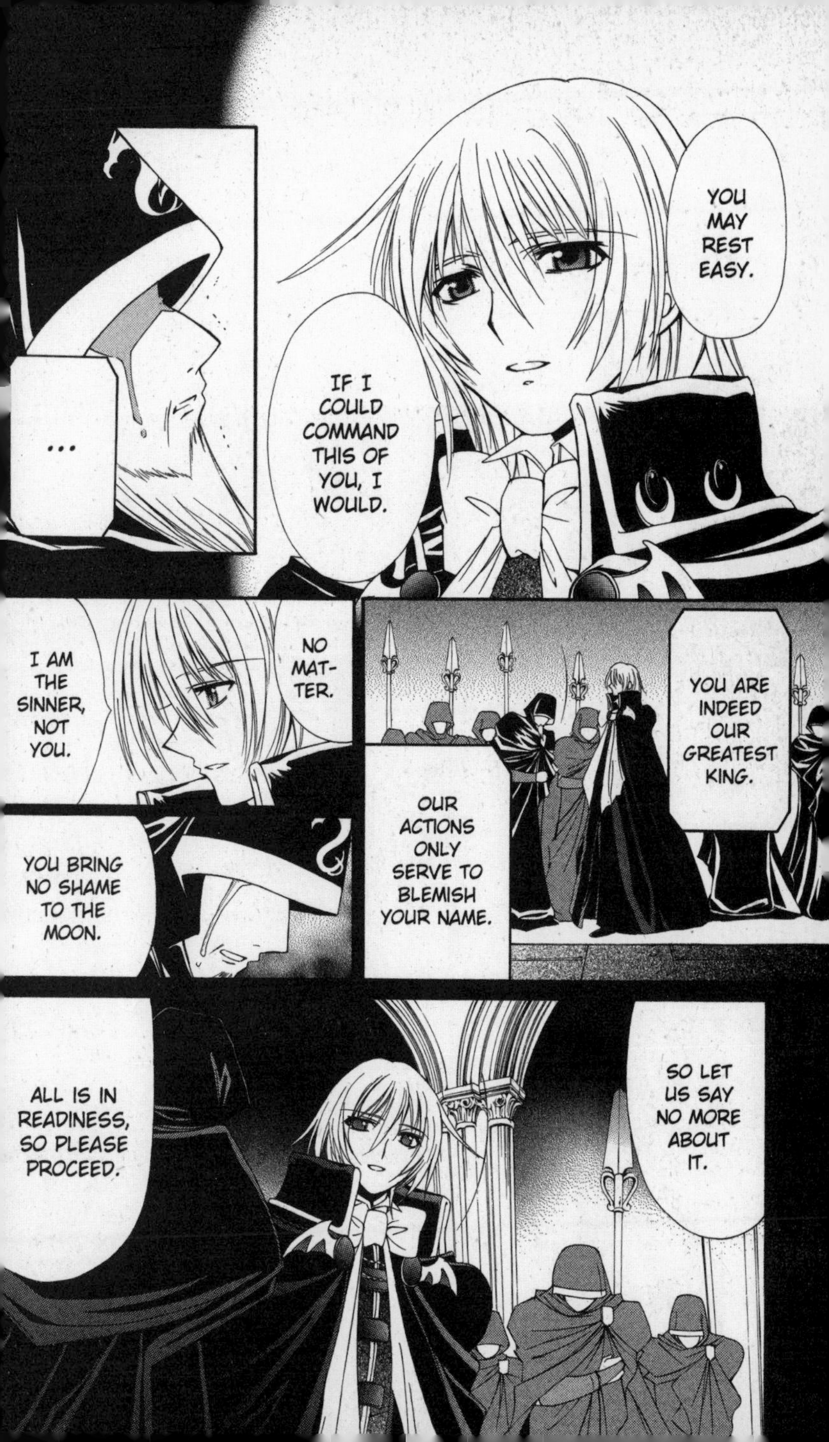
YOU MAY REST EASY.
IF I COULD COMMAND THIS OF YOU, I WOULD.
...
YOU ARE INDEED OUR GREATEST KING.
OUR ACTIONS ONLY SERVE TO BLEMISH YOUR NAME.
NO MAT-TER.
I AM THE SINNER, NOT YOU.
YOU BRING NO SHAME TO THE MOON.
SO LET US SAY NO MORE ABOUT IT.
ALL IS IN READINESS, SO PLEASE PROCEED.

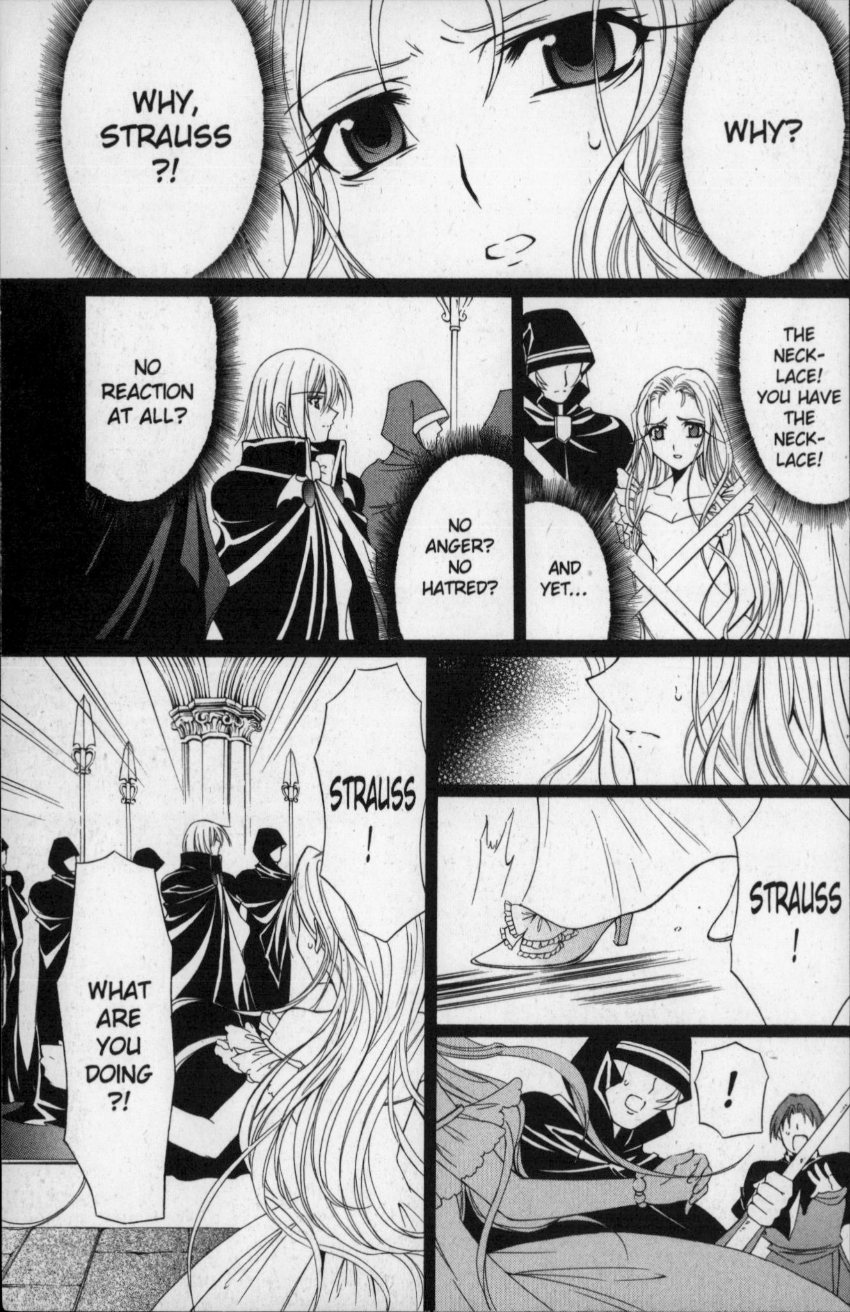
WHY?
WHY, STRAUSS?!
THE NECKLACE! YOU HAVE THE NECKLACE!
AND YET...
NO REACTION AT ALL?
NO ANGER? NO HATRED?
STRAUSS!
!
STRAUSS!
WHAT ARE YOU DOING?!

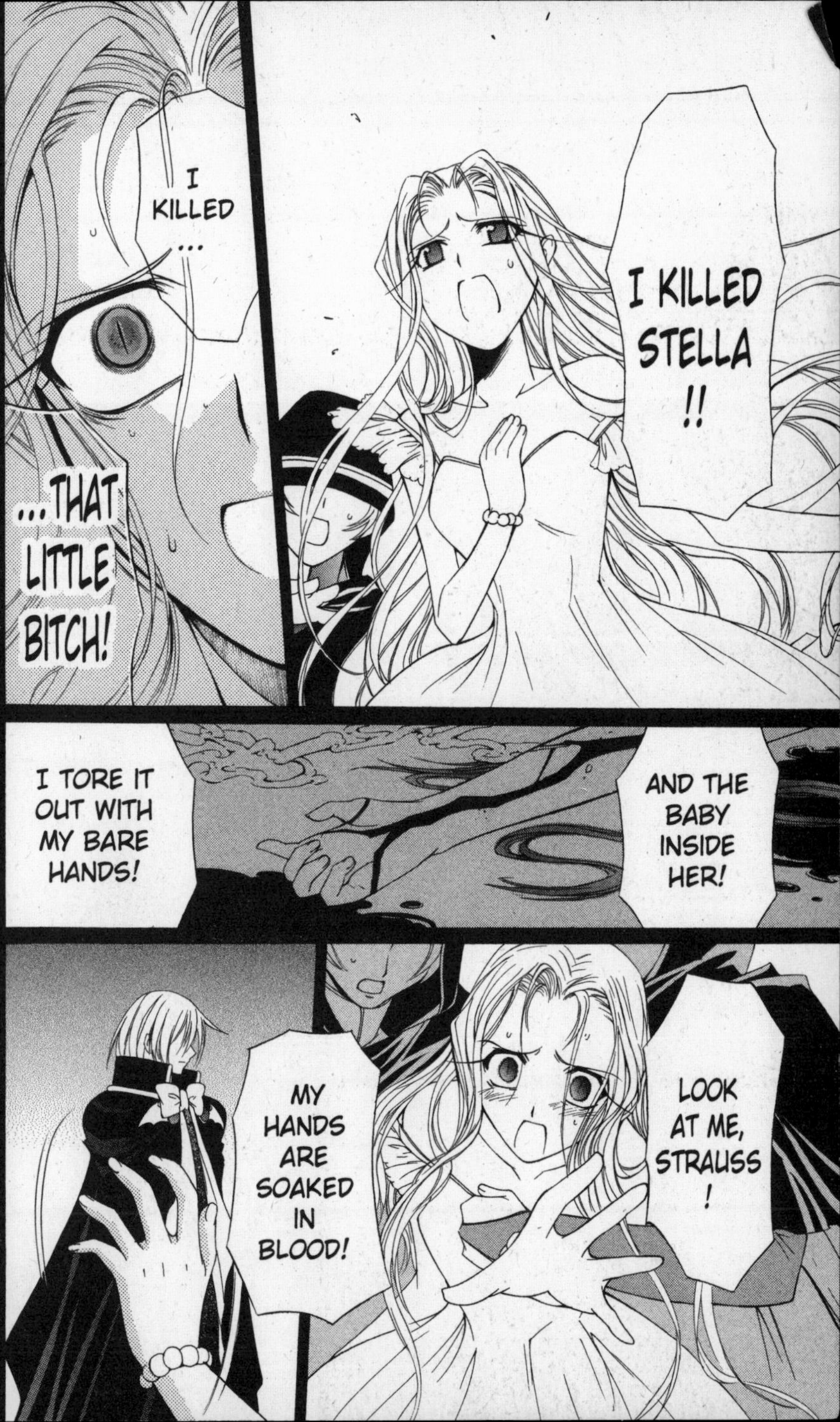
I KILLED STELLA!!
I KILLED...
...THAT LITTLE BITCH!
AND THE BABY INSIDE HER!
I TORE IT OUT WITH MY BARE HANDS!
LOOK AT ME, STRAUSS!
MY HANDS ARE SOAKED IN BLOOD!

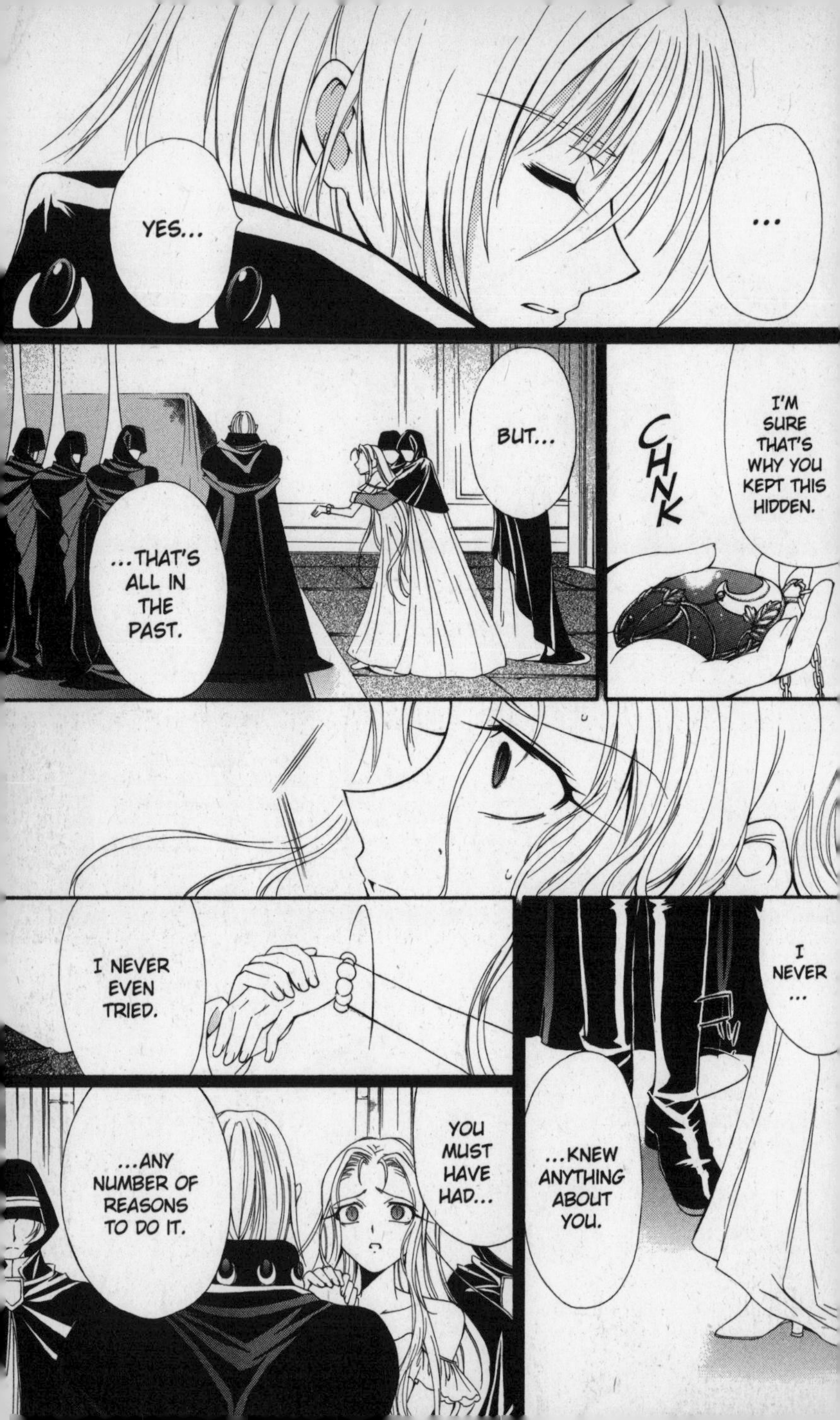
...
YES...
I'M SURE THAT'S WHY YOU KEPT THIS HIDDEN.
CHNK
BUT...
...THAT'S ALL IN THE PAST.
I NEVER ...
...KNEW ANYTHING ABOUT YOU.
I NEVER EVEN TRIED.
YOU MUST HAVE HAD...
...ANY NUMBER OF REASONS TO DO IT.

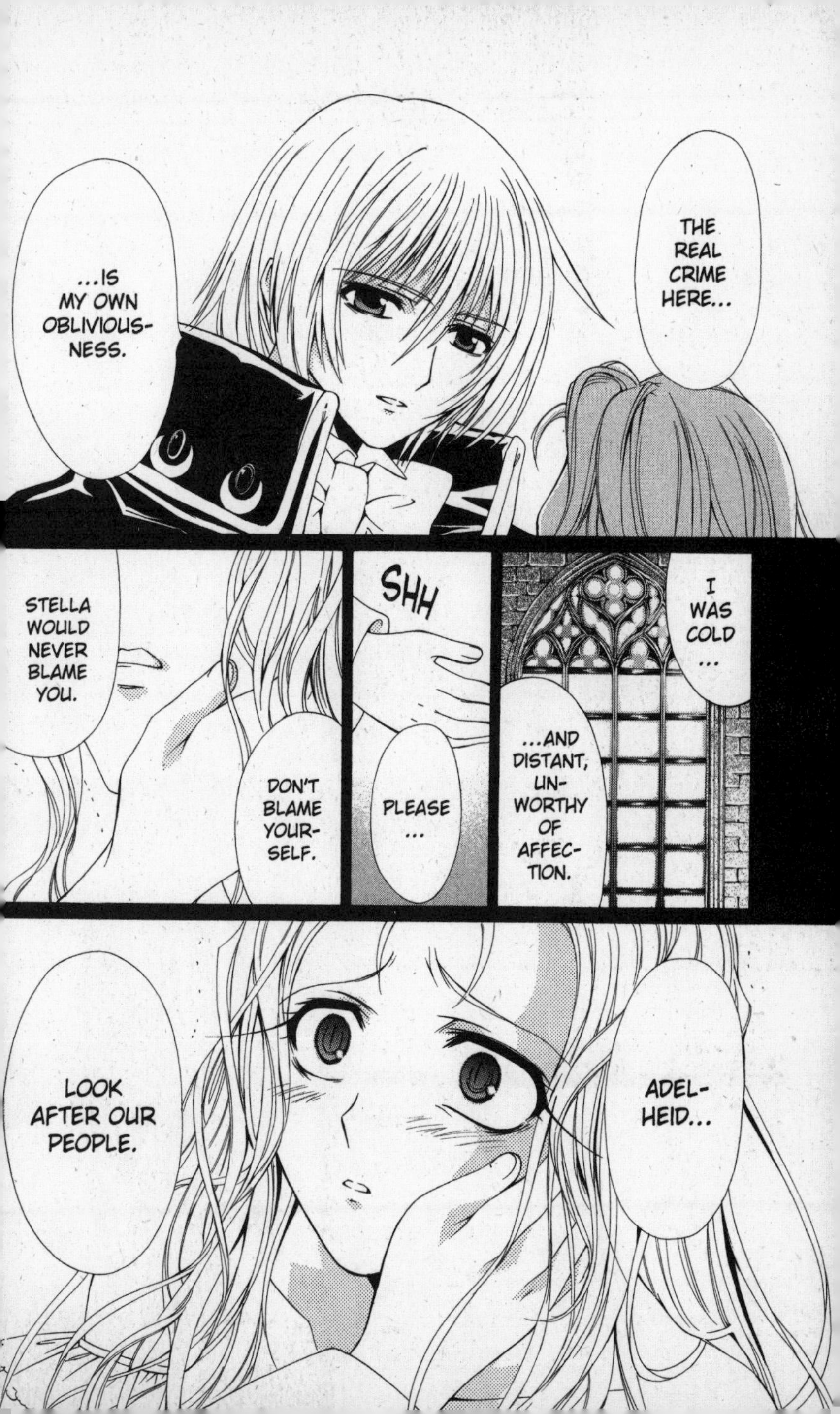
THE REAL CRIME HERE...
...IS MY OWN OBLIVIOUS-NESS.
I WAS COLD ...
...AND DISTANT, UN-WORTHY OF AFFEC-TION.
SHH
PLEASE ...
STELLA WOULD NEVER BLAME YOU.
DON'T BLAME YOUR-SELF.
ADEL-HEID...
LOOK AFTER OUR PEOPLE.

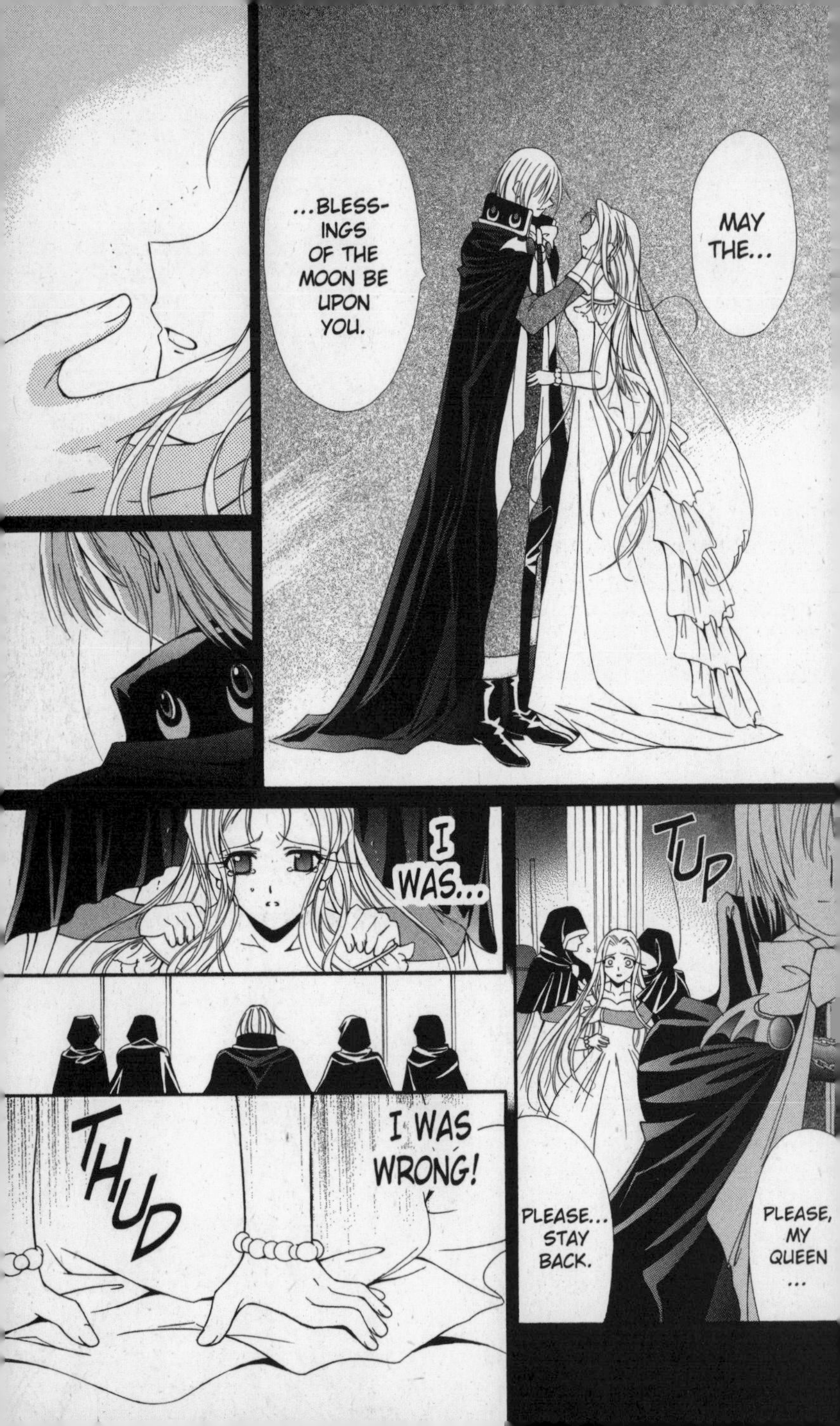
MAY THE...
...BLESS-INGS OF THE MOON BE UPON YOU.
TUP
PLEASE, MY QUEEN ...
PLEASE... STAY BACK.
I WAS...
I WAS WRONG!
THUD

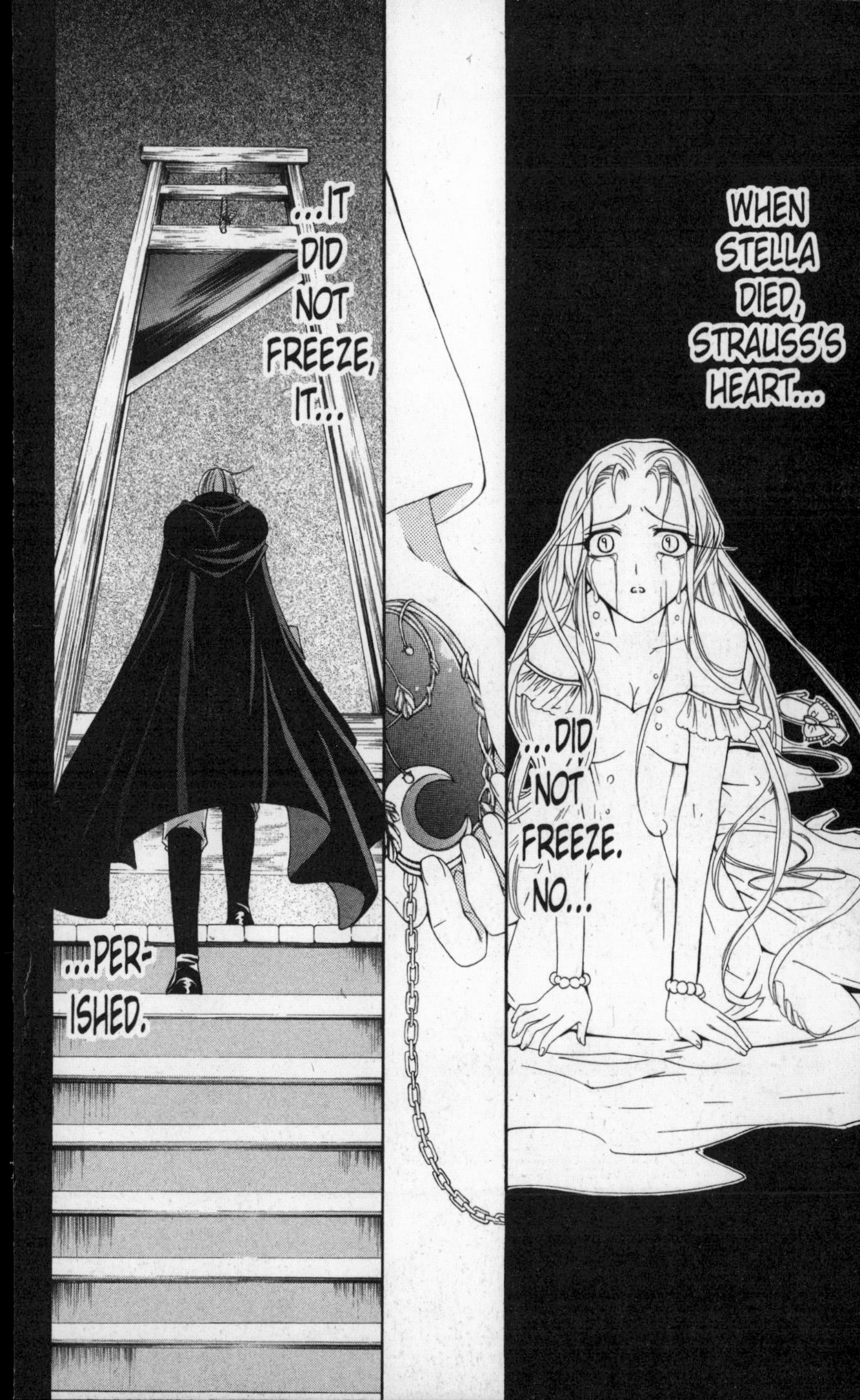
WHEN STELLA DIED, STRAUSS'S HEART...
...DID NOT FREEZE. NO...
...IT DID NOT FREEZE, IT...
...PER-ISHED.

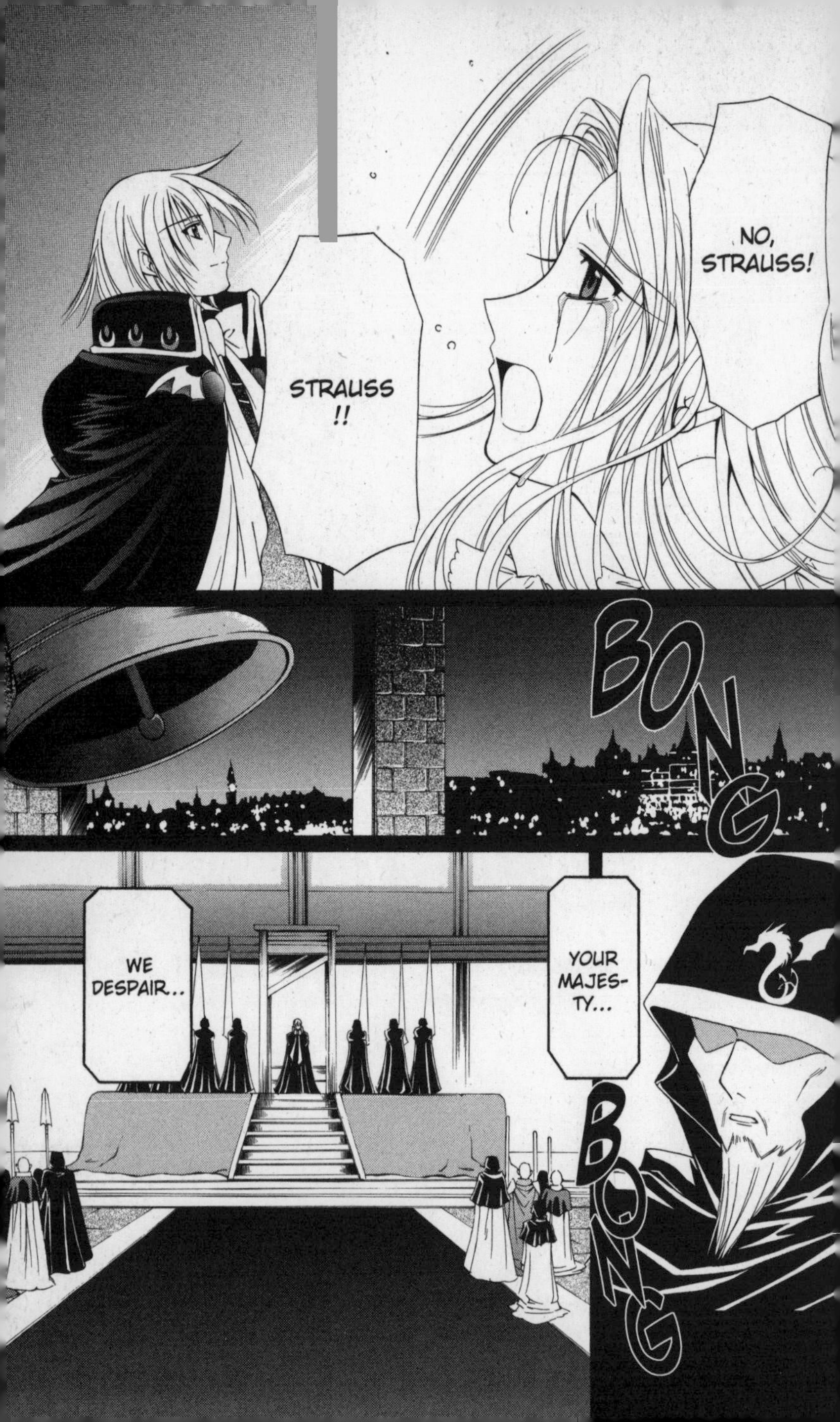
NO, STRAUSS!
STRAUSS !!
BONG
YOUR MAJESTY...
BONG
BONG
WE DESPAIR...

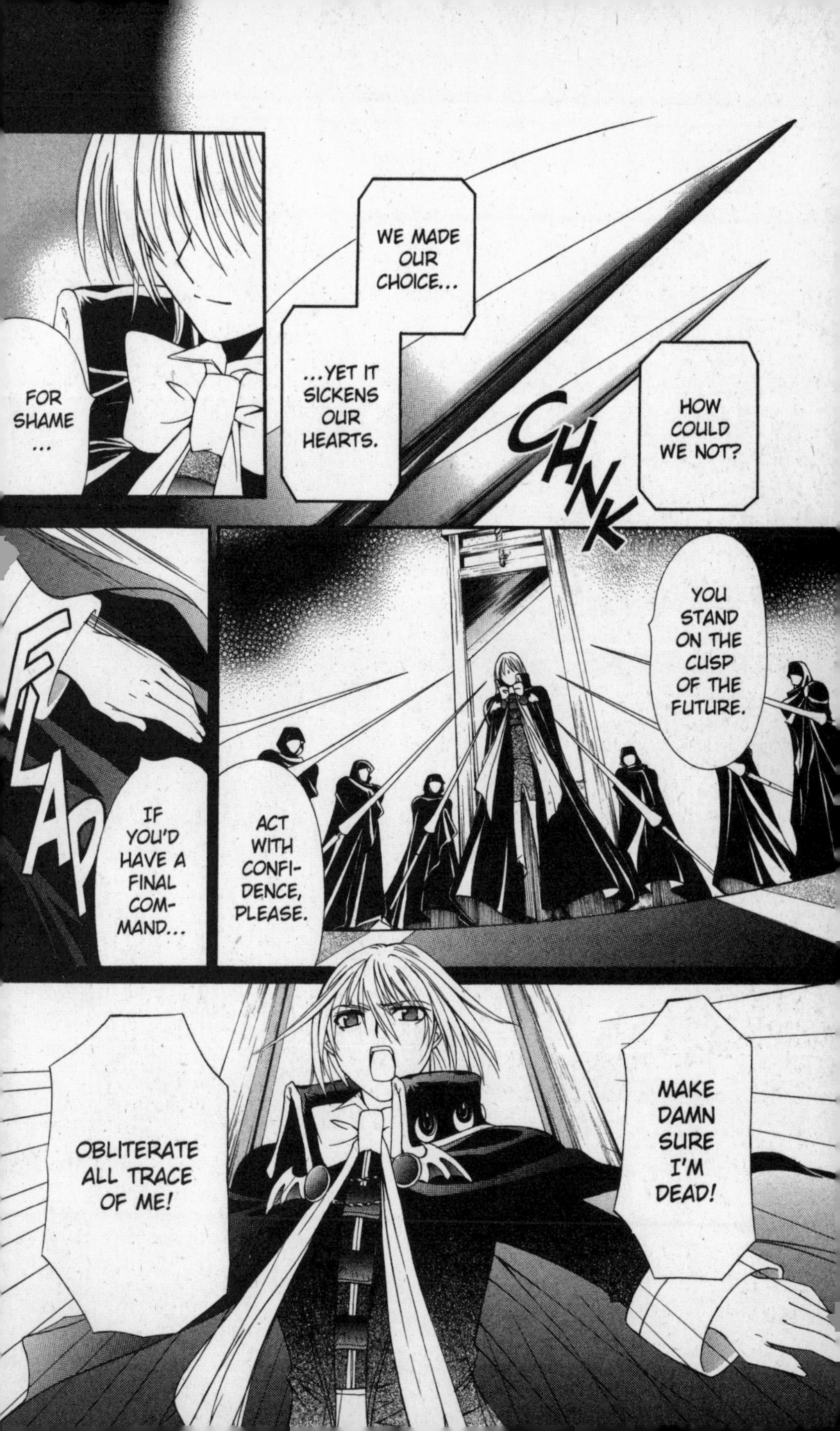
WE MADE OUR CHOICE...
...YET IT SICKENS OUR HEARTS.
CHNK
HOW COULD WE NOT?
FOR SHAME ...
YOU STAND ON THE CUSP OF THE FUTURE.
ACT WITH CONFI-DENCE, PLEASE.
FLAP
IF YOU'D HAVE A FINAL COM-MAND...
MAKE DAMN SURE I'M DEAD!
OBLITERATE ALL TRACE OF ME!

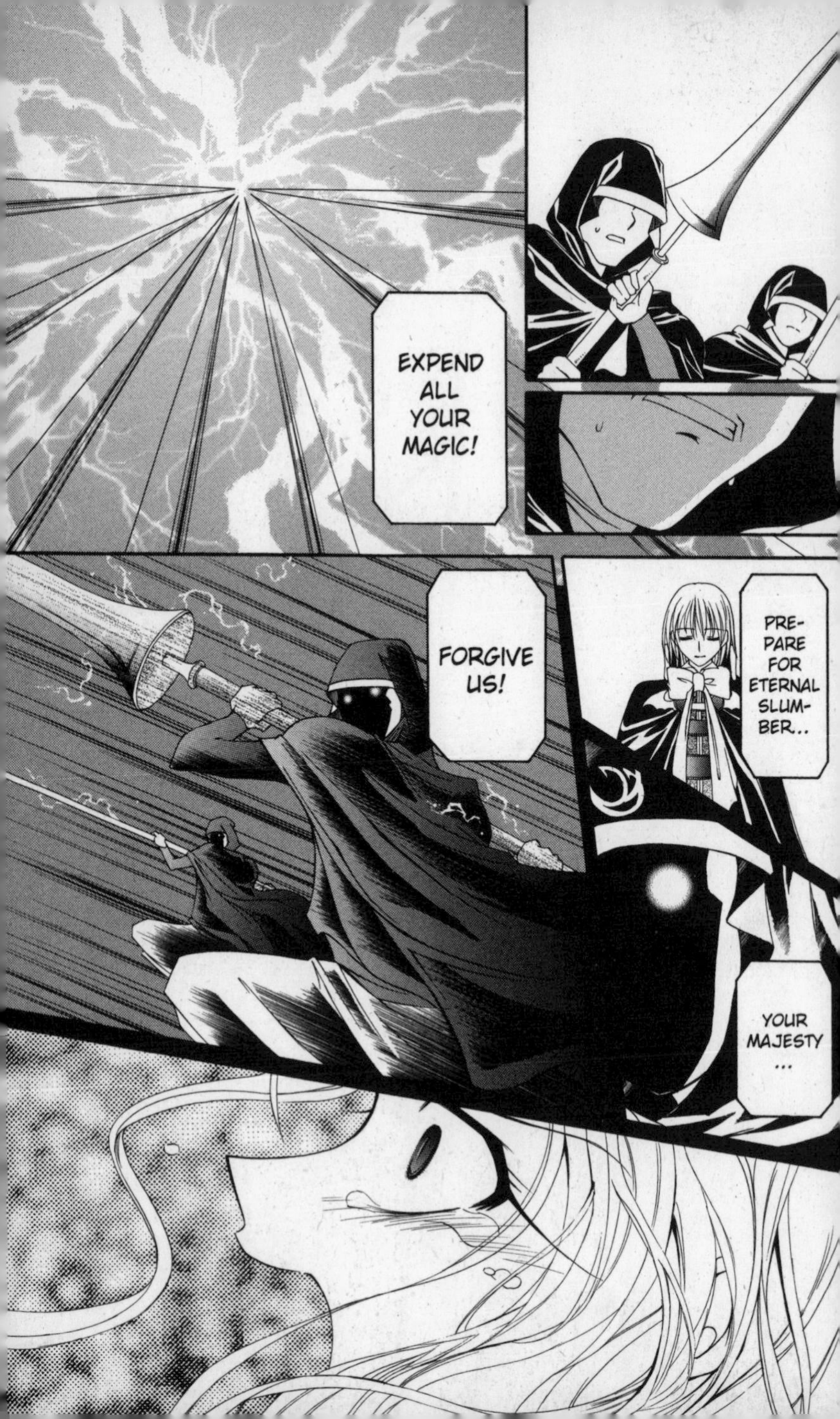
EXPEND ALL YOUR MAGIC!
PRE-PARE FOR ETERNAL SLUM-BER...
FORGIVE US!
YOUR MAJESTY...

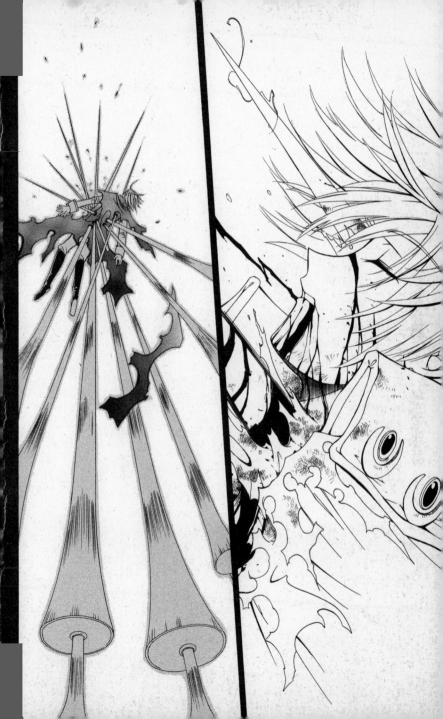

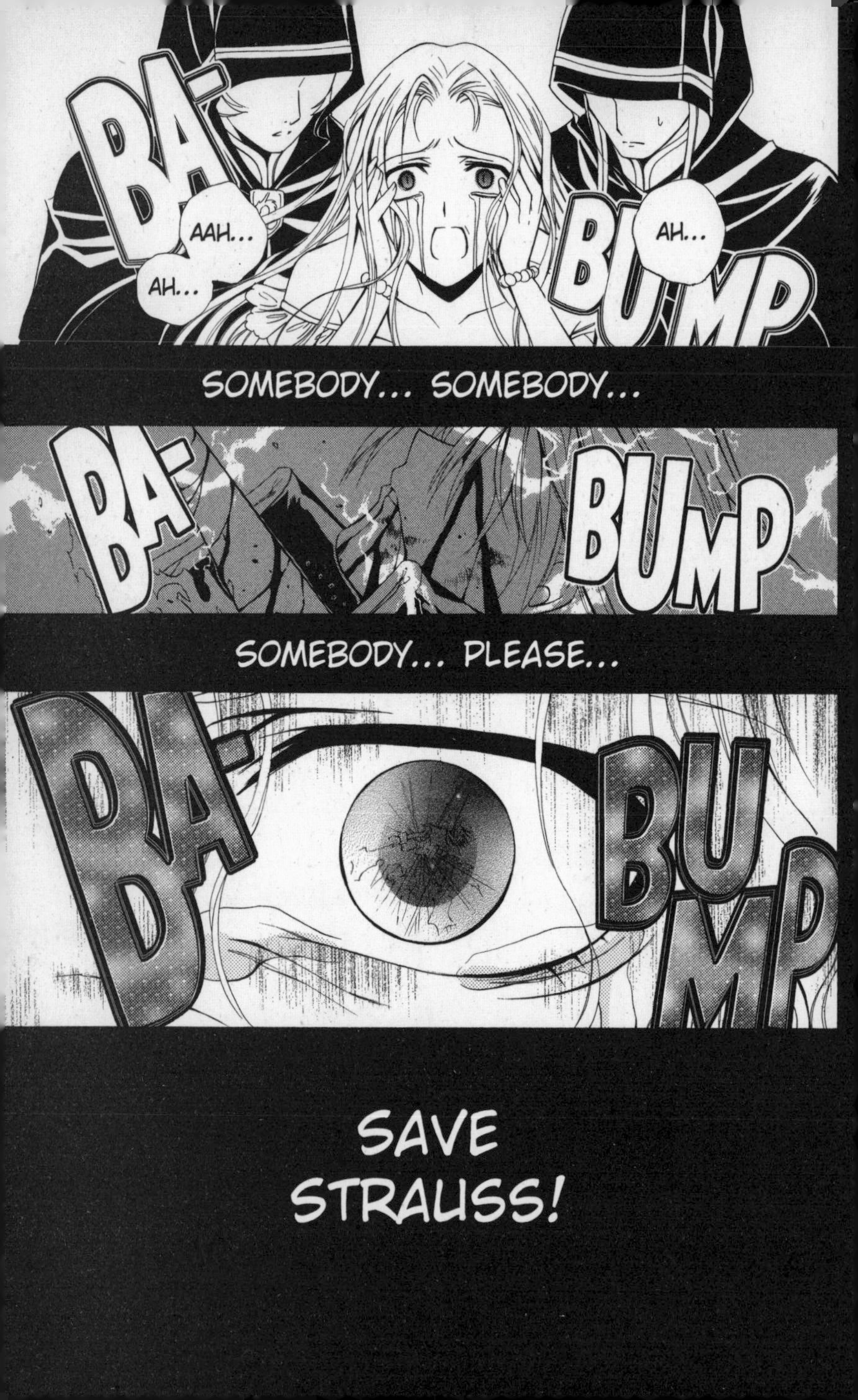
AH...
AAH...
AH...
BA-BUMP
SOMEBODY... SOMEBODY...
BA-BUMP
SOMEBODY... PLEASE...
BA-BUMP
SAVE STRAUSS!

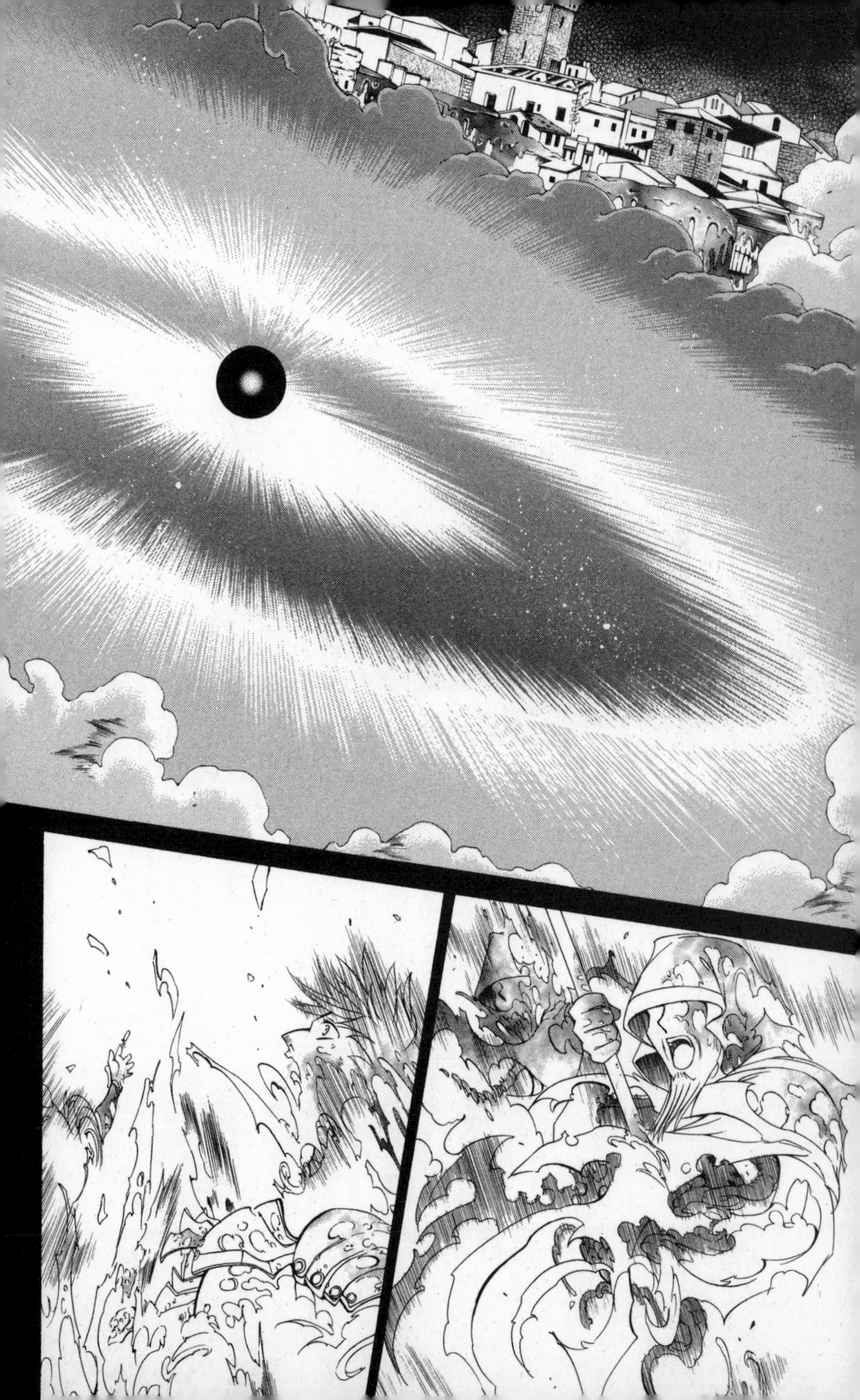

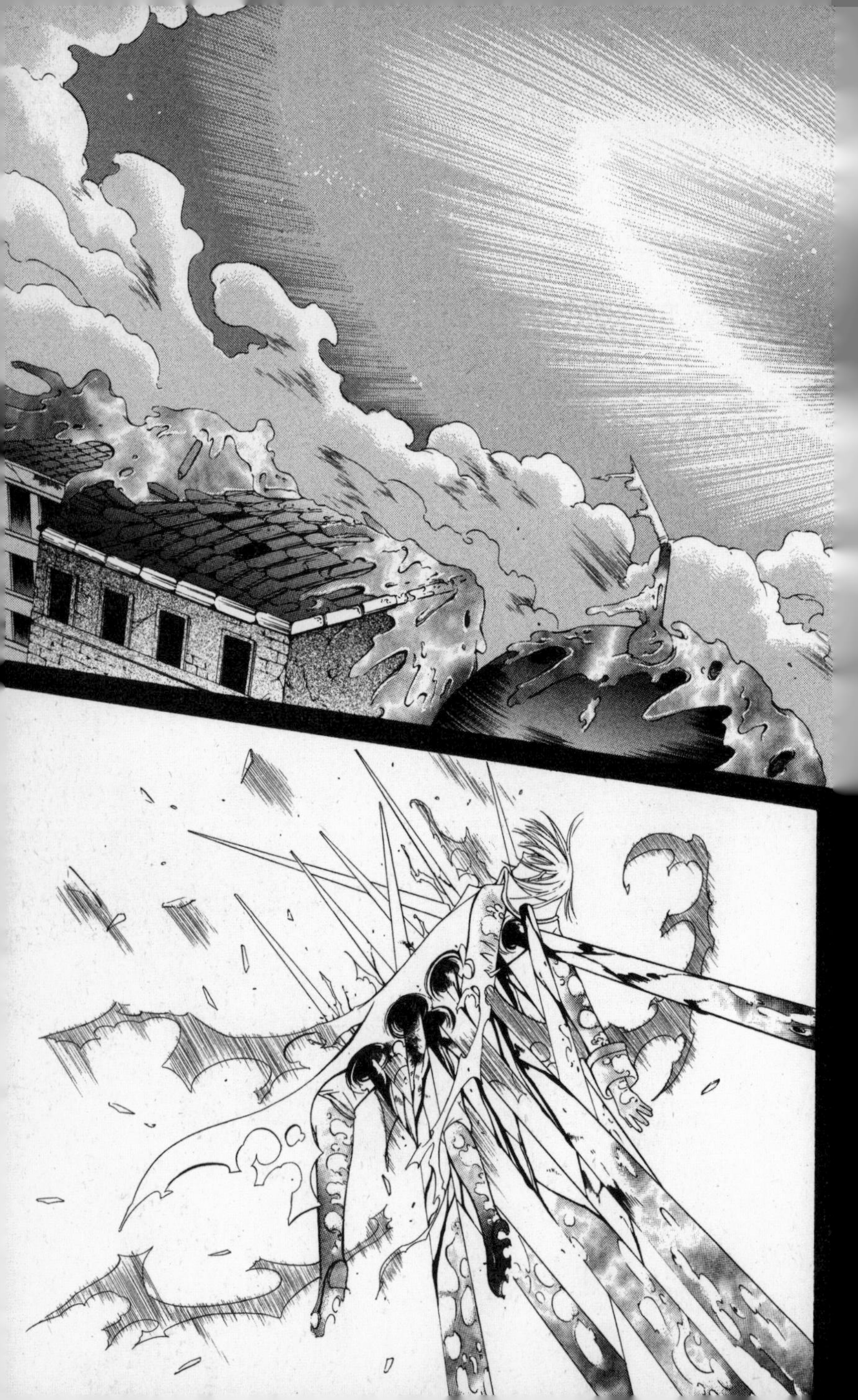

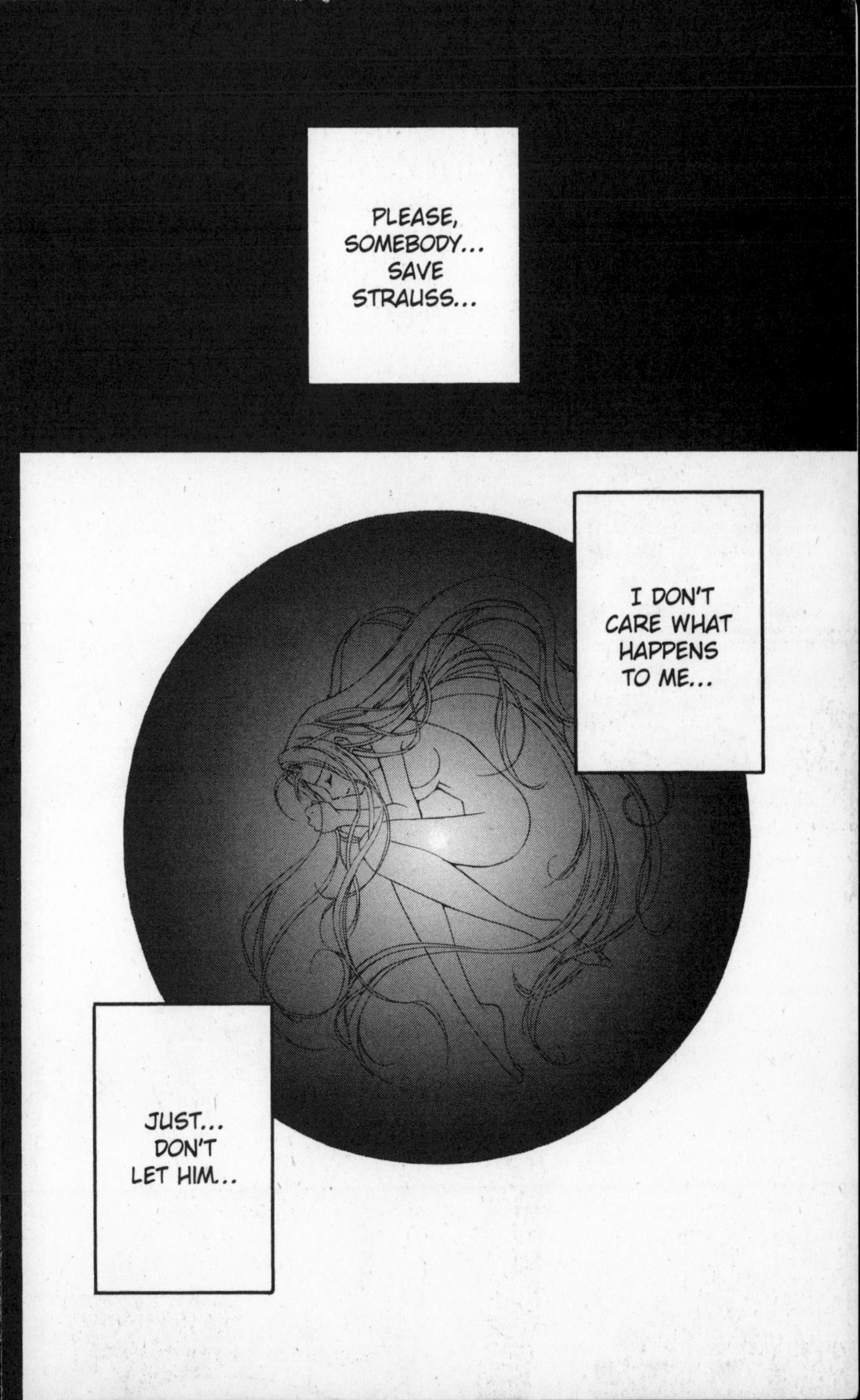
PLEASE, SOMEBODY... SAVE STRAUSS...
I DON'T CARE WHAT HAPPENS TO ME...
JUST... DON'T LET HIM...

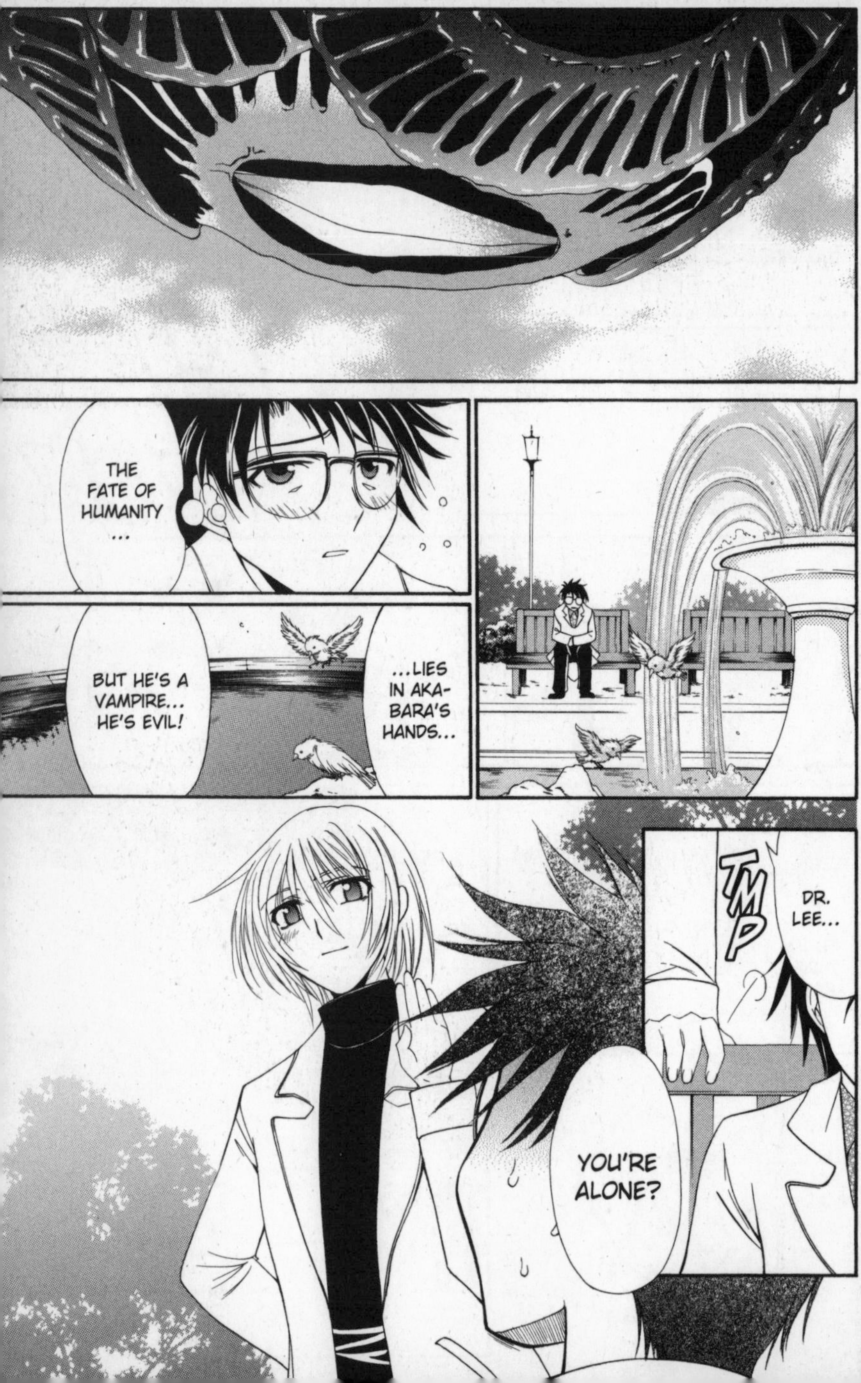
THE FATE OF HUMANITY...
...LIES IN AKA-BARA'S HANDS...
BUT HE'S A VAMPIRE... HE'S EVIL!
DR. LEE...
TMP
YOU'RE ALONE?

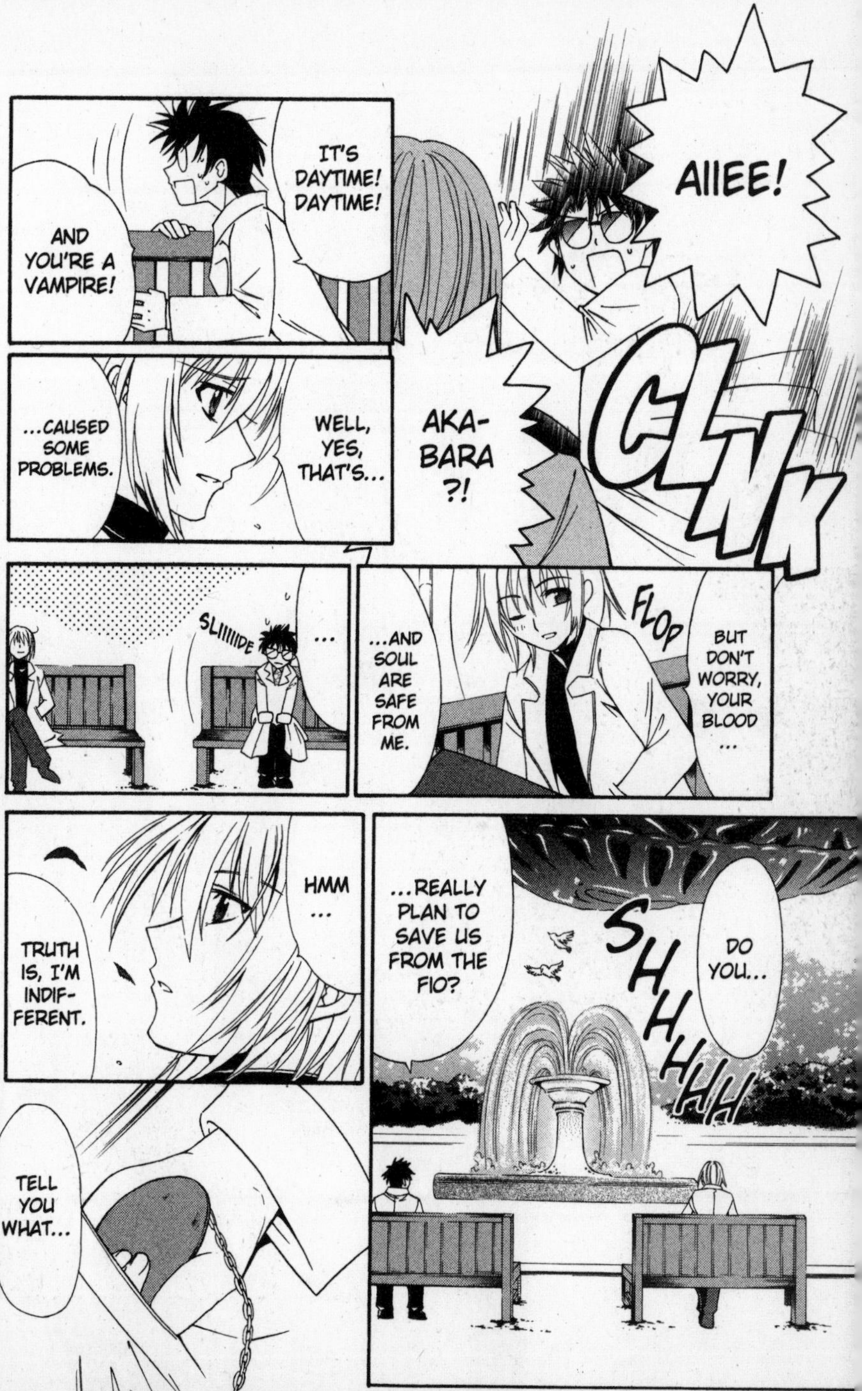
AIIEE!
AKA-BARA ?!
CLINK
IT'S DAYTIME! DAYTIME!
AND YOU'RE A VAMPIRE!
WELL, YES, THAT'S...
...CAUSED SOME PROBLEMS.
FLOP
BUT DON'T WORRY, YOUR BLOOD...
...AND SOUL ARE SAFE FROM ME.
...
SLIIIIIDE
DO YOU...
SHHHHHH
...REALLY PLAN TO SAVE US FROM THE FIO?
HMM...
TRUTH IS, I'M INDIF-FERENT.
TELL YOU WHAT...

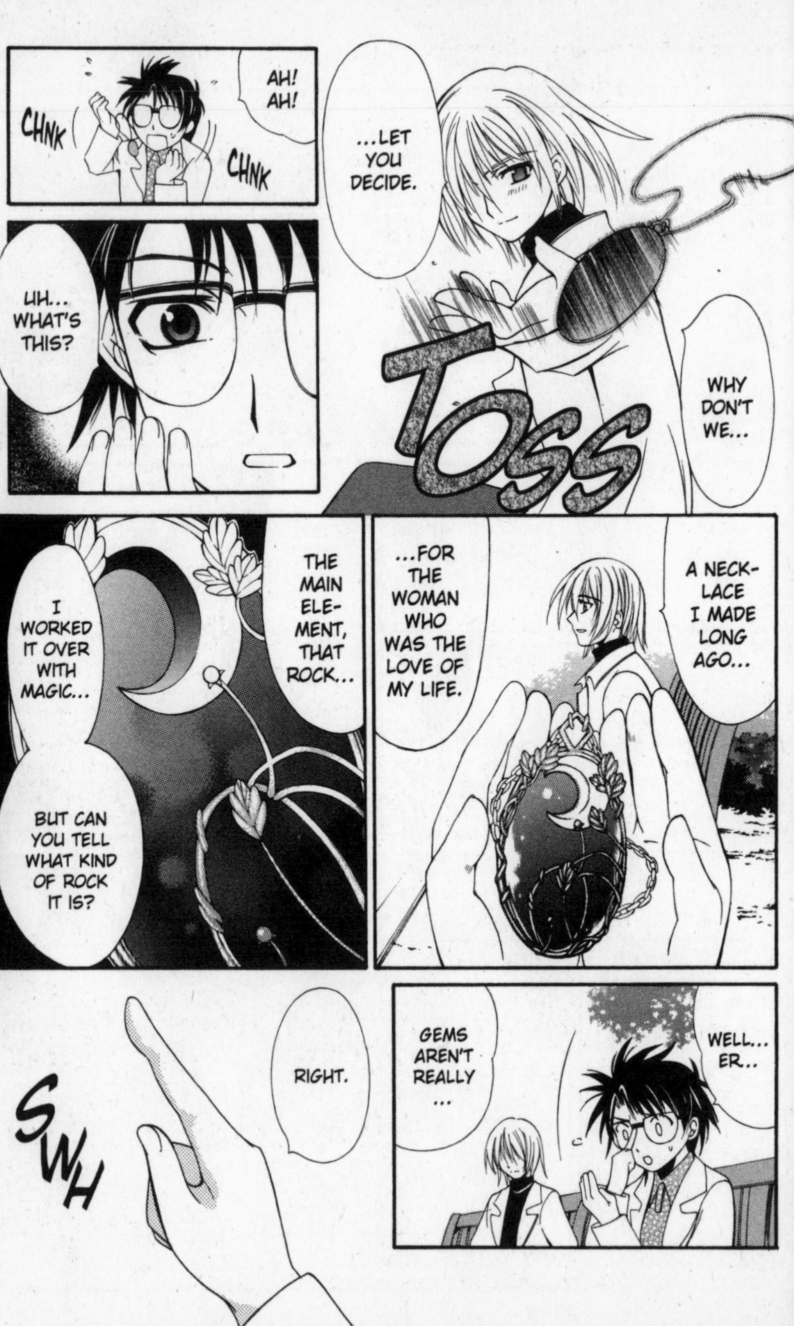
WHY DON'T WE...
...LET YOU DECIDE.
TOSS
AH! AH!
CHNK
CHNK
UH... WHAT'S THIS?
A NECK-LACE I MADE LONG AGO...
...FOR THE WOMAN WHO WAS THE LOVE OF MY LIFE.
THE MAIN ELE-MENT, THAT ROCK...
I WORKED IT OVER WITH MAGIC...
BUT CAN YOU TELL WHAT KIND OF ROCK IT IS?
WELL... ER...
GEMS AREN'T REALLY ...
RIGHT.
SWH

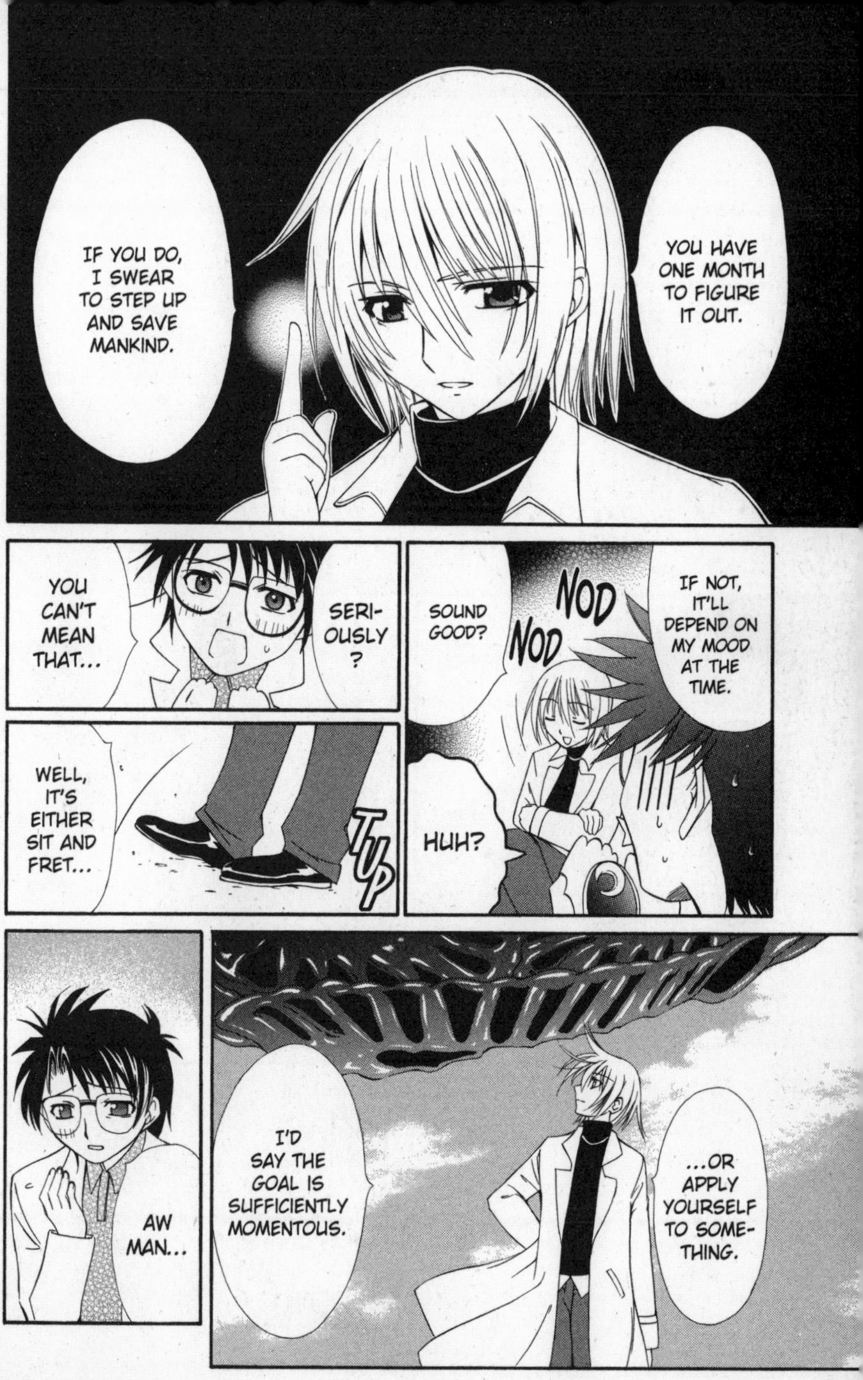
YOU HAVE ONE MONTH TO FIGURE IT OUT.
IF YOU DO, I SWEAR TO STEP UP AND SAVE MANKIND.
IF NOT, IT'LL DEPEND ON MY MOOD AT THE TIME.
NOD
NOD
SOUND GOOD?
HUH?
SERI-OUSLY?
YOU CAN'T MEAN THAT...
TUP
WELL, IT'S EITHER SIT AND FRET...
...OR APPLY YOURSELF TO SOME-THING.
I'D SAY THE GOAL IS SUFFICIENTLY MOMENTOUS.
AW MAN...

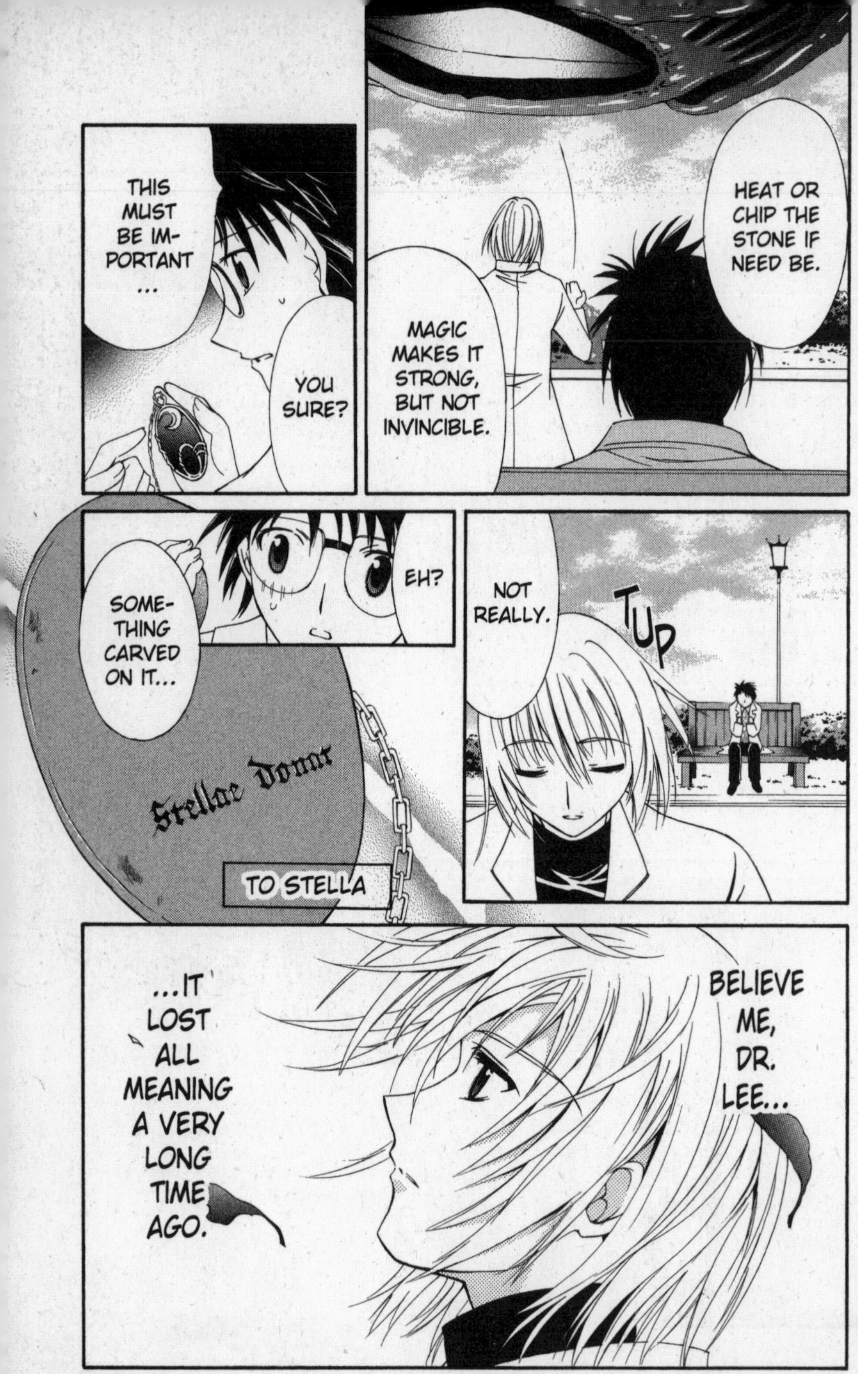
HEAT OR CHIP THE STONE IF NEED BE.
MAGIC MAKES IT STRONG, BUT NOT INVINCIBLE.
THIS MUST BE IM-PORTANT ...
YOU SURE?
NOT REALLY.
TUP
EH?
SOME-THING CARVED ON IT...
Stellae Donum
TO STELLA
BELIEVE ME, DR. LEE...
...IT LOST ALL MEANING A VERY LONG TIME AGO.

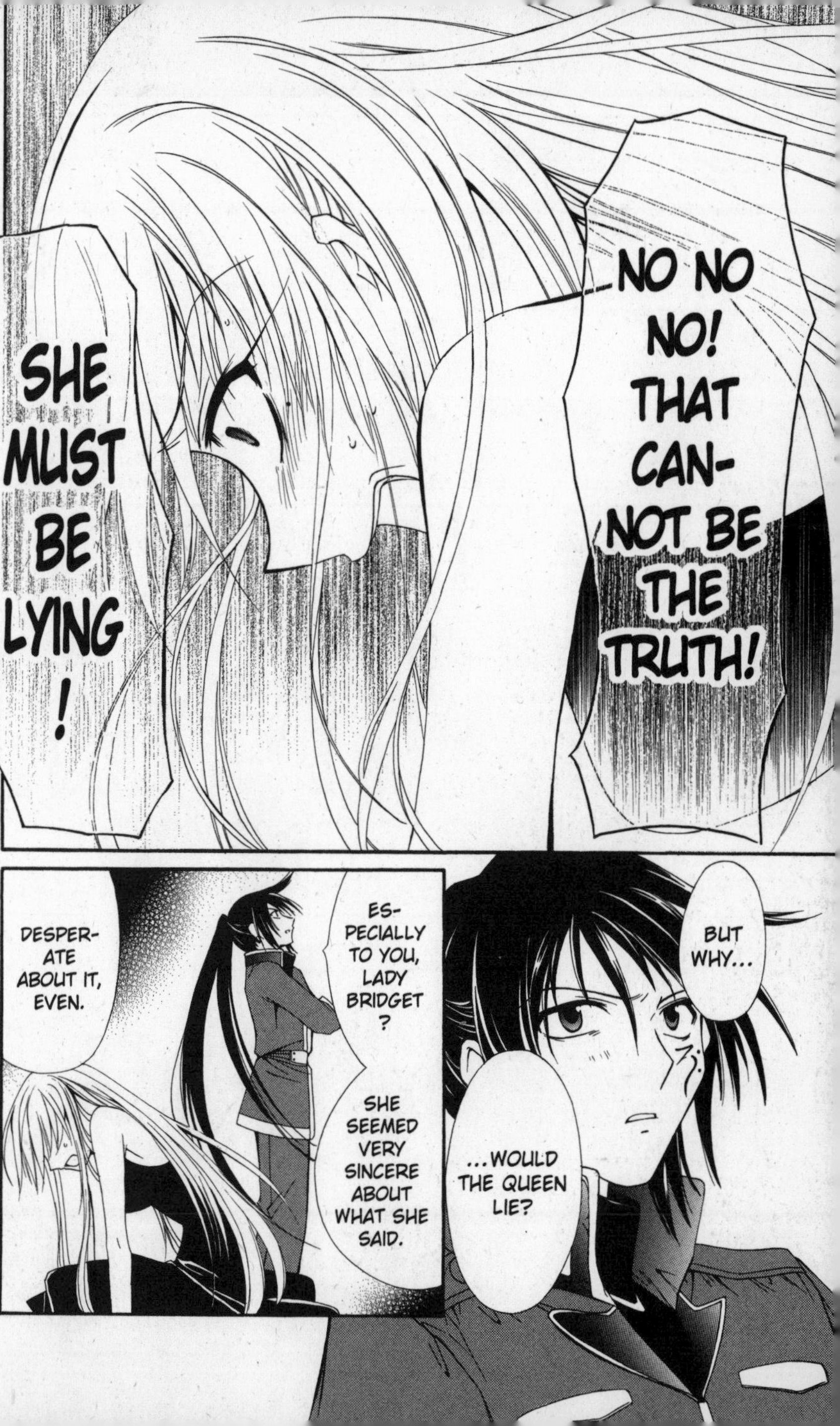
NO NO NO! THAT CANNOT BE THE TRUTH!
SHE MUST BE LYING!
BUT WHY...
...WOULD THE QUEEN LIE?
ESPECIALLY TO YOU, LADY BRIDGET?
SHE SEEMED VERY SINCERE ABOUT WHAT SHE SAID.
DESPERATE ABOUT IT, EVEN.

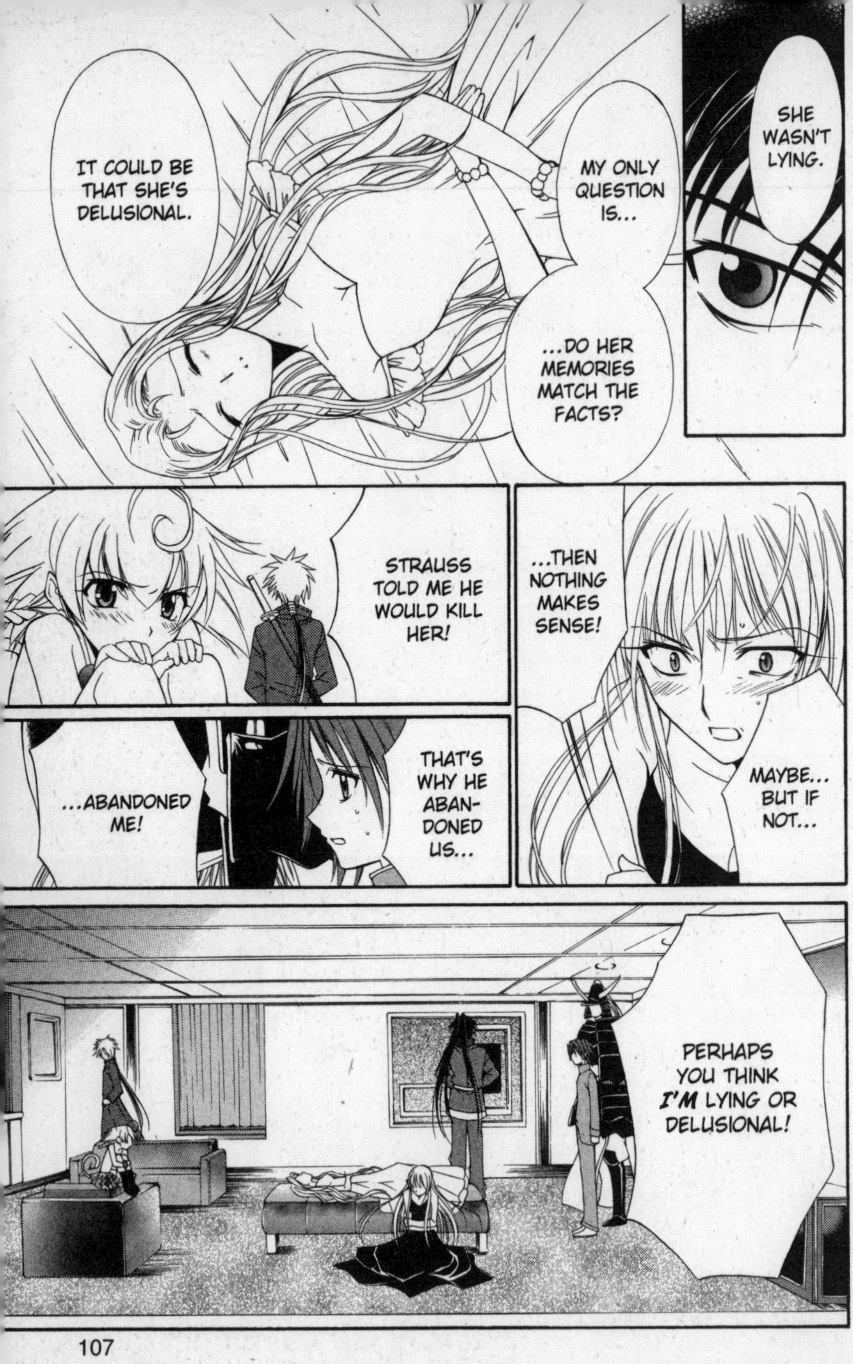
SHE WASN'T LYING.
MY ONLY QUESTION IS...
...DO HER MEMORIES MATCH THE FACTS?
IT COULD BE THAT SHE'S DELUSIONAL.
MAYBE... BUT IF NOT...
...THEN NOTHING MAKES SENSE!
STRAUSS TOLD ME HE WOULD KILL HER!
THAT'S WHY HE ABAN-DONED US...
...ABANDONED ME!
PERHAPS YOU THINK *I'M* LYING OR DELUSIONAL!

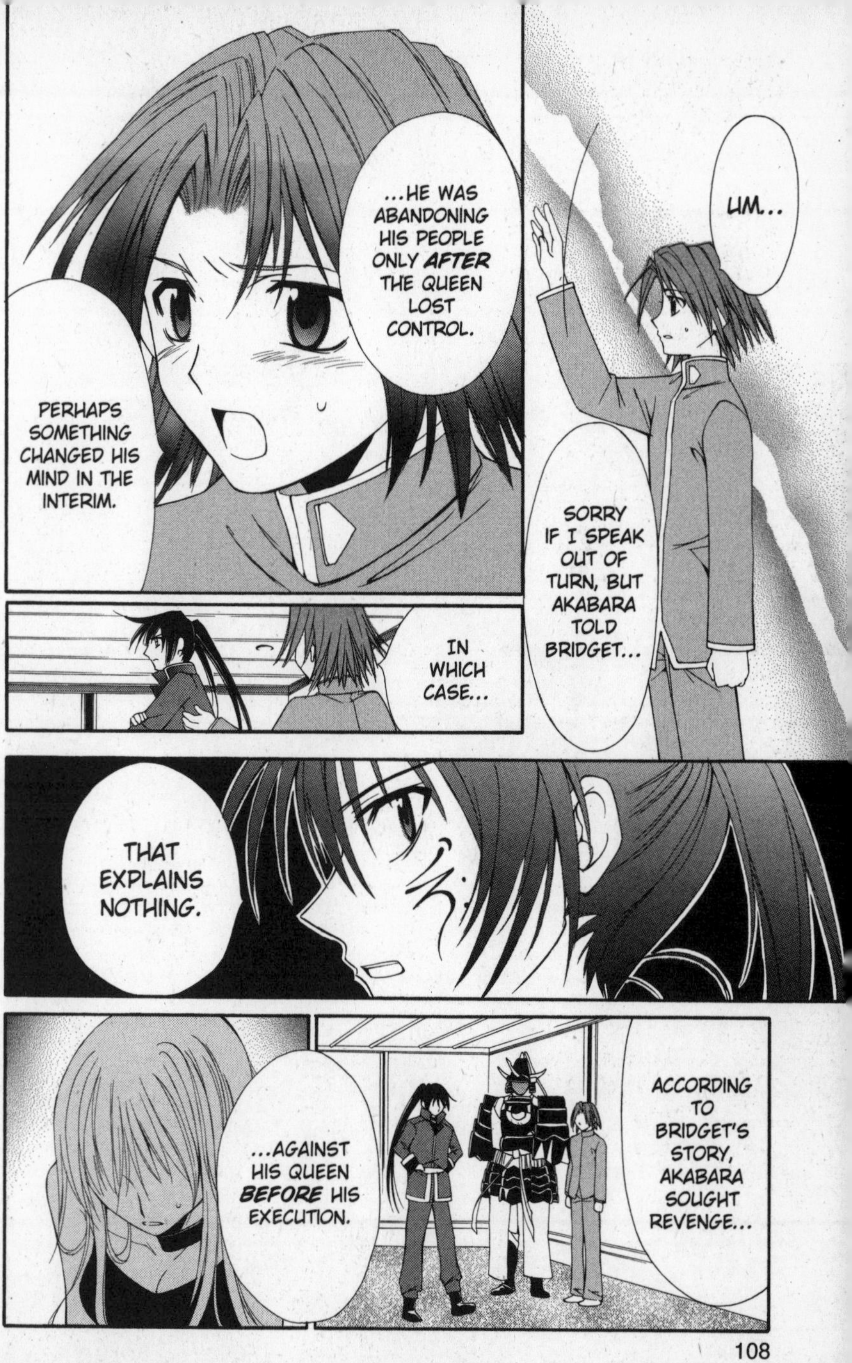
UM...
SORRY IF I SPEAK OUT OF TURN, BUT AKABARA TOLD BRIDGET...
...HE WAS ABANDONING HIS PEOPLE ONLY ***AFTER*** THE QUEEN LOST CONTROL.
PERHAPS SOMETHING CHANGED HIS MIND IN THE INTERIM.
IN WHICH CASE...
THAT EXPLAINS NOTHING.
ACCORDING TO BRIDGET'S STORY, AKABARA SOUGHT REVENGE...
...AGAINST HIS QUEEN ***BEFORE*** HIS EXECUTION.

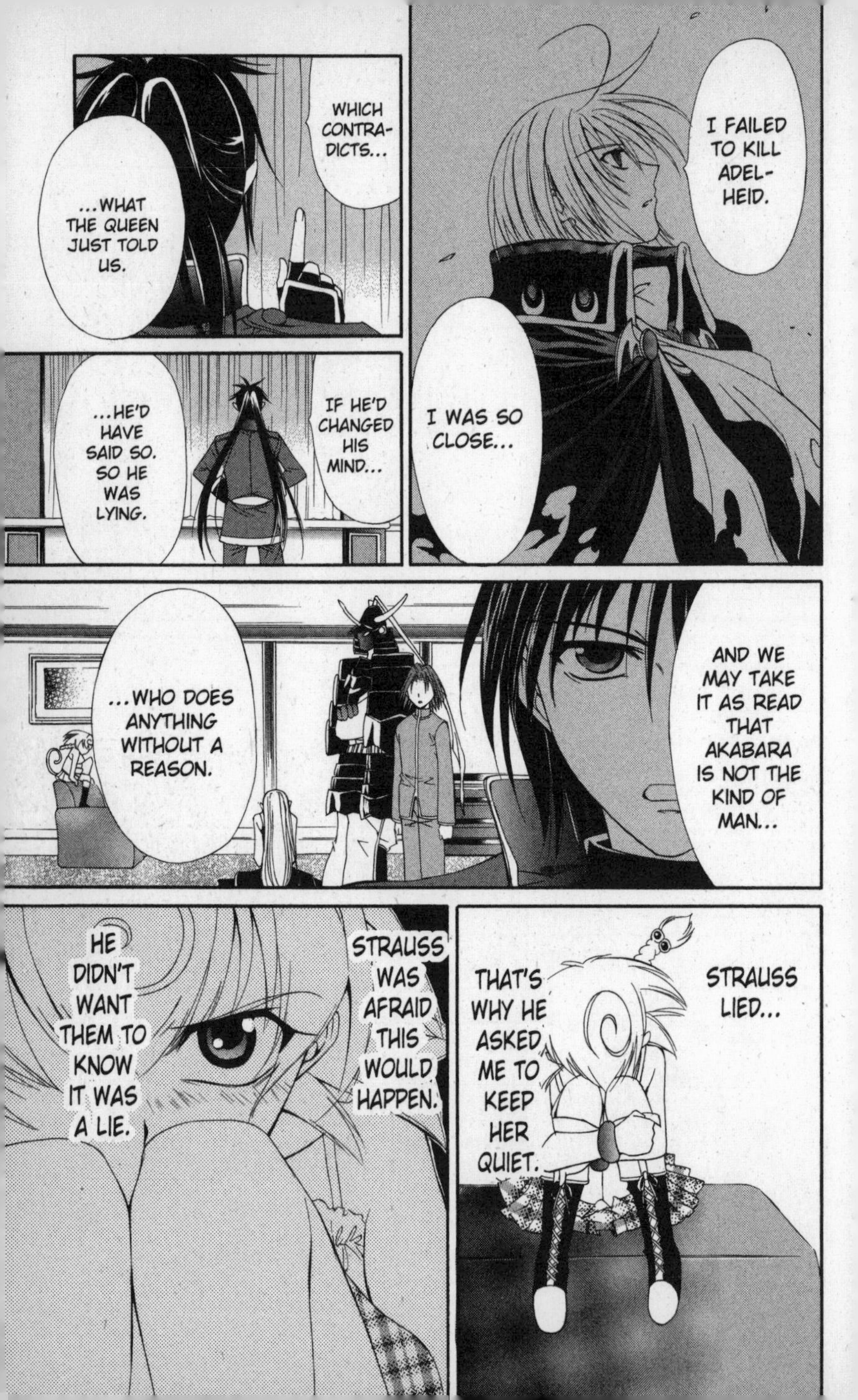
I FAILED TO KILL ADEL-HEID.
I WAS SO CLOSE...
WHICH CONTRA-DICTS...
...WHAT THE QUEEN JUST TOLD US.
IF HE'D CHANGED HIS MIND...
...HE'D HAVE SAID SO. SO HE WAS LYING.
AND WE MAY TAKE IT AS READ THAT AKABARA IS NOT THE KIND OF MAN...
...WHO DOES ANYTHING WITHOUT A REASON.
STRAUSS LIED...
THAT'S WHY HE ASKED ME TO KEEP HER QUIET.
STRAUSS WAS AFRAID THIS WOULD HAPPEN.
HE DIDN'T WANT THEM TO KNOW IT WAS A LIE.

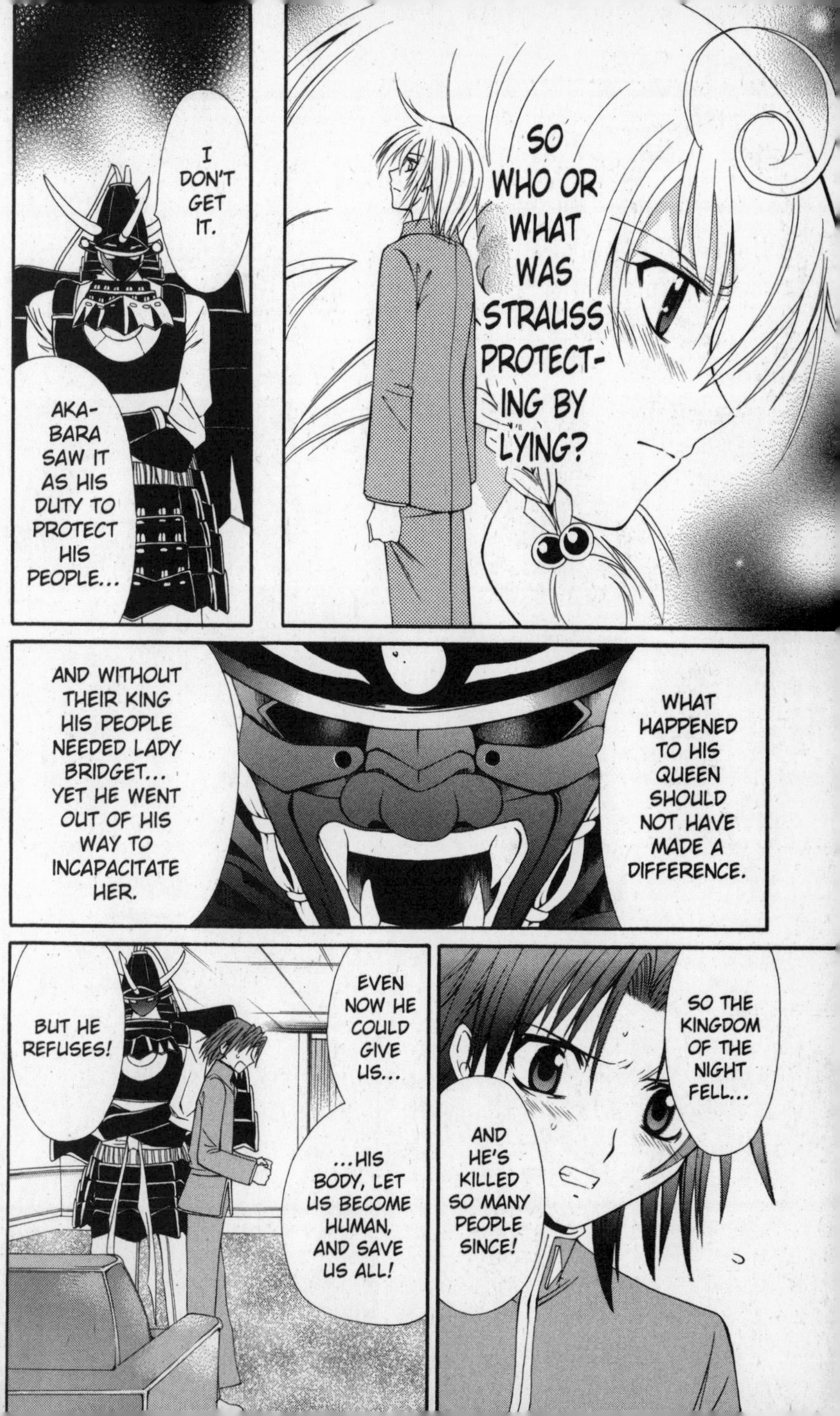
SO WHO OR WHAT WAS STRAUSS PROTECTING BY LYING?
I DON'T GET IT.
AKABARA SAW IT AS HIS DUTY TO PROTECT HIS PEOPLE...
WHAT HAPPENED TO HIS QUEEN SHOULD NOT HAVE MADE A DIFFERENCE.
AND WITHOUT THEIR KING HIS PEOPLE NEEDED LADY BRIDGET... YET HE WENT OUT OF HIS WAY TO INCAPACITATE HER.
SO THE KINGDOM OF THE NIGHT FELL...
AND HE'S KILLED SO MANY PEOPLE SINCE!
EVEN NOW HE COULD GIVE US...
...HIS BODY, LET US BECOME HUMAN, AND SAVE US ALL!
BUT HE REFUSES!

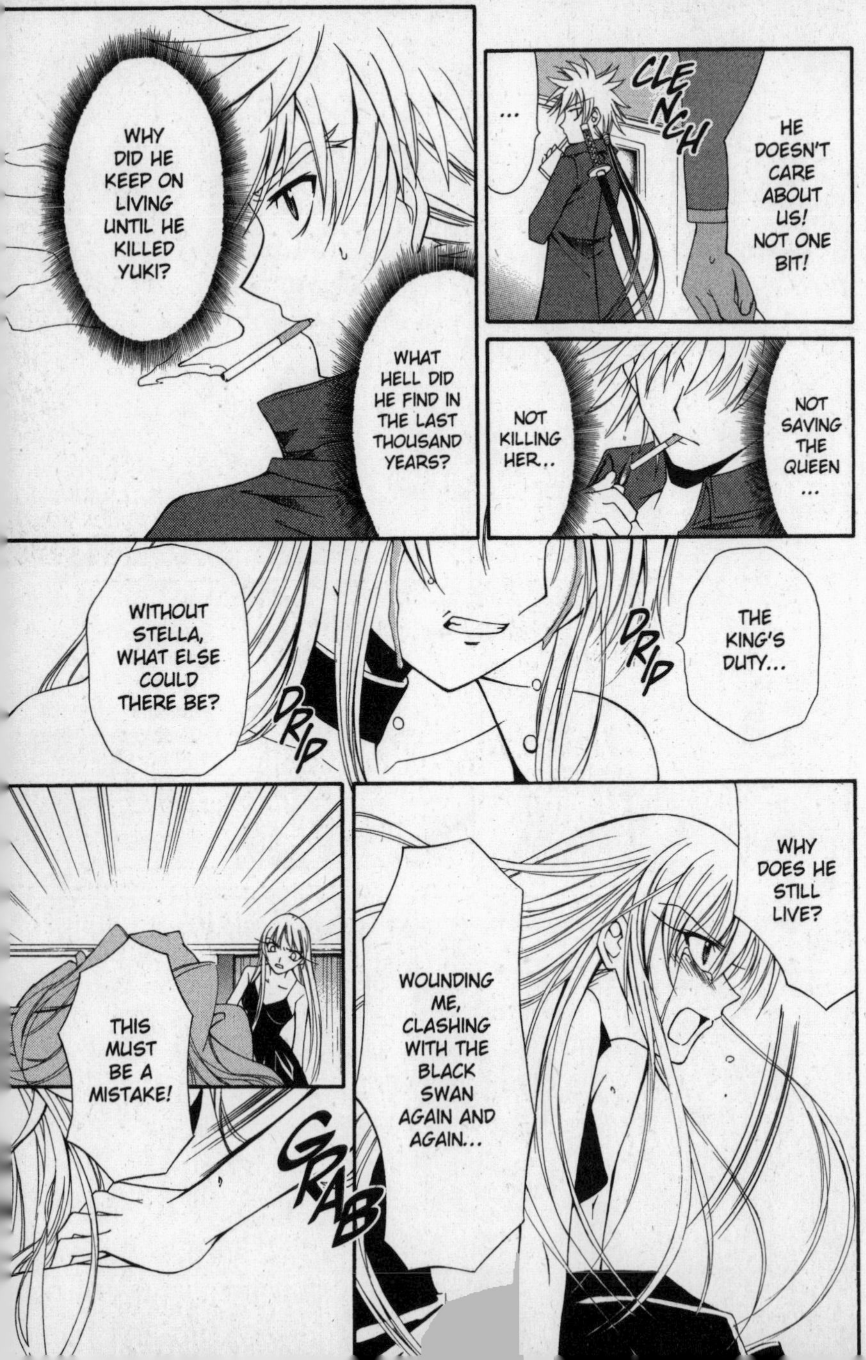
...
CLENCH
HE DOESN'T CARE ABOUT US! NOT ONE BIT!
NOT SAVING THE QUEEN...
NOT KILLING HER...
WHY DID HE KEEP ON LIVING UNTIL HE KILLED YUKI?
WHAT HELL DID HE FIND IN THE LAST THOUSAND YEARS?
THE KING'S DUTY...
DRIP
WITHOUT STELLA, WHAT ELSE COULD THERE BE?
DRIP
WHY DOES HE STILL LIVE?
WOUNDING ME, CLASHING WITH THE BLACK SWAN AGAIN AND AGAIN...
GRAB
THIS MUST BE A MISTAKE!

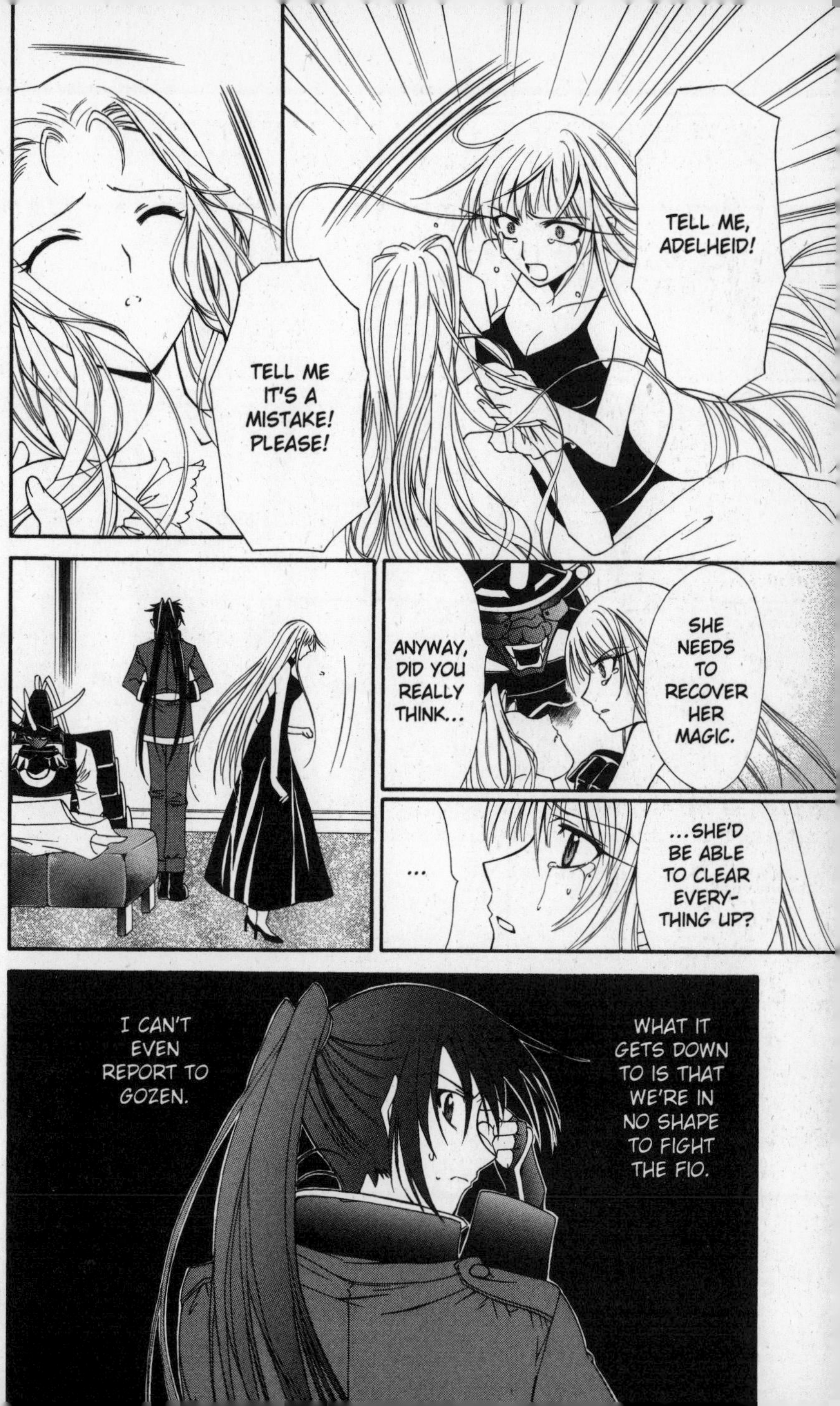
TELL ME, ADELHEID!
TELL ME IT'S A MISTAKE! PLEASE!
SHE NEEDS TO RECOVER HER MAGIC.
ANYWAY, DID YOU REALLY THINK...
...SHE'D BE ABLE TO CLEAR EVERY-THING UP?
...
WHAT IT GETS DOWN TO IS THAT WE'RE IN NO SHAPE TO FIGHT THE FIO.
I CAN'T EVEN REPORT TO GOZEN.

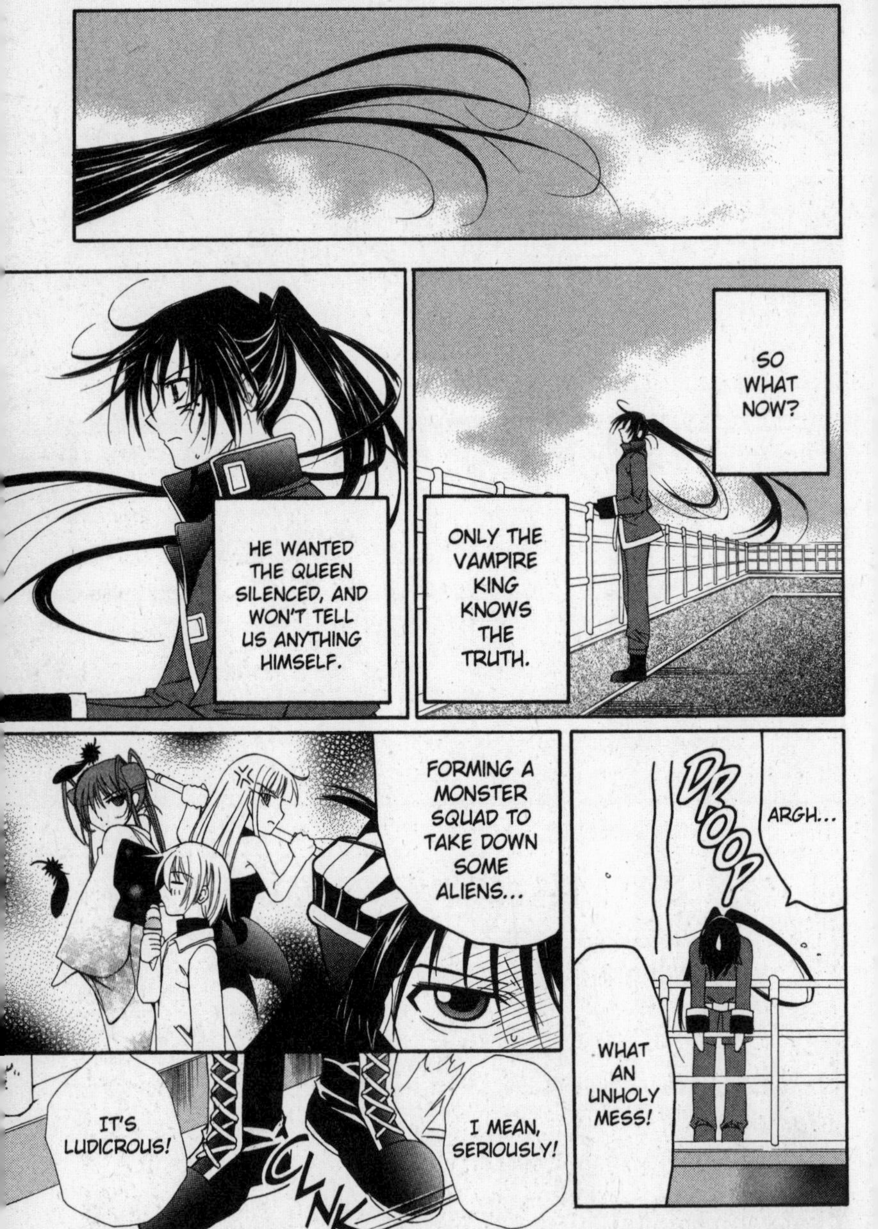
SO WHAT NOW?
ONLY THE VAMPIRE KING KNOWS THE TRUTH.
HE WANTED THE QUEEN SILENCED, AND WON'T TELL US ANYTHING HIMSELF.
DROOP
ARGH...
WHAT AN UNHOLY MESS!
FORMING A MONSTER SQUAD TO TAKE DOWN SOME ALIENS...
I MEAN, SERIOUSLY!
IT'S LUDICROUS!
CLNK

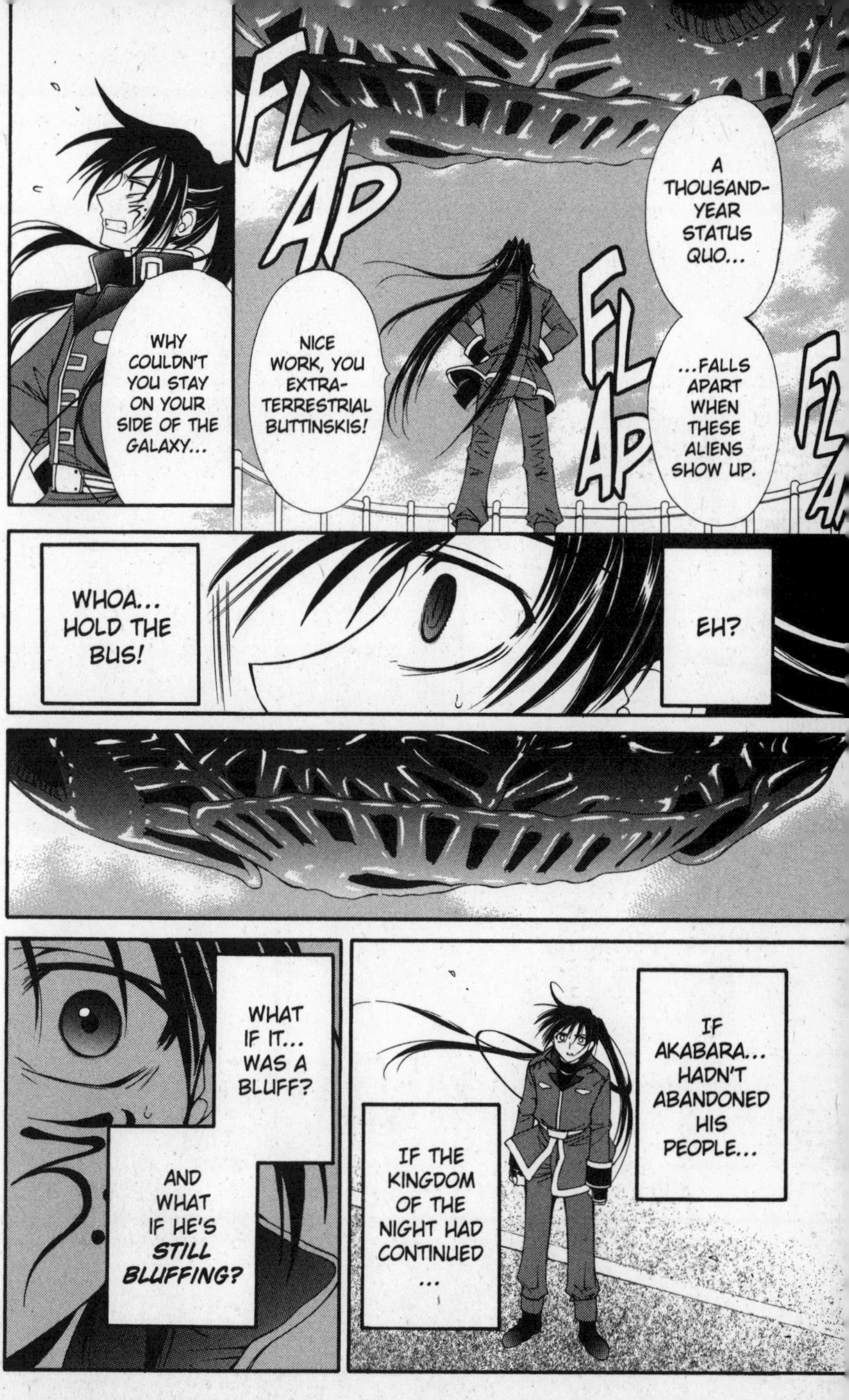
A THOUSAND-YEAR STATUS QUO...
...FALLS APART WHEN THESE ALIENS SHOW UP.
FLAP
FLAP
NICE WORK, YOU EXTRA-TERRESTRIAL BUTTINSKIS!
FLAP
WHY COULDN'T YOU STAY ON YOUR SIDE OF THE GALAXY...
EH?
WHOA... HOLD THE BUS!
IF AKABARA... HADN'T ABANDONED HIS PEOPLE...
IF THE KINGDOM OF THE NIGHT HAD CONTINUED ...
WHAT IF IT... WAS A BLUFF?
AND WHAT IF HE'S *STILL BLUFFING?*

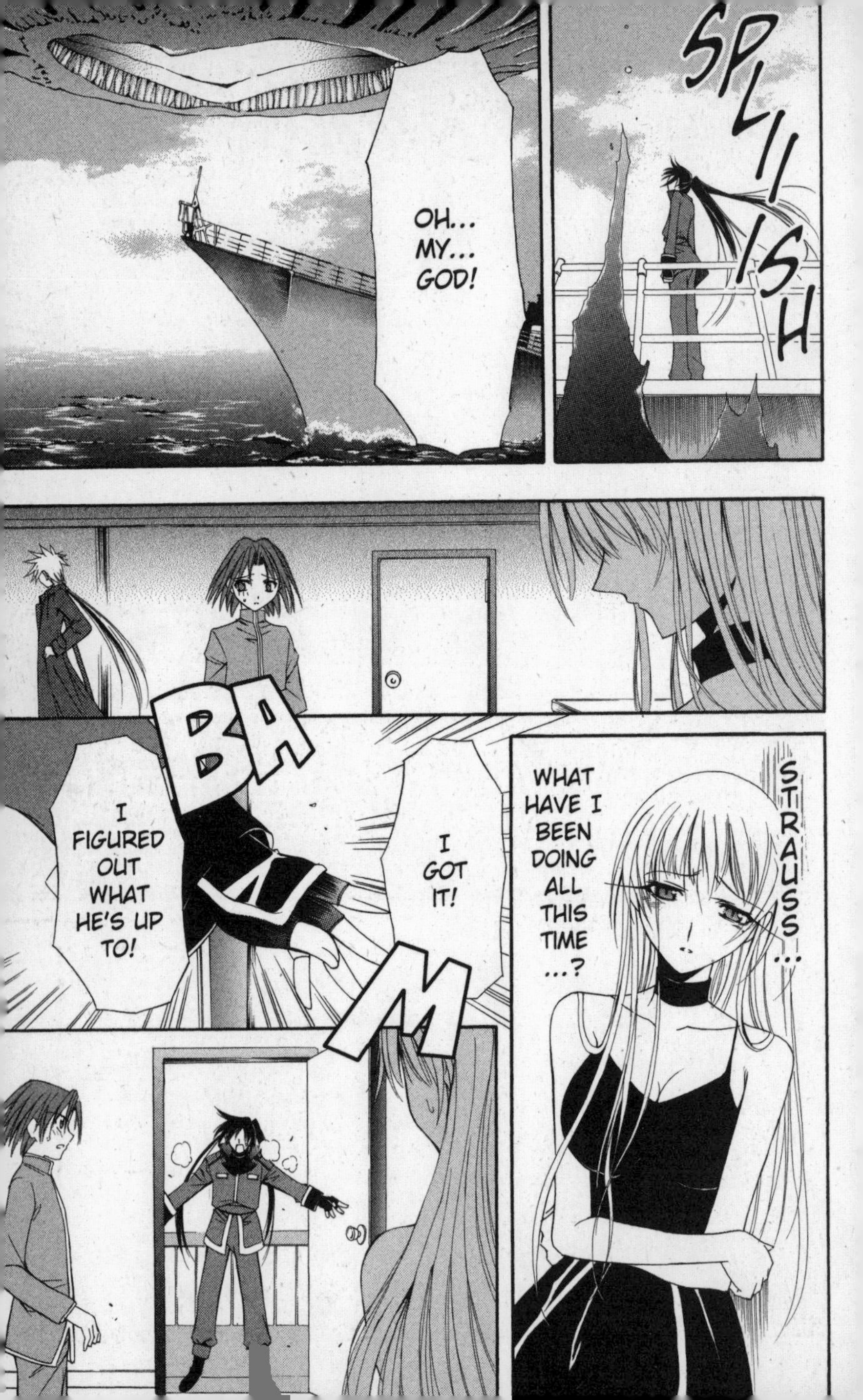
SPLIISH
OH... MY... GOD!
STRAUSS...
WHAT HAVE I BEEN DOING ALL THIS TIME ...?
BAM
I GOT IT!
I FIGURED OUT WHAT HE'S UP TO!

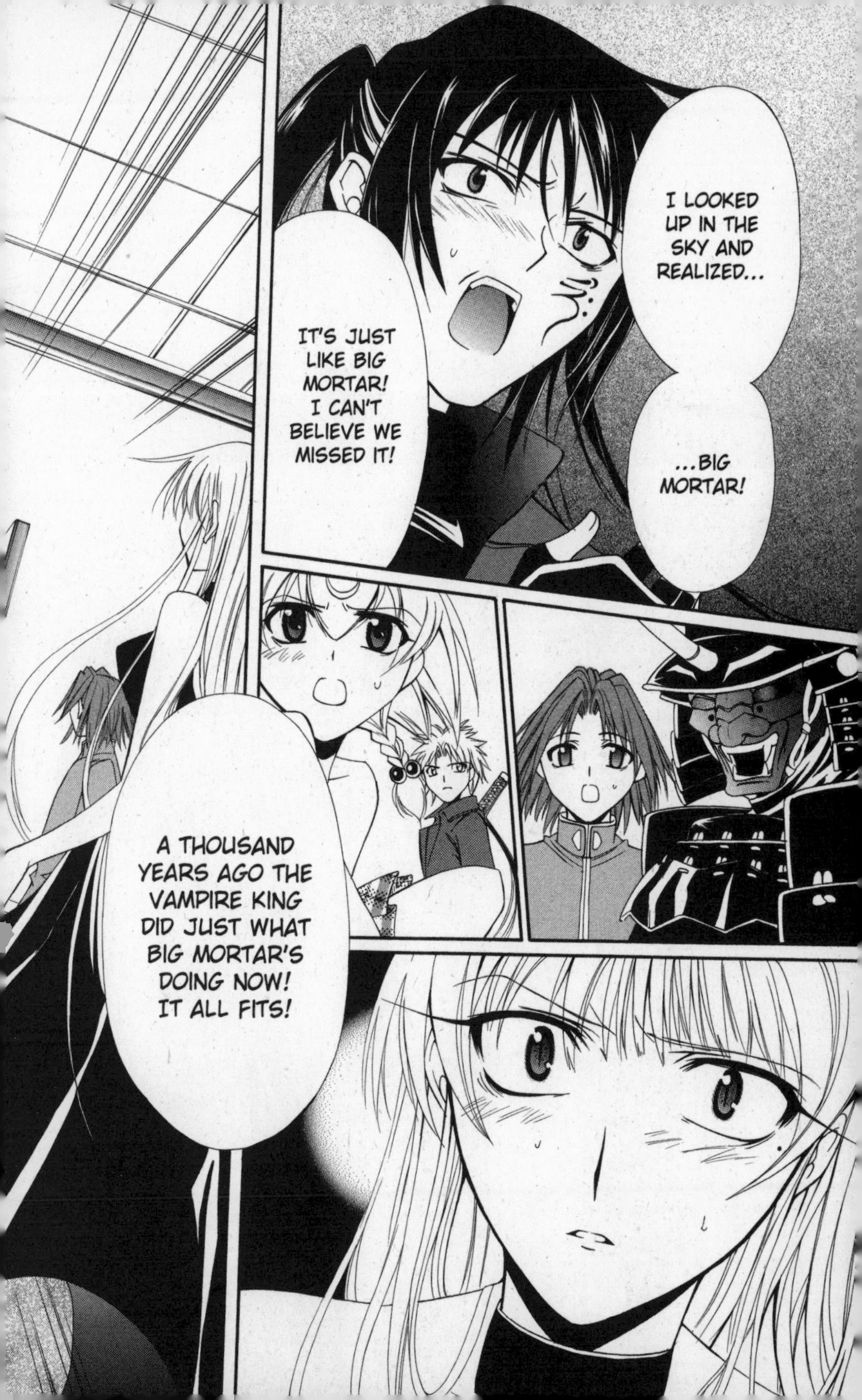
I LOOKED UP IN THE SKY AND REALIZED...
...BIG MORTAR!
IT'S JUST LIKE BIG MORTAR! I CAN'T BELIEVE WE MISSED IT!
A THOUSAND YEARS AGO THE VAMPIRE KING DID JUST WHAT BIG MORTAR'S DOING NOW! IT ALL FITS!

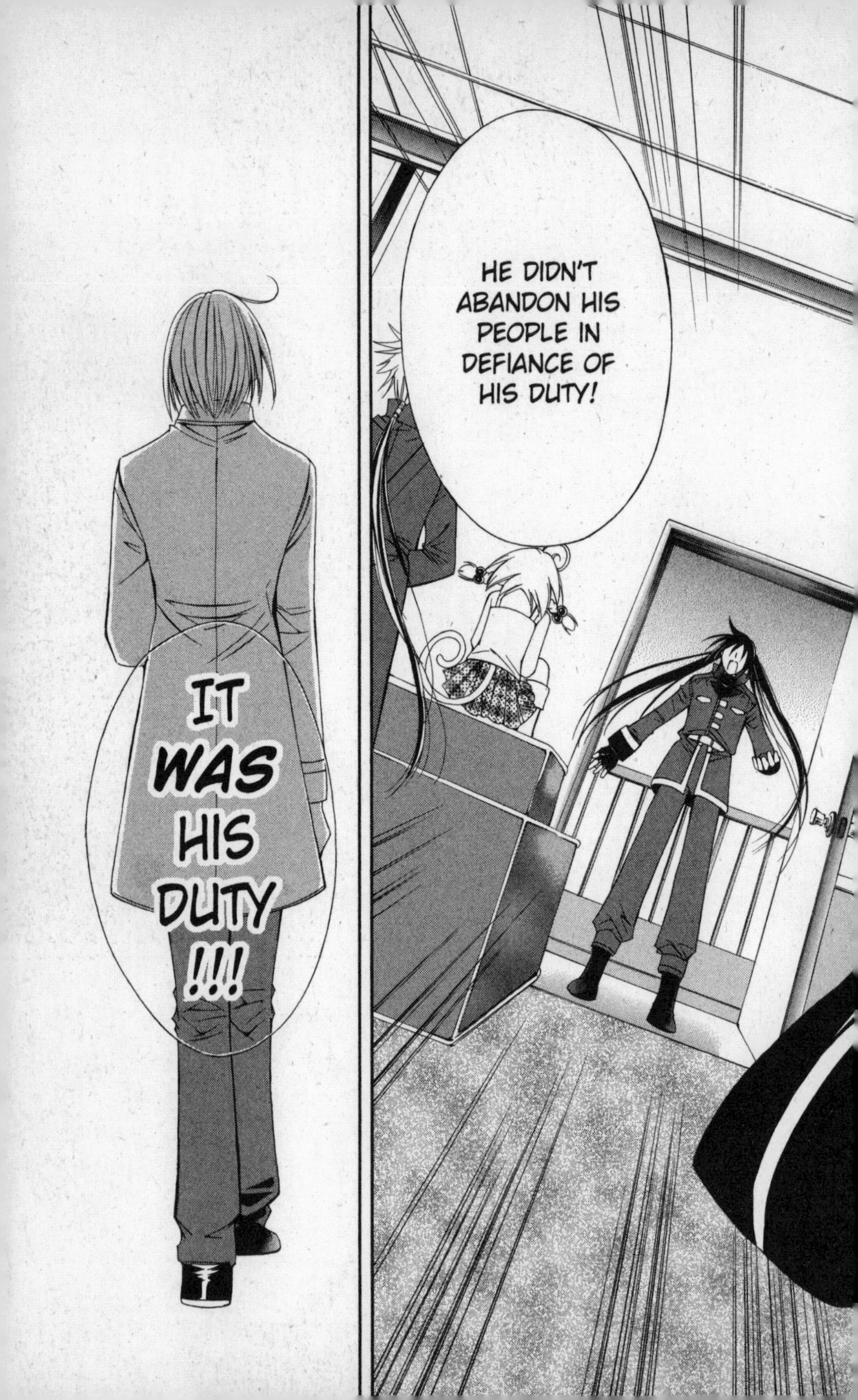
HE DIDN'T ABANDON HIS PEOPLE IN DEFIANCE OF HIS DUTY!
IT WAS HIS DUTY!!!

THE RECORD OF A

FALLEN VAMPIRE

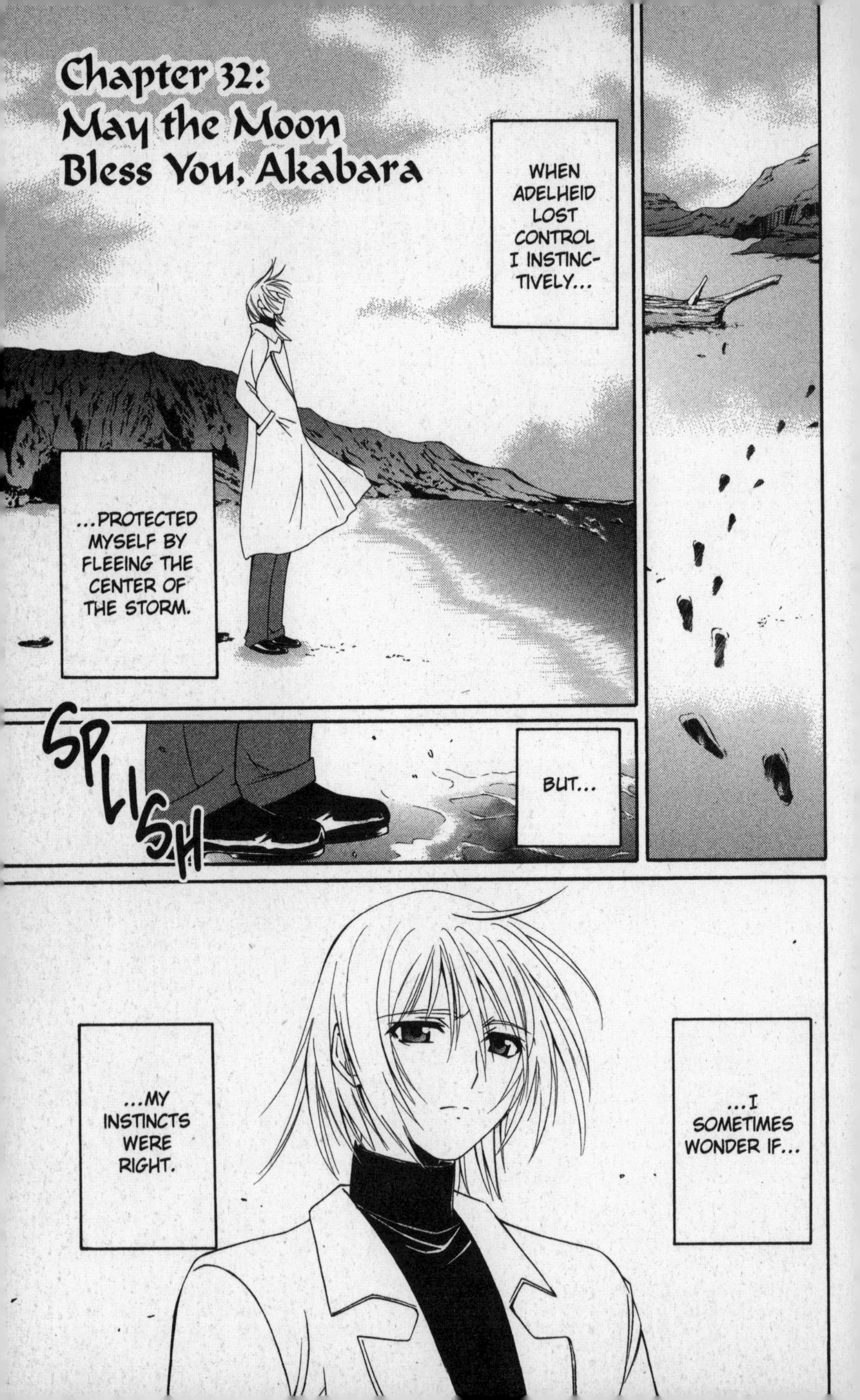
Chapter 32:
May the Moon Bless You, Akabara
WHEN ADELHEID LOST CONTROL I INSTINCTIVELY...
...PROTECTED MYSELF BY FLEEING THE CENTER OF THE STORM.
BUT...
SPLISH
...I SOMETIMES WONDER IF...
...MY INSTINCTS WERE RIGHT.

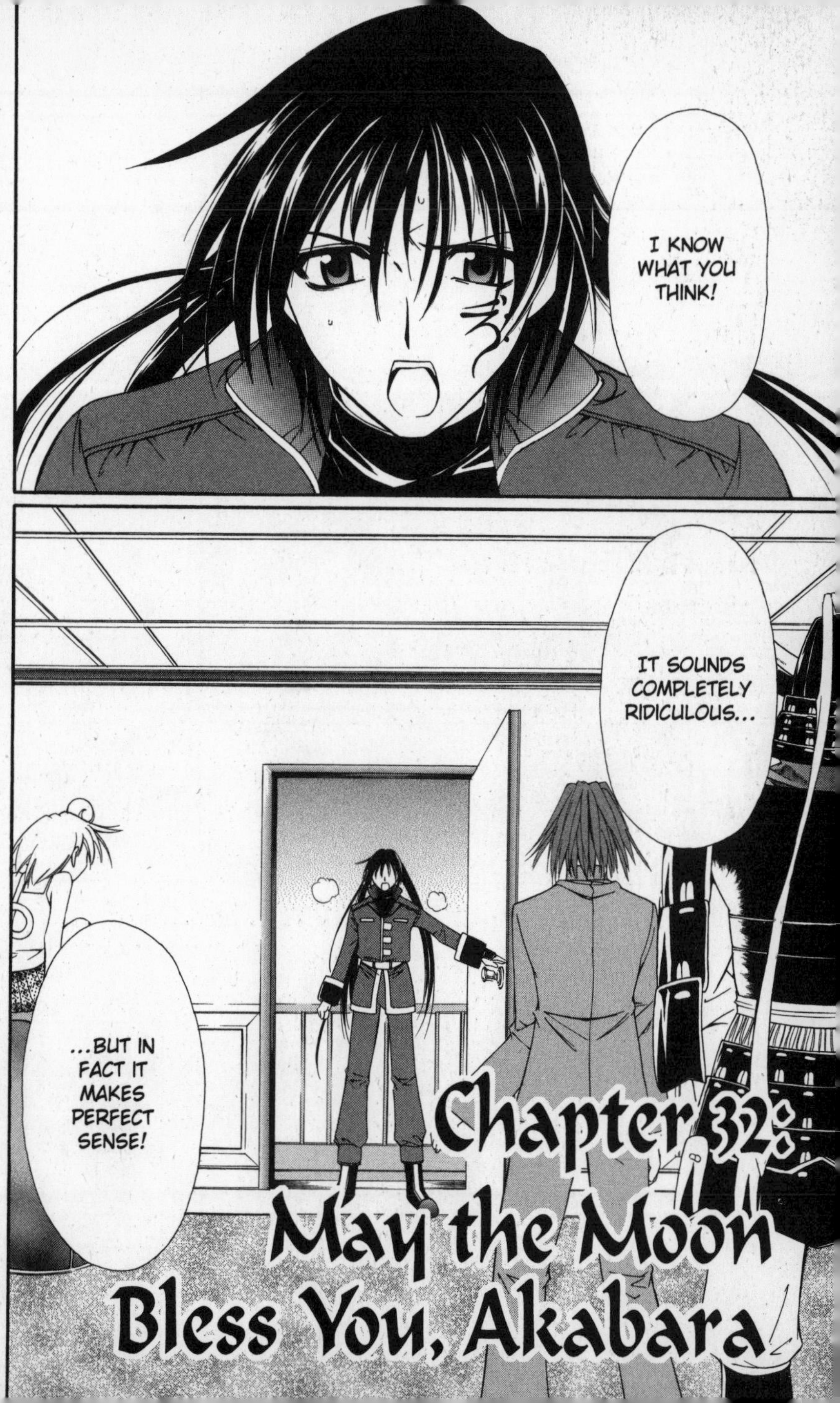
I KNOW WHAT YOU THINK!
IT SOUNDS COMPLETELY RIDICULOUS...
...BUT IN FACT IT MAKES PERFECT SENSE!
Chapter 32: May the Moon Bless You, Akabara

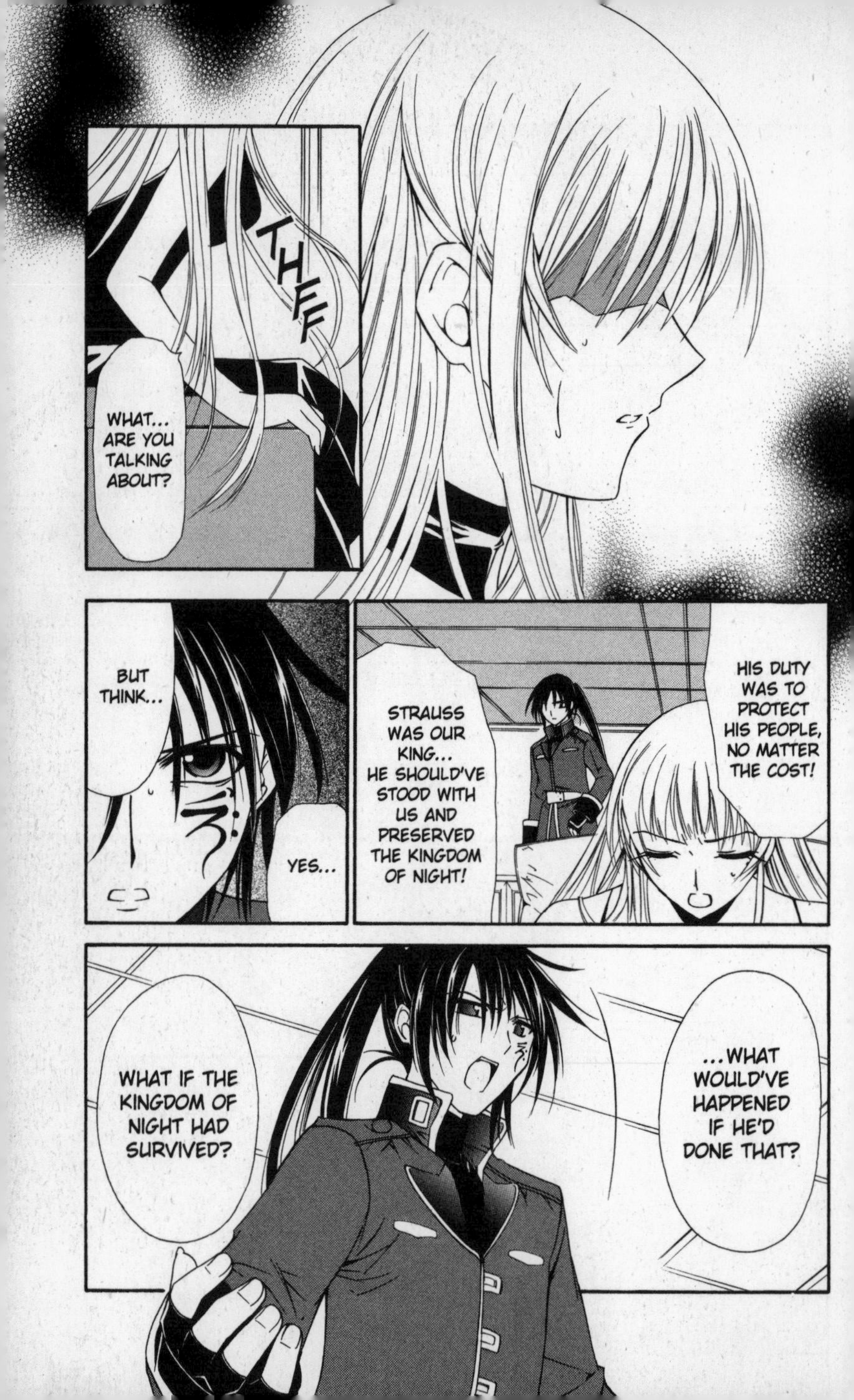
THFF
WHAT... ARE YOU TALKING ABOUT?
HIS DUTY WAS TO PROTECT HIS PEOPLE, NO MATTER THE COST!
STRAUSS WAS OUR KING... HE SHOULD'VE STOOD WITH US AND PRESERVED THE KINGDOM OF NIGHT!
YES...
BUT THINK...
...WHAT WOULD'VE HAPPENED IF HE'D DONE THAT?
WHAT IF THE KINGDOM OF NIGHT HAD SURVIVED?

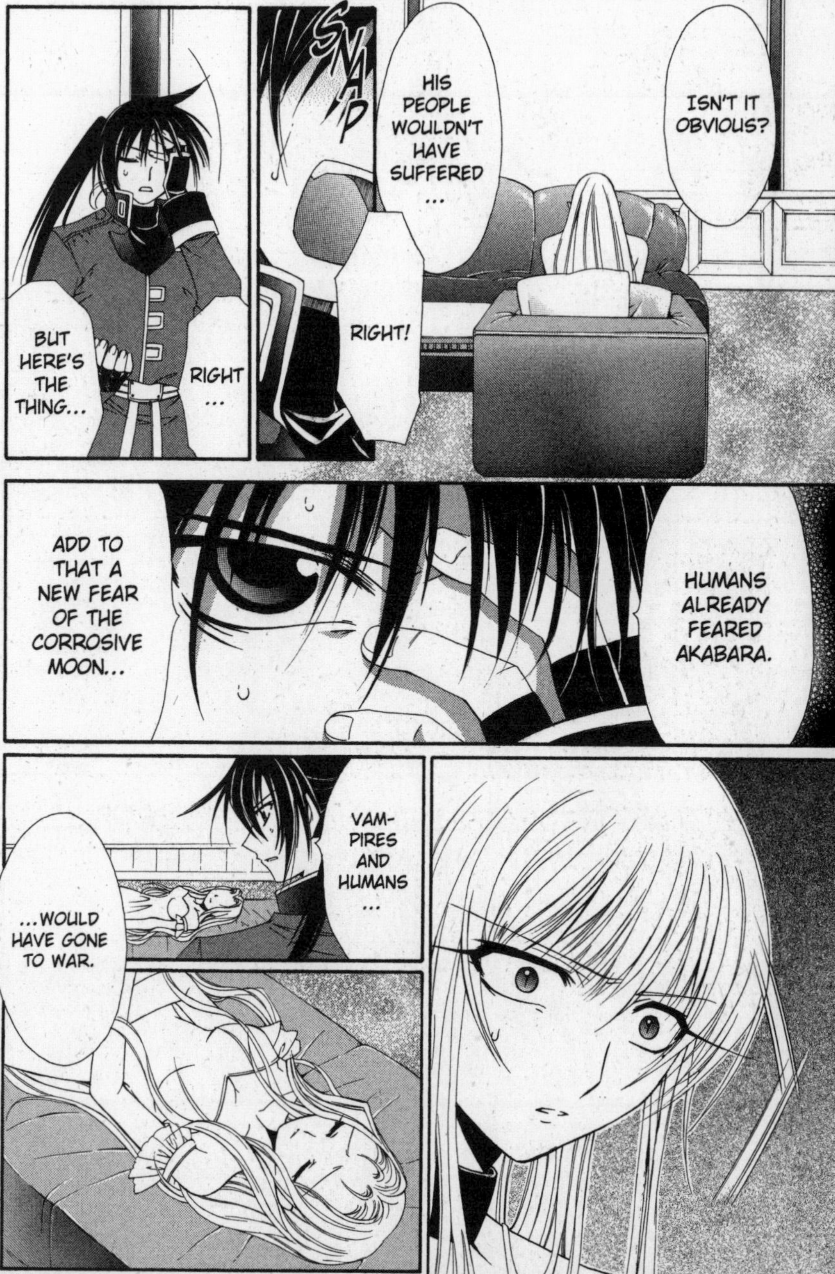
ISN'T IT OBVIOUS?
HIS PEOPLE WOULDN'T HAVE SUFFERED...
SNAP
RIGHT!
RIGHT...
BUT HERE'S THE THING...
HUMANS ALREADY FEARED AKABARA.
ADD TO THAT A NEW FEAR OF THE CORROSIVE MOON...
VAMPIRES AND HUMANS...
...WOULD HAVE GONE TO WAR.

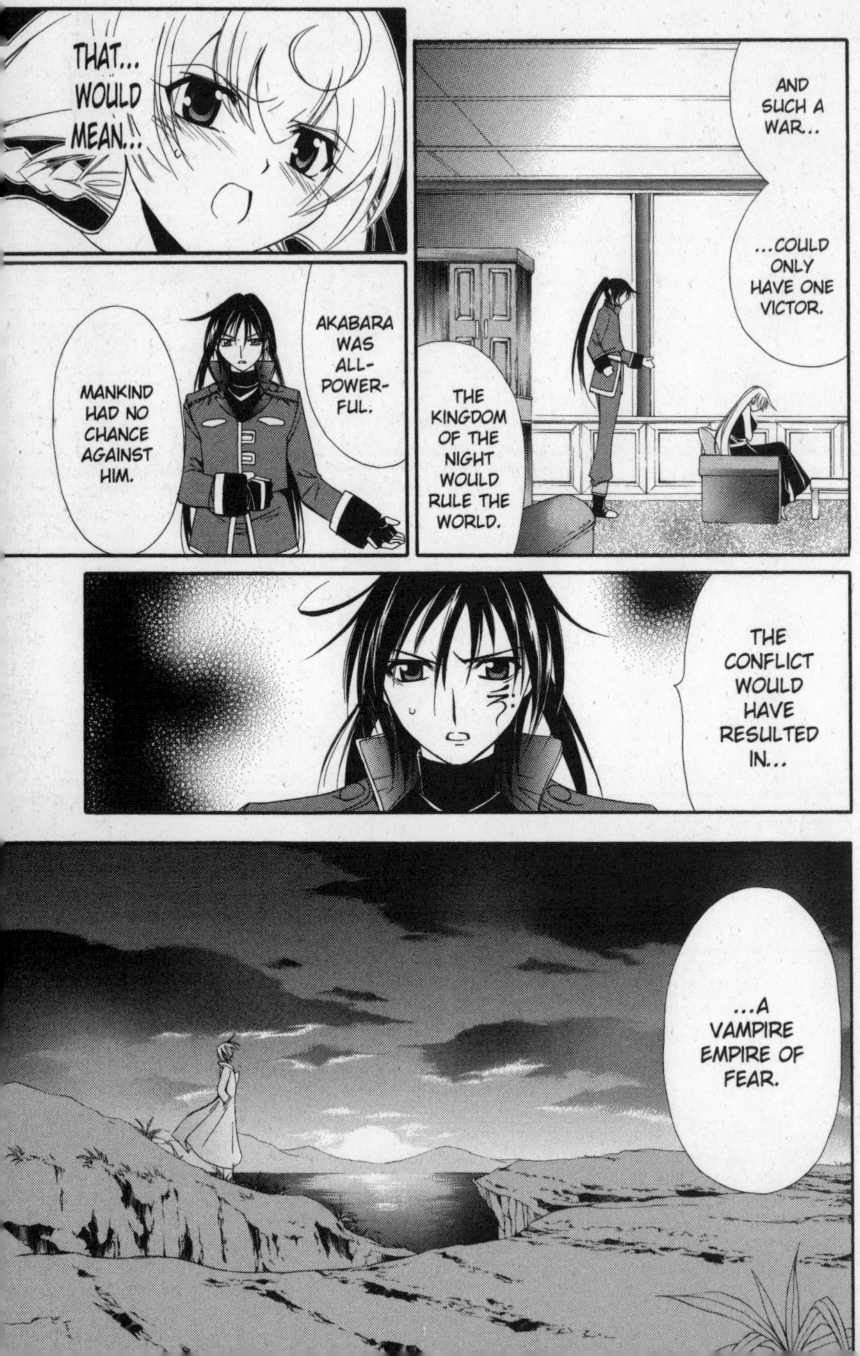
AND SUCH A WAR..
...COULD ONLY HAVE ONE VICTOR.
THE KINGDOM OF THE NIGHT WOULD RULE THE WORLD.
THAT... WOULD MEAN...
AKABARA WAS ALL-POWERFUL.
MANKIND HAD NO CHANCE AGAINST HIM.
THE CONFLICT WOULD HAVE RESULTED IN...
...A VAMPIRE EMPIRE OF FEAR.

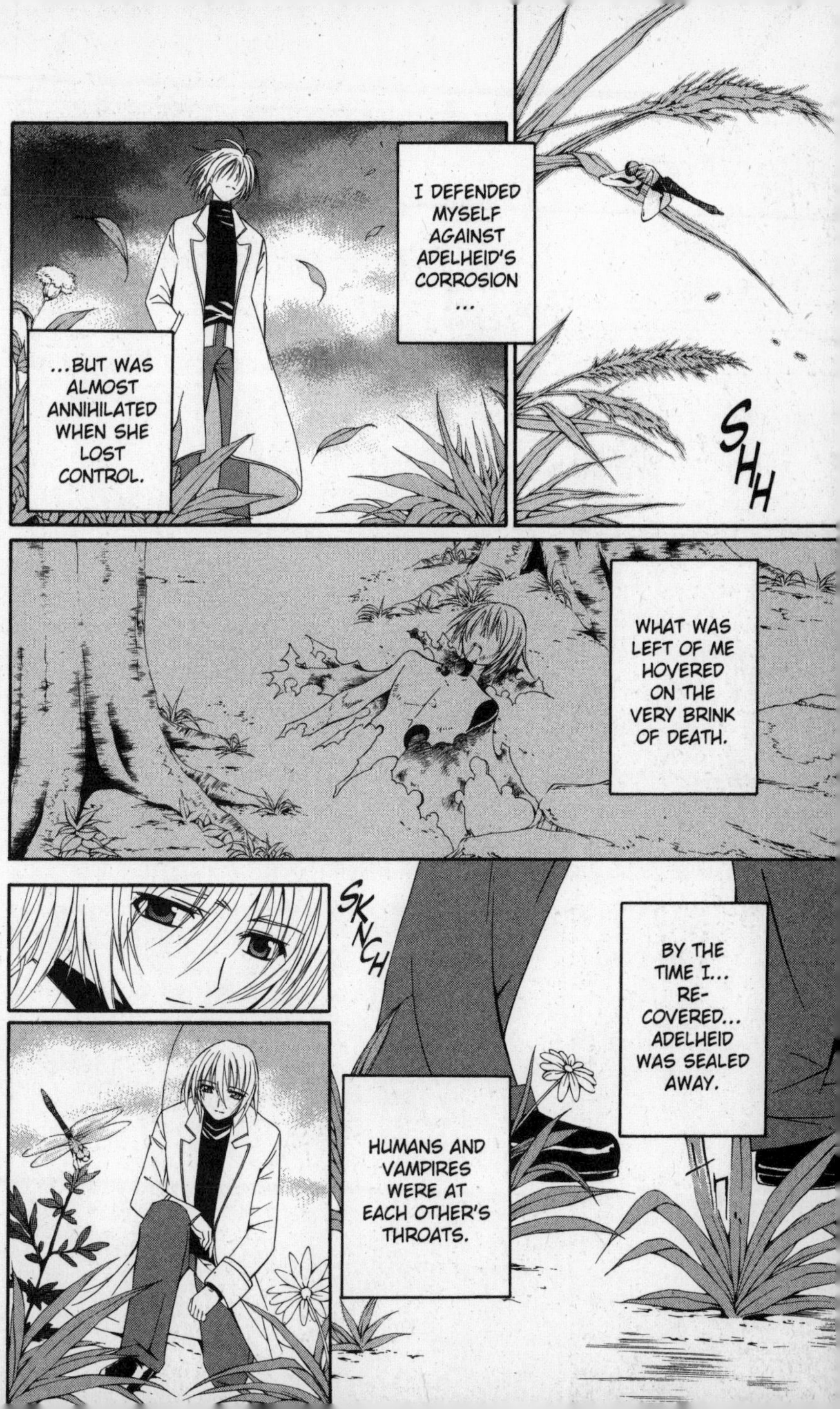
SHH
I DEFENDED MYSELF AGAINST ADELHEID'S CORROSION...
...BUT WAS ALMOST ANNIHILATED WHEN SHE LOST CONTROL.
WHAT WAS LEFT OF ME HOVERED ON THE VERY BRINK OF DEATH.
SKNCH
BY THE TIME I... RE-COVERED... ADELHEID WAS SEALED AWAY.
HUMANS AND VAMPIRES WERE AT EACH OTHER'S THROATS.

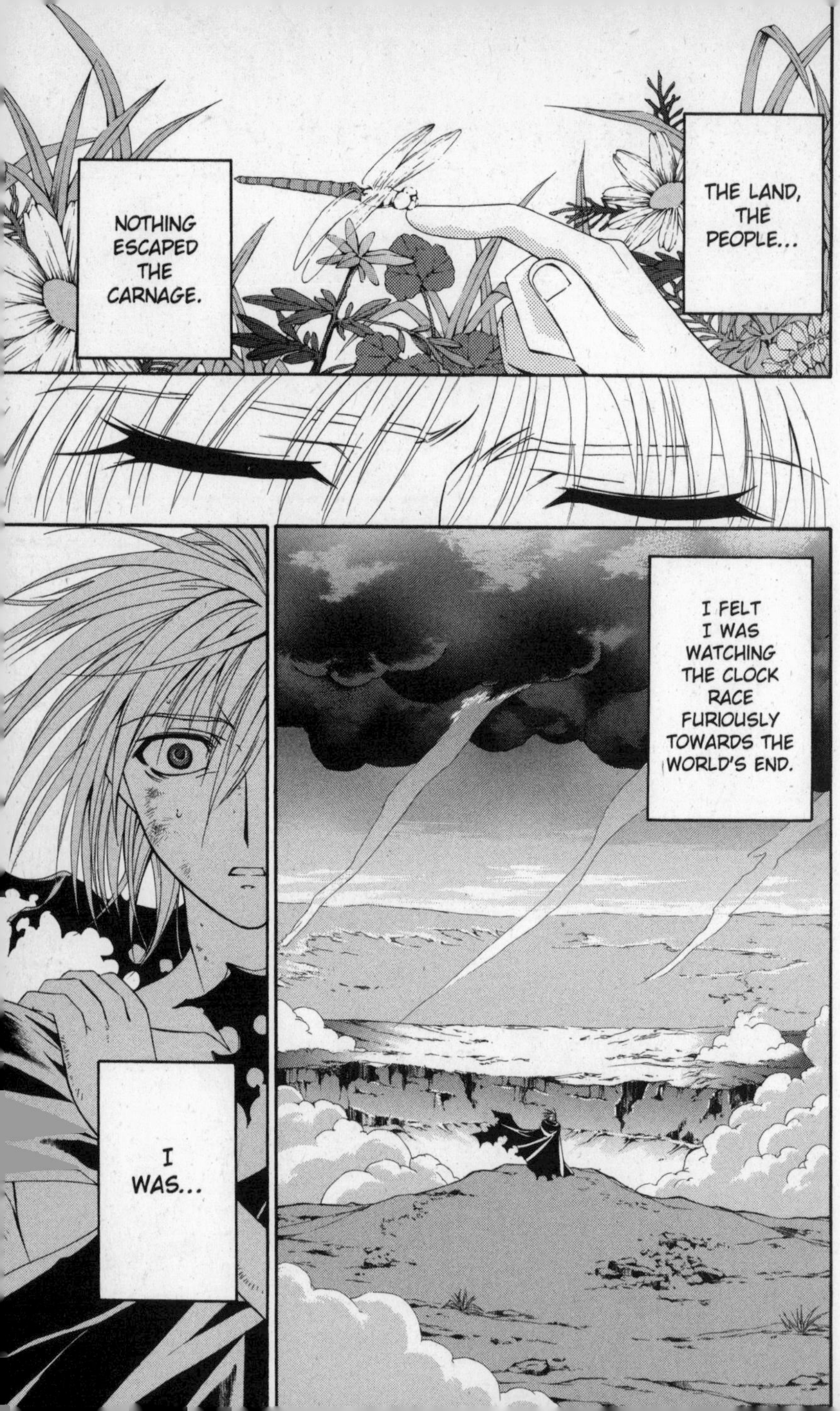
THE LAND, THE PEOPLE...
NOTHING ESCAPED THE CARNAGE.
I FELT I WAS WATCHING THE CLOCK RACE FURIOUSLY TOWARDS THE WORLD'S END.
I WAS...

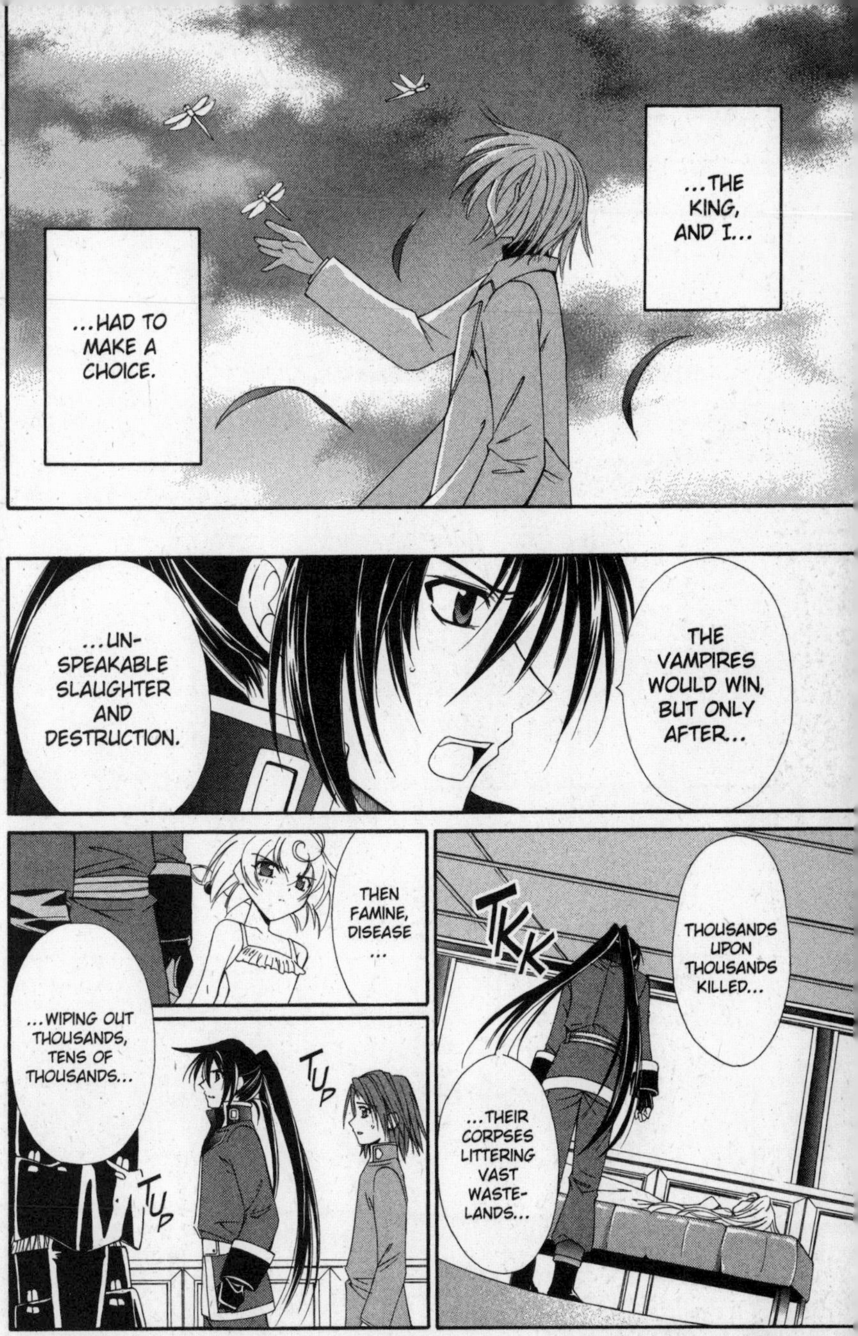
...THE KING, AND I...
...HAD TO MAKE A CHOICE.
THE VAMPIRES WOULD WIN, BUT ONLY AFTER...
...UN-SPEAKABLE SLAUGHTER AND DESTRUCTION.
TKK
THOUSANDS UPON THOUSANDS KILLED...
...THEIR CORPSES LITTERING VAST WASTE-LANDS...
THEN FAMINE, DISEASE ...
TUP
...WIPING OUT THOUSANDS, TENS OF THOUSANDS...
TUP

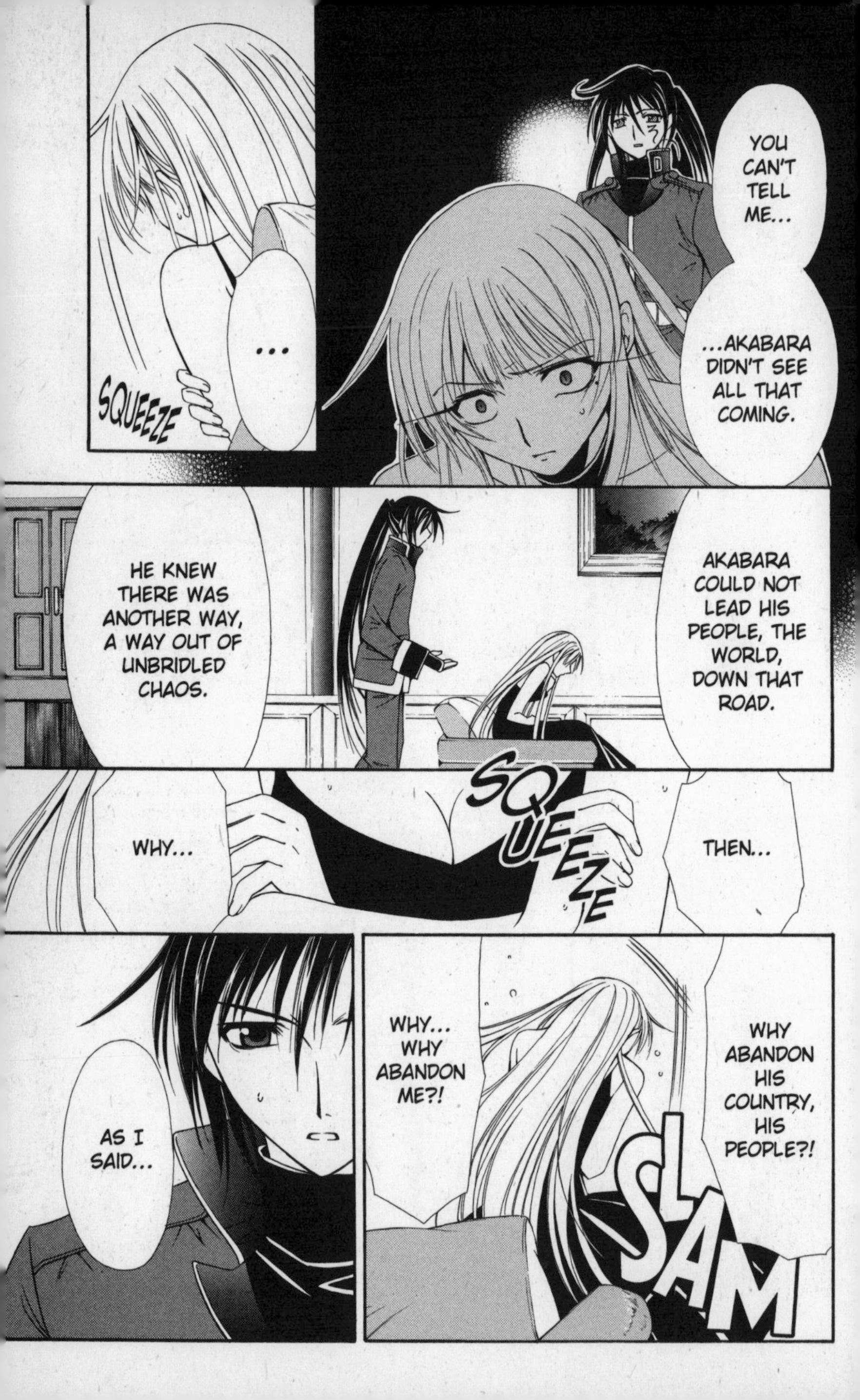
YOU CAN'T TELL ME...
...AKABARA DIDN'T SEE ALL THAT COMING.
...
SQUEEZE
AKABARA COULD NOT LEAD HIS PEOPLE, THE WORLD, DOWN THAT ROAD.
HE KNEW THERE WAS ANOTHER WAY, A WAY OUT OF UNBRIDLED CHAOS.
THEN...
SQUEEZE
WHY...
WHY ABANDON HIS COUNTRY, HIS PEOPLE?!
WHY... WHY ABANDON ME?!
SLAM
AS I SAID...

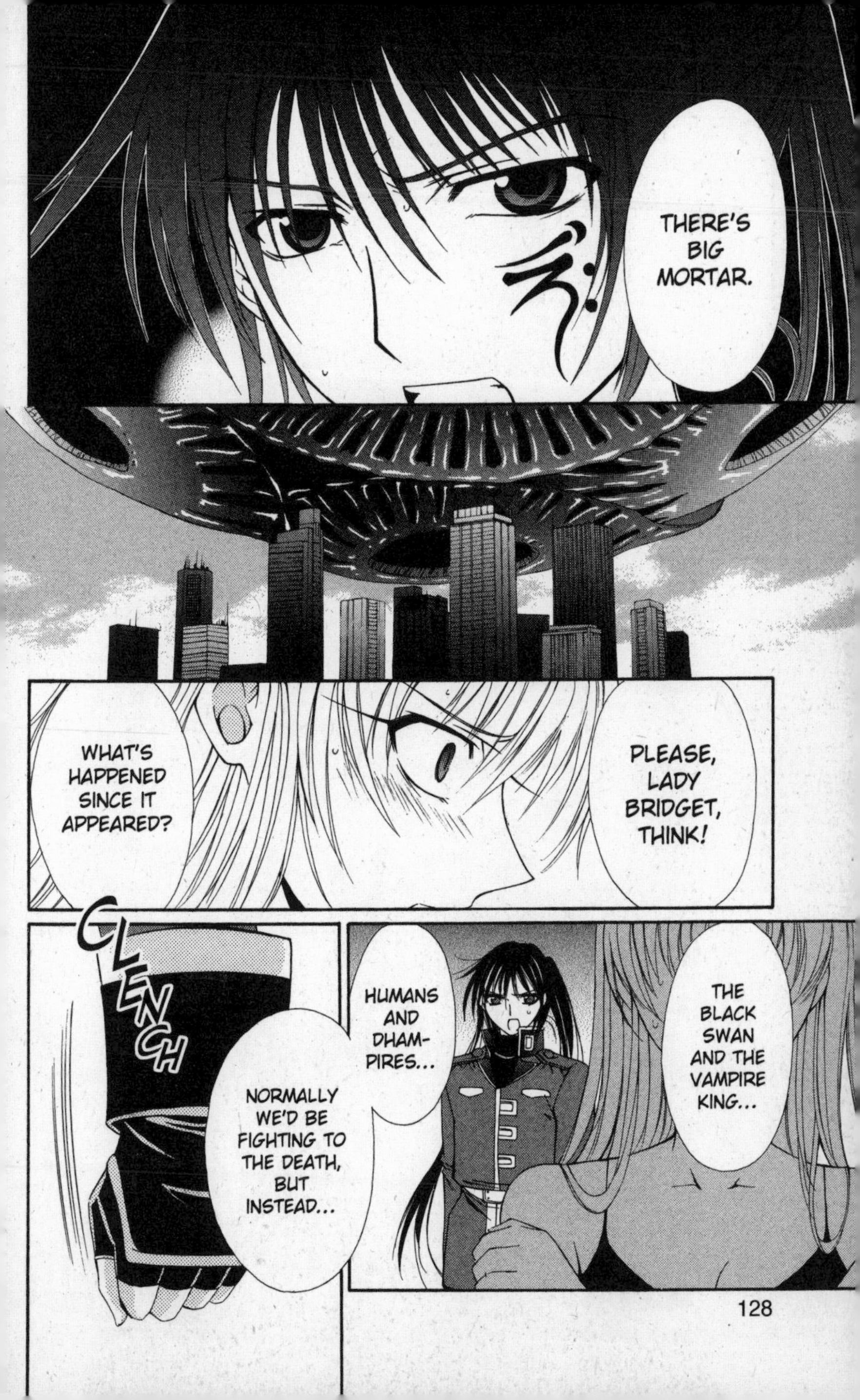
THERE'S BIG MORTAR.
PLEASE, LADY BRIDGET, THINK!
WHAT'S HAPPENED SINCE IT APPEARED?
THE BLACK SWAN AND THE VAMPIRE KING...
HUMANS AND DHAM-PIRES...
NORMALLY WE'D BE FIGHTING TO THE DEATH, BUT INSTEAD...
CLENCH

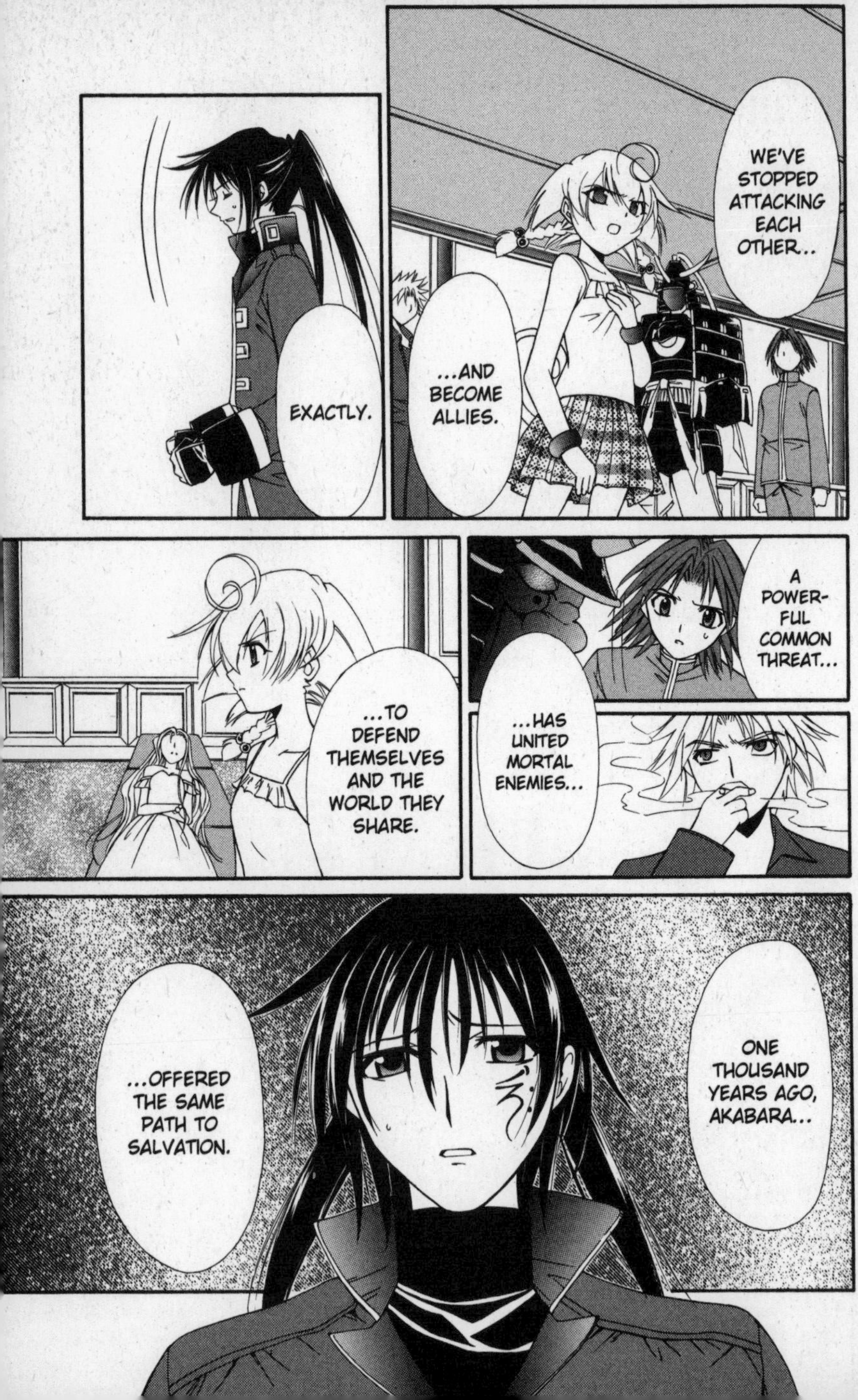
WE'VE STOPPED ATTACKING EACH OTHER...
...AND BECOME ALLIES.
EXACTLY.
A POWER-FUL COMMON THREAT...
...HAS UNITED MORTAL ENEMIES...
...TO DEFEND THEMSELVES AND THE WORLD THEY SHARE.
ONE THOUSAND YEARS AGO, AKABARA...
...OFFERED THE SAME PATH TO SALVATION.

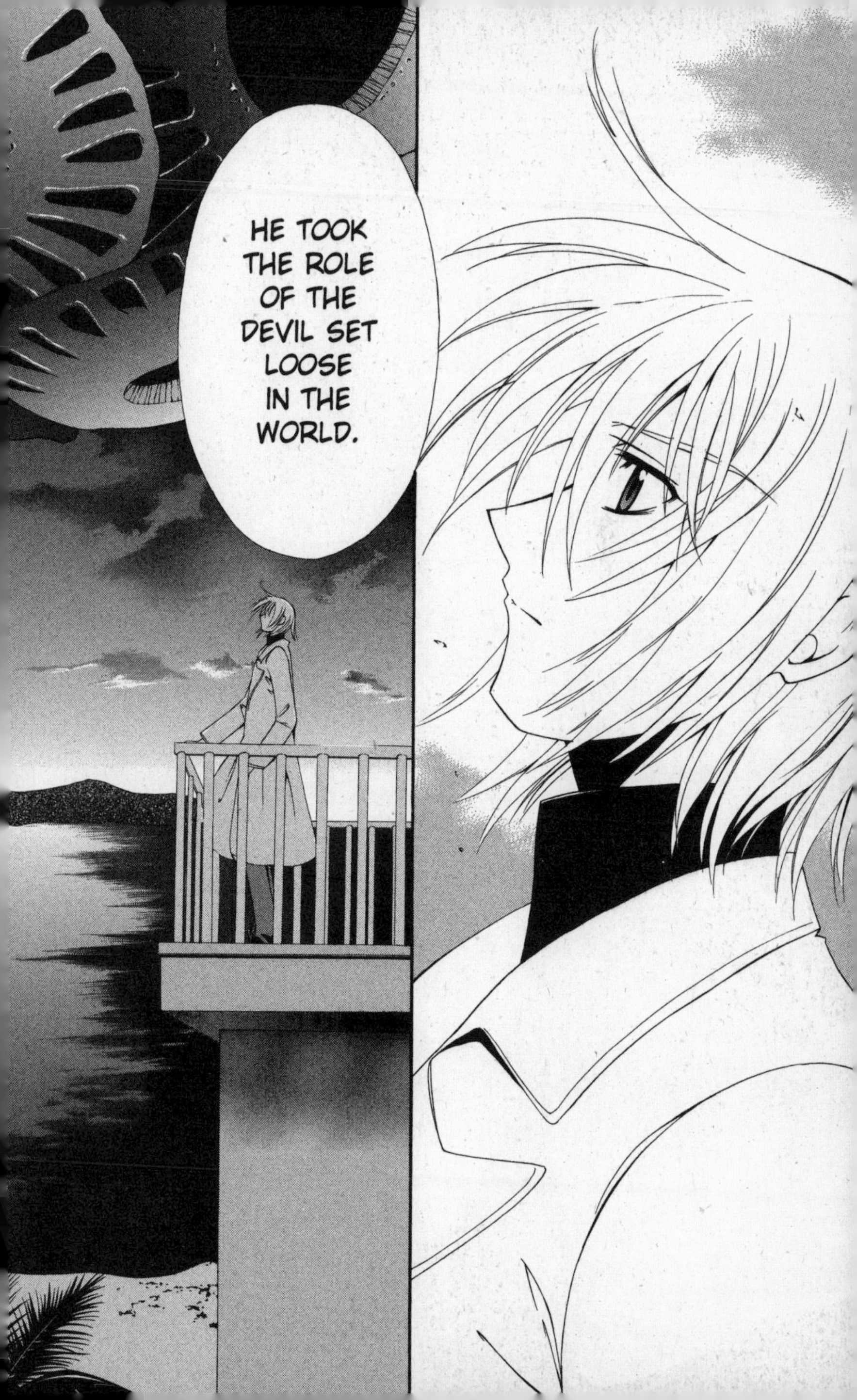
HE TOOK THE ROLE OF THE DEVIL SET LOOSE IN THE WORLD.

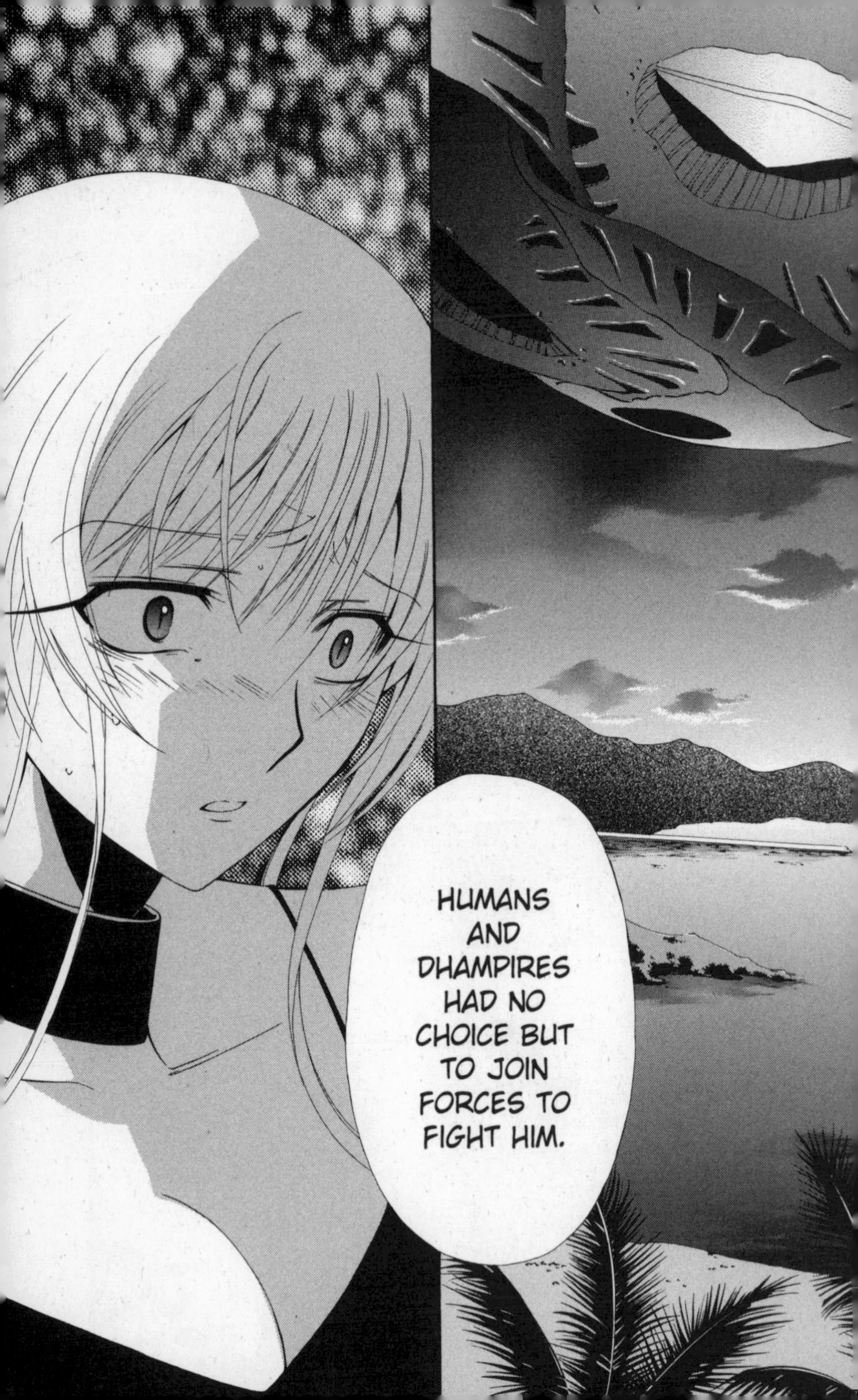
HUMANS AND DHAMPIRES HAD NO CHOICE BUT TO JOIN FORCES TO FIGHT HIM.

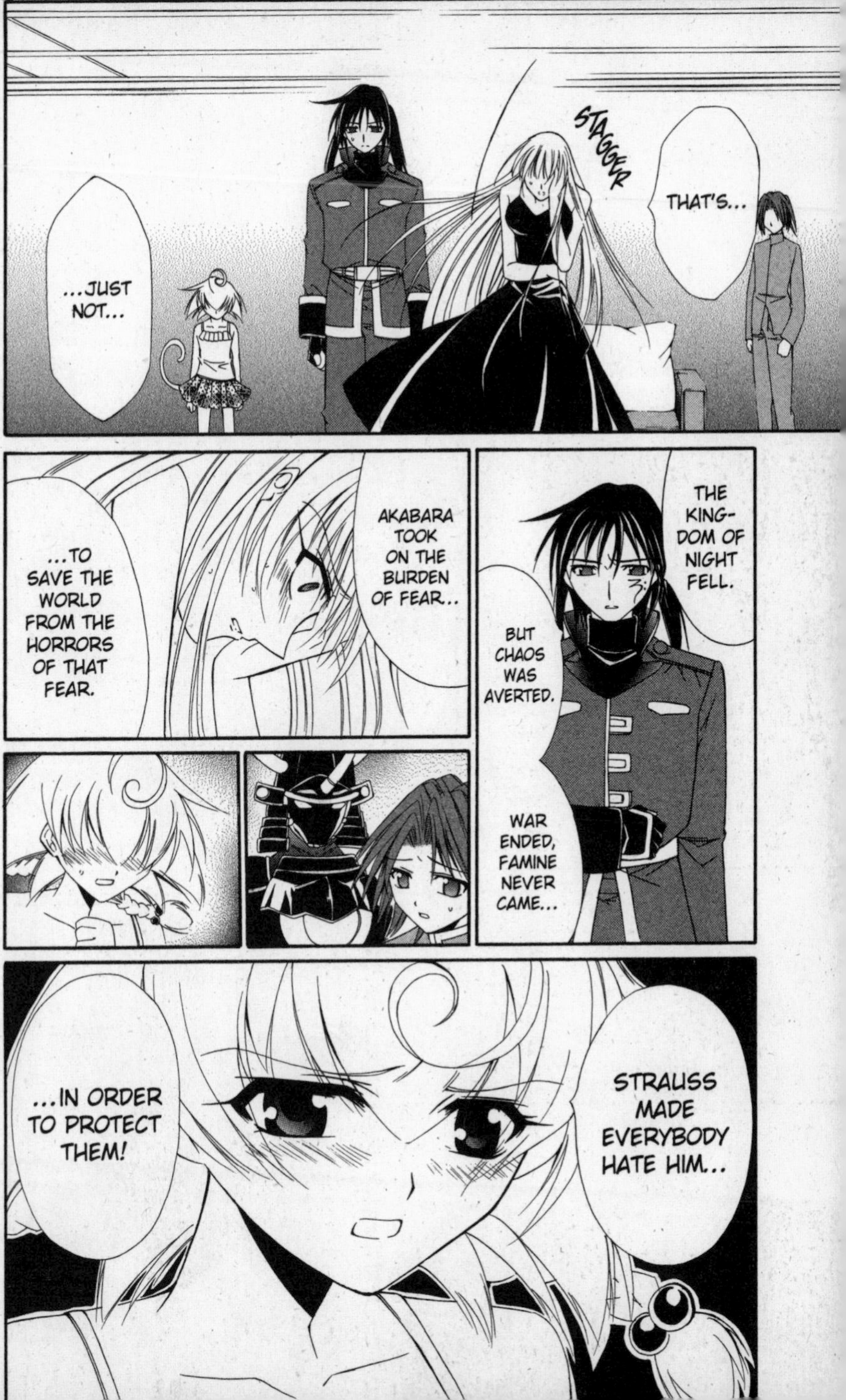
THAT'S...
STAGGER
...JUST NOT...
THE KING-DOM OF NIGHT FELL.
BUT CHAOS WAS AVERTED.
WAR ENDED, FAMINE NEVER CAME...
AKABARA TOOK ON THE BURDEN OF FEAR...
...TO SAVE THE WORLD FROM THE HORRORS OF THAT FEAR.
STRAUSS MADE EVERYBODY HATE HIM...
...IN ORDER TO PROTECT THEM!

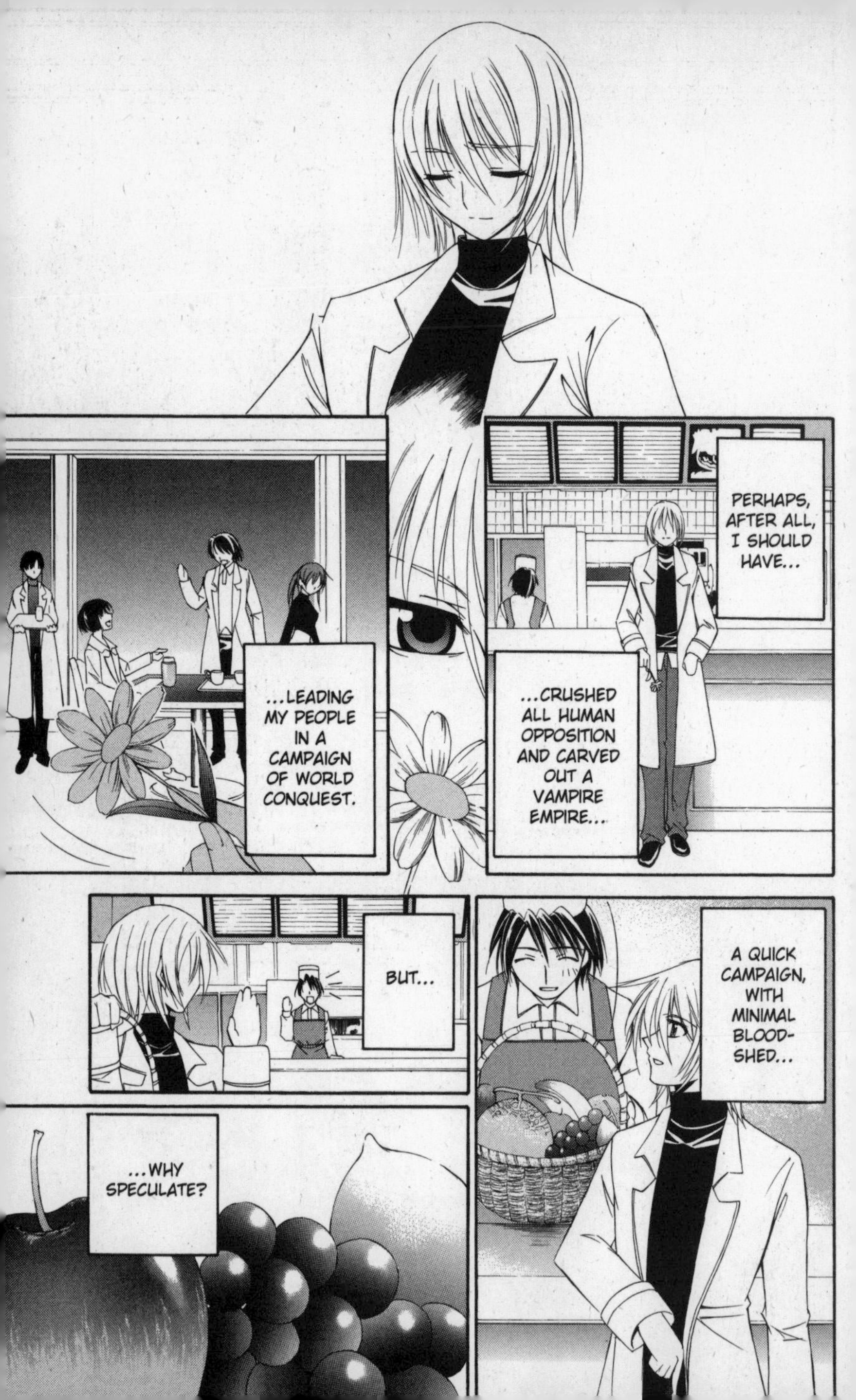
PERHAPS, AFTER ALL, I SHOULD HAVE...
...CRUSHED ALL HUMAN OPPOSITION AND CARVED OUT A VAMPIRE EMPIRE...
...LEADING MY PEOPLE IN A CAMPAIGN OF WORLD CONQUEST.
A QUICK CAMPAIGN, WITH MINIMAL BLOOD-SHED...
BUT...
...WHY SPECULATE?

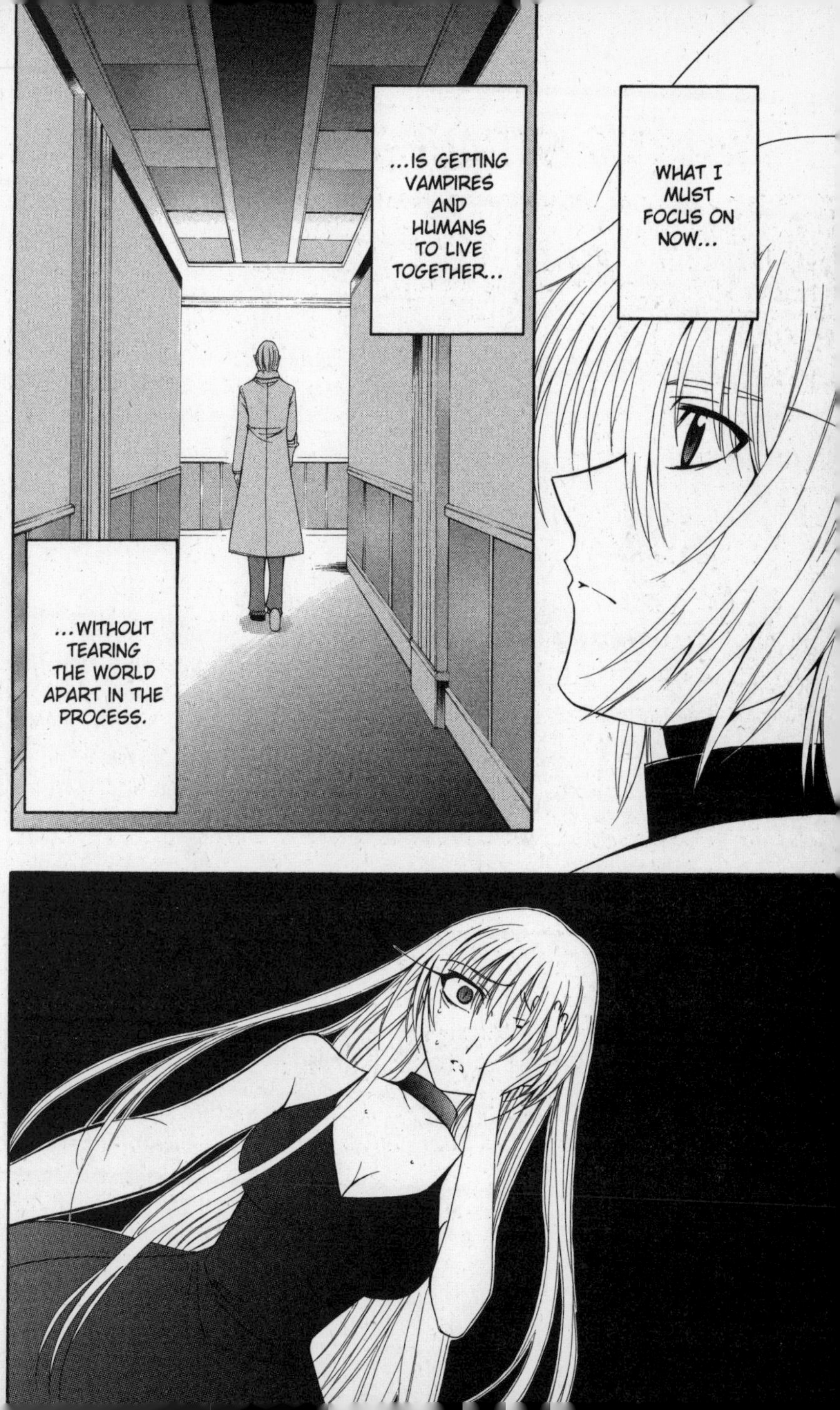
WHAT I MUST FOCUS ON NOW...
...IS GETTING VAMPIRES AND HUMANS TO LIVE TOGETHER...
...WITHOUT TEARING THE WORLD APART IN THE PROCESS.

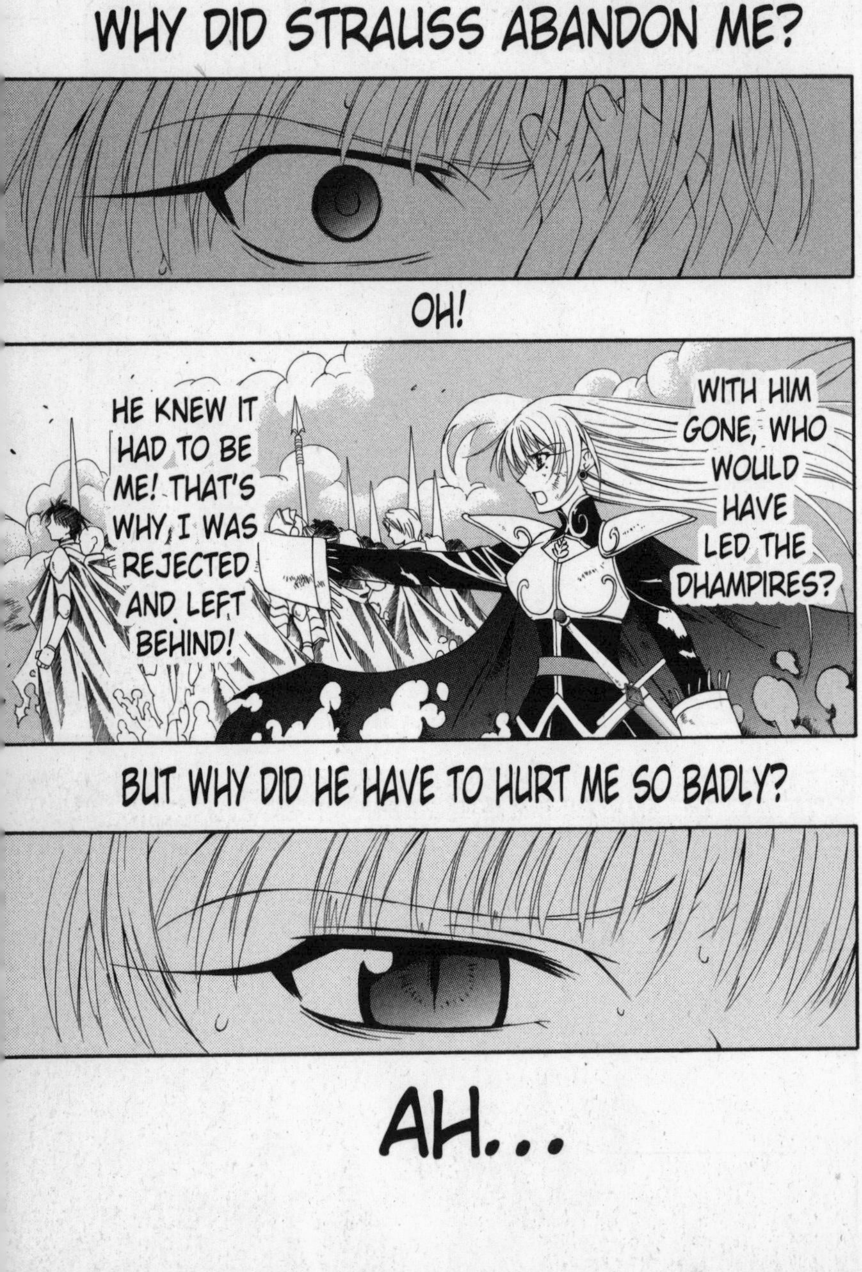
WHY DID STRAUSS ABANDON ME?
OH!
WITH HIM GONE, WHO WOULD HAVE LED THE DHAMPIRES?
HE KNEW IT HAD TO BE ME! THAT'S WHY I WAS REJECTED AND LEFT BEHIND!
BUT WHY DID HE HAVE TO HURT ME SO BADLY?
AH...

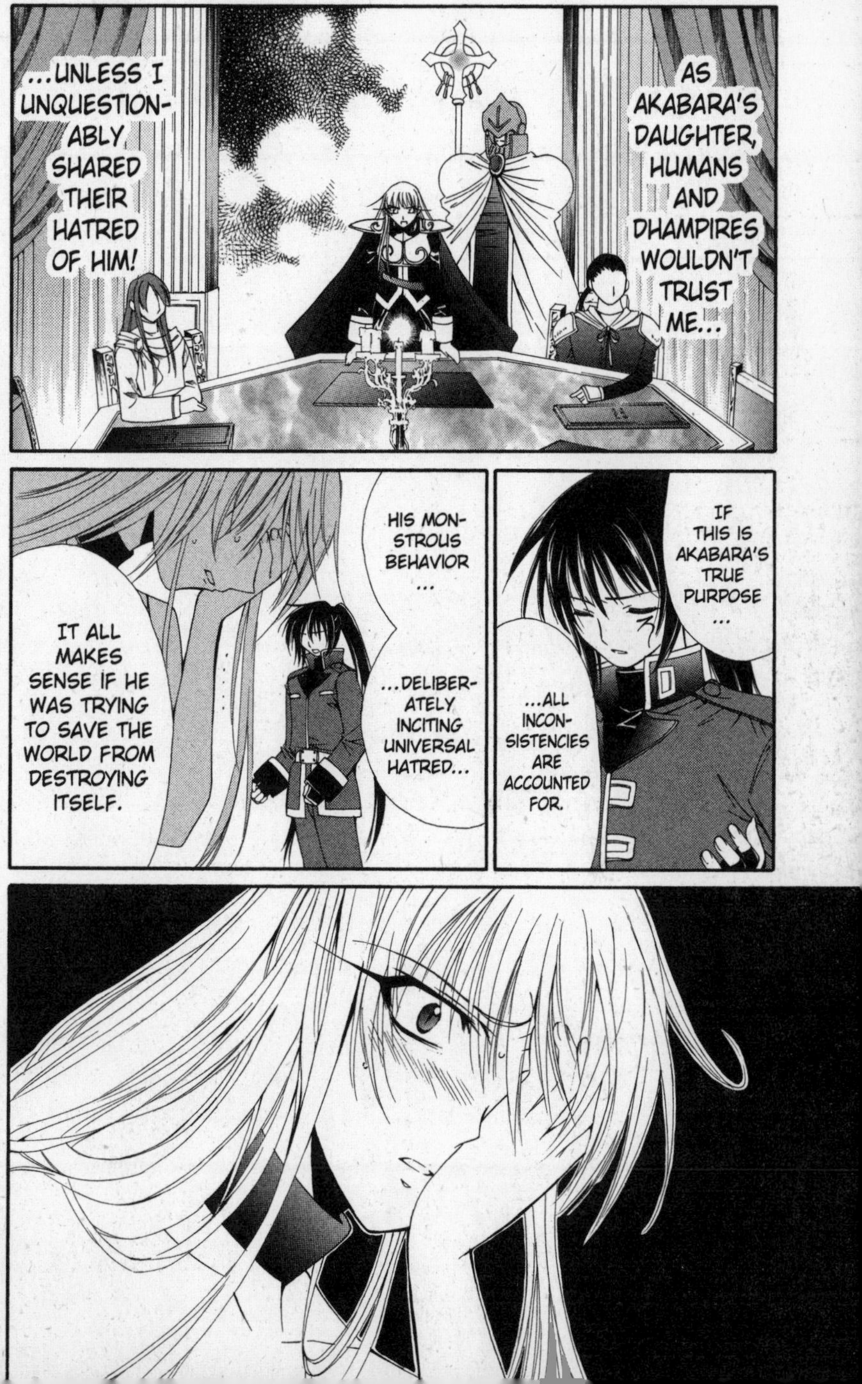
AS AKABARA'S DAUGHTER, HUMANS AND DHAMPIRES WOULDN'T TRUST ME...
...UNLESS I UNQUESTION-ABLY SHARED THEIR HATRED OF HIM!
IF THIS IS AKABARA'S TRUE PURPOSE...
...ALL INCON-SISTENCIES ARE ACCOUNTED FOR.
HIS MON-STROUS BEHAVIOR...
...DELIBER-ATELY INCITING UNIVERSAL HATRED...
IT ALL MAKES SENSE IF HE WAS TRYING TO SAVE THE WORLD FROM DESTROYING ITSELF.

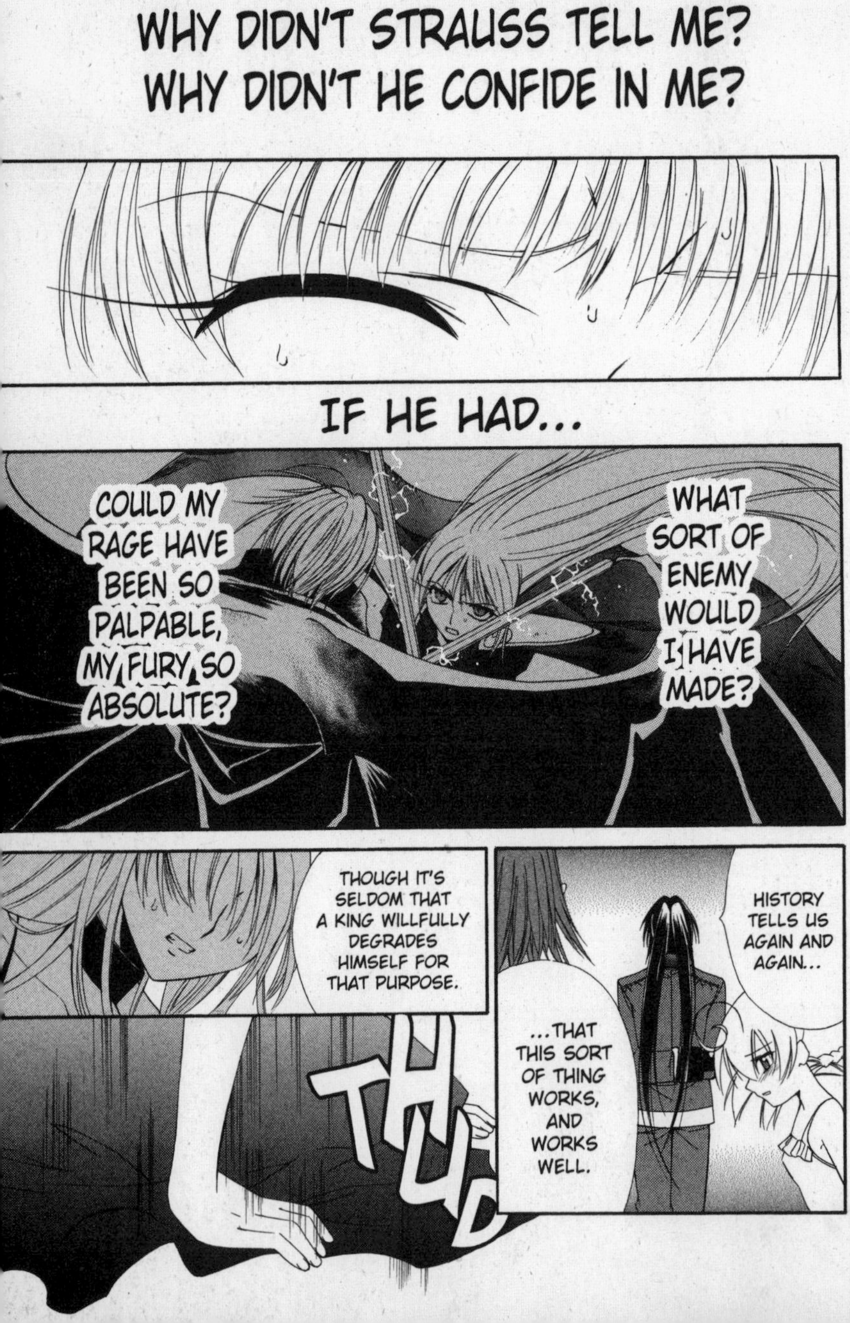
WHY DIDN'T STRAUSS TELL ME? WHY DIDN'T HE CONFIDE IN ME?
IF HE HAD...
WHAT SORT OF ENEMY WOULD I HAVE MADE?
COULD MY RAGE HAVE BEEN SO PALPABLE, MY FURY SO ABSOLUTE?
HISTORY TELLS US AGAIN AND AGAIN...
...THAT THIS SORT OF THING WORKS, AND WORKS WELL.
THOUGH IT'S SELDOM THAT A KING WILLFULLY DEGRADES HIMSELF FOR THAT PURPOSE.
THUD

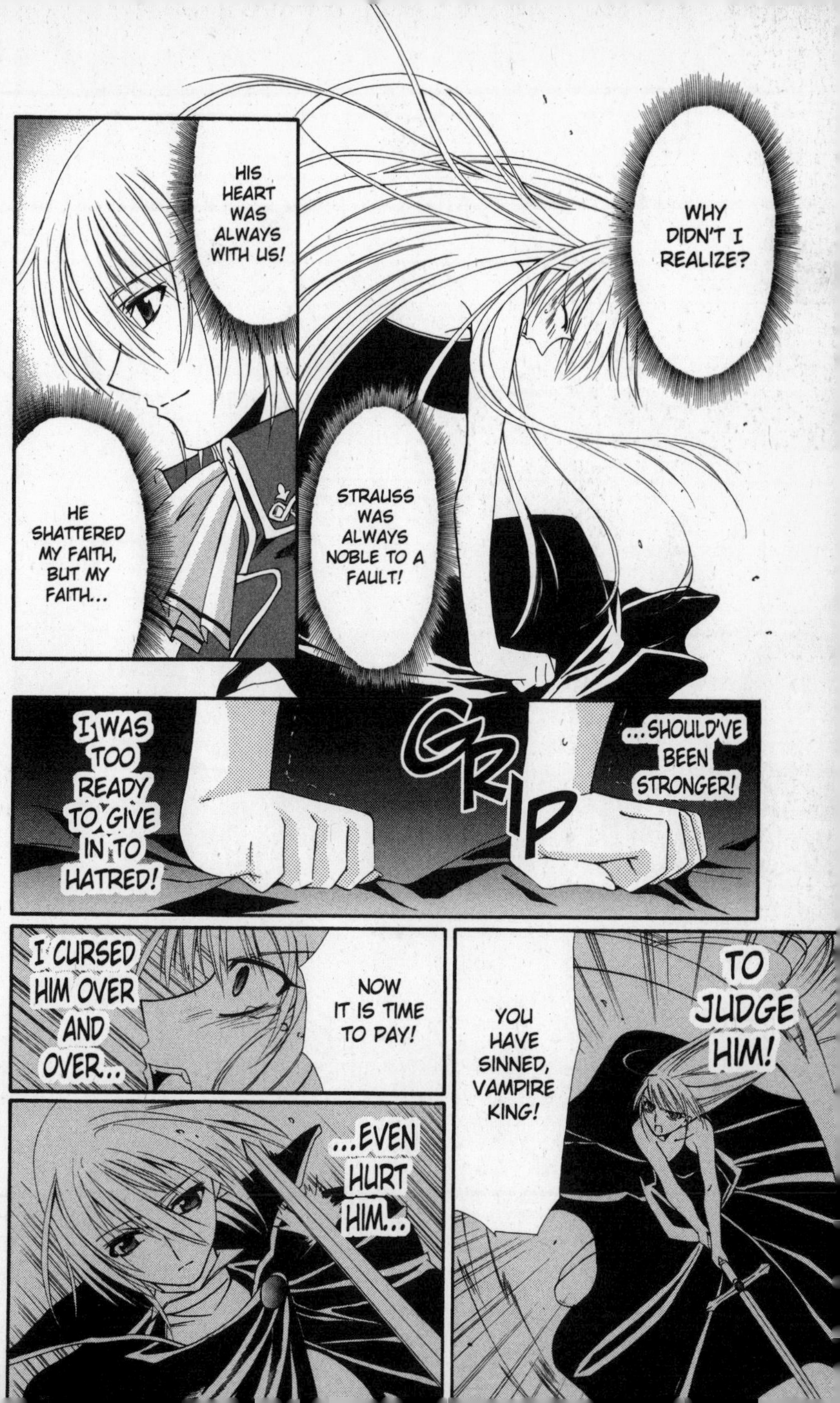
WHY DIDN'T I REALIZE?
STRAUSS WAS ALWAYS NOBLE TO A FAULT!
HIS HEART WAS ALWAYS WITH US!
HE SHATTERED MY FAITH, BUT MY FAITH...
...SHOULD'VE BEEN STRONGER!
GRIP
I WAS TOO READY TO GIVE IN TO HATRED!
TO JUDGE HIM!
YOU HAVE SINNED, VAMPIRE KING!
NOW IT IS TIME TO PAY!
I CURSED HIM OVER AND OVER...
...EVEN HURT HIM...

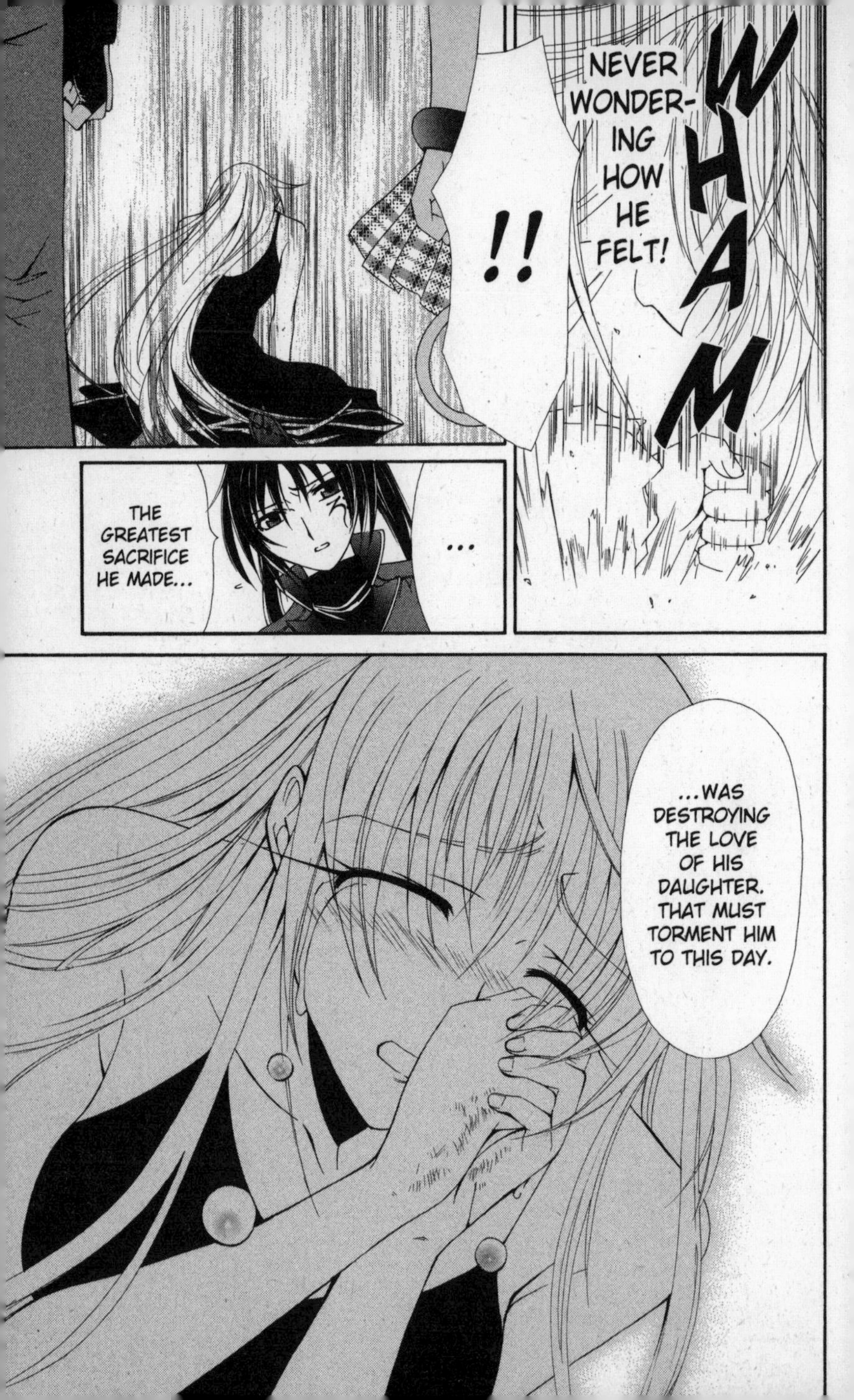
NEVER WONDERING HOW HE FELT!
WHAM
!!
THE GREATEST SACRIFICE HE MADE...
...
...WAS DESTROYING THE LOVE OF HIS DAUGHTER. THAT MUST TORMENT HIM TO THIS DAY.

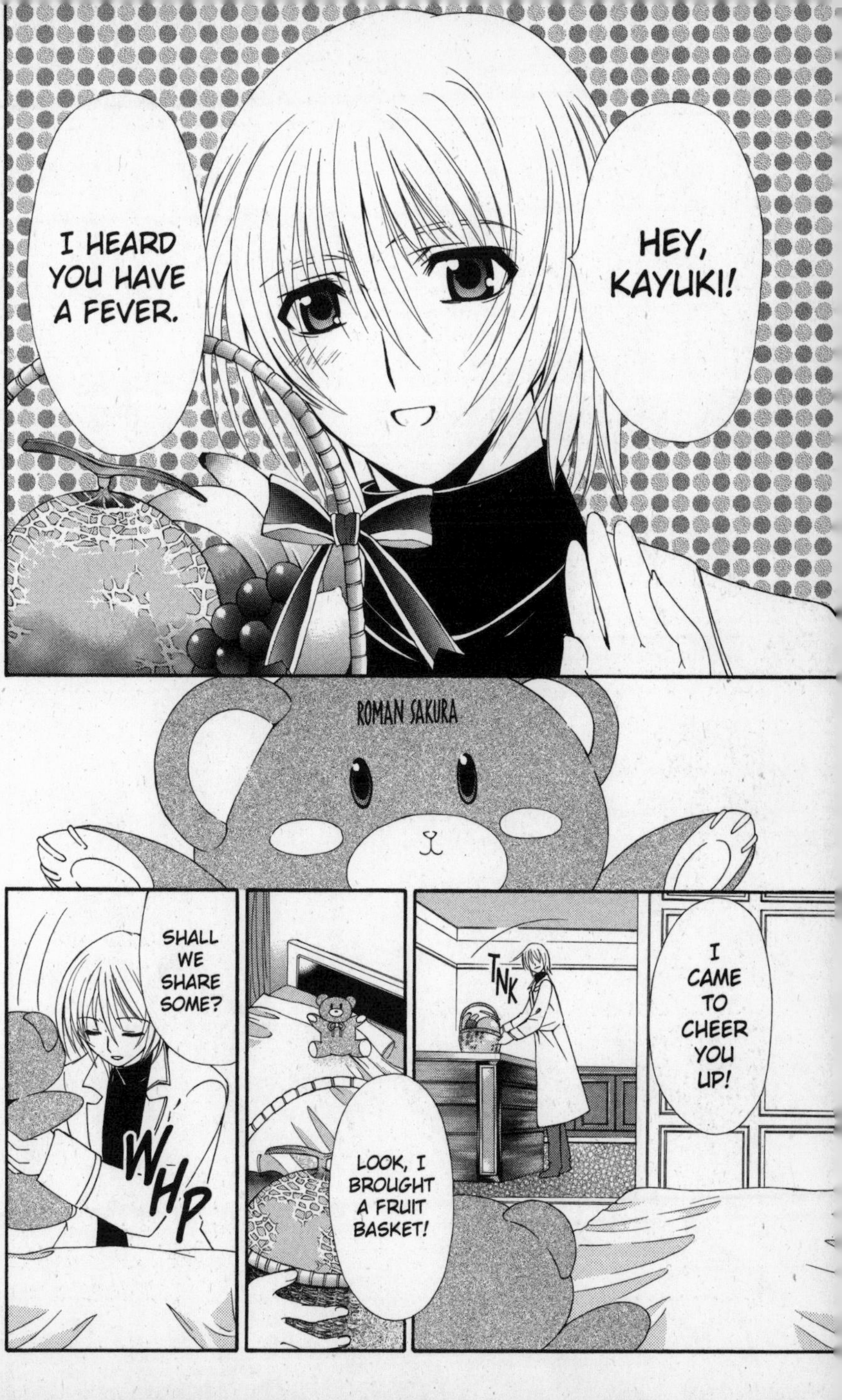

HEY, KAYUKI!
I HEARD YOU HAVE A FEVER.
ROMAN SAKURA
I CAME TO CHEER YOU UP!
TNK
LOOK, I BROUGHT A FRUIT BASKET!
SHALL WE SHARE SOME?
WHP

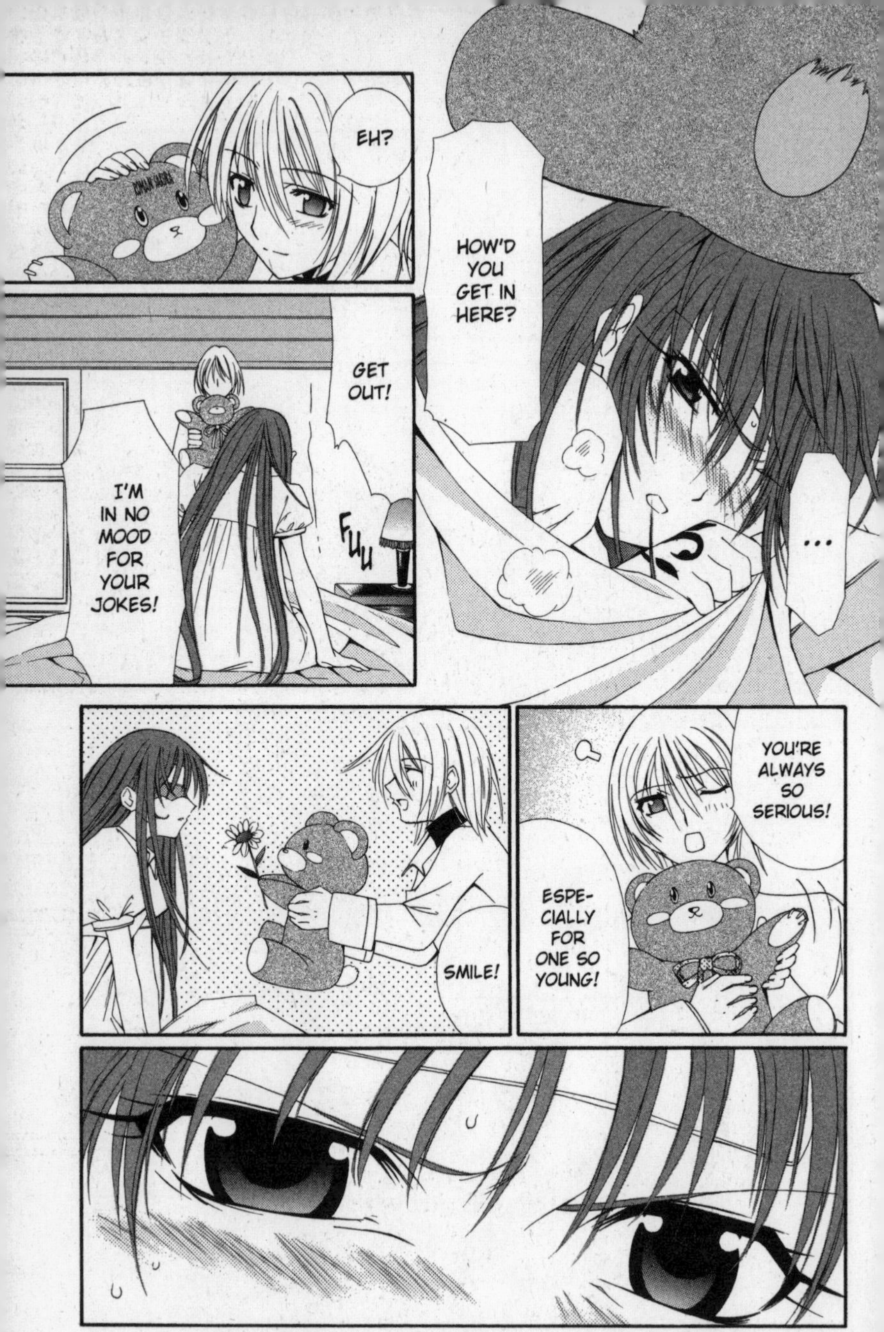
HOW'D YOU GET IN HERE?
...
EH?
GET OUT!
I'M IN NO MOOD FOR YOUR JOKES!
FUU
YOU'RE ALWAYS SO SERIOUS!
ESPE-CIALLY FOR ONE SO YOUNG!
SMILE!

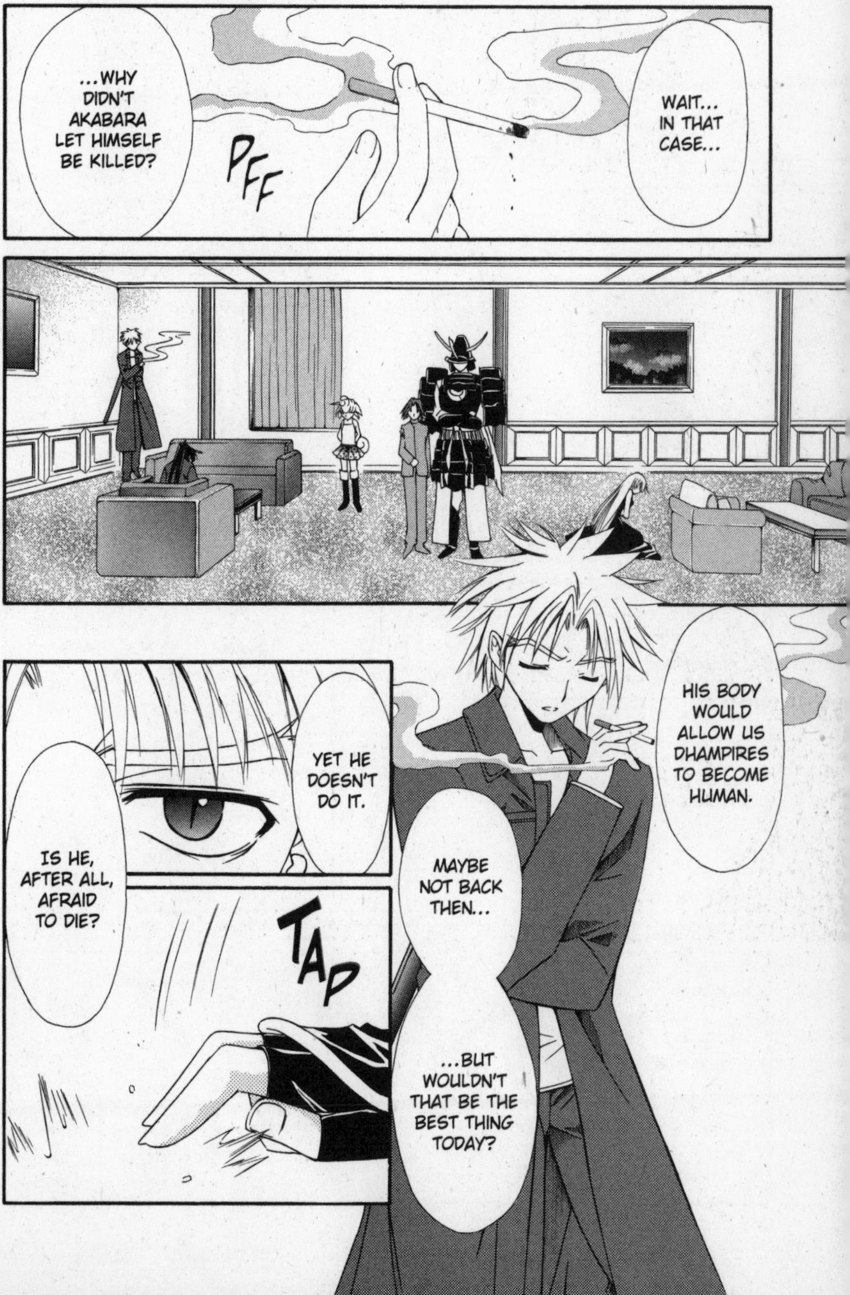
WAIT... IN THAT CASE...
PFF
...WHY DIDN'T AKABARA LET HIMSELF BE KILLED?
HIS BODY WOULD ALLOW US DHAMPIRES TO BECOME HUMAN.
YET HE DOESN'T DO IT.
IS HE, AFTER ALL, AFRAID TO DIE?
TAP
MAYBE NOT BACK THEN...
...BUT WOULDN'T THAT BE THE BEST THING TODAY?

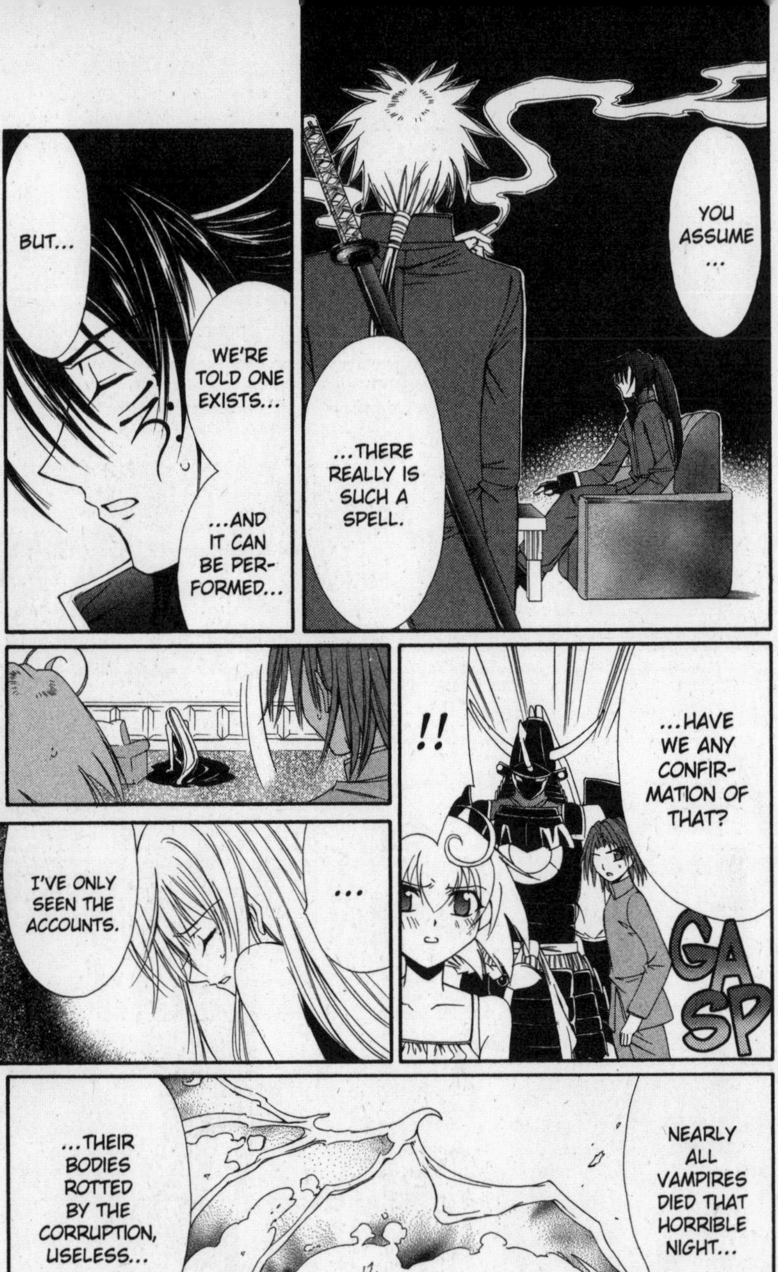
YOU ASSUME ...
...THERE REALLY IS SUCH A SPELL.
BUT...
WE'RE TOLD ONE EXISTS...
...AND IT CAN BE PERFORMED...
!!
...HAVE WE ANY CONFIRMATION OF THAT?
GASP
...
I'VE ONLY SEEN THE ACCOUNTS.
NEARLY ALL VAMPIRES DIED THAT HORRIBLE NIGHT...
...THEIR BODIES ROTTED BY THE CORRUPTION, USELESS...

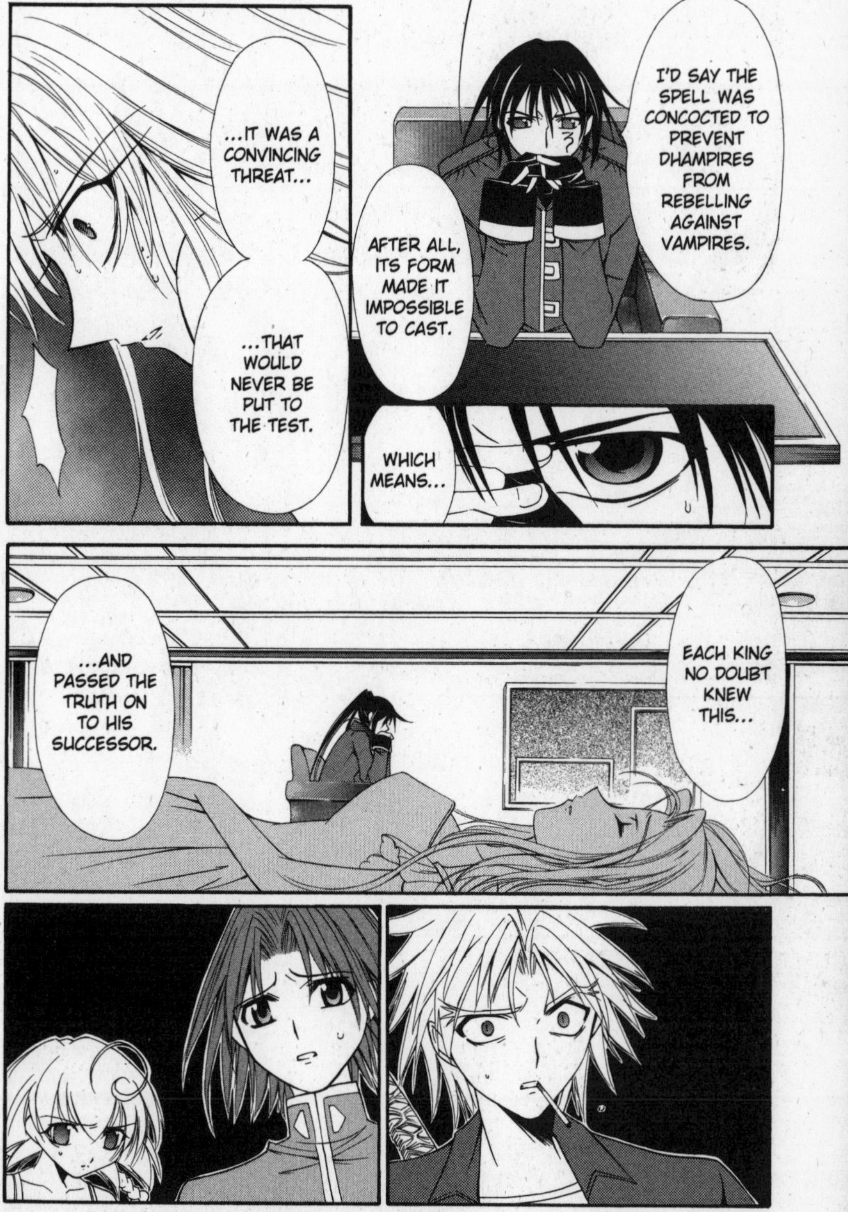
I'D SAY THE SPELL WAS CONCOCTED TO PREVENT DHAMPIRES FROM REBELLING AGAINST VAMPIRES.
AFTER ALL, ITS FORM MADE IT IMPOSSIBLE TO CAST.
WHICH MEANS...
...IT WAS A CONVINCING THREAT...
...THAT WOULD NEVER BE PUT TO THE TEST.
EACH KING NO DOUBT KNEW THIS...
...AND PASSED THE TRUTH ON TO HIS SUCCESSOR.

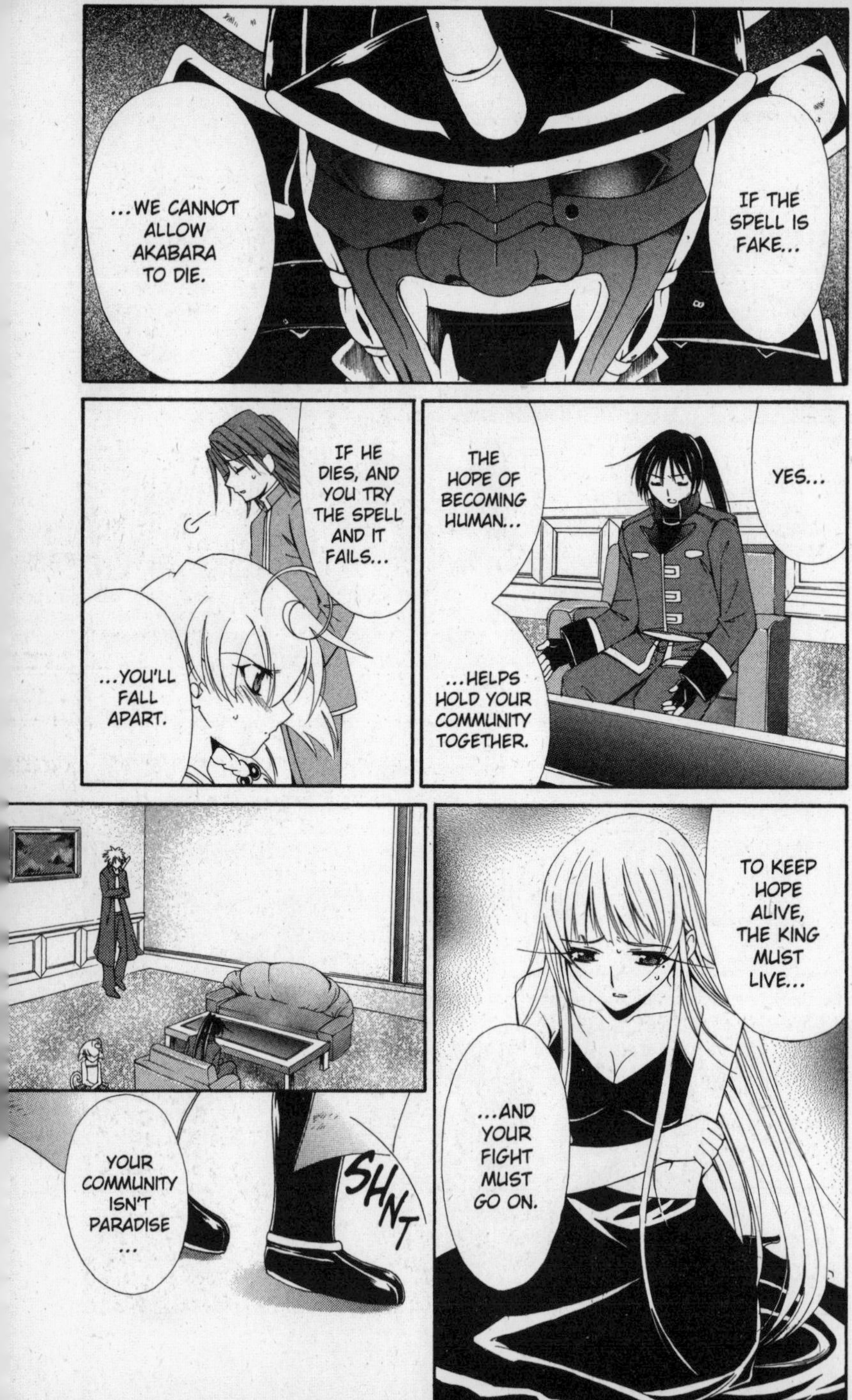
IF THE SPELL IS FAKE...
...WE CANNOT ALLOW AKABARA TO DIE.
YES...
THE HOPE OF BECOMING HUMAN...
...HELPS HOLD YOUR COMMUNITY TOGETHER.
IF HE DIES, AND YOU TRY THE SPELL AND IT FAILS...
...YOU'LL FALL APART.
TO KEEP HOPE ALIVE, THE KING MUST LIVE...
...AND YOUR FIGHT MUST GO ON.
SHNT
YOUR COMMUNITY ISN'T PARADISE ...

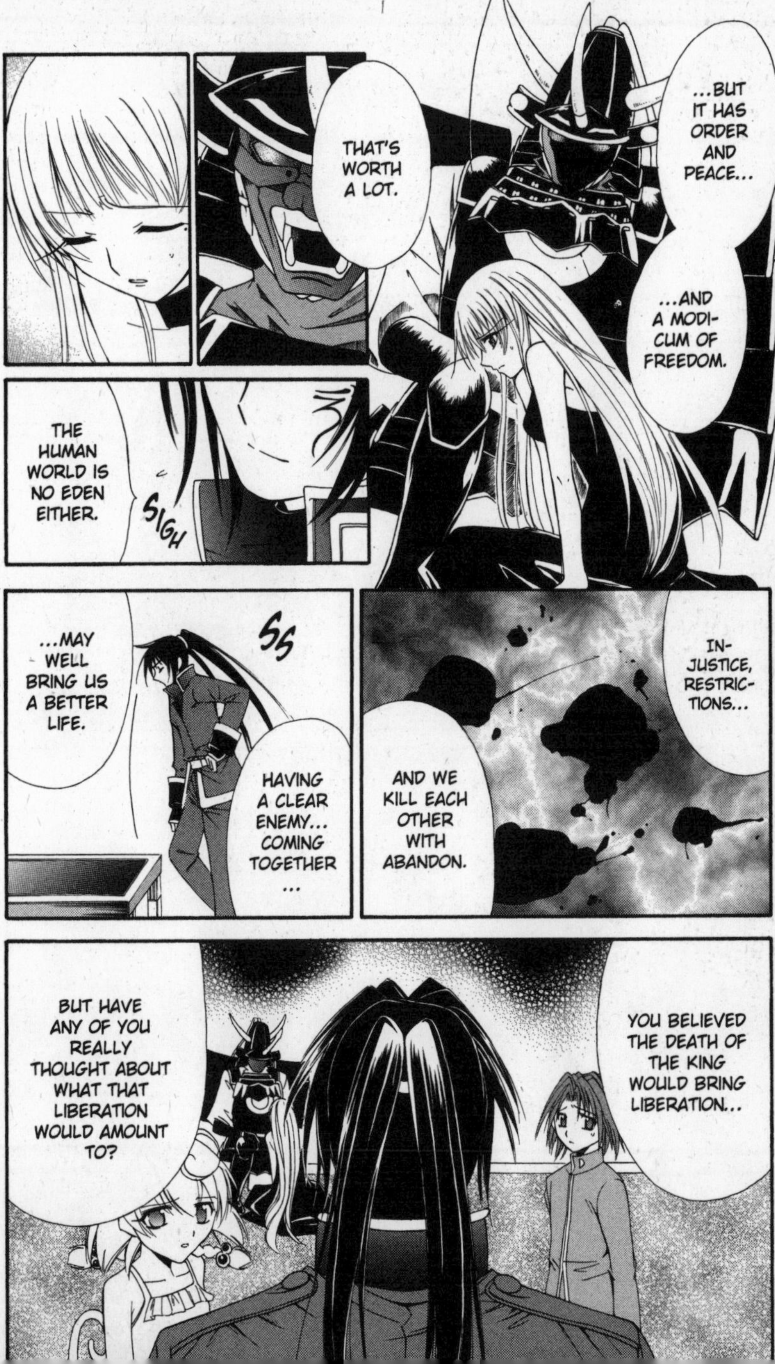
...BUT IT HAS ORDER AND PEACE...
...AND A MODI-CUM OF FREEDOM.
THAT'S WORTH A LOT.
THE HUMAN WORLD IS NO EDEN EITHER.
SIGH
IN-JUSTICE, RESTRIC-TIONS...
AND WE KILL EACH OTHER WITH ABANDON.
HAVING A CLEAR ENEMY... COMING TOGETHER ...
...MAY WELL BRING US A BETTER LIFE.
SS
YOU BELIEVED THE DEATH OF THE KING WOULD BRING LIBERATION...
BUT HAVE ANY OF YOU REALLY THOUGHT ABOUT WHAT THAT LIBERATION WOULD AMOUNT TO?

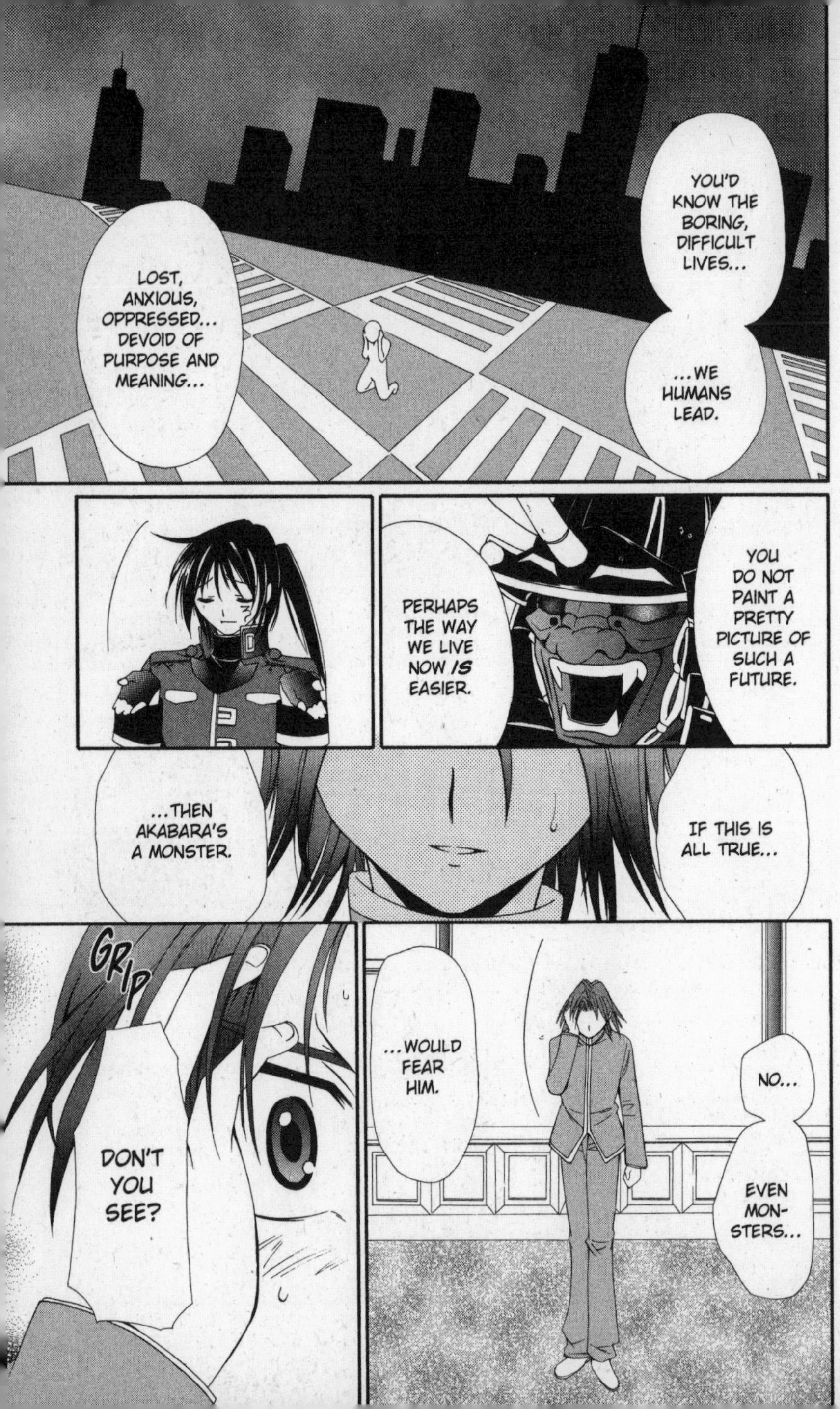
YOU'D KNOW THE BORING, DIFFICULT LIVES...
...WE HUMANS LEAD.
LOST, ANXIOUS, OPPRESSED... DEVOID OF PURPOSE AND MEANING...
YOU DO NOT PAINT A PRETTY PICTURE OF SUCH A FUTURE.
PERHAPS THE WAY WE LIVE NOW *IS* EASIER.
IF THIS IS ALL TRUE...
...THEN AKABARA'S A MONSTER.
NO...
EVEN MON-STERS...
...WOULD FEAR HIM.
GRIP
DON'T YOU SEE?

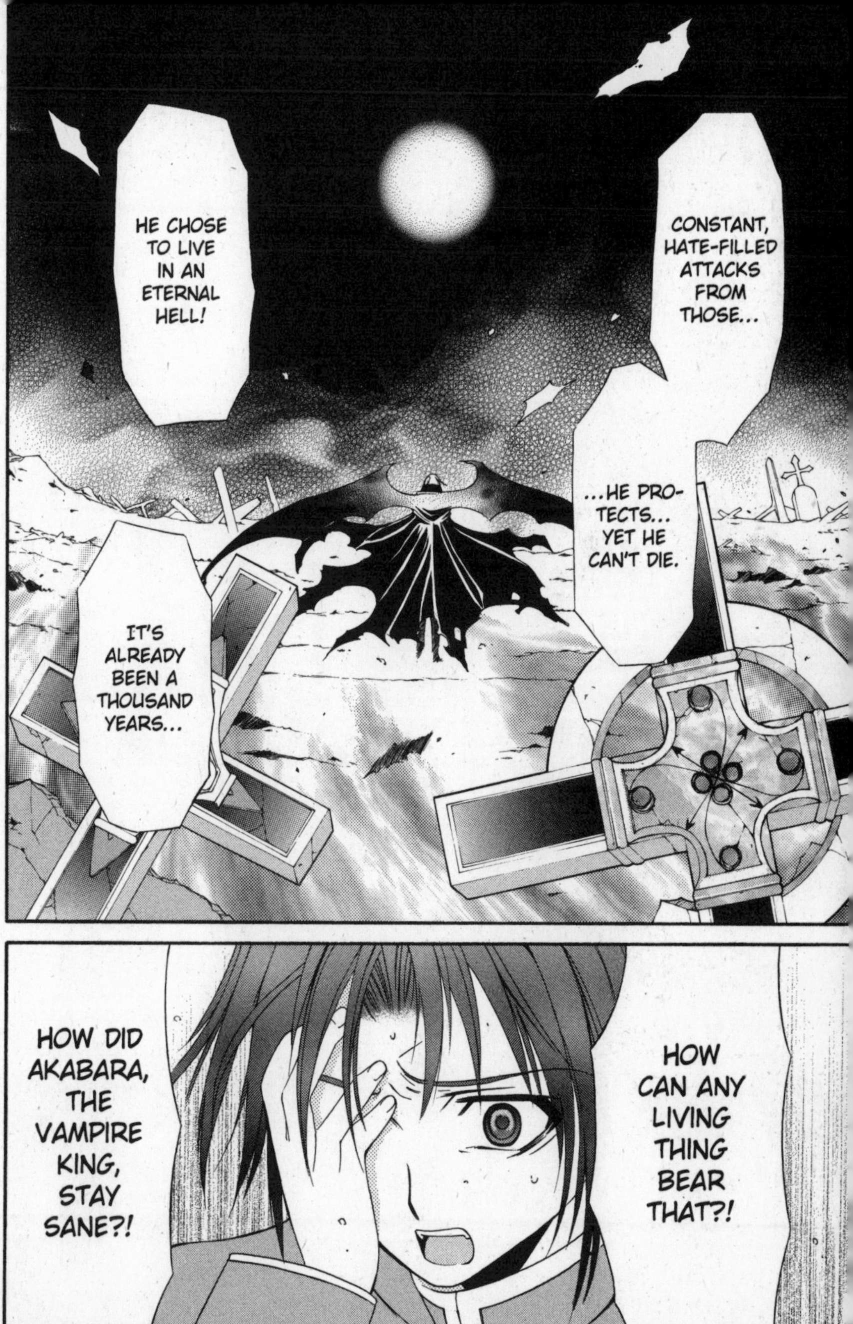
CONSTANT, HATE-FILLED ATTACKS FROM THOSE...
...HE PROTECTS... YET HE CAN'T DIE.
HE CHOSE TO LIVE IN AN ETERNAL HELL!
IT'S ALREADY BEEN A THOUSAND YEARS...
HOW CAN ANY LIVING THING BEAR THAT?!
HOW DID AKABARA, THE VAMPIRE KING, STAY SANE?!

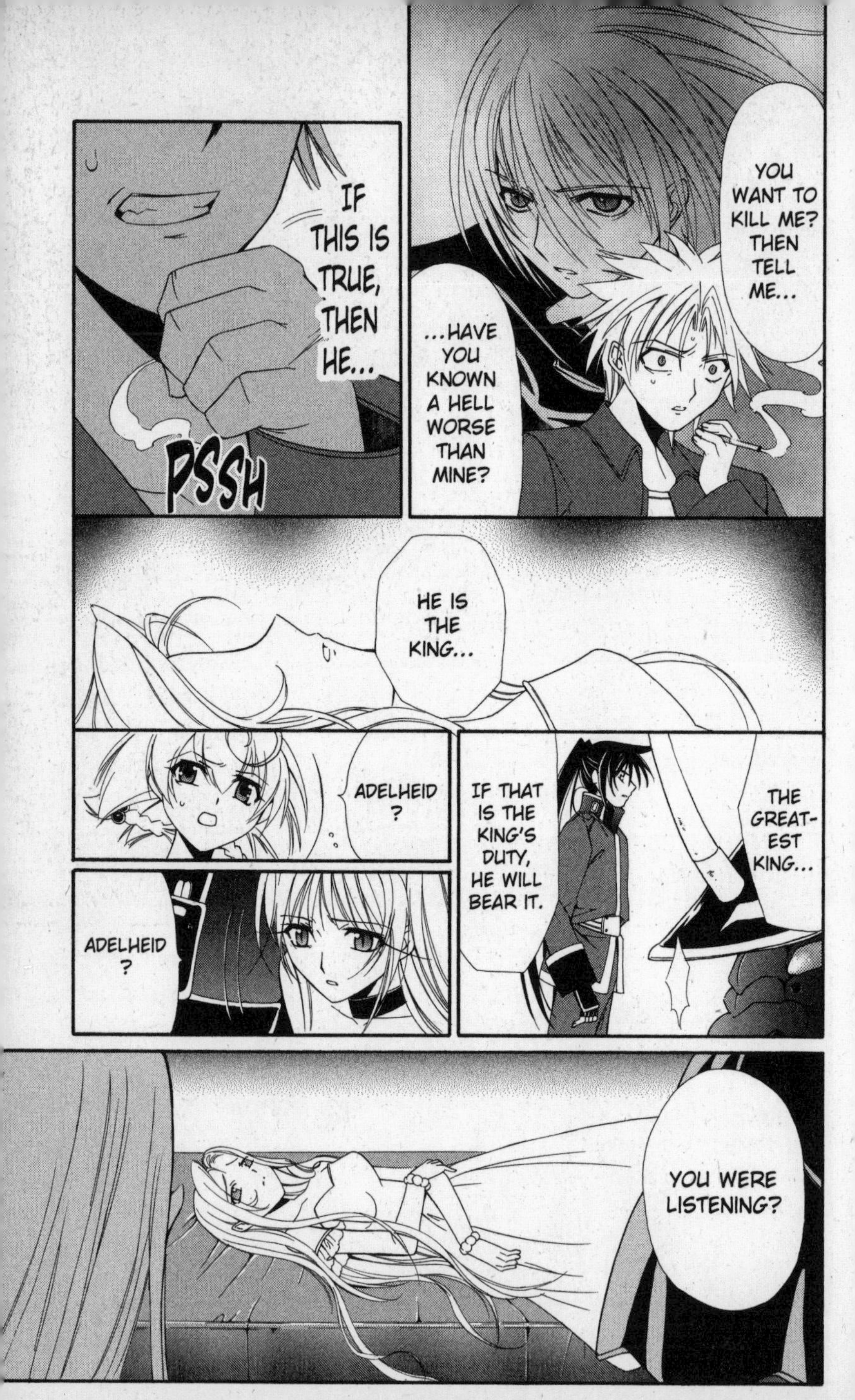
YOU WANT TO KILL ME? THEN TELL ME...
...HAVE YOU KNOWN A HELL WORSE THAN MINE?
IF THIS IS TRUE, THEN HE...
PSSH
HE IS THE KING...
THE GREAT-EST KING...
IF THAT IS THE KING'S DUTY, HE WILL BEAR IT.
ADELHEID?
ADELHEID?
YOU WERE LISTENING?

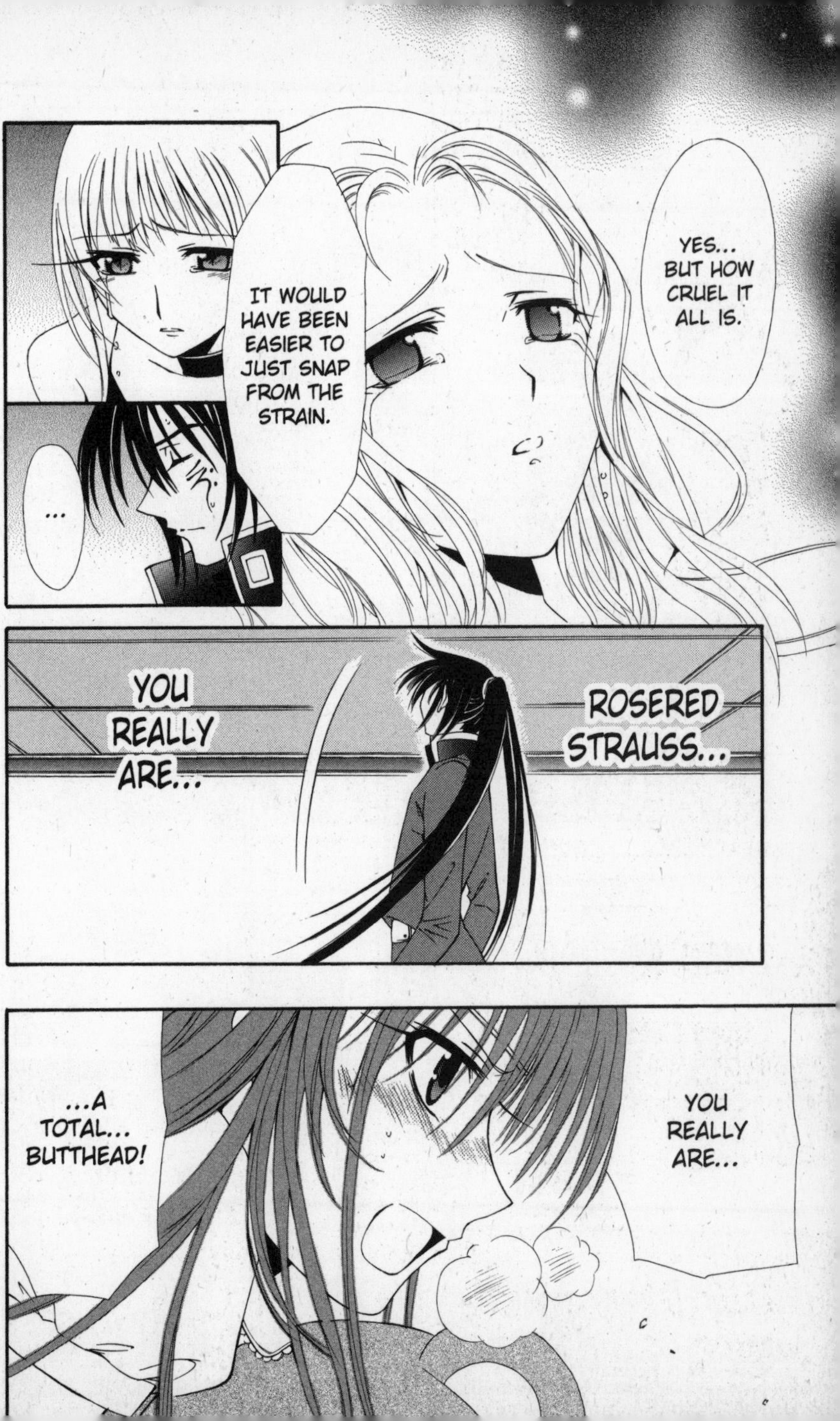
YES... BUT HOW CRUEL IT ALL IS.
IT WOULD HAVE BEEN EASIER TO JUST SNAP FROM THE STRAIN.
...
ROSERED STRAUSS...
YOU REALLY ARE...
YOU REALLY ARE...
...A TOTAL... BUTTHEAD!

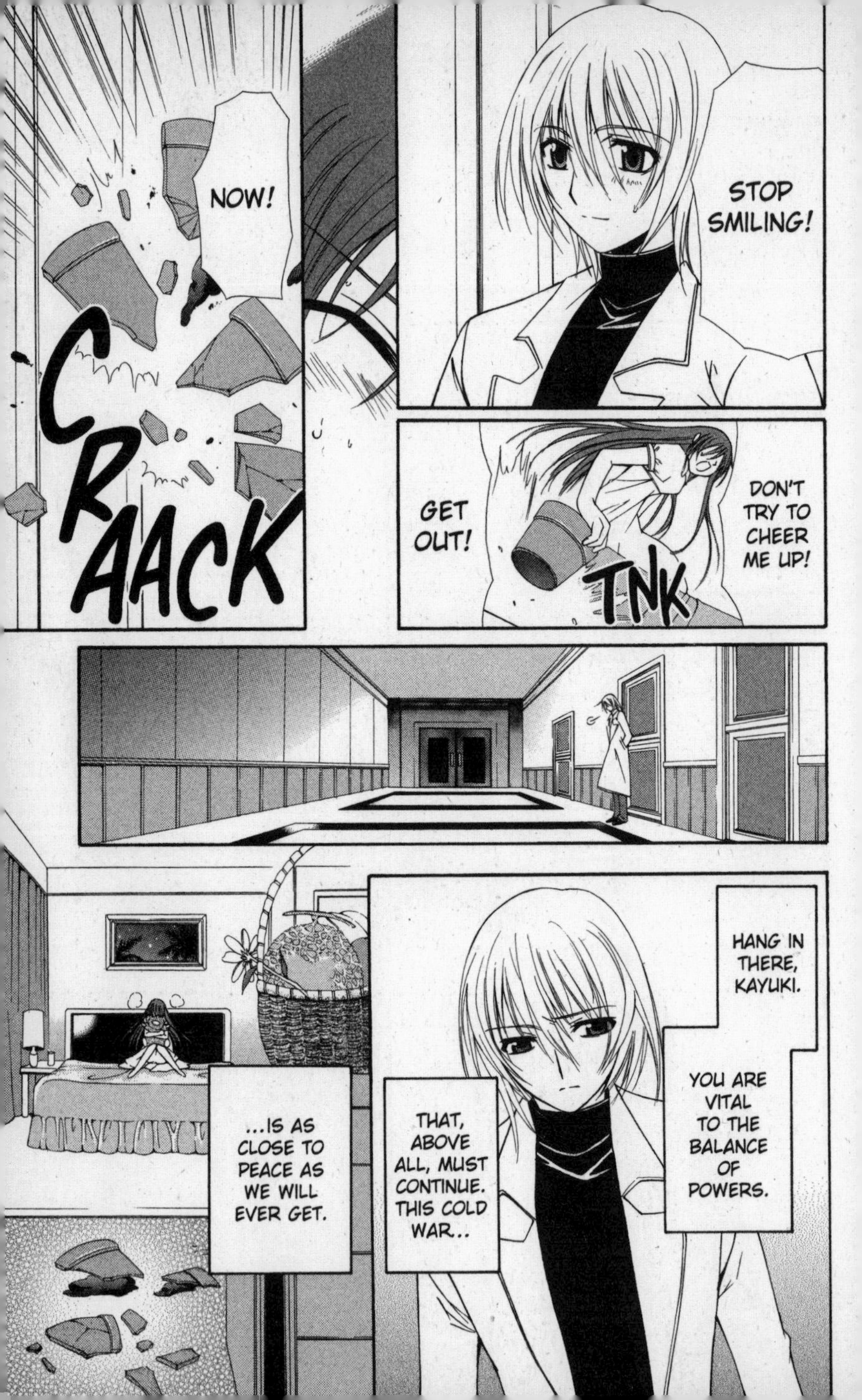
STOP SMILING!
DON'T TRY TO CHEER ME UP!
GET OUT!
TNK
NOW!
CRAACK
HANG IN THERE, KAYUKI.
YOU ARE VITAL TO THE BALANCE OF POWERS.
THAT, ABOVE ALL, MUST CONTINUE. THIS COLD WAR...
...IS AS CLOSE TO PEACE AS WE WILL EVER GET.

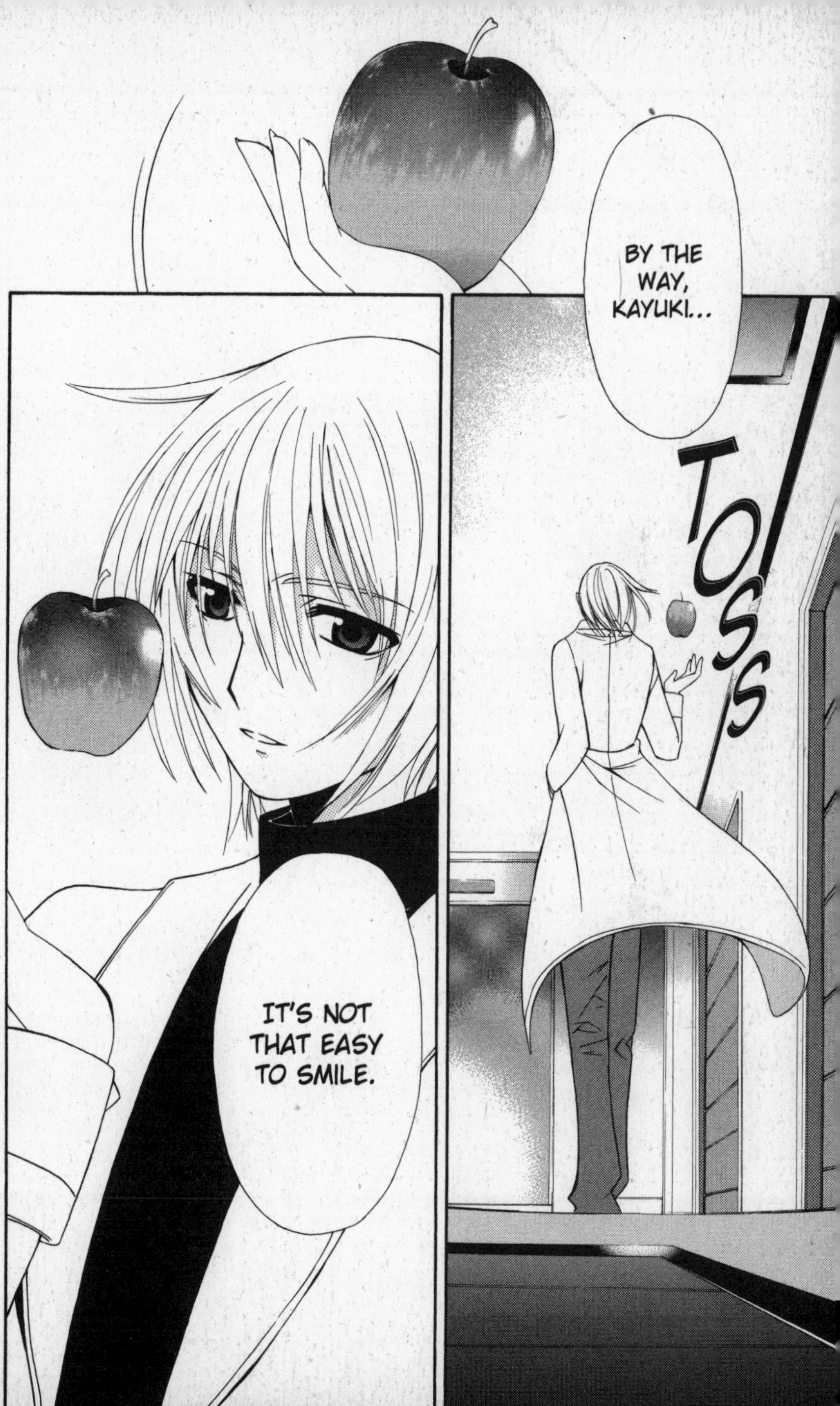
BY THE WAY, KAYUKI...
TOSS
IT'S NOT THAT EASY TO SMILE.

THE RECORD OF A

FALLEN VAMPIRE

THE RECORD OF A

FALLEN VAMPIRE

Chapter 33: Whose Hands Are Soaked in Blood?

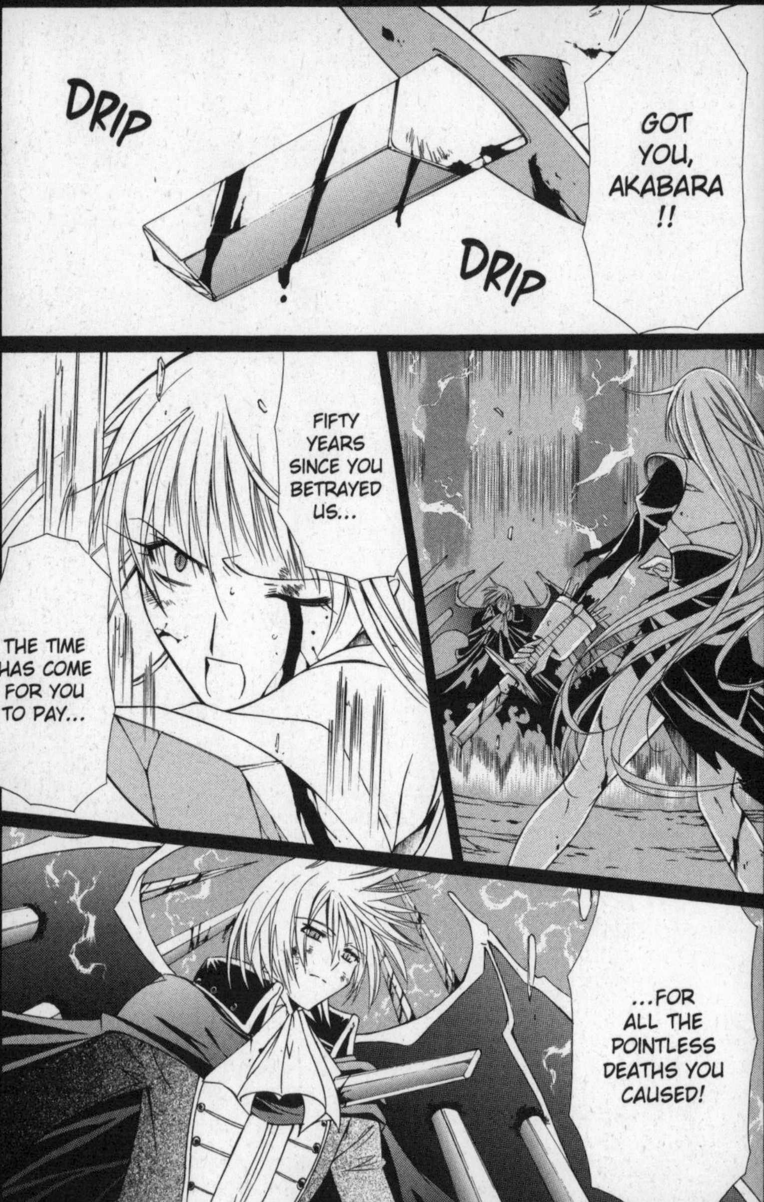
GOT YOU, AKABARA !!
DRIP
DRIP
FIFTY YEARS SINCE YOU BETRAYED US...
THE TIME HAS COME FOR YOU TO PAY...
...FOR ALL THE POINTLESS DEATHS YOU CAUSED!

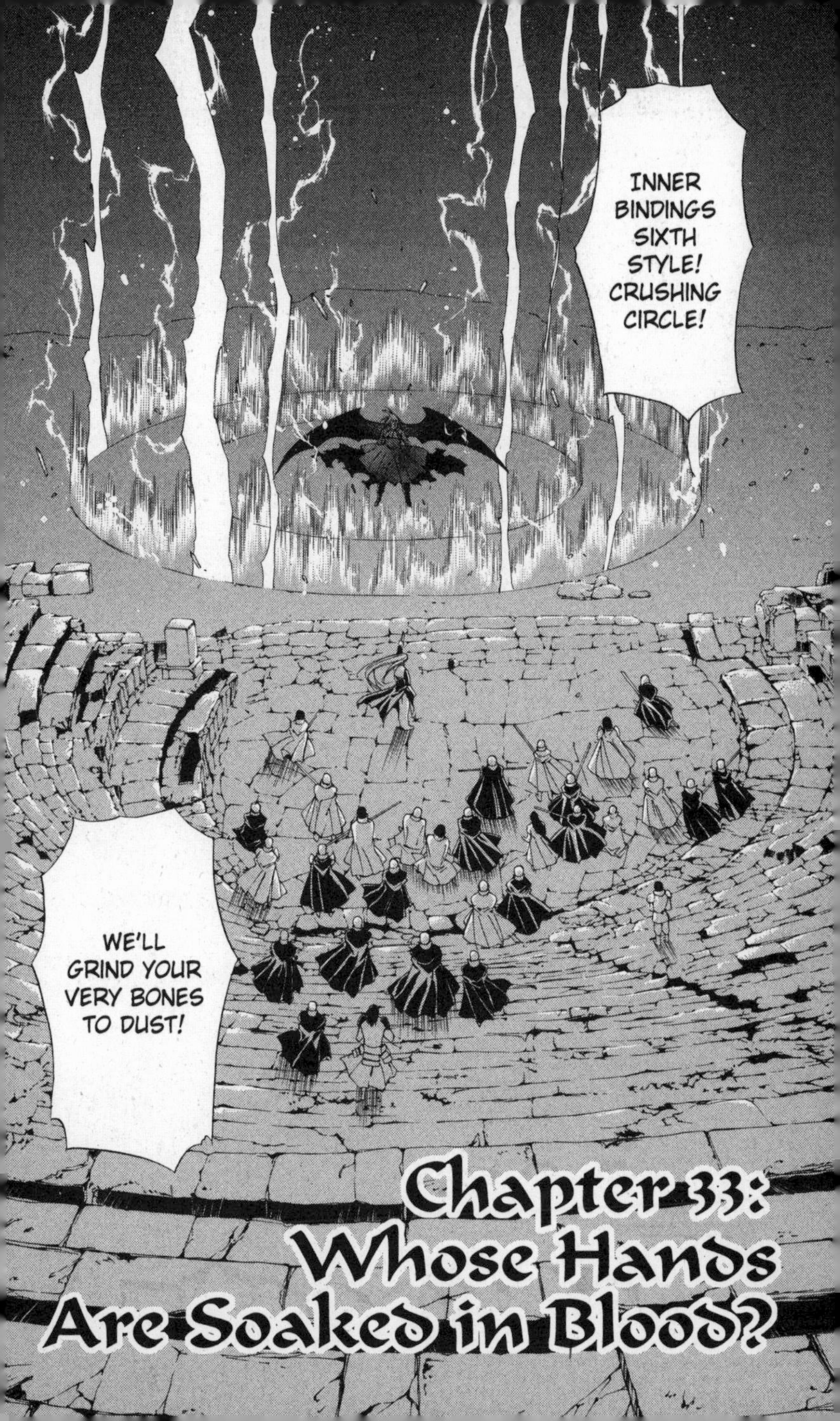
INNER BINDINGS SIXTH STYLE! CRUSHING CIRCLE!
WE'LL GRIND YOUR VERY BONES TO DUST!
Chapter 33: Whose Hands Are Soaked in Blood?

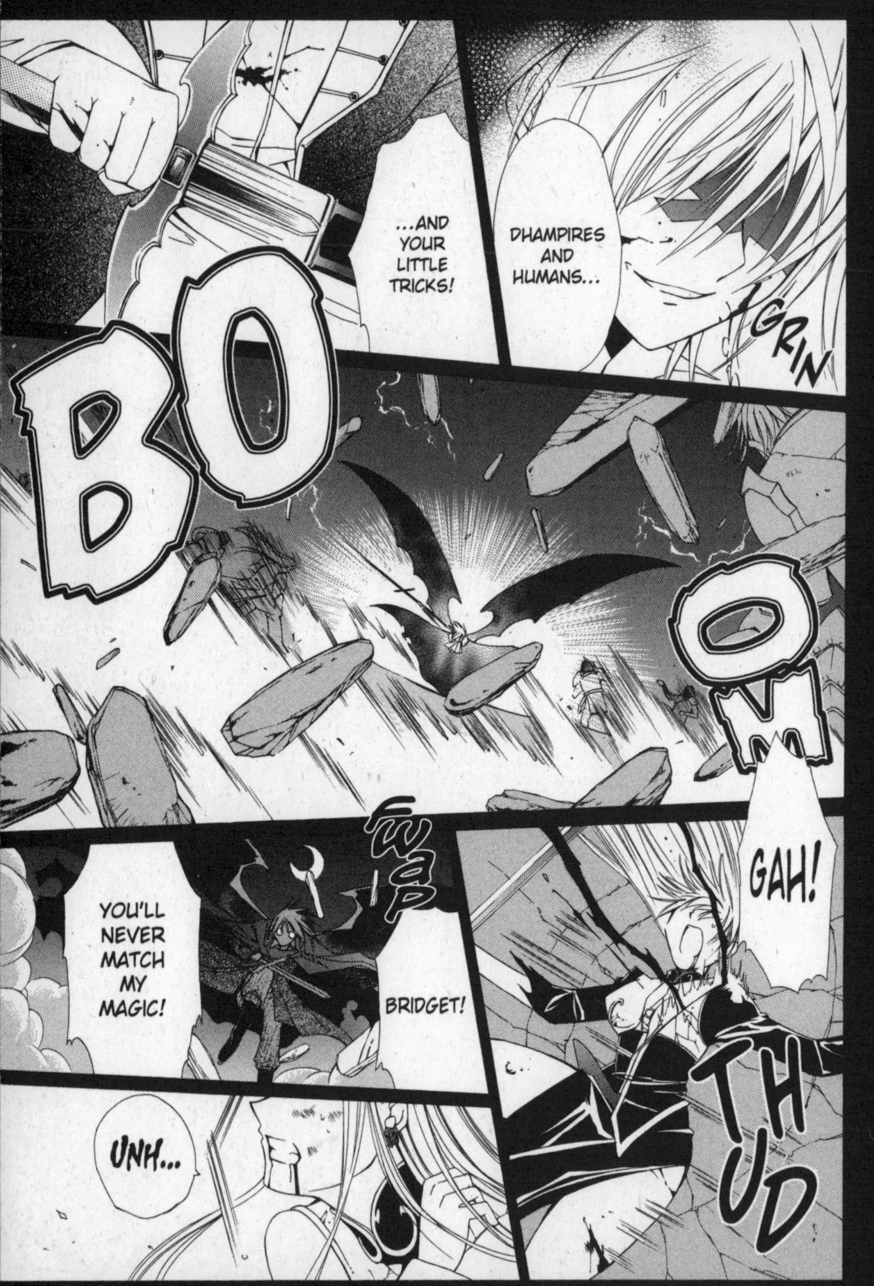
DHAMPIRES AND HUMANS...
GRIN
...AND YOUR LITTLE TRICKS!
BOOM
GAH!
THUD
fwap
BRIDGET!
YOU'LL NEVER MATCH MY MAGIC!
UNH...

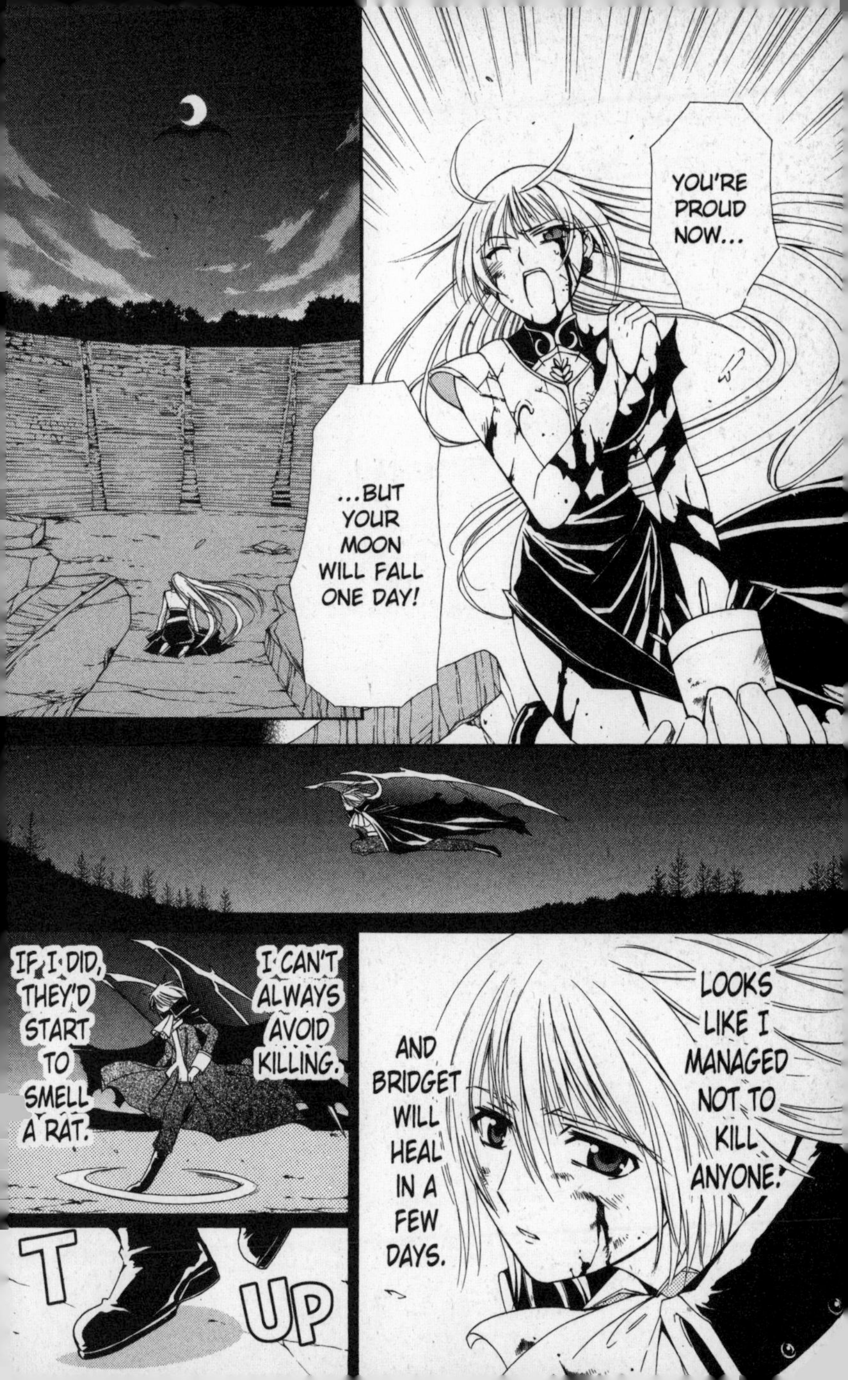
YOU'RE PROUD NOW...
...BUT YOUR MOON WILL FALL ONE DAY!
LOOKS LIKE I MANAGED NOT TO KILL ANYONE.
AND BRIDGET WILL HEAL IN A FEW DAYS.
I CAN'T ALWAYS AVOID KILLING.
IF I DID, THEY'D START TO SMELL A RAT.
T
UP

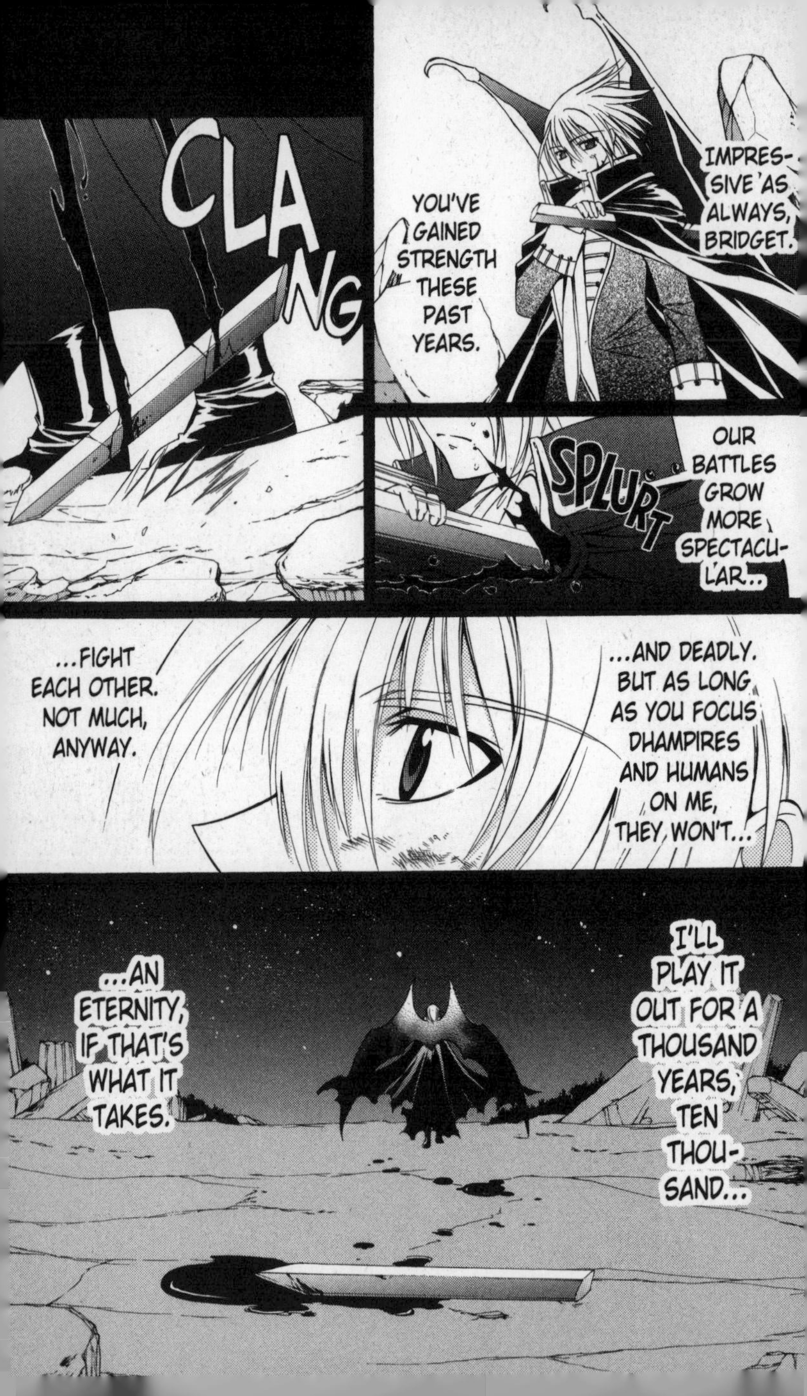
IMPRESSIVE AS ALWAYS, BRIDGET.
YOU'VE GAINED STRENGTH THESE PAST YEARS.
SPLURT
OUR BATTLES GROW MORE SPECTACULAR...
CLANG
...AND DEADLY. BUT AS LONG AS YOU FOCUS DHAMPIRES AND HUMANS ON ME, THEY WON'T...
...FIGHT EACH OTHER. NOT MUCH, ANYWAY.
I'LL PLAY IT OUT FOR A THOUSAND YEARS, TEN THOUSAND...
...AN ETERNITY, IF THAT'S WHAT IT TAKES.

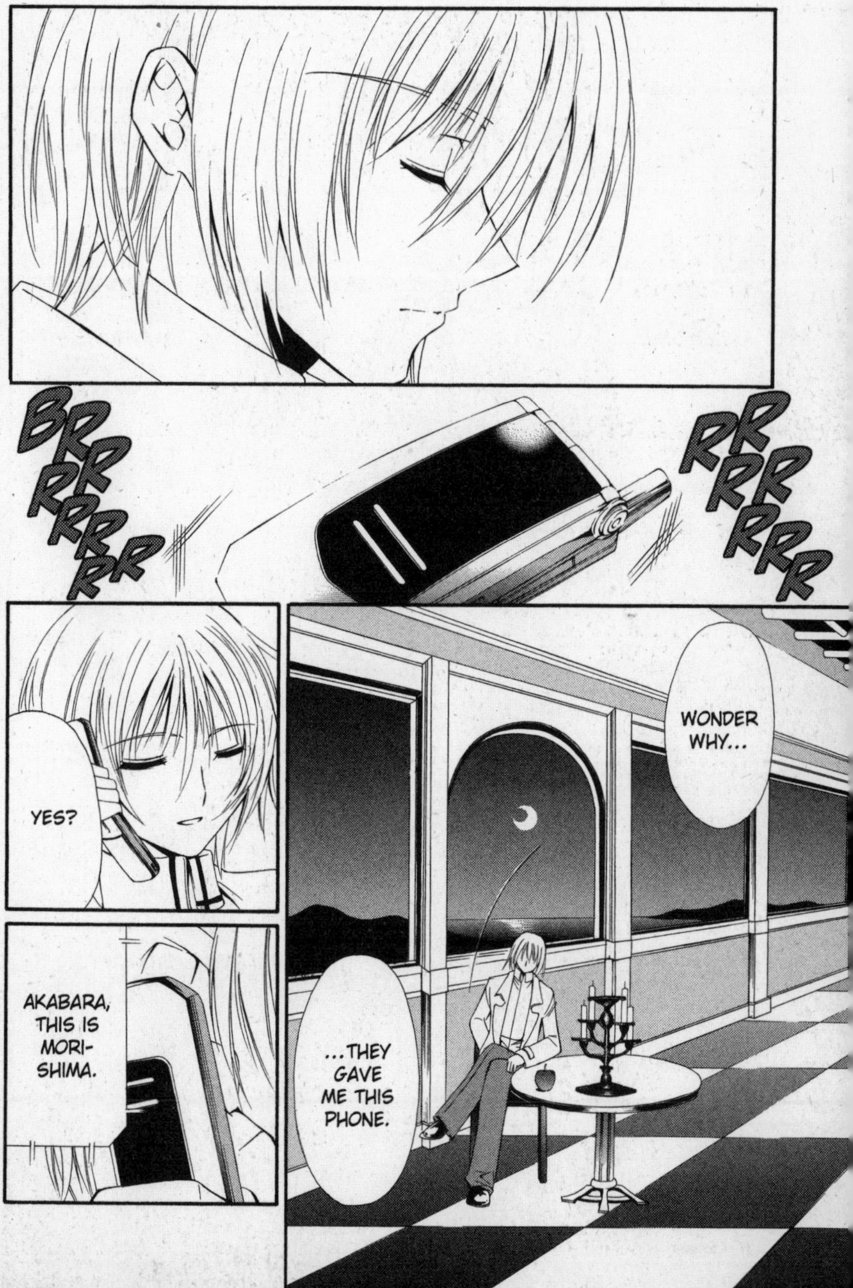
BRRRRRRR
RRRRRRRR
WONDER WHY...
...THEY GAVE ME THIS PHONE.
YES?
AKABARA, THIS IS MORI-SHIMA.

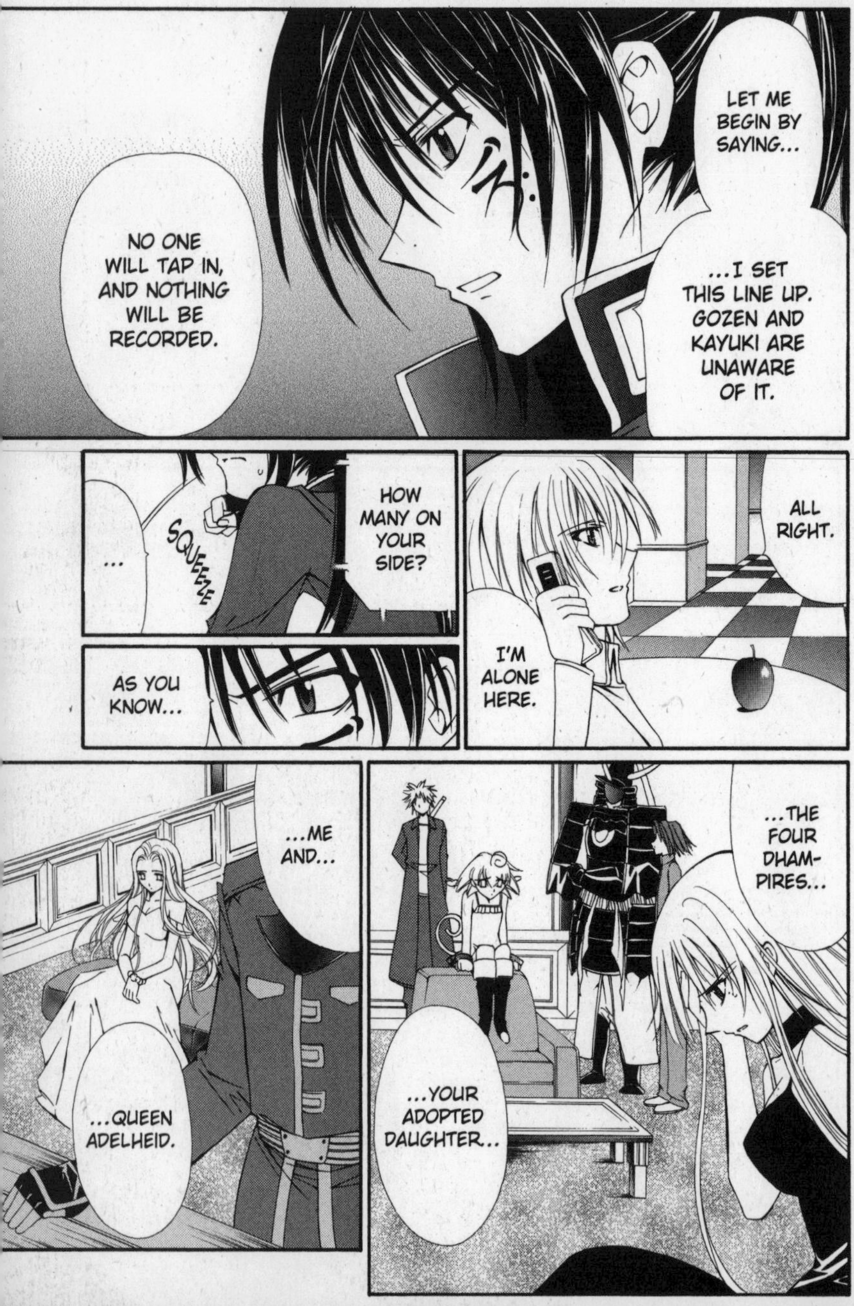
LET ME BEGIN BY SAYING...
...I SET THIS LINE UP. GOZEN AND KAYUKI ARE UNAWARE OF IT.
NO ONE WILL TAP IN, AND NOTHING WILL BE RECORDED.
ALL RIGHT.
I'M ALONE HERE.
HOW MANY ON YOUR SIDE?
SQUEEZE
...
AS YOU KNOW...
...THE FOUR DHAMPIRES...
...YOUR ADOPTED DAUGHTER...
...ME AND...
...QUEEN ADELHEID.

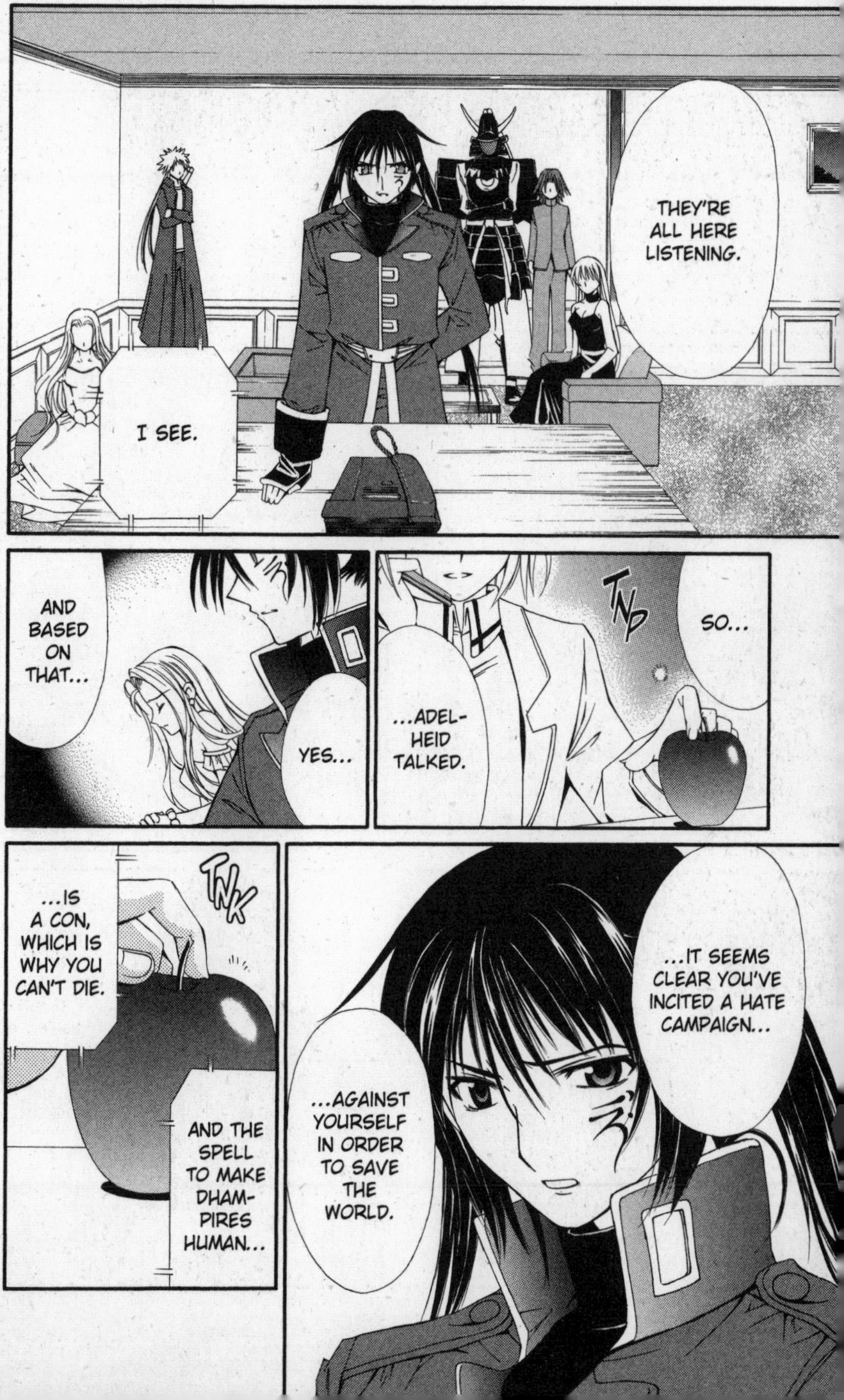
THEY'RE ALL HERE LISTENING.
I SEE.
TNP
SO...
...ADEL-HEID TALKED.
YES...
AND BASED ON THAT...
...IT SEEMS CLEAR YOU'VE INCITED A HATE CAMPAIGN...
...AGAINST YOURSELF IN ORDER TO SAVE THE WORLD.
TNK
AND THE SPELL TO MAKE DHAM-PIRES HUMAN...
...IS A CON, WHICH IS WHY YOU CAN'T DIE.

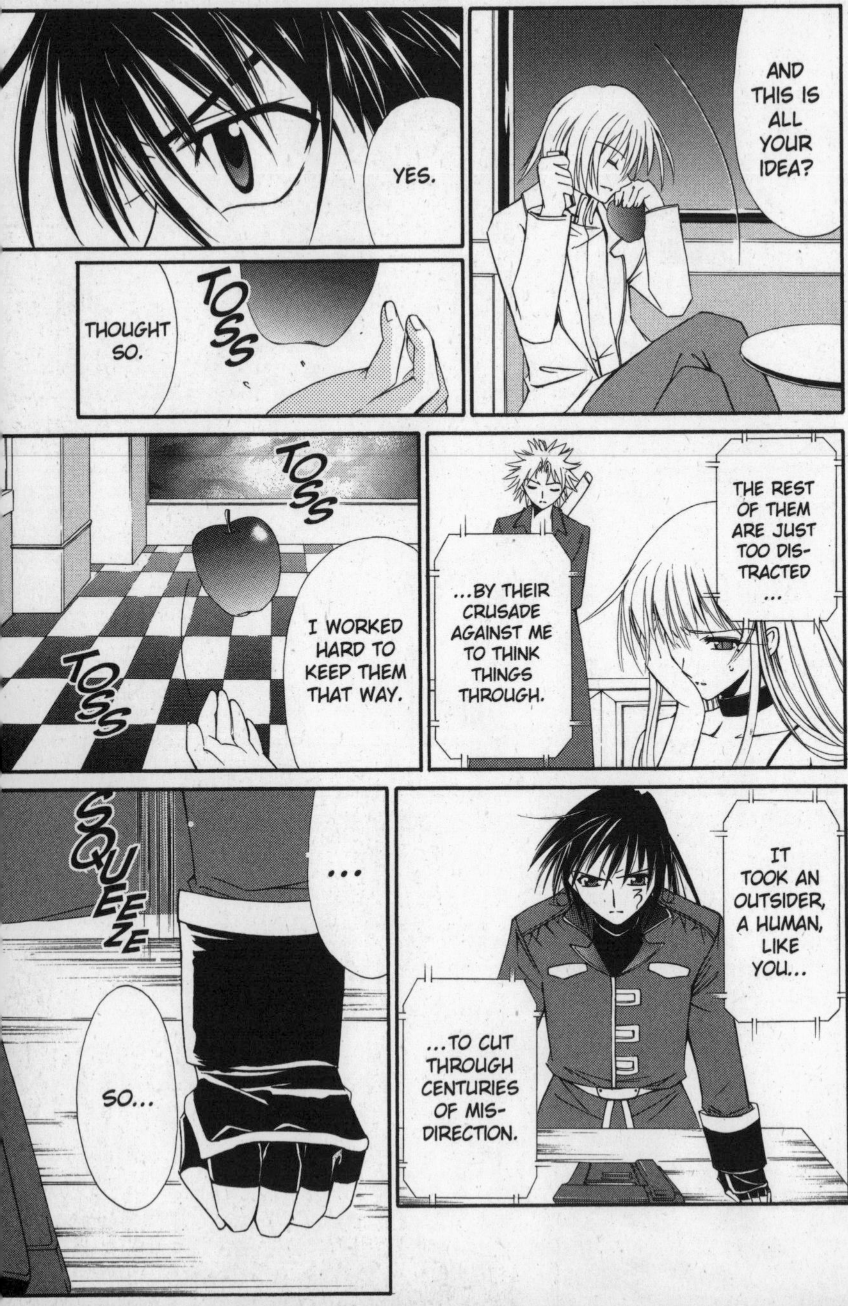
AND THIS IS ALL YOUR IDEA?
YES.
TOSS
THOUGHT SO.
THE REST OF THEM ARE JUST TOO DIS-TRACTED ...
...BY THEIR CRUSADE AGAINST ME TO THINK THINGS THROUGH.
TOSS
I WORKED HARD TO KEEP THEM THAT WAY.
TOSS
IT TOOK AN OUTSIDER, A HUMAN, LIKE YOU...
...TO CUT THROUGH CENTURIES OF MIS-DIRECTION.
SQUEEZE
...
SO...

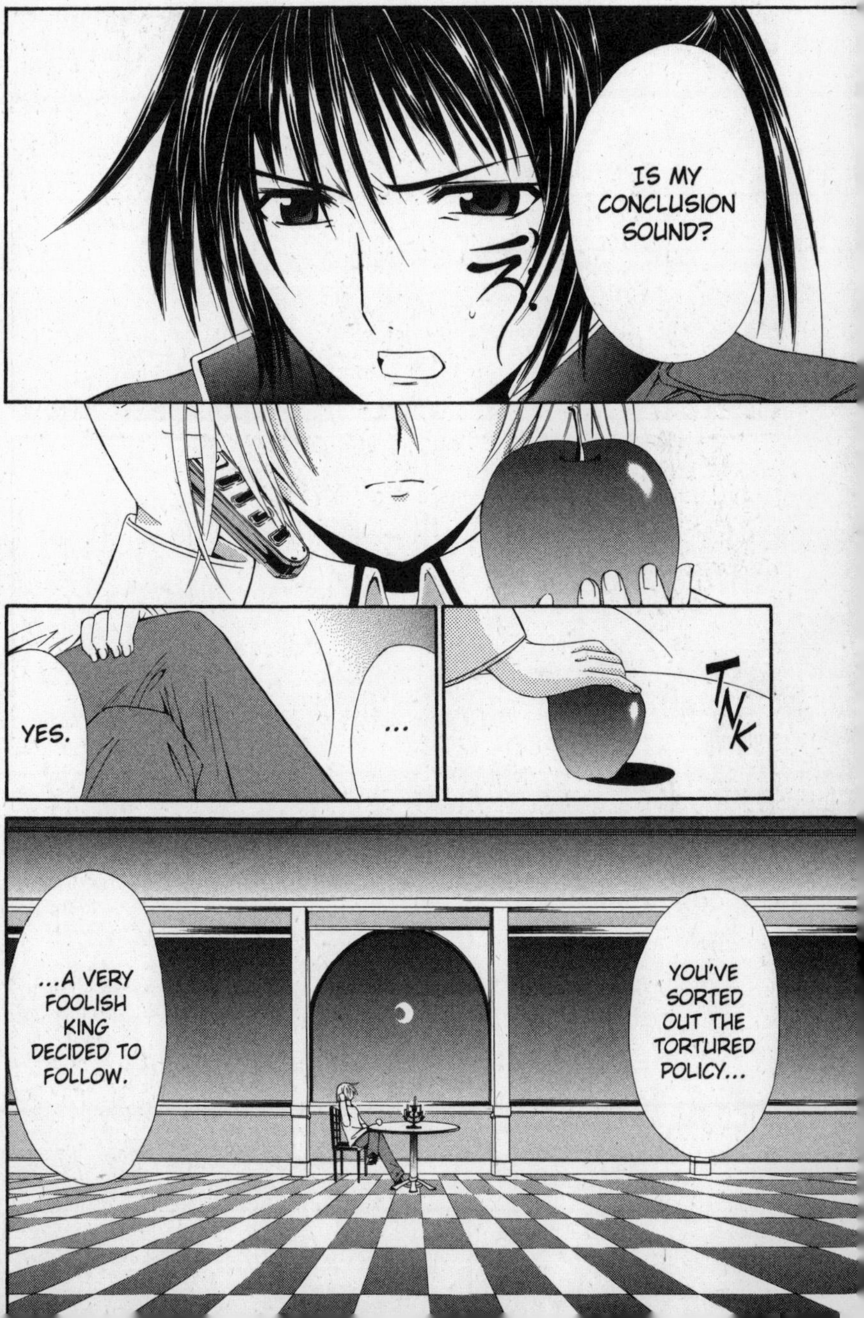
IS MY CONCLUSION SOUND?
TNK
...
YES.
YOU'VE SORTED OUT THE TORTURED POLICY...
...A VERY FOOLISH KING DECIDED TO FOLLOW.

OKAY...

GOT TO PICK MY WORDS CARE-FULLY...

I KEPT CHAOS IN CHECK...

...BUT AS A RESULT BROUGHT MANY...

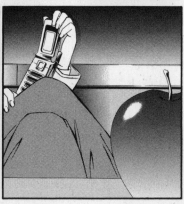

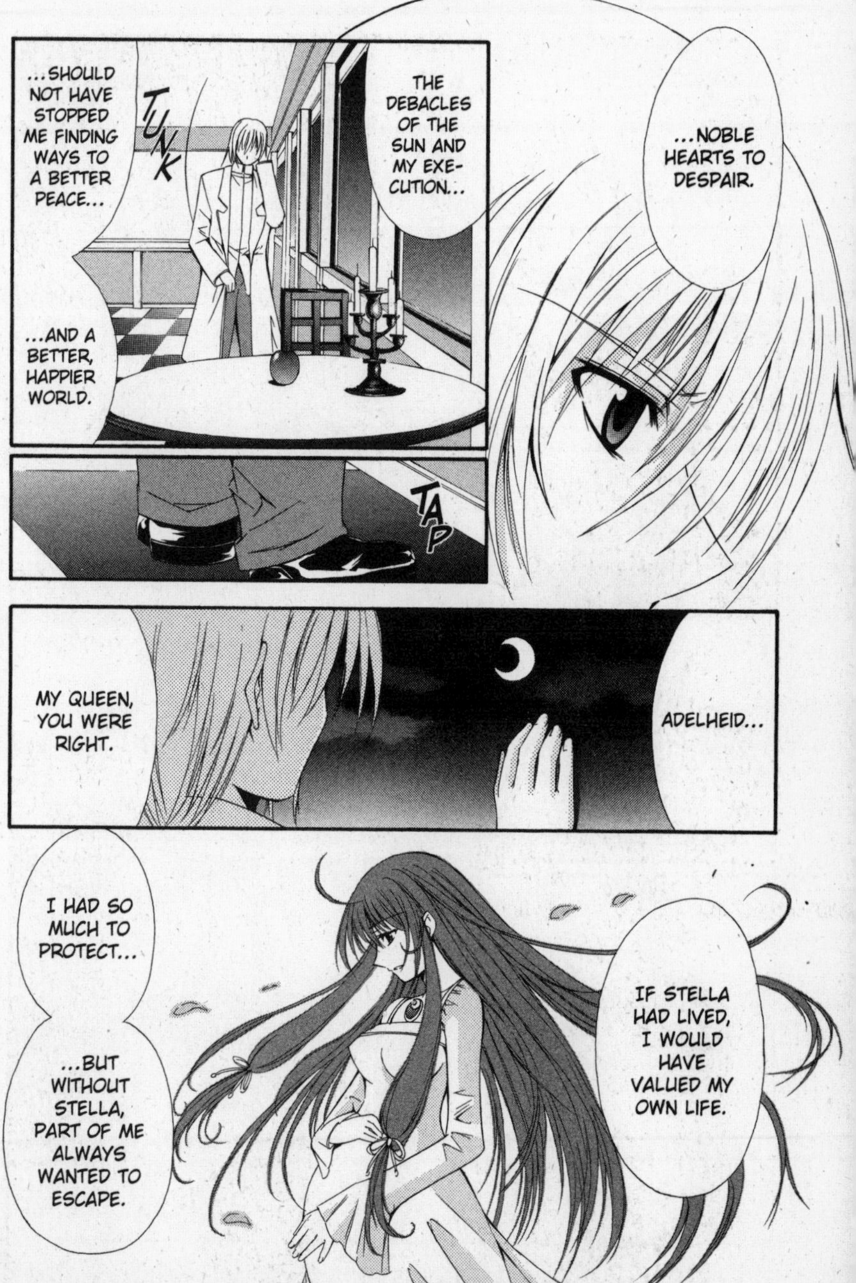
...NOBLE HEARTS TO DESPAIR.
THE DEBACLES OF THE SUN AND MY EXE-CUTION...
TUNK
...SHOULD NOT HAVE STOPPED ME FINDING WAYS TO A BETTER PEACE...
...AND A BETTER, HAPPIER WORLD.
TAP
ADELHEID...
MY QUEEN, YOU WERE RIGHT.
IF STELLA HAD LIVED, I WOULD HAVE VALUED MY OWN LIFE.
I HAD SO MUCH TO PROTECT...
...BUT WITHOUT STELLA, PART OF ME ALWAYS WANTED TO ESCAPE.

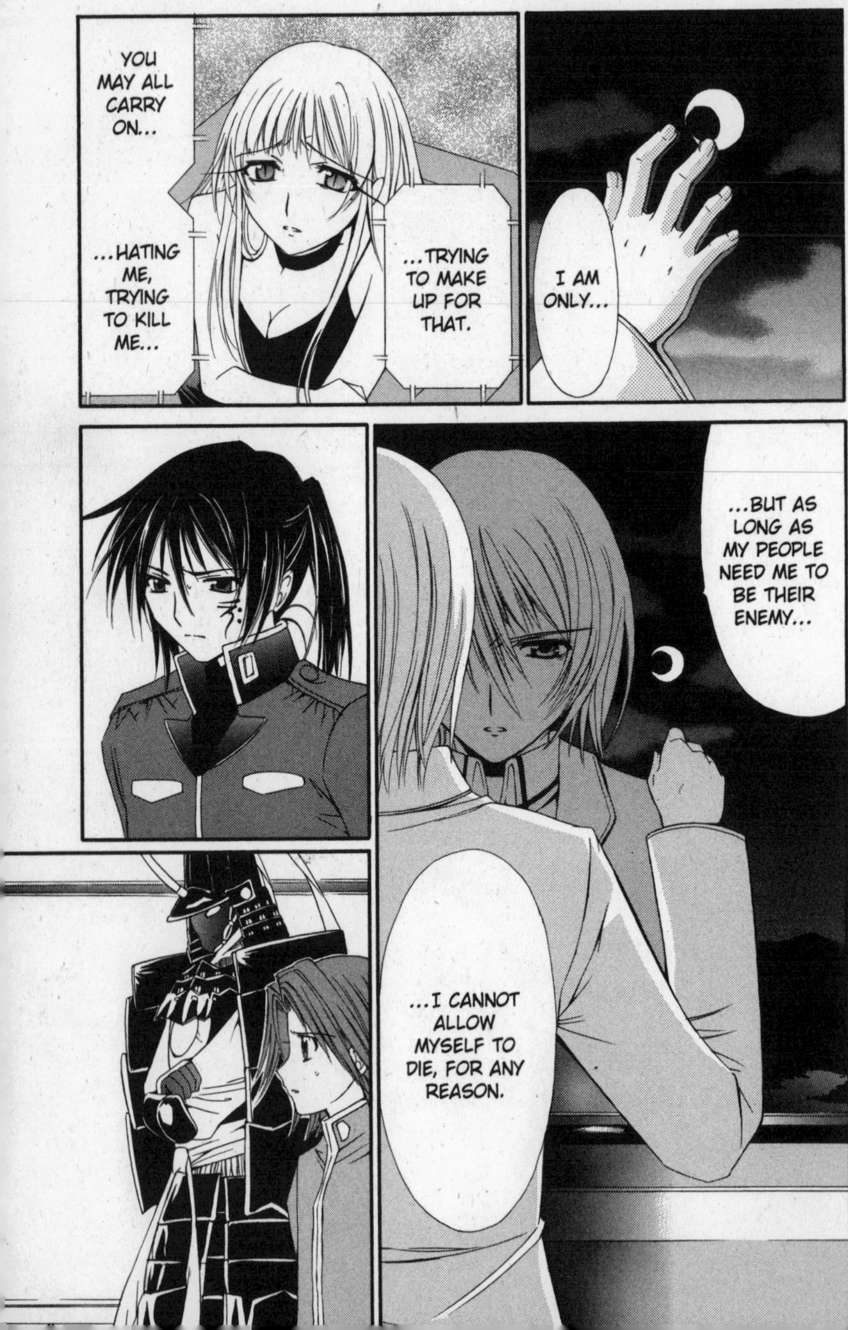
I AM ONLY...
...TRYING TO MAKE UP FOR THAT.
YOU MAY ALL CARRY ON...
...HATING ME, TRYING TO KILL ME...
...BUT AS LONG AS MY PEOPLE NEED ME TO BE THEIR ENEMY...
...I CANNOT ALLOW MYSELF TO DIE, FOR ANY REASON.

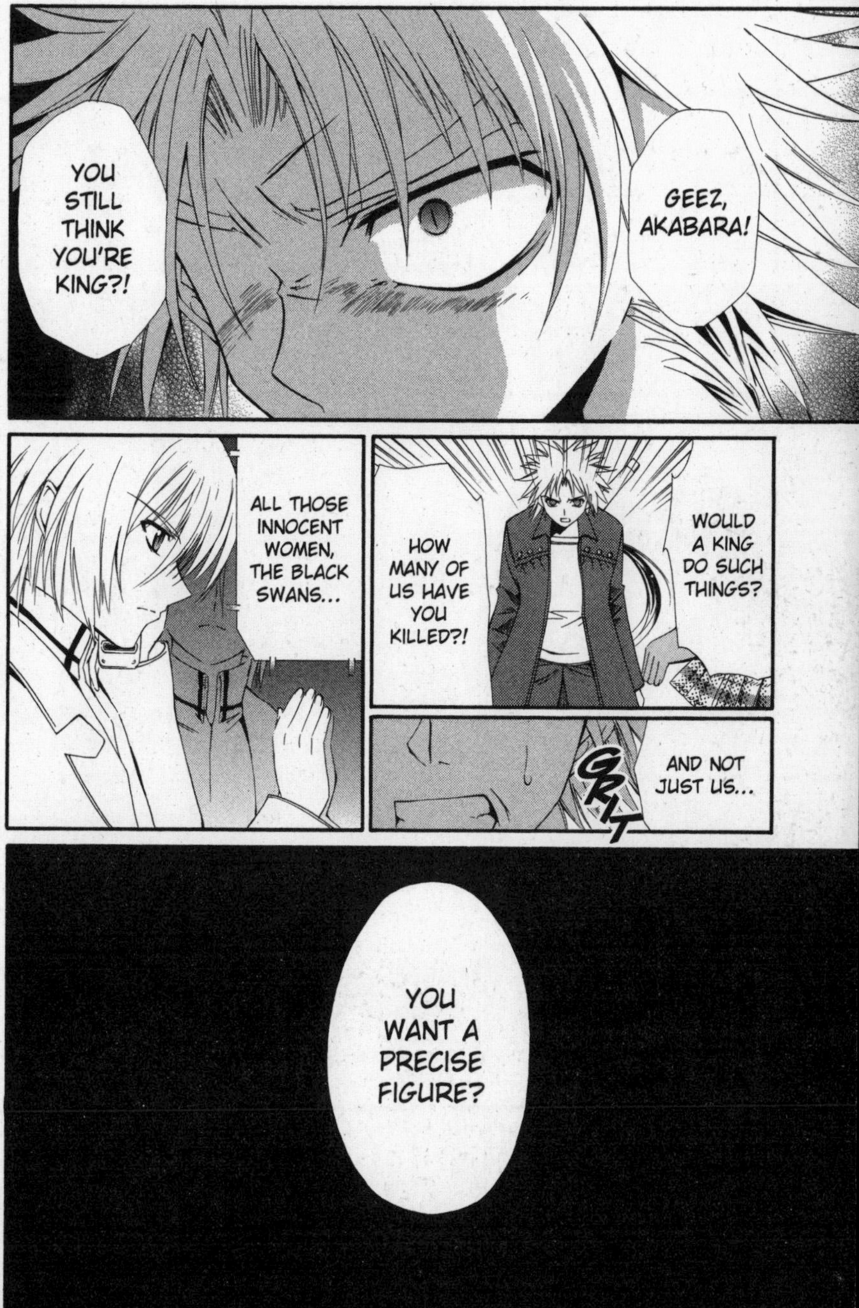
GEEZ, AKABARA!
YOU STILL THINK YOU'RE KING?!
WOULD A KING DO SUCH THINGS?
HOW MANY OF US HAVE YOU KILLED?!
AND NOT JUST US...
GRIT
ALL THOSE INNOCENT WOMEN, THE BLACK SWANS...
YOU WANT A PRECISE FIGURE?

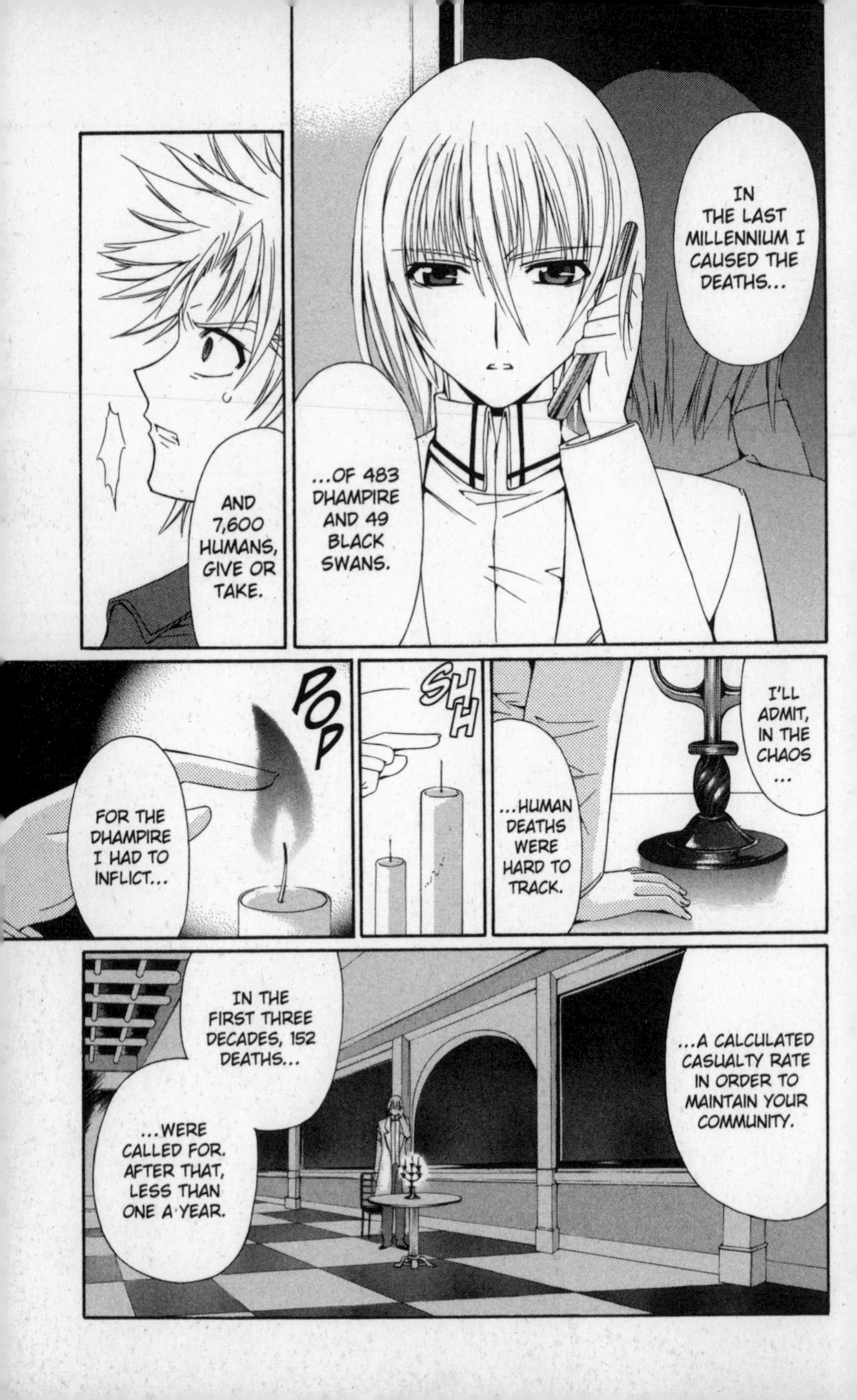
IN THE LAST MILLENNIUM I CAUSED THE DEATHS...
...OF 483 DHAMPIRE AND 49 BLACK SWANS.
AND 7,600 HUMANS, GIVE OR TAKE.
I'LL ADMIT, IN THE CHAOS...
...HUMAN DEATHS WERE HARD TO TRACK.
SHH
POP
FOR THE DHAMPIRE I HAD TO INFLICT...
...A CALCULATED CASUALTY RATE IN ORDER TO MAINTAIN YOUR COMMUNITY.
IN THE FIRST THREE DECADES, 152 DEATHS...
...WERE CALLED FOR. AFTER THAT, LESS THAN ONE A YEAR.

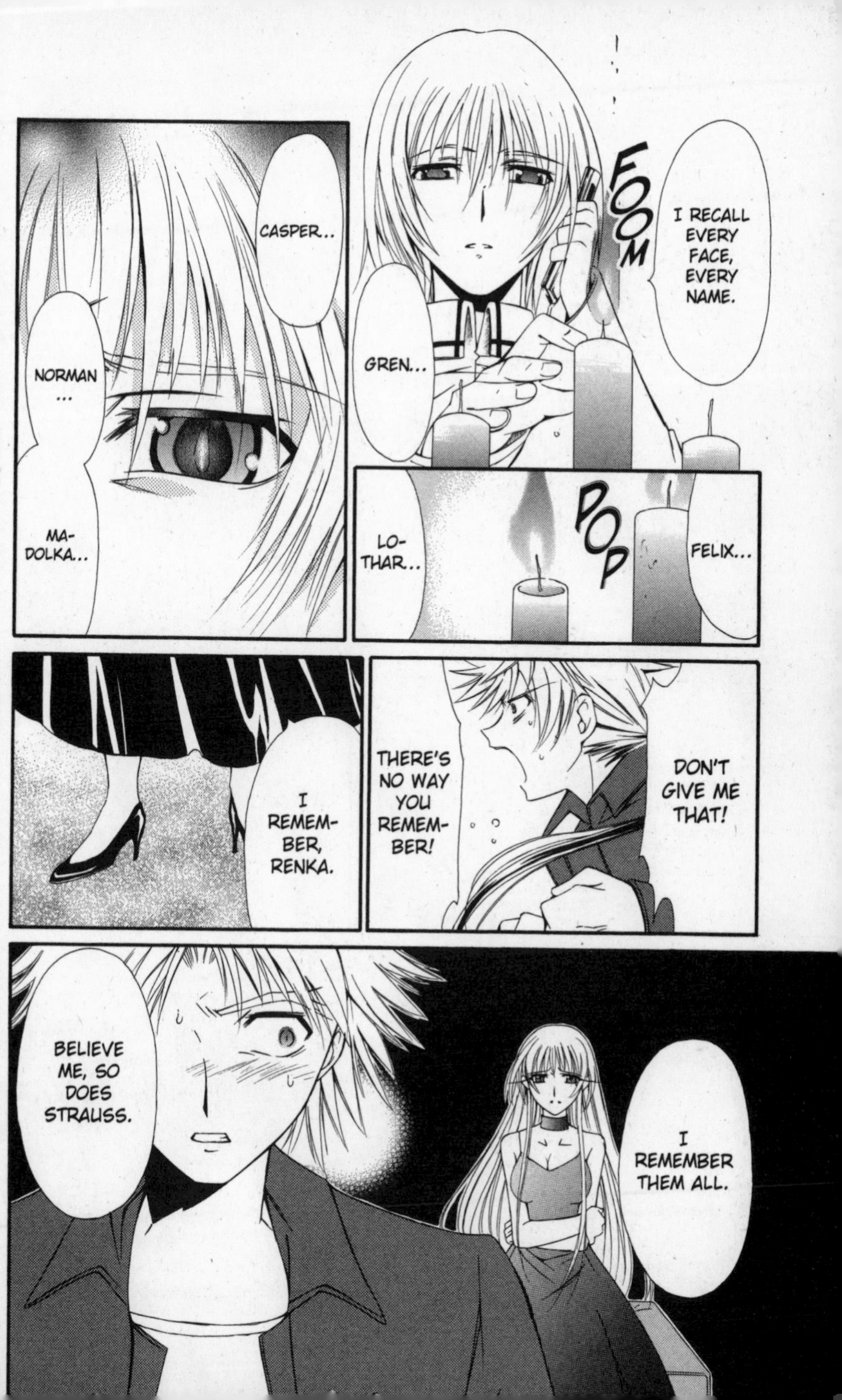
I RECALL EVERY FACE, EVERY NAME.
FOOM
GREN...
FELIX...
POP
LO-THAR...
CASPER...
NORMAN...
MA-DOLKA...
DON'T GIVE ME THAT!
THERE'S NO WAY YOU REMEMBER!
I REMEMBER, RENKA.
I REMEMBER THEM ALL.
BELIEVE ME, SO DOES STRAUSS.

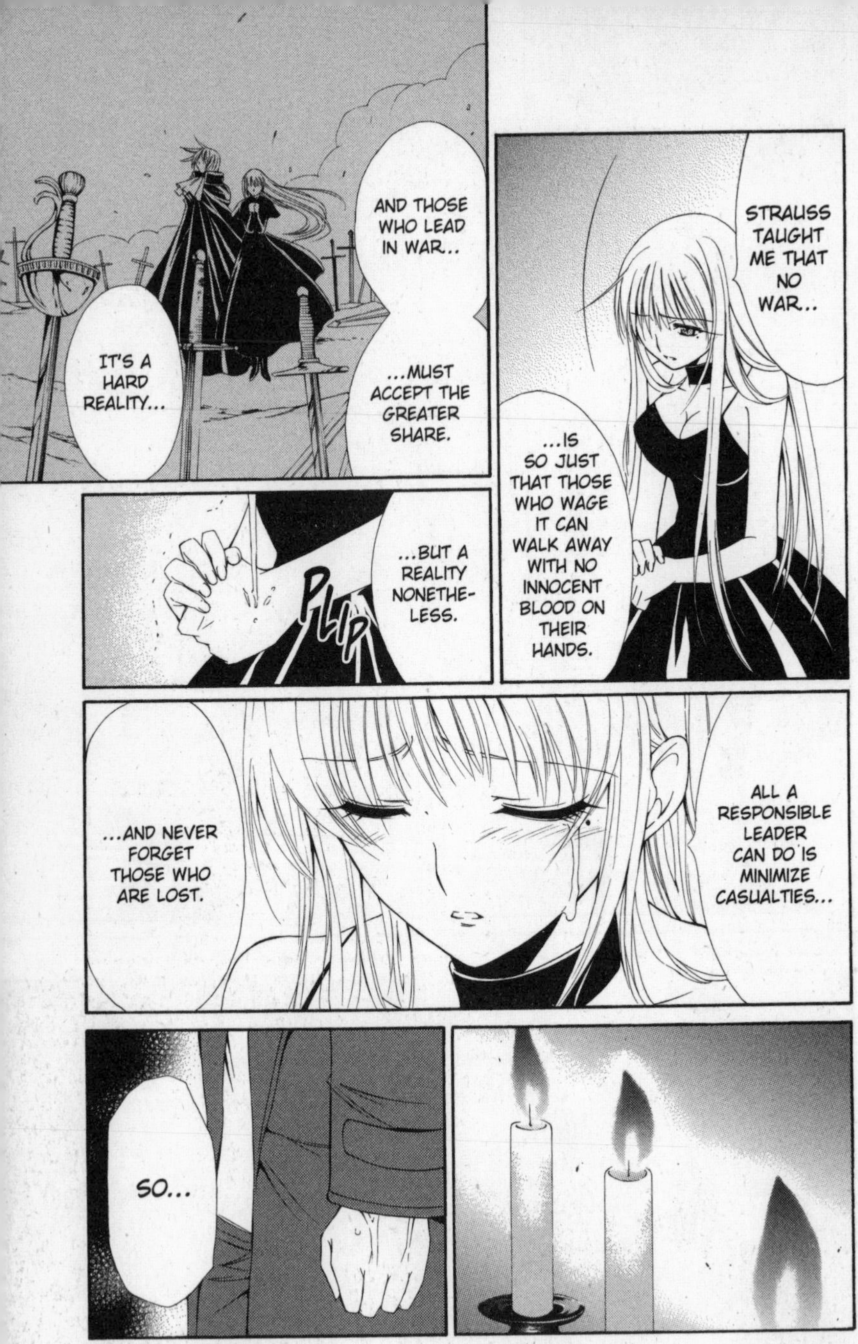
STRAUSS TAUGHT ME THAT NO WAR...
...IS SO JUST THAT THOSE WHO WAGE IT CAN WALK AWAY WITH NO INNOCENT BLOOD ON THEIR HANDS.
AND THOSE WHO LEAD IN WAR...
...MUST ACCEPT THE GREATER SHARE.
IT'S A HARD REALITY...
...BUT A REALITY NONETHELESS.
PLIP
ALL A RESPONSIBLE LEADER CAN DO IS MINIMIZE CASUALTIES...
...AND NEVER FORGET THOSE WHO ARE LOST.
SO...

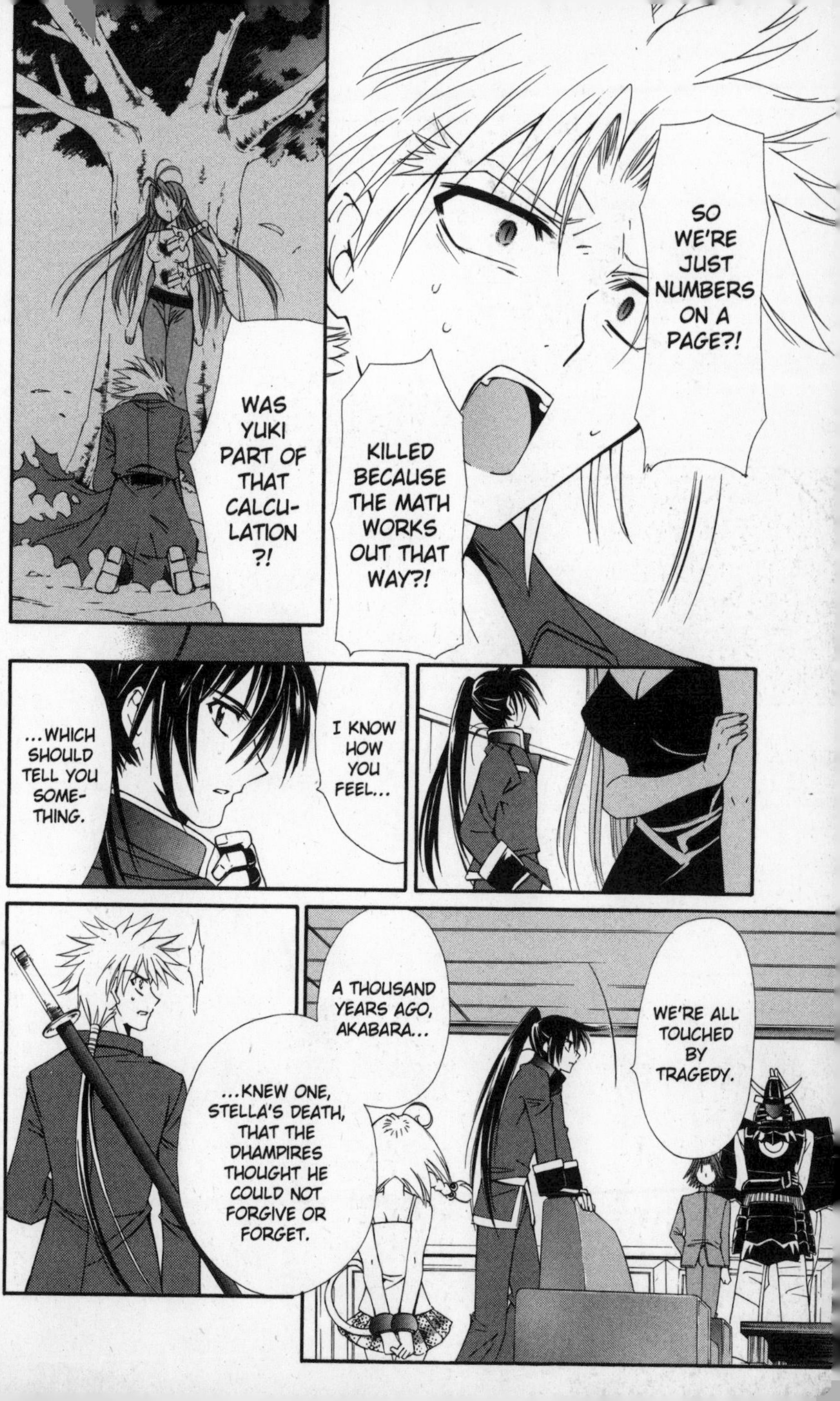
SO WE'RE JUST NUMBERS ON A PAGE?!
KILLED BECAUSE THE MATH WORKS OUT THAT WAY?!
WAS YUKI PART OF THAT CALCU-LATION?!
I KNOW HOW YOU FEEL...
...WHICH SHOULD TELL YOU SOME-THING.
WE'RE ALL TOUCHED BY TRAGEDY.
A THOUSAND YEARS AGO, AKABARA...
...KNEW ONE, STELLA'S DEATH, THAT THE DHAMPIRES THOUGHT HE COULD NOT FORGIVE OR FORGET.

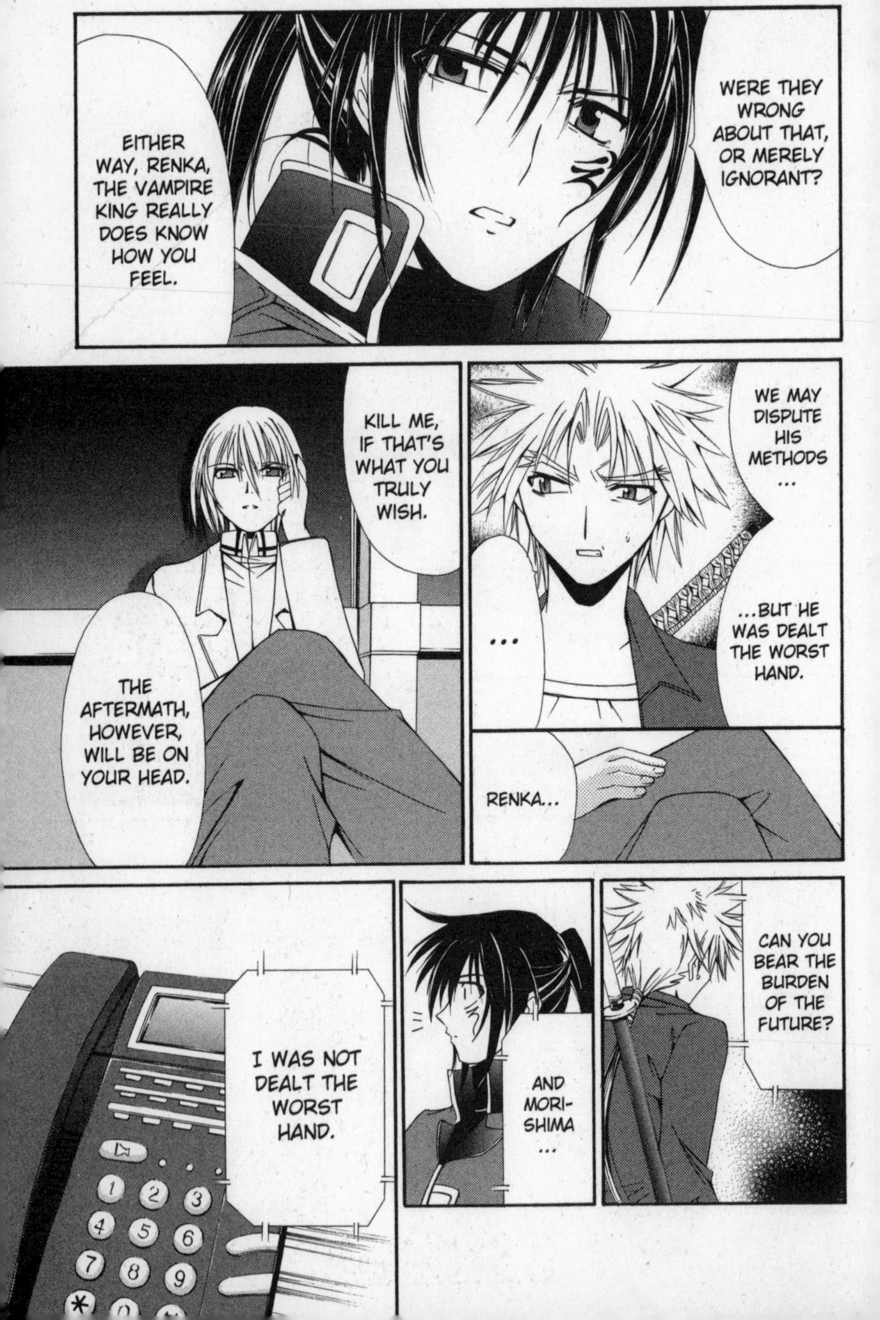
WERE THEY WRONG ABOUT THAT, OR MERELY IGNORANT?
EITHER WAY, RENKA, THE VAMPIRE KING REALLY DOES KNOW HOW YOU FEEL.
WE MAY DISPUTE HIS METHODS...
...BUT HE WAS DEALT THE WORST HAND.
...
RENKA...
KILL ME, IF THAT'S WHAT YOU TRULY WISH.
THE AFTERMATH, HOWEVER, WILL BE ON YOUR HEAD.
CAN YOU BEAR THE BURDEN OF THE FUTURE?
AND MORI-SHIMA...
I WAS NOT DEALT THE WORST HAND.

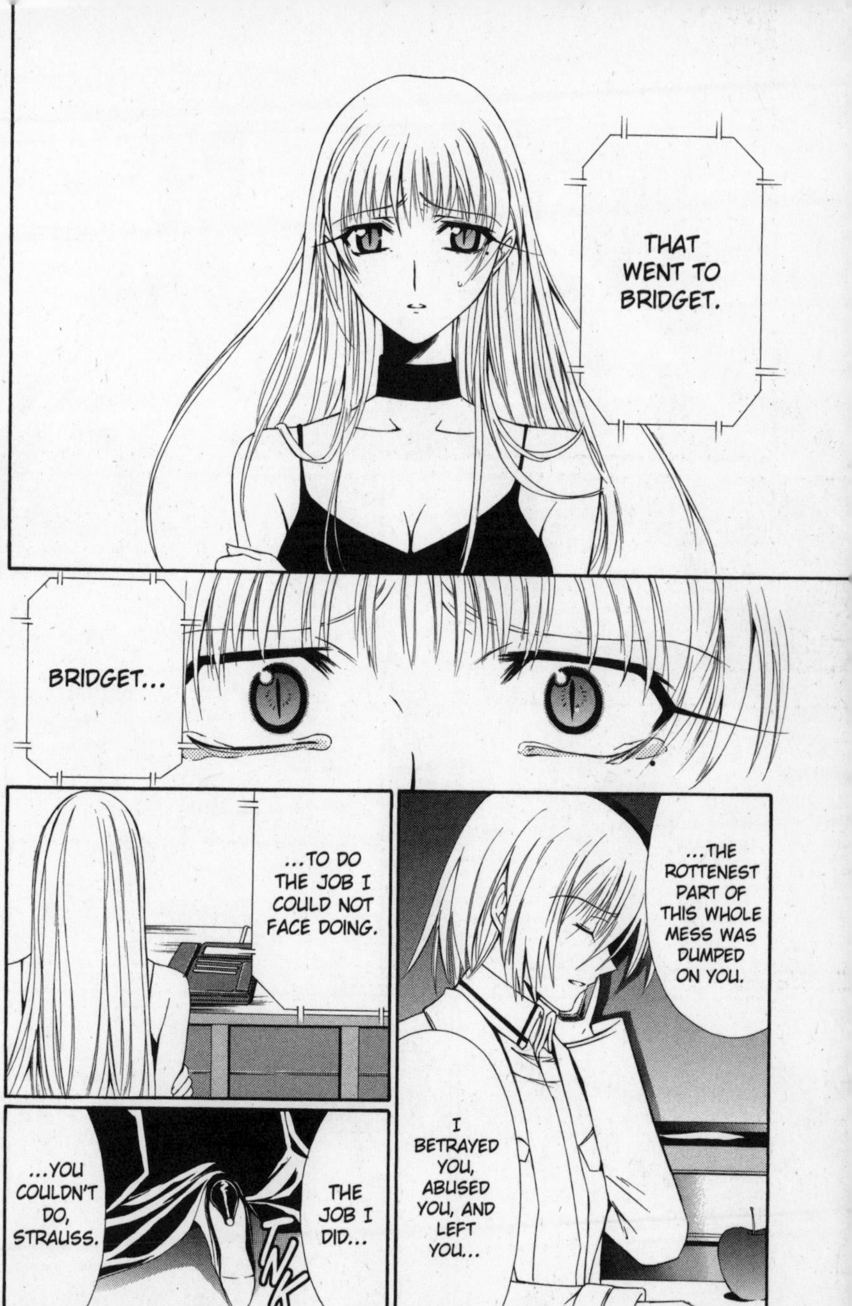
THAT WENT TO BRIDGET.
BRIDGET...
...THE ROTTENEST PART OF THIS WHOLE MESS WAS DUMPED ON YOU.
I BETRAYED YOU, ABUSED YOU, AND LEFT YOU...
...TO DO THE JOB I COULD NOT FACE DOING.
THE JOB I DID...
...YOU COULDN'T DO, STRAUSS.
TINK

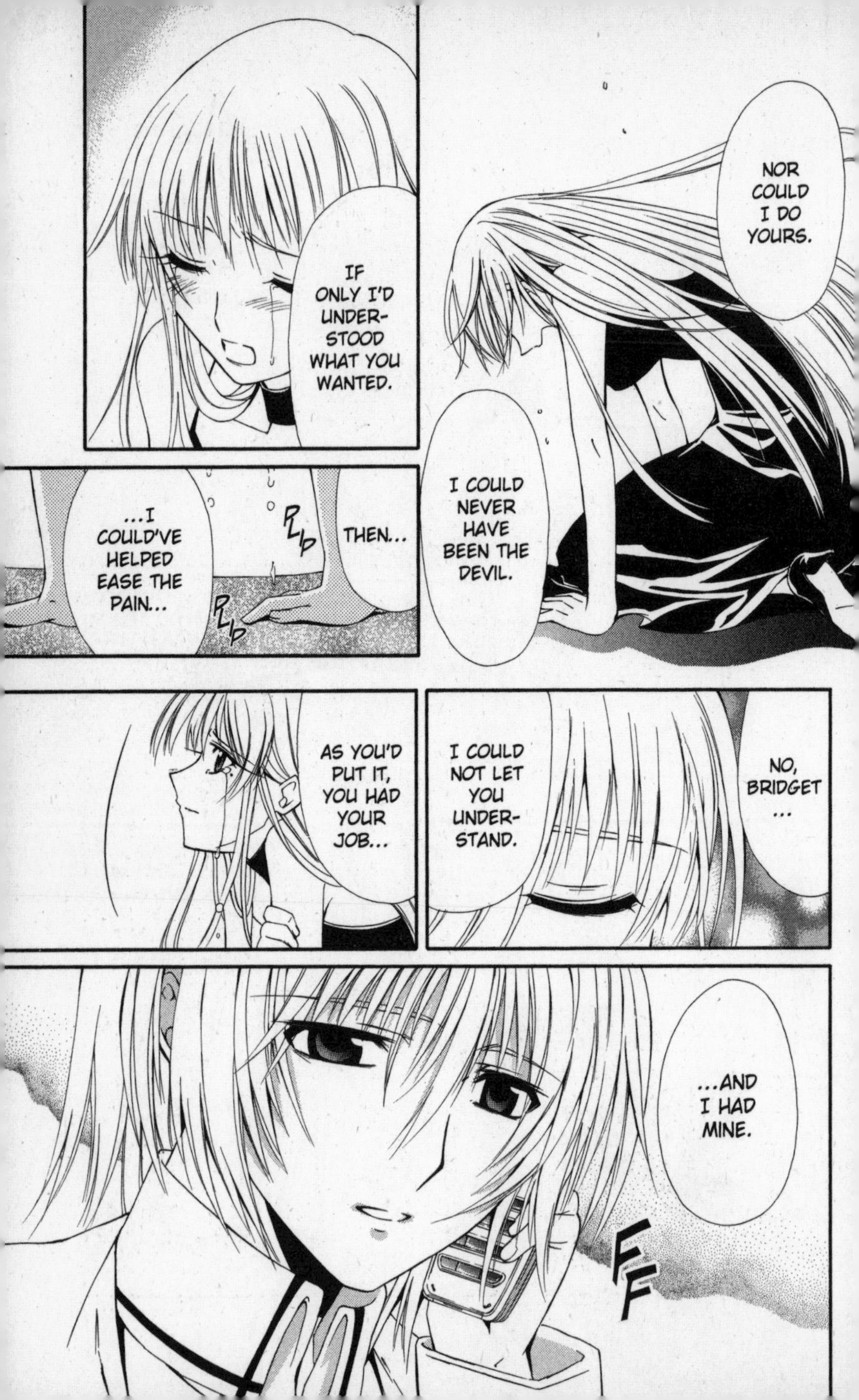
NOR COULD I DO YOURS.
I COULD NEVER HAVE BEEN THE DEVIL.
IF ONLY I'D UNDERSTOOD WHAT YOU WANTED.
THEN...
PLIP
...I COULD'VE HELPED EASE THE PAIN...
PLIP
NO, BRIDGET...
I COULD NOT LET YOU UNDERSTAND.
AS YOU'D PUT IT, YOU HAD YOUR JOB...
...AND I HAD MINE.
FF

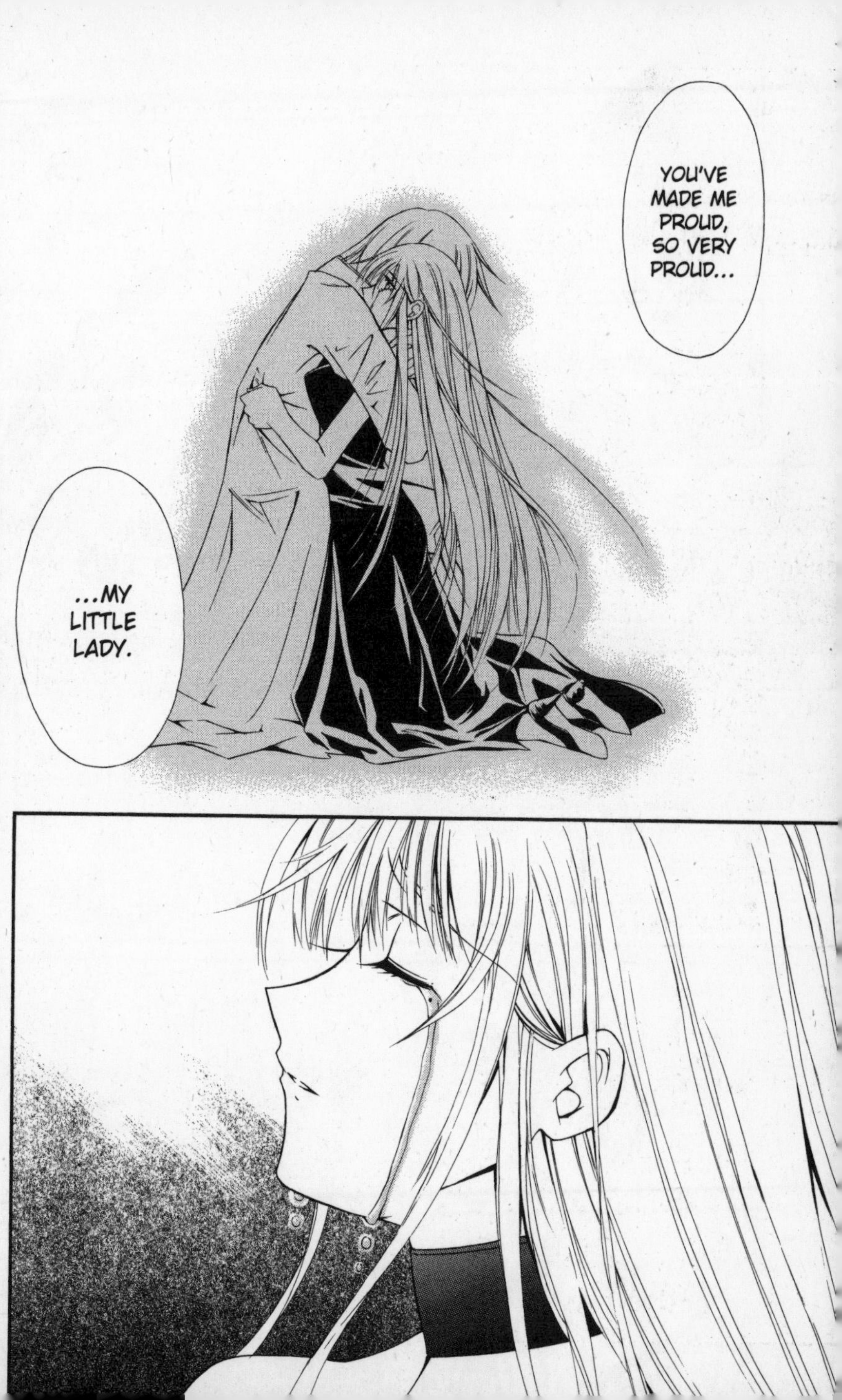
YOU'VE MADE ME PROUD, SO VERY PROUD...
...MY LITTLE LADY.

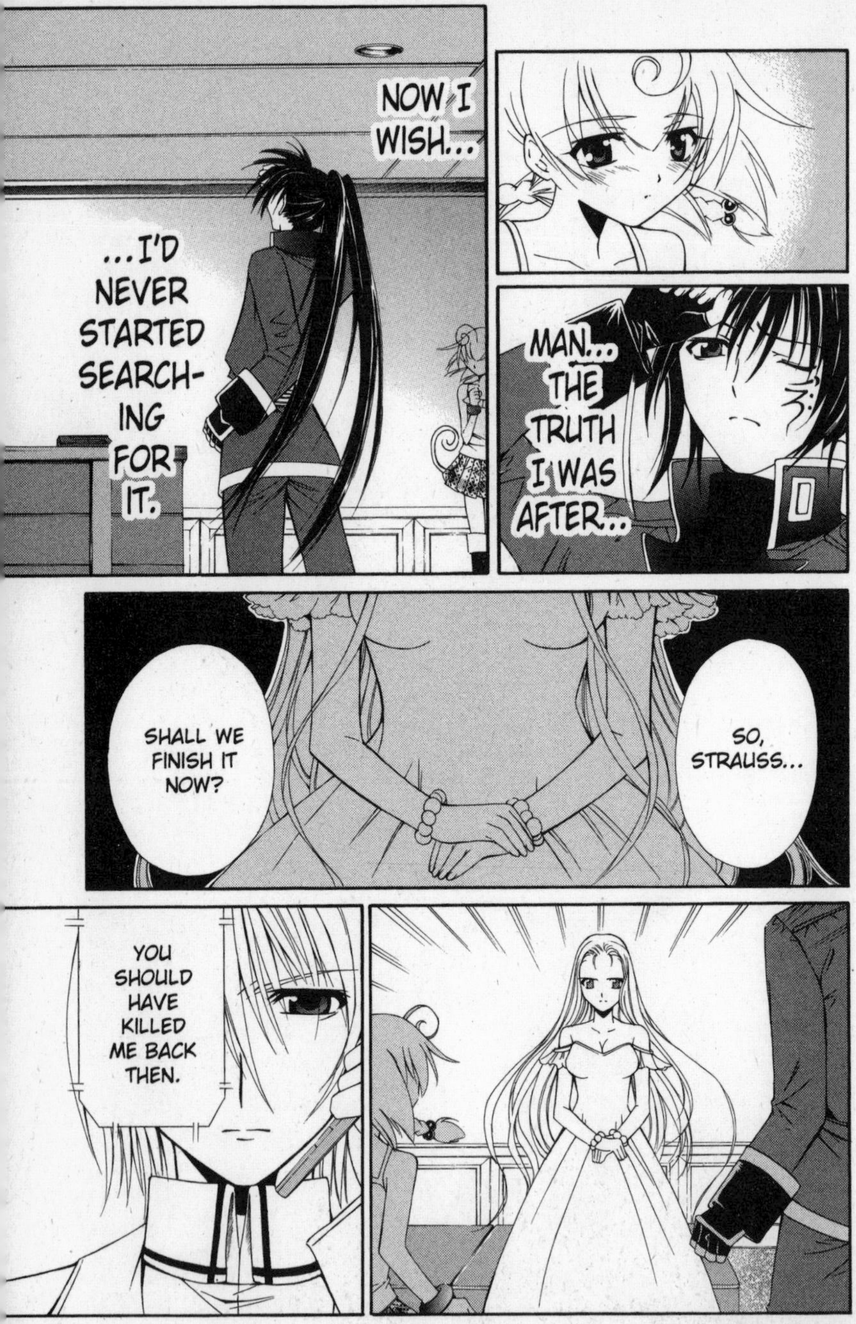
MAN... THE TRUTH I WAS AFTER...
NOW I WISH...
...I'D NEVER STARTED SEARCHING FOR IT.
SO, STRAUSS...
SHALL WE FINISH IT NOW?
YOU SHOULD HAVE KILLED ME BACK THEN.

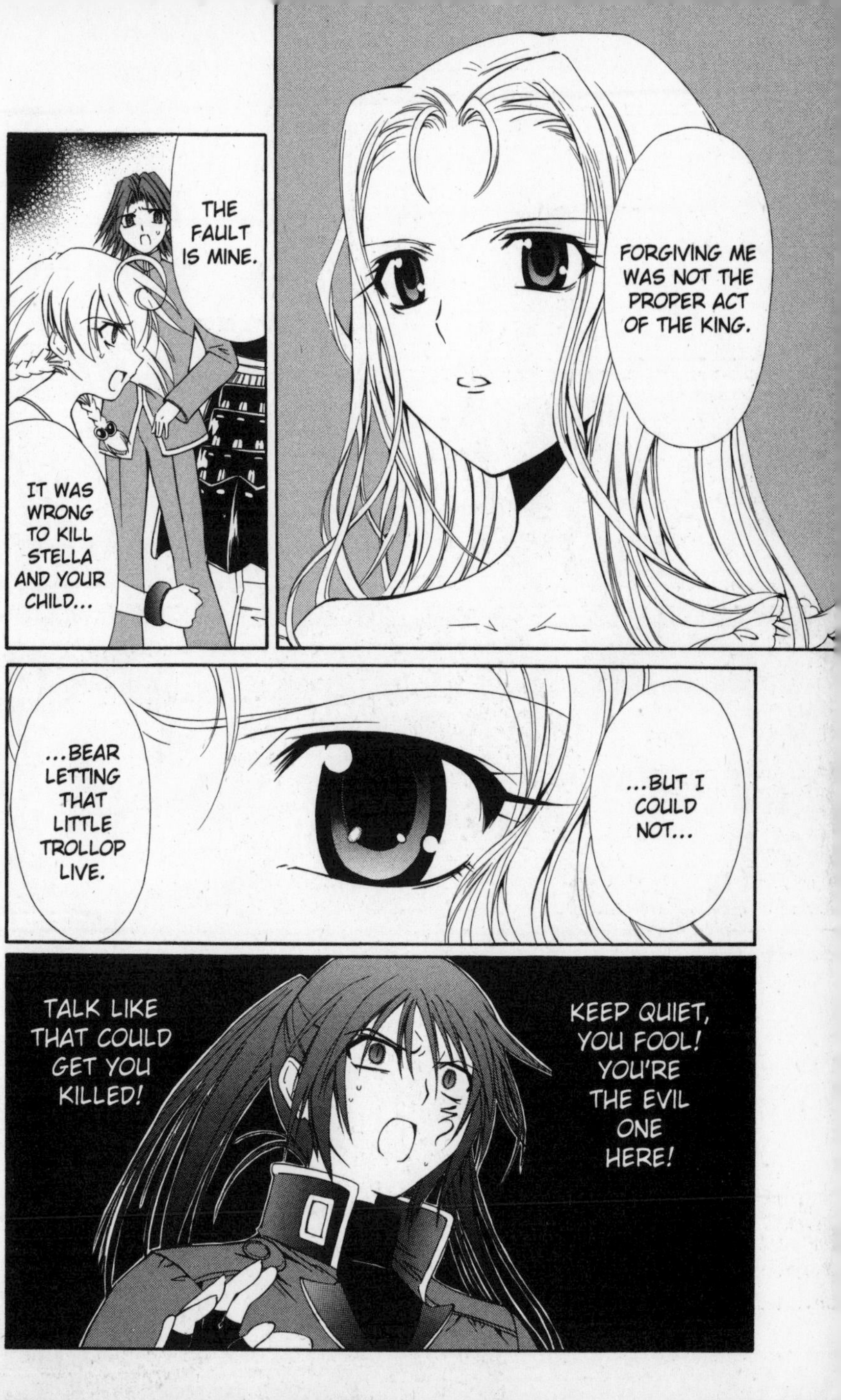
FORGIVING ME WAS NOT THE PROPER ACT OF THE KING.
THE FAULT IS MINE.
IT WAS WRONG TO KILL STELLA AND YOUR CHILD...
...BUT I COULD NOT...
...BEAR LETTING THAT LITTLE TROLLOP LIVE.
KEEP QUIET, YOU FOOL! YOU'RE THE EVIL ONE HERE!
TALK LIKE THAT COULD GET YOU KILLED!

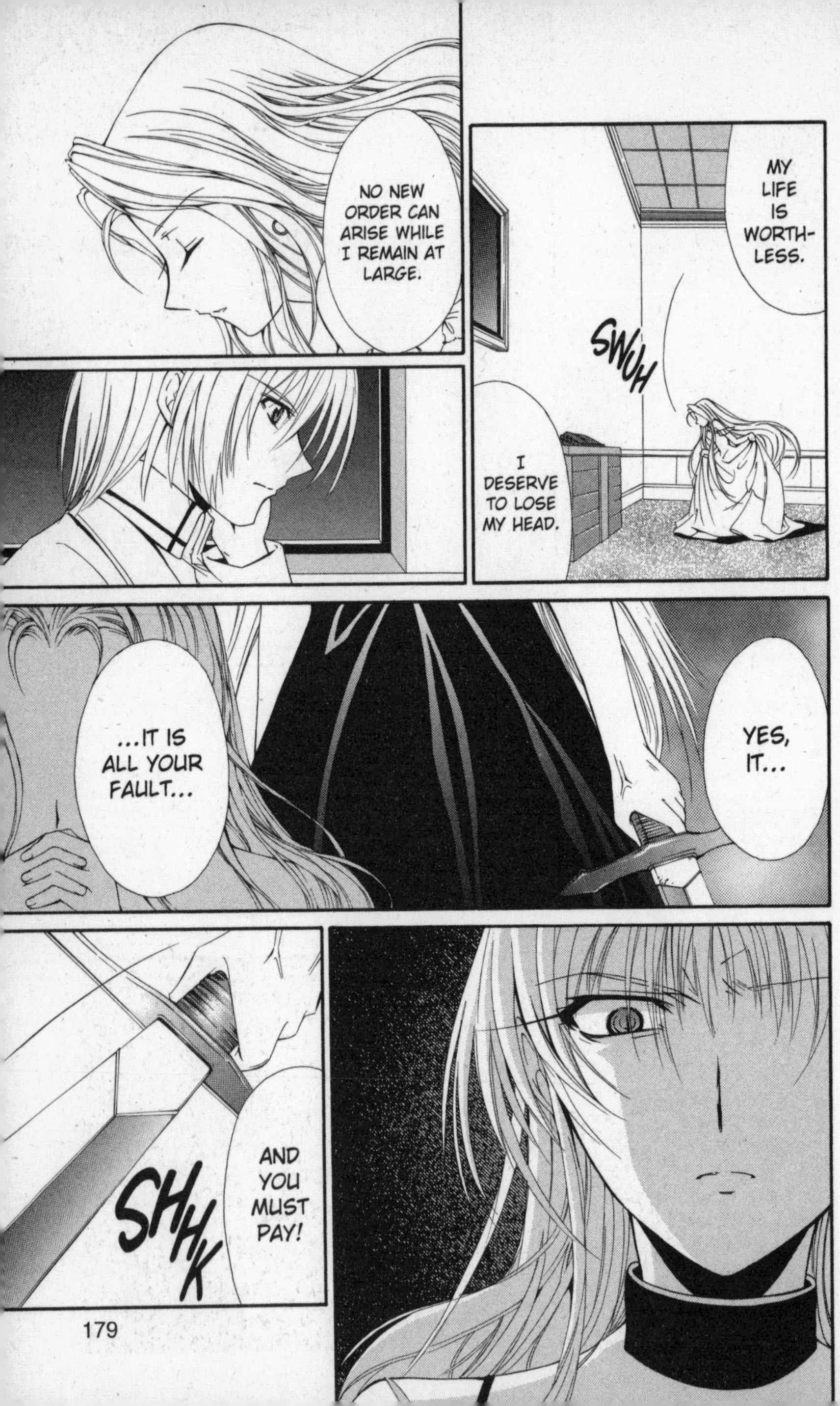
MY LIFE IS WORTHLESS.
SWUH
I DESERVE TO LOSE MY HEAD.
NO NEW ORDER CAN ARISE WHILE I REMAIN AT LARGE.
YES, IT...
...IT IS ALL YOUR FAULT...
AND YOU MUST PAY!
SHHK

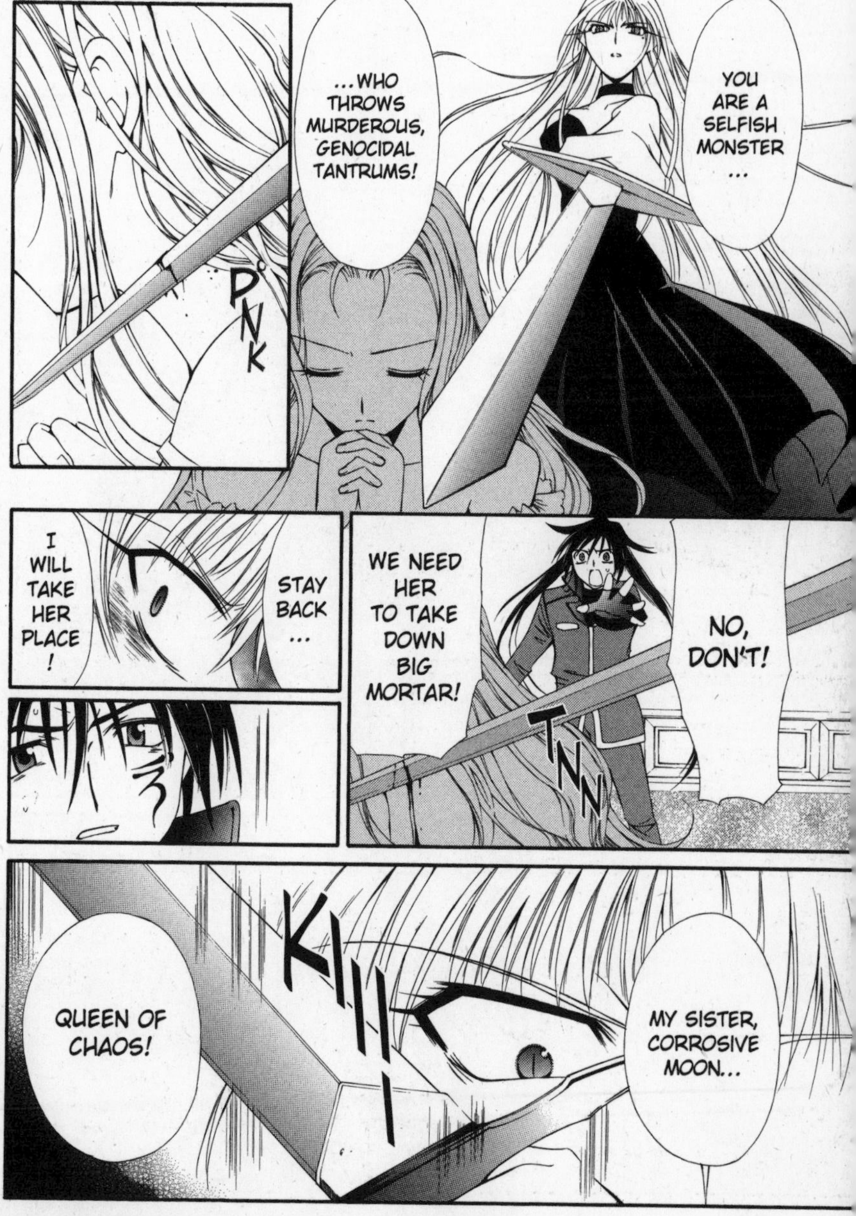
YOU ARE A SELFISH MONSTER...
...WHO THROWS MURDEROUS, GENOCIDAL TANTRUMS!
DNK
NO, DON'T!
WE NEED HER TO TAKE DOWN BIG MORTAR!
TNN
STAY BACK...
I WILL TAKE HER PLACE!
MY SISTER, CORROSIVE MOON...
KIIII
QUEEN OF CHAOS!

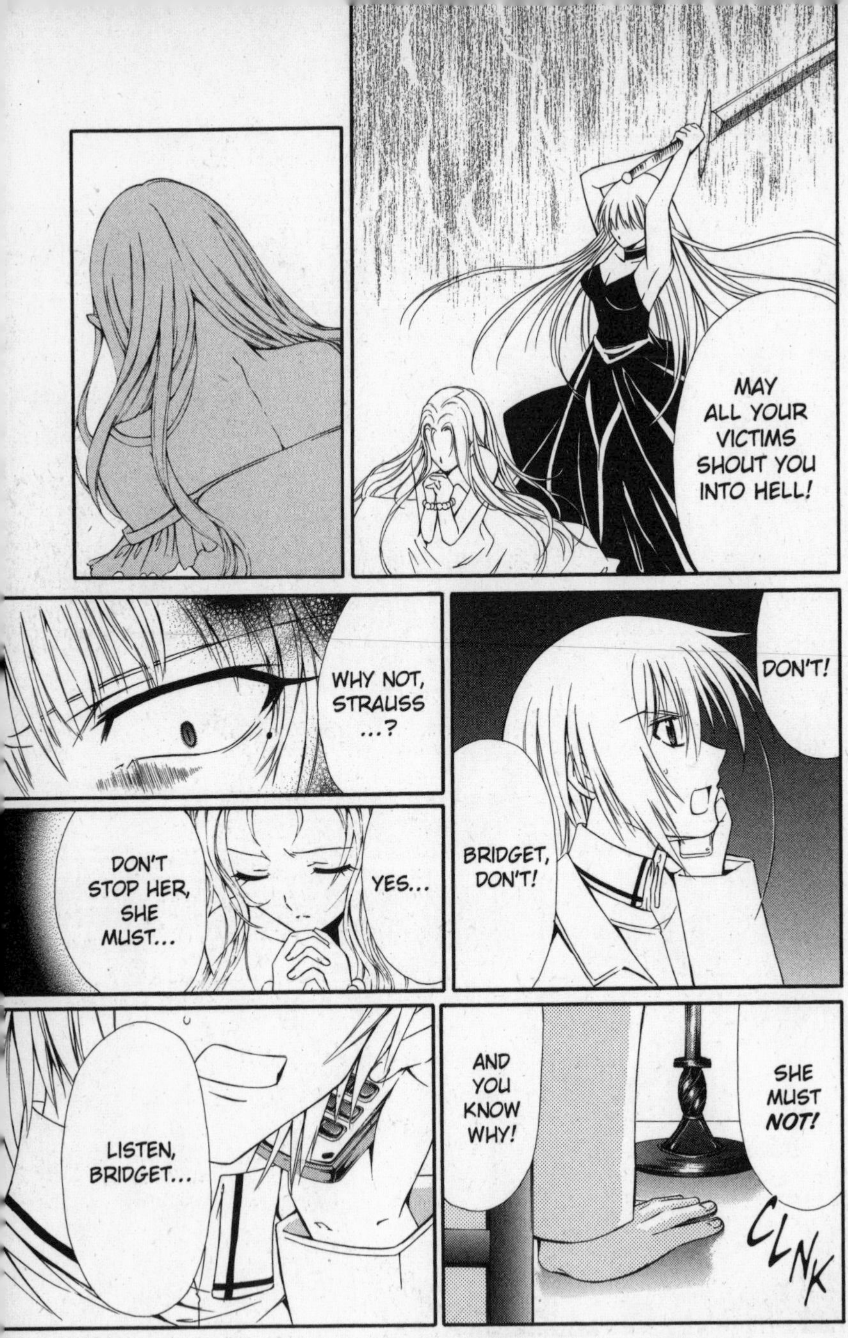
MAY ALL YOUR VICTIMS SHOUT YOU INTO HELL!
DON'T!
BRIDGET, DON'T!
WHY NOT, STRAUSS ...?
YES...
DON'T STOP HER, SHE MUST...
SHE MUST *NOT!*
AND YOU KNOW WHY!
CLNK
LISTEN, BRIDGET...

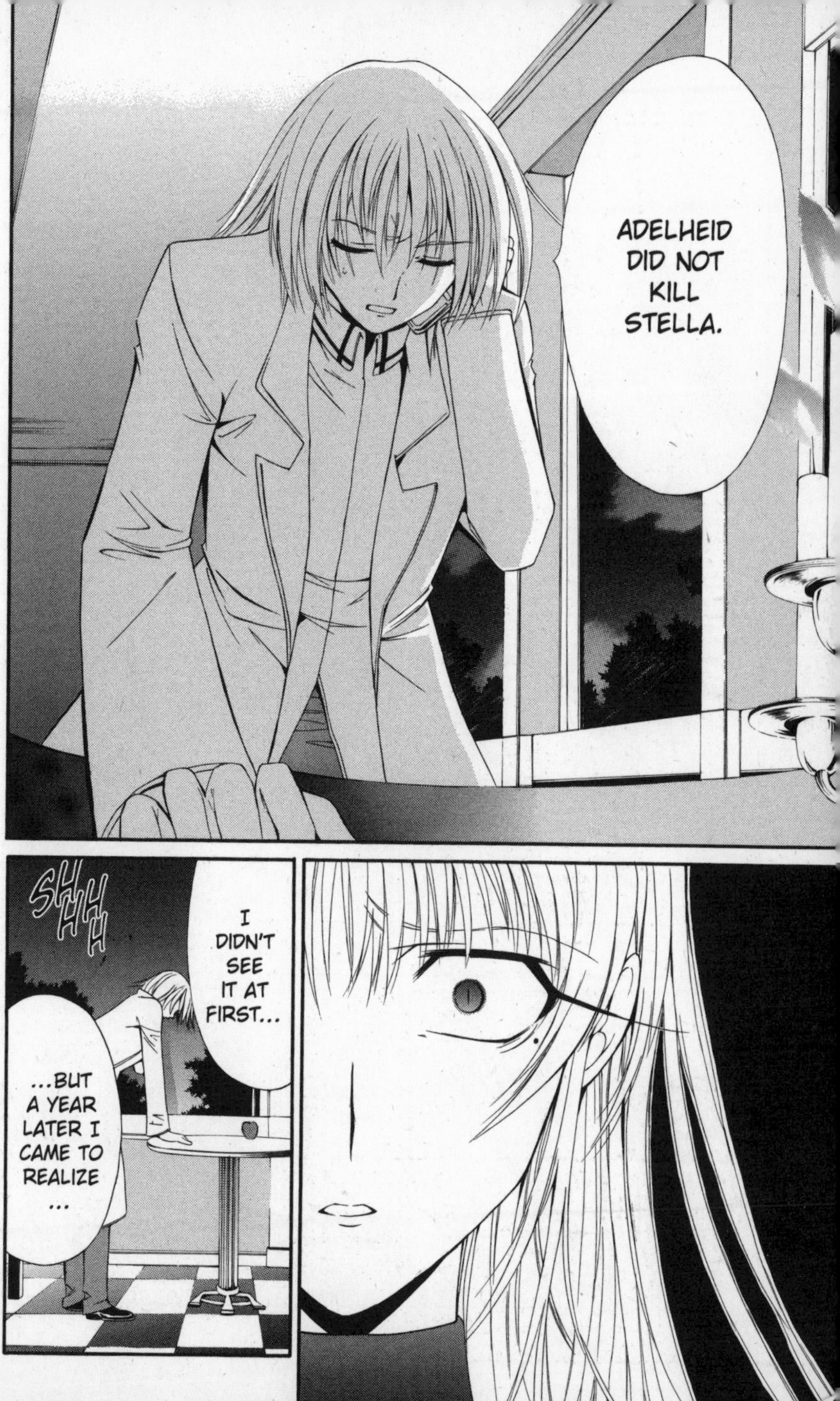
ADELHEID DID NOT KILL STELLA.
I DIDN'T SEE IT AT FIRST...
SHHHH
...BUT A YEAR LATER I CAME TO REALIZE ...

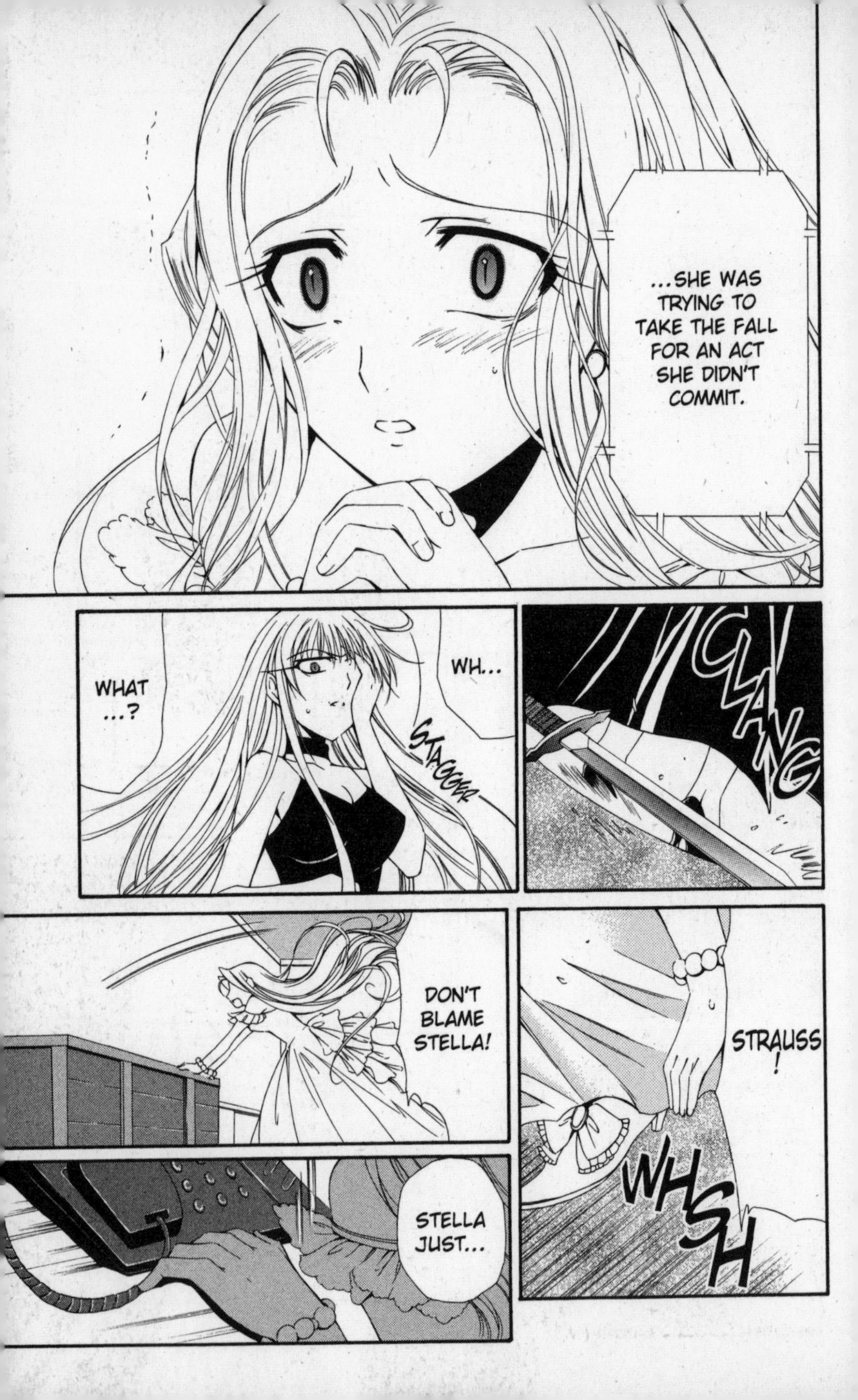
...SHE WAS TRYING TO TAKE THE FALL FOR AN ACT SHE DIDN'T COMMIT.
CLANG
WH...
WHAT ...?
STAGGER
STRAUSS!
WHSH
DON'T BLAME STELLA!
STELLA JUST...

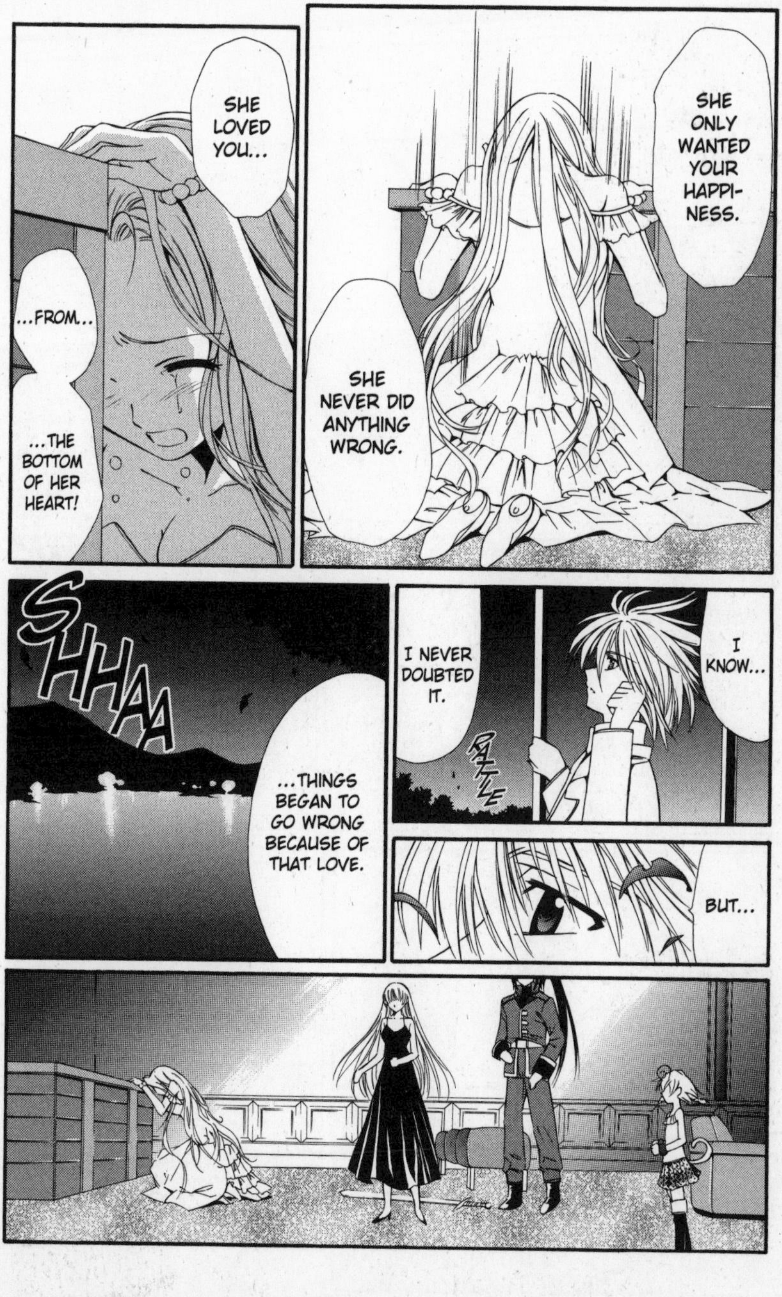
SHE ONLY WANTED YOUR HAPPINESS.
SHE NEVER DID ANYTHING WRONG.
SHE LOVED YOU...
...FROM...
...THE BOTTOM OF HER HEART!
I KNOW...
I NEVER DOUBTED IT.
RATTLE
BUT...
SHHAA
...THINGS BEGAN TO GO WRONG BECAUSE OF THAT LOVE.

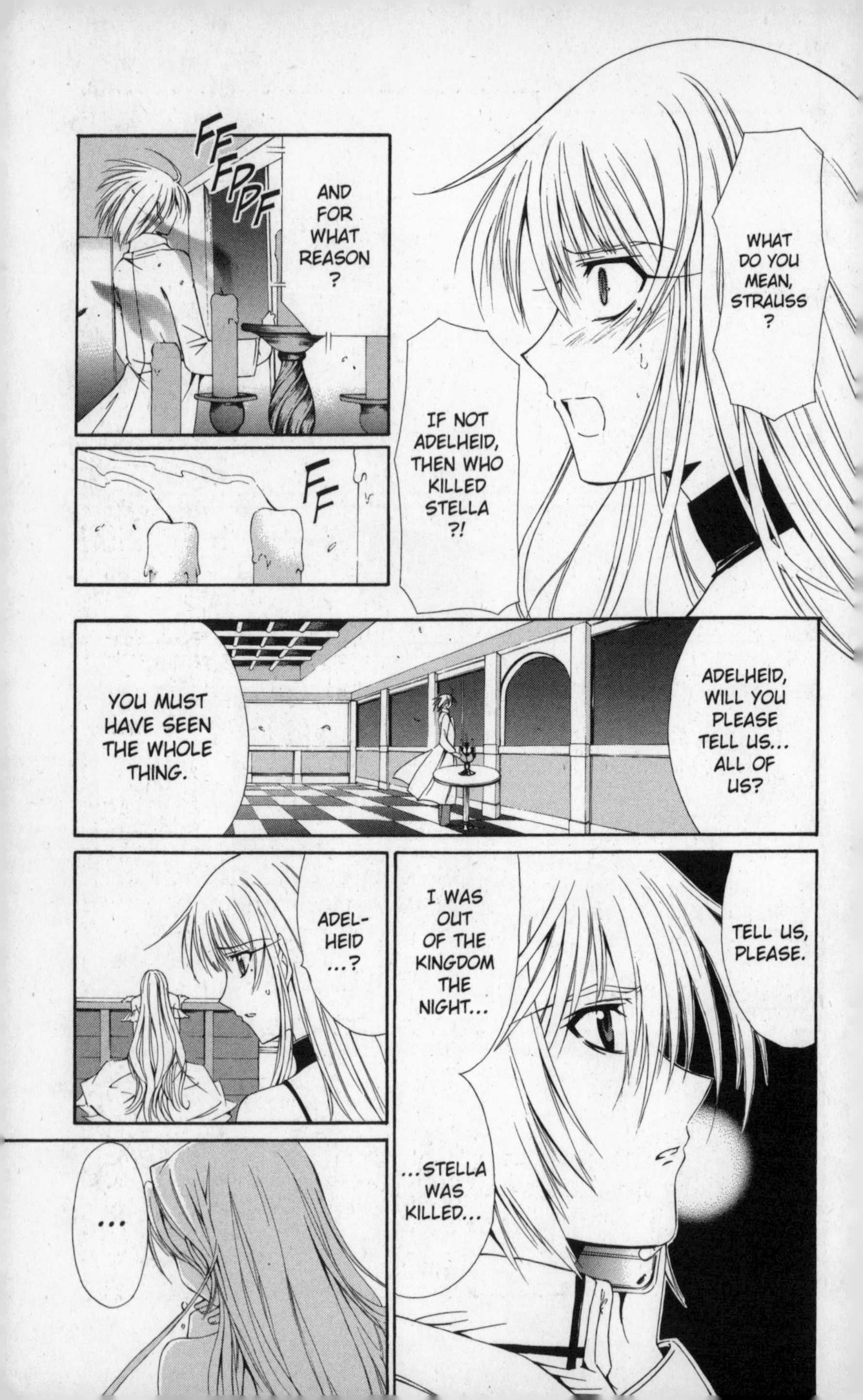
WHAT DO YOU MEAN, STRAUSS?
IF NOT ADELHEID, THEN WHO KILLED STELLA?!
FFFPPF
AND FOR WHAT REASON?
FF
ADELHEID, WILL YOU PLEASE TELL US... ALL OF US?
YOU MUST HAVE SEEN THE WHOLE THING.
TELL US, PLEASE.
I WAS OUT OF THE KINGDOM THE NIGHT...
...STELLA WAS KILLED...
ADEL-HEID...?
...

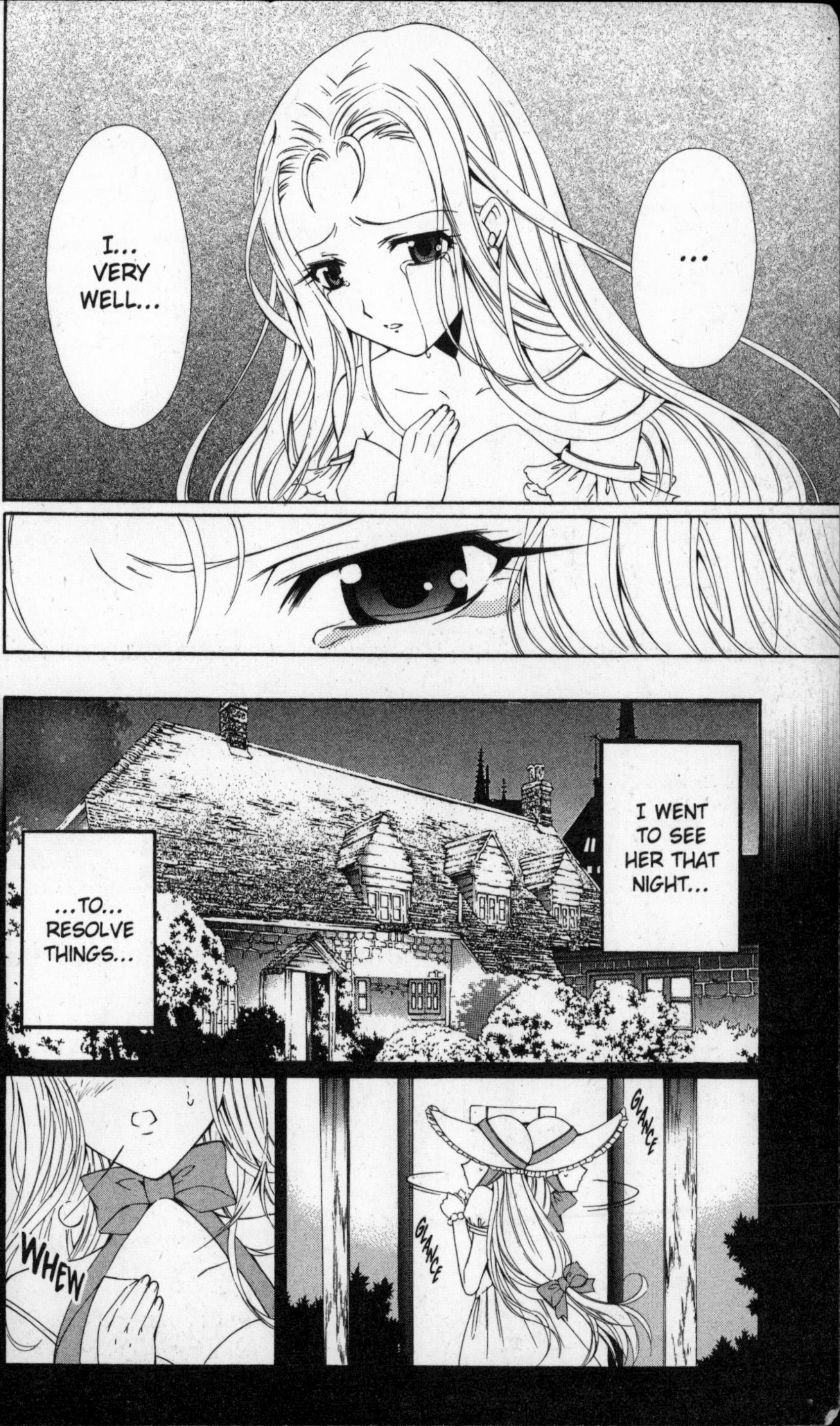
...
I... VERY WELL...
I WENT TO SEE HER THAT NIGHT...
...TO... RESOLVE THINGS...
GLANCE
GLANCE
WHEW

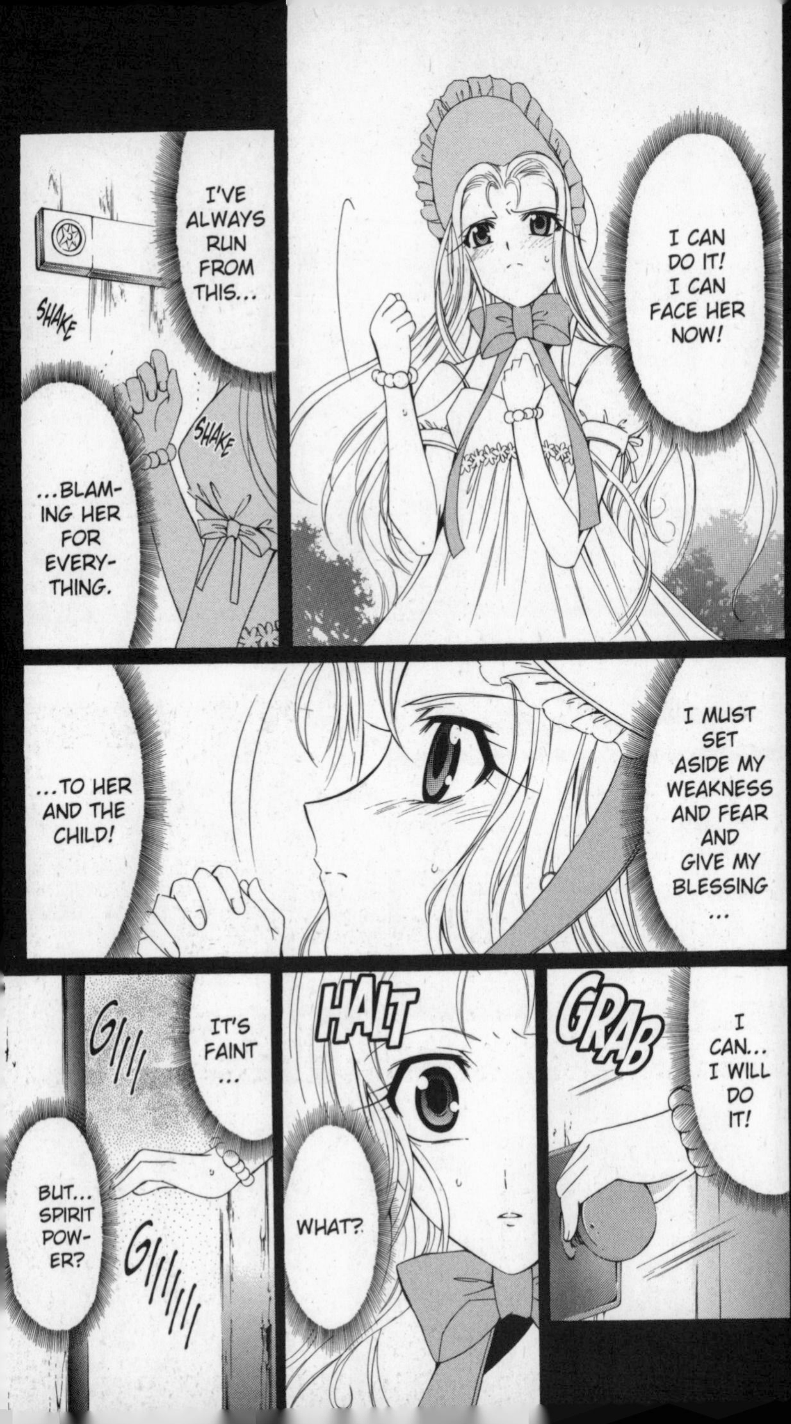
I CAN DO IT! I CAN FACE HER NOW!
I'VE ALWAYS RUN FROM THIS...
SHAKE
SHAKE
...BLAMING HER FOR EVERYTHING.
I MUST SET ASIDE MY WEAKNESS AND FEAR AND GIVE MY BLESSING...
...TO HER AND THE CHILD!
GRAB
I CAN... I WILL DO IT!
HALT
WHAT?
GIIII
IT'S FAINT...
BUT... SPIRIT POWER?
GIIIIIII

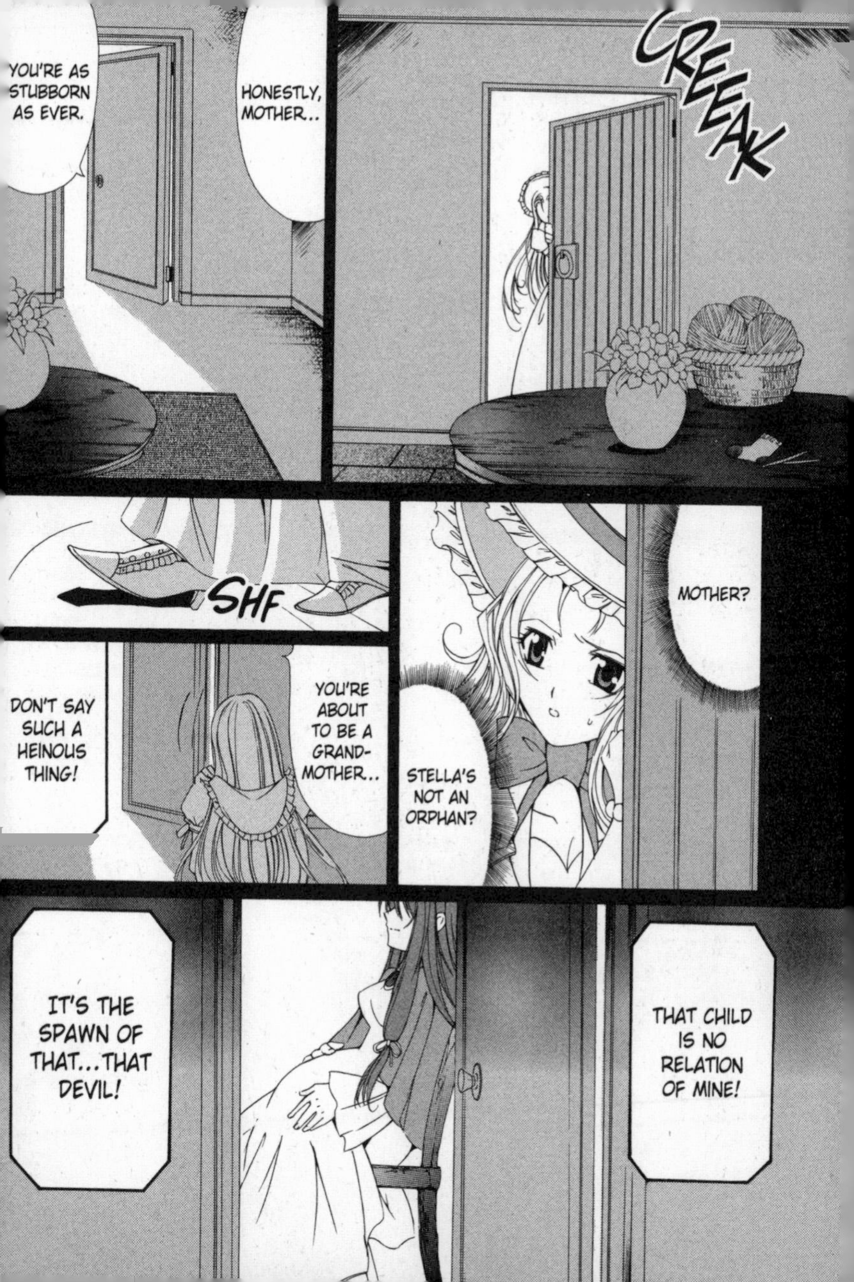
CREEEAK
HONESTLY, MOTHER...
YOU'RE AS STUBBORN AS EVER.
MOTHER?
STELLA'S NOT AN ORPHAN?
SHF
YOU'RE ABOUT TO BE A GRAND-MOTHER...
DON'T SAY SUCH A HEINOUS THING!
THAT CHILD IS NO RELATION OF MINE!
IT'S THE SPAWN OF THAT...THAT DEVIL!

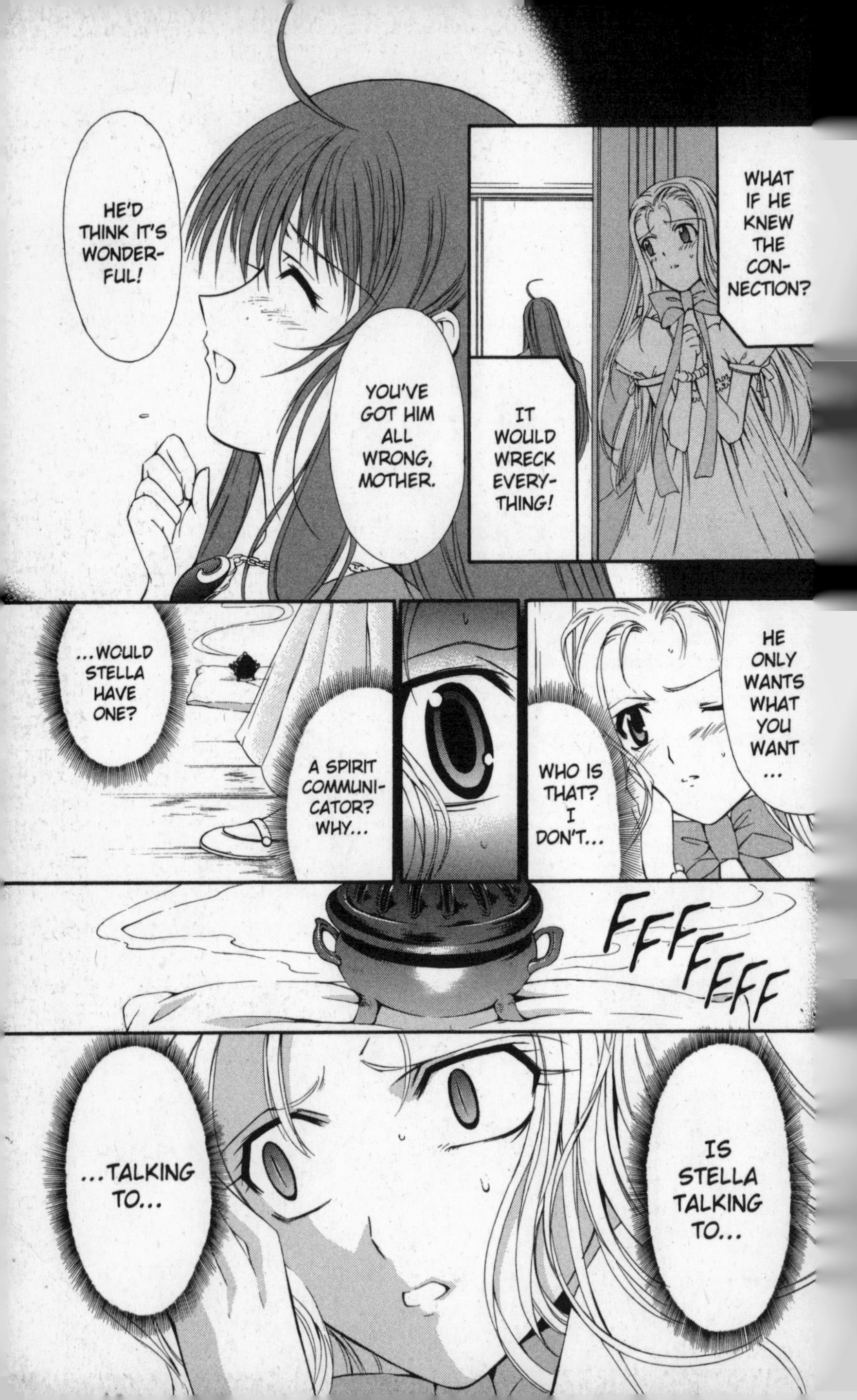
WHAT IF HE KNEW THE CON- NECTION?
IT WOULD WRECK EVERY- THING!
YOU'VE GOT HIM ALL WRONG, MOTHER.
HE'D THINK IT'S WONDER- FUL!
HE ONLY WANTS WHAT YOU WANT ...
WHO IS THAT? I DON'T...
A SPIRIT COMMUNI- CATOR? WHY...
...WOULD STELLA HAVE ONE?
FFFFFFFF
IS STELLA TALKING TO...
...TALKING TO...

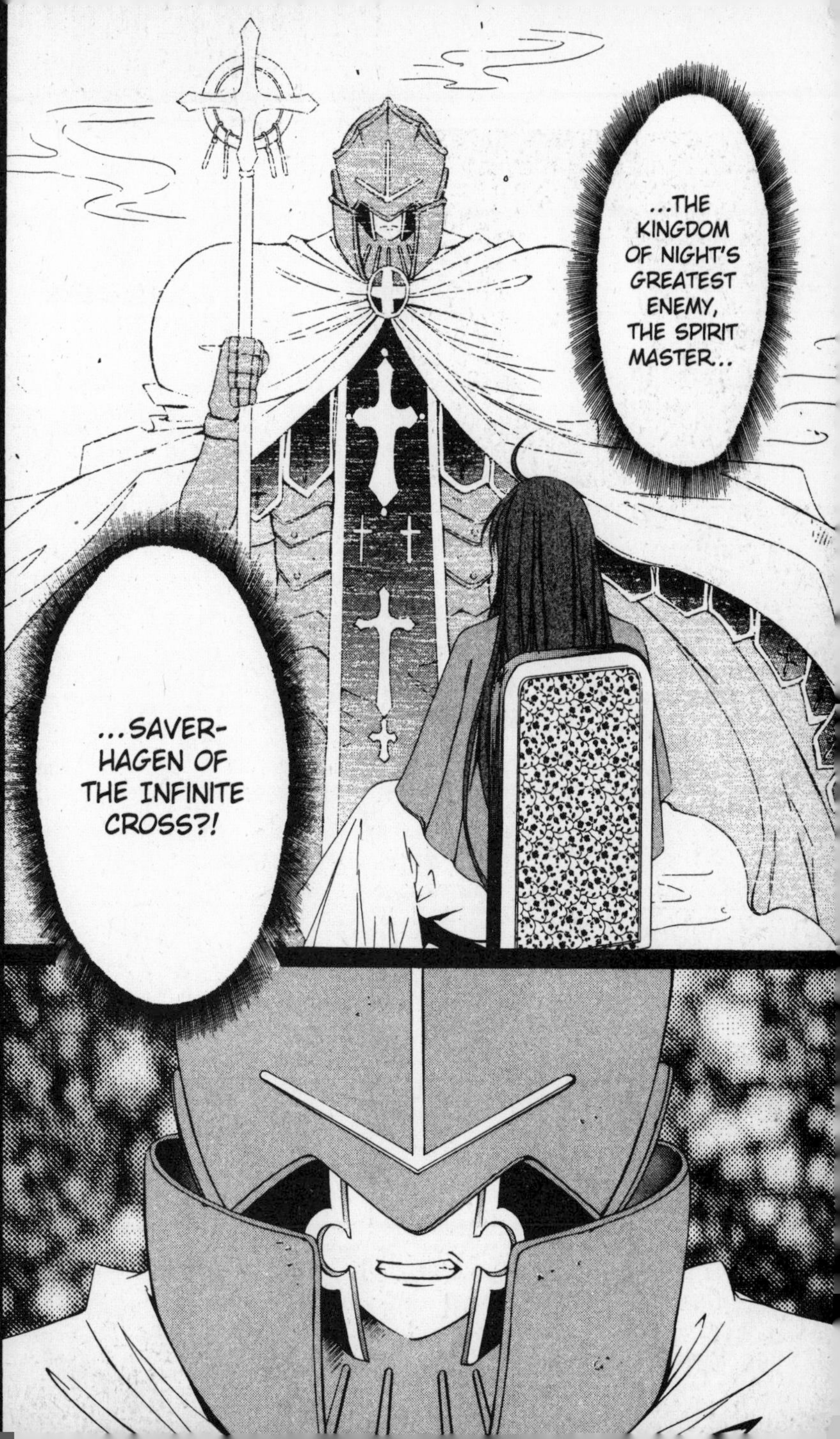
...THE KINGDOM OF NIGHT'S GREATEST ENEMY, THE SPIRIT MASTER...
...SAVER-HAGEN OF THE INFINITE CROSS?!

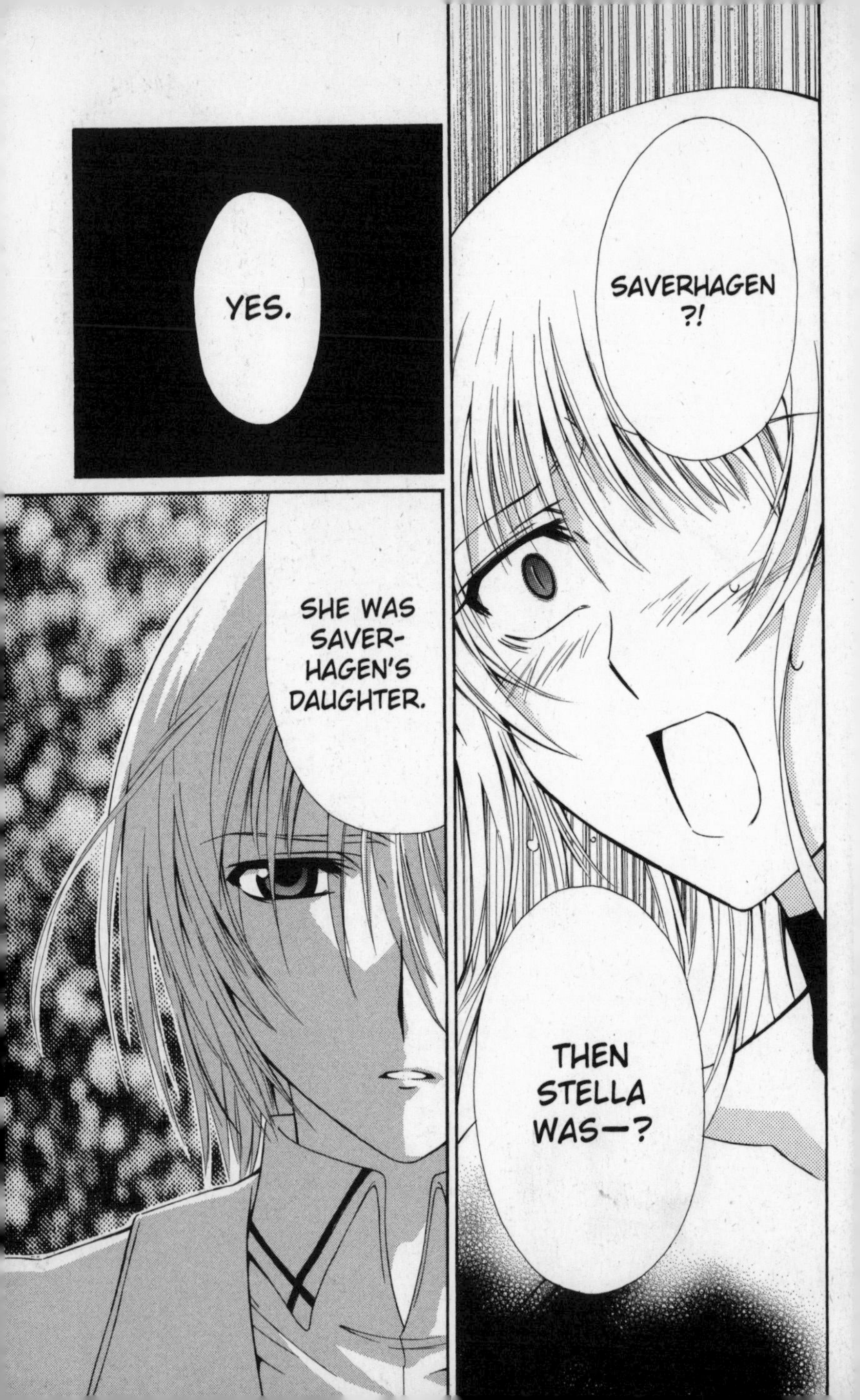
SAVERHAGEN ?!
THEN STELLA WAS—?
YES.
SHE WAS SAVER-HAGEN'S DAUGHTER.

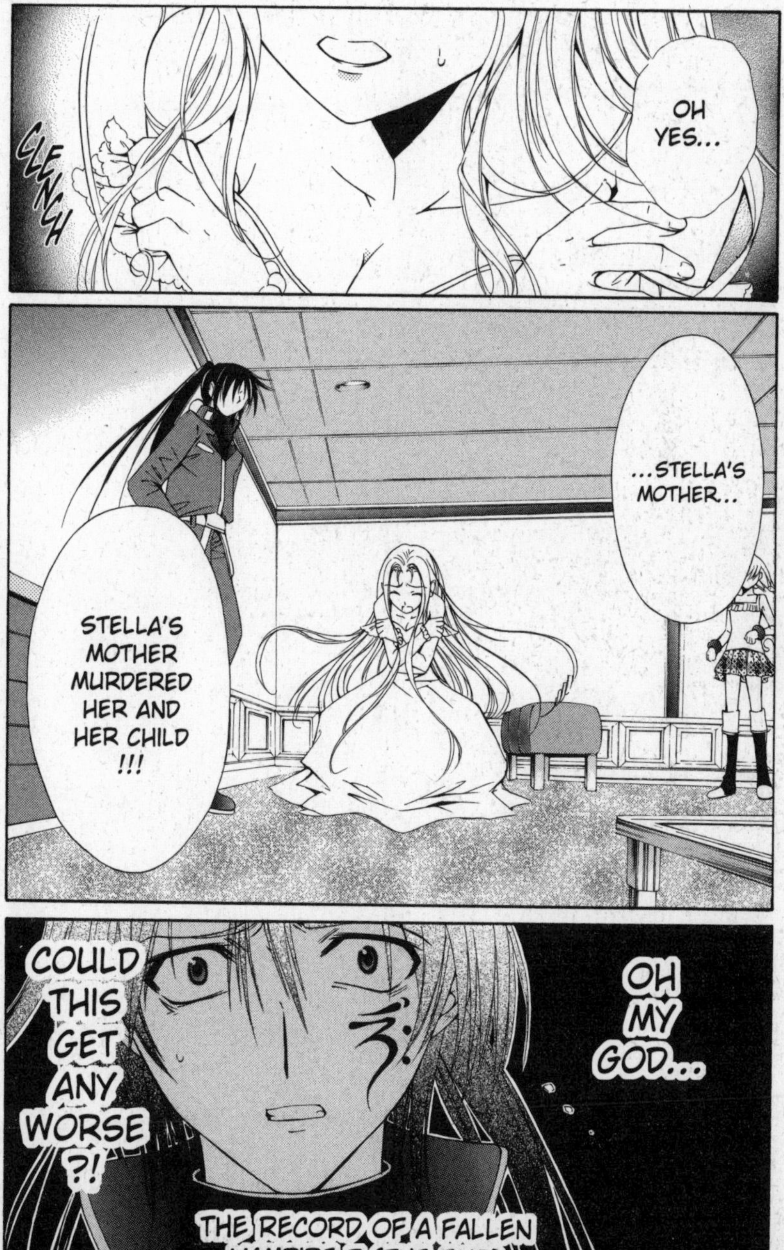
OH YES...
CLENCH
...STELLA'S MOTHER...
STELLA'S MOTHER MURDERED HER AND HER CHILD !!!
OH MY GOD...
COULD THIS GET ANY WORSE ?!
THE RECORD OF A FALLEN VAMPIRE 7 (THE END)

THE RECORD OF A

FALLEN VAMPIRE

THE RECORD OF A FALLEN VAMPIRE VOLUME 7!

I SPENT A LOT OF TIME ON THESE ILLUSTRATIONS THIS TIME! I HOPE YOU LIKE THEM.

AND I HOPE WE MEET AGAIN NEXT VOLUME!

—YURI KIMURA

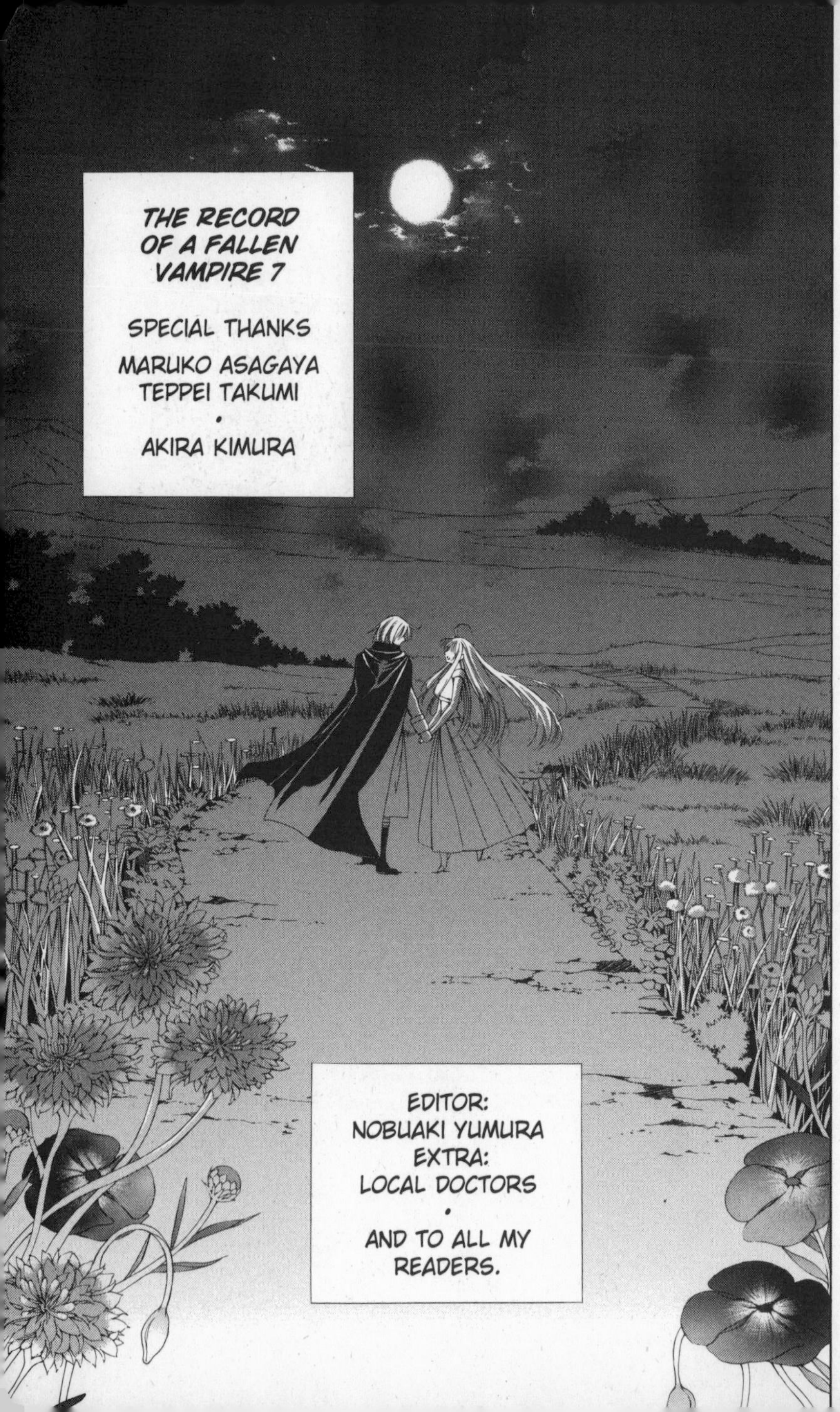
THE RECORD OF A FALLEN VAMPIRE 7
SPECIAL THANKS
MARUKO ASAGAYA
TEPPEI TAKUMI
•
AKIRA KIMURA
EDITOR: NOBUAKI YUMURA
EXTRA: LOCAL DOCTORS
•
AND TO ALL MY READERS.

AUTHOR'S AFTERWORD

SCENES IN WHICH CHARACTERS EXPLAIN TO THOSE AROUND THEM WHAT HAPPENED IN THE PAST ARE FAIRLY COMMON NOT ONLY IN MANGA BUT ALSO IN NOVELS, MOVIES AND TV SHOWS. IN THESE FLASHBACKS, THERE IS ONE THING WE ALL THINK BUT NEVER SAY ALOUD: "NOBODY REALLY REMEMBERS EXACTLY WHAT THEY SAID, MUCH LESS WHAT OTHER PEOPLE SAID..."

HUMAN MEMORY IS HORRIBLY UNRELIABLE. VERY FEW OF US CAN ACCURATELY DESCRIBE A CONVERSATION WE HAD A HALF HOUR BEFORE. AND A DAY LATER, A WEEK LATER, A YEAR LATER, RELATING ALL PERTINENT DETAILS OF A STORY BASED ON MEMORY ALONE CALLS FOR SUPERHUMAN RECALL. EVEN MEMORABLE EXPERIENCES ARE EXTREMELY DIFFICULT TO REMEMBER ACCURATELY, MUCH LESS RELATE TO OTHERS. DISTORTIONS AND MISTAKES INEVITABLY CREEP IN.

I WAS ONCE CONFIDENT AN AUTHOR WHO'D DIED YOUNG HAD DONE SO IN A TRAIN ACCIDENT AND WAS STUNNED TO READ ONE DAY THAT IT HAD BEEN A CAR ACCIDENT INSTEAD. A SMALL ERROR, BUT I HAD BEEN A FAN, AND I WAS VERY DEPRESSED THAT I HAD FAILED TO REMEMBER THIS CORRECTLY.

SINCE MEMORY IS SO UNRELIABLE, IN REAL LIFE NO ONE WOULD BE ABLE TO RECOLLECT A STORY ABOUT THE PAST IN VERY ACCURATE DETAIL. BUT THOUGH WE MAY KNOW THIS, WE HAVE ALL TACITLY AGREED TO PUT SUCH CONCERNS ASIDE TO ENSURE THE STORY PROGRESSES SMOOTHLY. OCCASIONALLY I FOLD MY ARMS AND TRY TO FIGURE OUT WAYS AROUND THIS PROBLEM.

INCIDENTALLY, I LATER LEARNED THAT THE WRITER IN QUESTION HAD ACTUALLY DIED WHEN THE TAXI HE WAS IN HAD BEEN HIT BY A TRAIN. I WAS RELIEVED TO DISCOVER THAT MY MEMORY HADN'T COMPLETELY BUNGLED THAT BIT OF INFORMATION.

BUT I CHECKED AGAIN WHEN WRITING THIS, AND MY INITIAL SOURCE ONLY SAID "CAR ACCIDENT." NO MENTION OF THE CAR BEING HIT BY A TRAIN. AND I CANNOT REMEMBER WHERE I READ THIS LATER INFORMATION, SO MY OWN MEMORIES ARE ONCE AGAIN IN DOUBT.

I'M STILL WONDERING WHAT THE TRUTH IS.

LET ME BELATEDLY SAY I'M KYO SHIRODAIRA AND THIS IS VOLUME 7. AS THE QUEEN WAKES UP, THE TRUTH AT THE CORE OF THIS STORY IS BECOMING CLEAR. DON'T WORRY, I HAVE NO PLANS TO OVERTURN EVERYTHING REVEALED IN THIS VOLUME. FROM THIS POINT ON WE'RE JUST WRAPPING UP LOOSE ENDS AND BRINGING THE STORY TO A CLOSE. HOPEFULLY ALL THE SEEDS I'VE PLANTED WILL BEAR FRUIT.

NEXT VOLUME WILL REVEAL THE FULL TRUTH BEHIND STELLA'S DEATH, INVOLVING SECRETS THAT CONNECT TO THE PRESENT DAY. SO LOOK FORWARD TO IT! WE HAVE NOT MUCH FARTHER TO GO.

I MOST SINCERELY PRAY WE WILL MEET AGAIN IN VOLUME 8.

—KYO SHIRODAIRA

城平京

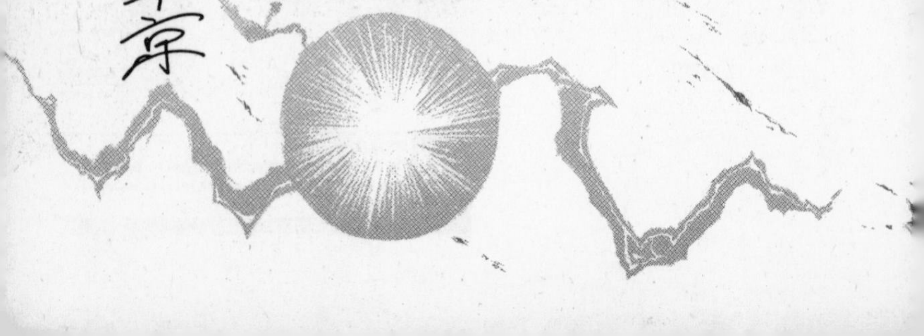

THE RECORD OF A FALLEN VAMPIRE

VOL. 7
VIZ MEDIA EDITION

STORY BY: KYO SHIRODAIRA ART BY: YURI KIMURA

Translation & Adaptation...Andrew Cunningham
Touch-up Art & Lettering...HudsonYards
Design...Ronnie Casson
Editor...Gary Leach

VP, Production...Alvin Lu
VP, Publishing Licensing...Rika Inouye
VP, Sales & Product Marketing...Gonzalo Ferreyra
VP, Creative...Linda Espinosa
Publisher...Hyoe Narita

Printed in the U.S.A.

Published by VIZ Media, LLC
P.O. Box 77010
San Francisco, CA 94107

10 9 8 7 6 5 4 3 2 1
First printing, November 2009

www.viz.com

NTAL ADVISORY
RECORD OF A FALLEN VAMPIRE is rated T for Teen and is
mmended for ages 13 and up. Contains strong language and
sy violence.
ratings.viz.com

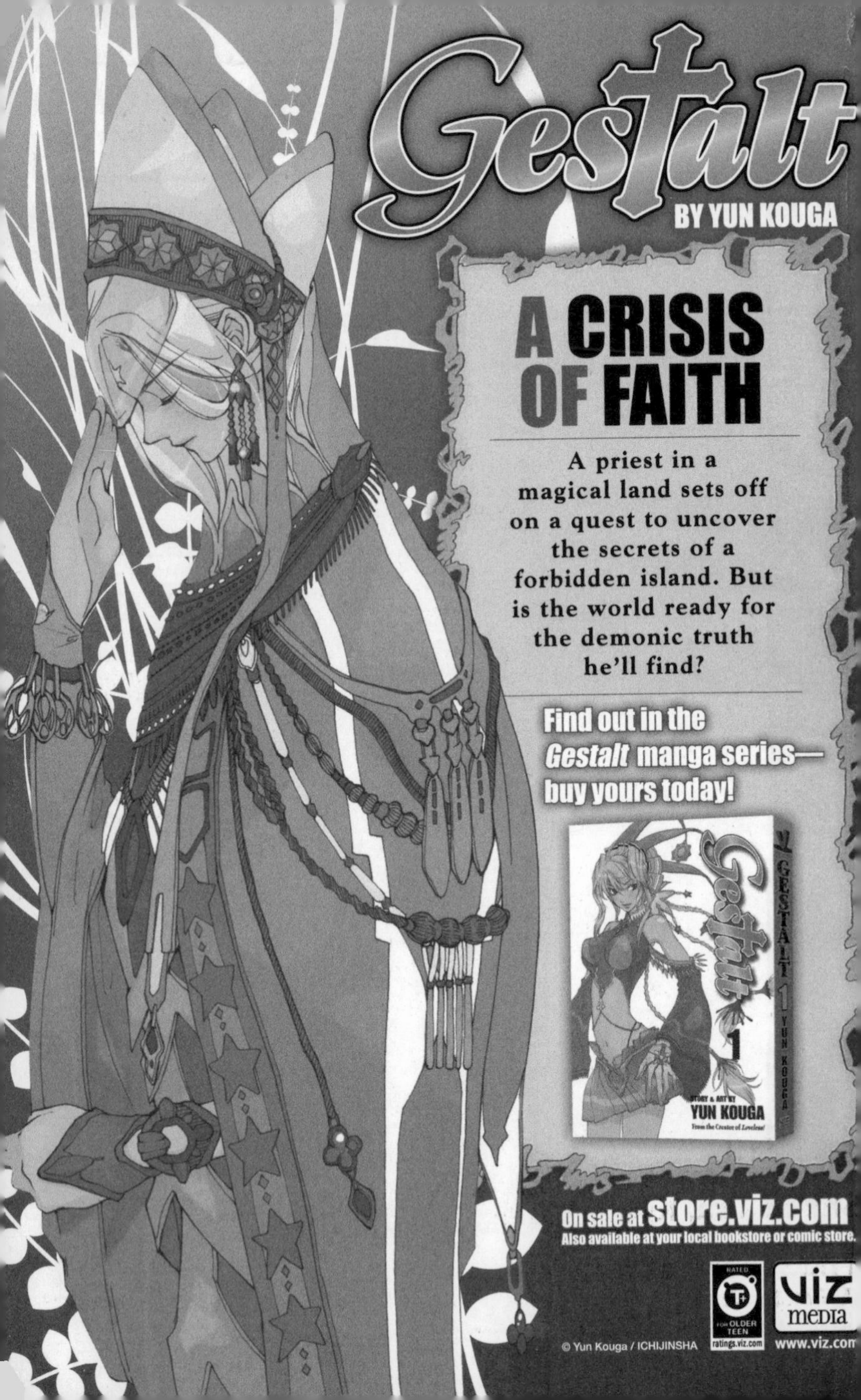
Gestalt
BY YUN KOUGA
A CRISIS OF FAITH
A priest in a magical land sets off on a quest to uncover the secrets of a forbidden island. But is the world ready for the demonic truth he'll find?
Find out in the Gestalt manga series—buy yours today!
Gestalt
1
STORY & ART BY
YUN KOUGA
From the Creator of Loveless!
GESTALT 1 YUN KOUGA
On sale at store.viz.com
Also available at your local bookstore or comic store.
RATED
T+
FOR OLDER TEEN
ratings.viz.com
VIZ media
www.viz.com
© Yun Kouga / ICHIJINSHA